REPETITIVE STRAIN INJURIES

THE COMPLETE GUIDE TO ALTERNATIVE TREATMENTS AND PREVENTION

REPETITIVE STRAIN INJURIES

THE COMPLETE GUIDE TO ALTERNATIVE TREATMENTS AND PREVENTION

TIMOTHY J. JAMESON, D.C.

Illustrations by Judie Funicelli
Photographs by Wanda Worthington

KEATS PUBLISHING, INC. NEW CANAAN, CONNECTICUT

Repetitive Strain Injuries is not intended as medical advice. Its intent is solely informational and educational. Please consult a health professional should the need for one be indicated.

REPETITIVE STRAIN INJURIES
Copyright © 1998 by Timothy J. Jameson, D.C.
All Rights Reserved

No part of this book may be reproduced in any form without the written consent of the publisher.

Library of Congress Cataloging-in-Publication Data

Jameson, Timothy J.
    Repetitive strain injuries : the complete guide to alternative treatment and prevention / Timothy J. Jameson : illustrations by Judy Funicelli : photographs by Laura Main.
        p.   cm.
    Includes bibliographical references and index.
    ISBN 0-87983-802-7
    1. Overuse injuries—Prevention.   2. Overuse injuries—Alternative treatment.   3. Overuse injuries—Popular works.   I. Title.
RD97.6.J36   1998
617.1—dc21   98-15967
                                                                        CIP

Printed in the United States of America

Keats Publishing, Inc.
27 Pine Street (Box 876)
New Canaan, Connecticut 06840-0876
Website Address: www.keats.com

To my mother and father, Warren and Louise Jameson

Your dedication toward my education,
both in undergraduate and chiropractic school,
enabled me to write this book.

CONTENTS

PREFACE

The idea for this book came about in late 1995 as I began noticing an increasing number of people with repetitive strain injuries enter my chiropractic practice for treatment. As I studied the repetitive strain disease process, it occurred to me that not much information was available to the public regarding natural and alternative health treatments for these injuries. At the time, Pascarelli and Quilter's book, *Repetitive Strain Injuries, A Computer User's Guide,* was the standard for treatment procedures and RSI information. I found the book very helpful in developing my examination procedures and my understanding of the condition. But at the same time, I knew that a book discussing conservative treatments was desperately needed to counterbalance the medical viewpoint of Pascarelli's book.

The decision to begin the book-writing process came naturally to me. I began an impassioned search for information regarding diagnosis, treatment and rehabilitation of the repetitive strain injuries (RSIs) mentioned in this book. I have learned a tremendous amount through this process, which has benefited my patients and, I hope, all of those people throughout the world with whom I communicate via e-mail through the Internet SOREHAND newsgroup.

I need to preface this book by explaining an important fact about myself. I adhere to the chiropractic philosophy regarding the body's innate healing ability, which means that I believe that our bodies have an ability to heal naturally when assisted with the correct treatments and rehabilitation techniques. I abhor the indiscriminate, overprescribed use of drugs, medications and useless surgeries that so many RSI sufferers are subjected to. Through my private practice, I have seen people's lives drastically changed by hand, elbow and spinal surgeries which proved ineffective. Some of my patients come to me after being put on one medication after another, all in the hope of finding the "miracle" drug that will help their condition. Thus, I have written this book to help those who may be contemplating treatments such as these and are desperately looking for alternatives.

Please read through this book with an open mind. Consider the alternatives in healthcare. Open your eyes to the many disciplines and healers who want to help you overcome your RSI. A recent survey in 1994 by the Robert Wood Johnson Foundation regarding national access to health care indicates that "nearly 10 percent of the population, almost 25 million persons, saw a professional in 1994 for at least one of the following four therapies: chiropractic, relaxation techniques, therapeutic massage or acupuncture." There are healers out there—all you need to do is educate yourself about them. This book is a starting point toward that process. In the Resource Section, I've included a number of books that will guide you even further in the learning process. A person with an RSI who does not educate himself on the disease process is destined toward disability. Since you are reading this, you are taking the first steps toward healing yourself. Congratulations!

ACKNOWLEDGMENTS

I would like to thank a number of people for their help in producing this book. To begin with, I would like to thank the Keats Publishing staff for believing in my book and my abilities as an author. I would also like to thank my editor Phyllis Herman for her skills and support along with those informative snippets from the *New York Times* regarding RSIs that she sent to me every other month or so.

Thanks also goes to my wife Dr. Laurie Gossett for putting up with the time I spent in front of the computer over the past nine months (without developing an RSI, thank goodness!). Whenever I consulted her for advice on topics, she was there to help me organize my thoughts. She proved to be an excellent editor as well. I also want to thank my three year-old daughter Jillian for always bringing me back to what is really important when life seemed difficult. I am also grateful to my wife's family, especially Gene and RaeJean Gossett, who were always there to care for Jillian when work needed to be done.

There were a number of contributors to this book I want to acknowledge. Many thanks go to my friend and compatriot in the quest to educate the public about natural health care, Dr. Robert Wright, Ph.D., L.Ac. Dr. Wright contributed the chapter on acupuncture and traditional Chinese medicine and the case study for Reflex Sympathetic Dystrophy. Thanks also to Jan Maxwell, R.N., certified guided imagery instructor, for her input to the chapter on imagery techniques. Ralph Strauss, a Feldenkrais instructor from Los Angeles, reviewed the Feldenkrais section for accuracy. I would like to thank him for his notations, time and effort. Many thanks to my sister-in-law Jeanette Madsen, a naturopath and specialized kinesiologist, for her contributions to the chapter on naturopathy.

For helping out with the research, I want to thank Elizabeth Hesse (soon to be Dr. Hesse) a student at Life Chiropractic College West. Elizabeth was quite helpful in reading through the manuscript, offering good suggestions for changes. Many thanks to Nellie Rodriguez, the model for the stretching and exercise chapters. *Vogue* magazine is next, Nellie!

Two photographers provided their services for this book. The initial working photographs were taken by a good friend Laura Main. The final photo shoot was performed in the studio of Worthington Photography by Wanda Worthington. The author thanks both photographers for their help in producing this book. The illustrations were expertly drawn by a longtime friend, Judie Funicelli. Ms. Funicelli owns an airbrush illustration business in New Jersey called "Airbrush Plus." Thanks Judie!

I want to thank all of the writers on the SOREHAND Internet mailing list. This includes all of the unfortunate sufferers of repetitive injuries seeking advice and all of the health practitioners who unselfishly give their opinions on a daily basis purely to help others through difficult times. Reading the SOREHAND list has been a learning experience for me. My only wish is that I could help every person who writes their RSI story. My goal is that this book will bring a glimmer of hope to the RSI sufferer's plight.

Many thanks to my patients, whose stories you will read throughout the book. Their diligent compliance with treatment protocols, and their trust in my abilities as a doctor made this book possible.

Finally, I thank my parents, Warren and Louise Jameson, to whom this book is dedicated, for their continued love and support. I could not have achieved my level of education without their help and encouragement. Many thanks, Mom and Dad. I hope this book makes both of you proud!

PART 1

UNDERSTANDING THE BASICS OF A REPETITIVE STRAIN INJURY

CHAPTER ONE

RSI ANATOMY

A grasp of basic anatomical structures and terms is needed to understand the causes of repetitive strain injuries. Here is a list of terms to familiarize yourself with. It will help you to understand the syndromes explained in future chapters:

- **Muscle:** A tissue within the body containing cells that are contractile in nature. Muscle contraction allows for movement of the bones the muscles are attached to.
- **Tendon:** A tissue that affixes the muscle to a bone.
- **Ligament:** A fibrous material that joins bones together around and between joints.
- **Nerve:** The body's "electrical wiring," which conducts electrical impulses from the brain to organs, muscles and other body tissues.
- **Fascia:** A sheath of connective tissue that adjoins and wraps around organs, muscles, bones and other structures under the skin. It surrounds muscles like the wrapping on a sausage.
- **Bursa:** Bursas are fluid-filled sacs which protect areas where there is increased friction—for example, where a tendon rubs over a bone. These sacs are filled with a

substance called synovium. This is a clear fluid that acts as a lubricant.

- **Blood vessels:** Structures that carry blood to and from the heart. There are two types: arteries, which carry oxygen-rich blood away from the heart to the tissues of the body and veins, which carry oxygen-deficient blood back to the heart to be transported to the lungs for re-oxygenation.
- **Bones:** A living tissue composed of a fibrous matrix of calcium phosphate crystals and carbonates, giving them hardness. Blood-cell formation occurs within the soft gelatinous bone marrow of the spinal bones and long bones of the extremities.
- **The Spine:** The spine consists of five regions—the cervical spine (neck), thoracic spine (chest, mid-back area), lumbar spine (lower back), sacrum (tailbone) and coccyx. In this book, we will talk mostly about the cervical spine and its effect on upper-extremity disorders. The cervical spine consists of seven spinal bones or vertebrae. There are eight pairs of nerves that pass between each of the seven cervical spinal bones.
- **The Brain:** The master control panel for all of the body's functionings.

Repetitive strain injuries usually involve all of the above components, making treatment challenging. In this chapter, each of these structures will be addressed individually, and its role in the development of RSI conditions will be examined.

THE MUSCLES

Many repetitive strain injures develop because the muscles of the hands, wrists or arm are involved in movements that are

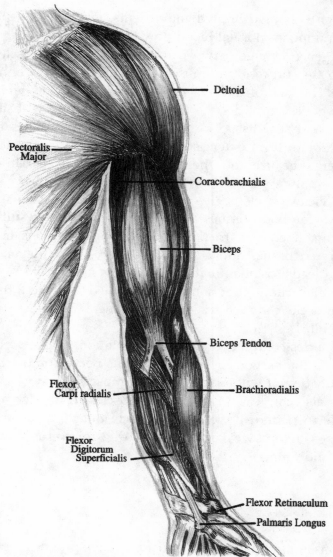

Deltoid

Pectoralis
Major

Coracobrachialis

Biceps

Biceps Tendon

Flexor
Carpi radialis

Brachioradialis

Flexor
Digitorum
Superficialis

Flexor Retinaculum

Palmaris Longus

Figure 1: The Forearm Muscles

quick and involve limited movements. This quick repetitive motion impedes normal blood flow to the tissues. It also inhibits oxygen exchange between the blood and the muscle cells. Due to this process, the muscles become more susceptible to injury. The lack of oxygen in the muscles, tendons and other involved tissues elicits the pain response, along with inflammation and scar tissue formation. The muscle begins to lose its contractility and tends to become weakened and easily fatigued because of the development of scarring and "microstrains."

A vicious cycle begins at this point, whereby the strained and oxygen-poor tissues lose contractile force, resulting in weakness. Increased friction and pressure develops between the injured tissues and adjacent structures. This degenerative process leads to inflammation, adhesions and further weakening. If the irritating motions are continued, chronic inflammation, muscle contractures, and permanent disability will be the result.[1]

Muscles contract because of information received from the brain via the nervous system. If there is nerve compression or inflammation, it will adversely affect muscle function. Irritated nerves also can lead to weakened muscles so the doctor must be able to discern a weakened muscle due to a nerve injury as opposed to a weakened muscle due to overuse, scarring, strain and fatigue.

THE TENDONS

Tendons are spaghetti-like extensions of the muscles that allow attachment to the bone. The muscle-tendon junction and the tendon-bone junction are two areas likely to be affected by repetitive strain injury.[2] Overuse of the muscle leads to "micro-

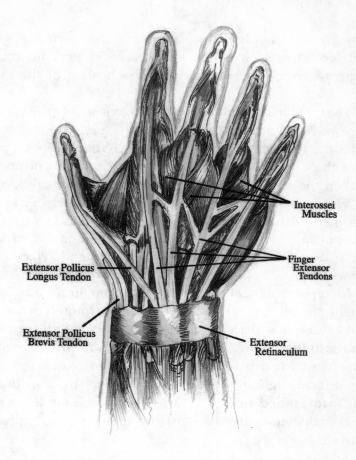

Interossei
Muscles

Extensor Pollicus
Longus Tendon

Finger
Extensor
Tendons

Extensor Pollicus
Brevis Tendon

Extensor
Retinaculum

Figure 2: Tendons of the Hand Extensors

tearing" of the tendon's attachment to the outer layer of bone, the periosteum. This leads to the pain and swelling that is typically felt along the bone's surface. In some cases, chronic tugging on the periosteum will lead to changes along the bone's surface that can be visualized on X-rays. For this reason, many clinicians apply a brace around tendon-periosteal attachment locations, such as the elbow area in the forearm. The compression aids in reattachment and healing of the injured area.

The tendons traveling to the fingers must pass under a structure called a retinaculum (see Figure 2). The retinaculum guides the tendon to its insertion point. When a tendon passes under these structures, it is wrapped by a sheath of material. Between the sheath and the tendon is the viscous fluid called synovium or synovial fluid. Synovial fluid is present in these tendon sheaths for a reason similar to the reason why motor oil is put in a car engine: It protects the tendon from friction. It also aids in the fluid motion of the tendon under the retinaculum.

In repetitive strain injuries, the synovium can thicken. Imagine the oil in a car getting thicker and more viscous. This would cause the parts to slow down and might even cause damage to the engine. A similar event occurs with the tendons of the hand when placed under repetitive strain. The tendons have difficulty gliding in the thick synovial fluid so they become swollen and thickened. This response leads to pain and inflammation until the stressor (the repetitive movements) is removed.

THE LIGAMENTS

Ligaments play an integral part in repetitive strain injuries. This is not because they tend to be injured (although they can be), but because they cover or enclose certain structures that are involved in the nerve entrapment syndromes mentioned later in this book. The most famous one is the transverse carpal ligament (also known as the flexor retinaculum) that encloses

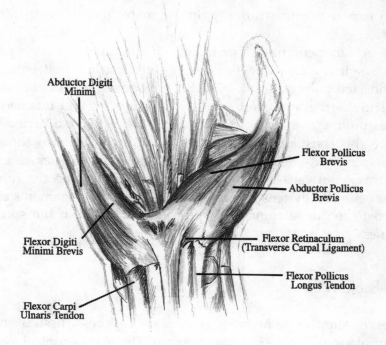

Figure 3: Palmar view of Wrist Tendons and Retinaculum

the carpal tunnel. Ligaments are tough, unyielding structures. In fact they are so tough that in some traumas the ligament will tear off its attachment site from the bone before it will break itself.

It is possible for the ligament to be injured (sprained) in RSI conditions. This would occur in strenuous work, such as carpentry, or in occupations involving heavy labor such as construction. Injured ligaments do not heal quickly, sometimes taking six months to a year to heal fully. This slow healing is due to the minimal blood supply to ligaments. Thus, the person suffering from an RSI along with sprained ligaments can experience frustrating pain for many months with little relief.

Another condition that ligaments and muscles play a part in is spinal strain due to poor posture. Each spinal bone is connected to its adjacent spinal bone by six different ligaments. Postural strain can exert stress on the muscles and ligaments, thus pulling or tugging on the spinal bones. Over a period of time, this constant tugging can actually distort the structure of the spine and affect the small openings where the nerves exit to travel outward to the body. Constant pulling on the spine from chronically tense muscles and strain on the ligaments can lead to the development of spurs emanating from the spinal bones.

THE NERVES

Nerves supply the muscles, organs, and all body tissues with information (impulses) from the brain. The nerves control muscular contractions and the amount of muscle fiber contracted. The nervous system plays a major part in all repetitive strain injuries. It consists of two major components: the central nervous system (brain and spinal cord) and the peripheral nervous system (nerves that travel from the spine to the tissues). RSIs involve injuries to the peripheral nervous system, but the central nervous system plays an important role as well.

Here is an example of how the nerve impulse process works. Impulses for muscle contraction in the fingers begin in the brain and then travel downward through the spinal cord, situated within the spine. When the nerves traveling to the arms and hands reach the level of the lower neck, they must exit out of the spine. (See Figure 4) There are two small openings, one on each side of the spine between each vertebra that

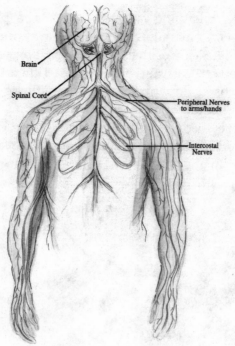

Figure 4: Nerves from Neck to the Hand

allow the passage of nerve roots along with arteries and veins and smaller nerves, out of both sides of the spinal column. These openings are called the intervertebral foraminae. Once the nerves have cleared these openings, they must then travel to their destination, in this case the muscles of the fingers. The peripheral nerves also send impulses to the organs, receive sensory information from organs and skin, and some are responsible for sympathetic and parasympathetic functions.

Nerves which are part of the sympathetic nervous system, emanating from the midback spinal region, are responsible for the "fight or flight" reaction. This reaction causes muscle tension, a release of adrenaline, a decrease of digestive functioning and increased breathing and heart rate. The parasympathetic nervous system, emanating from the brain and spinal region near the tailbone, causes the opposite reactions to occur: slower breathing, slower heart rate and increased digestive functioning.

An increased and prolonged sympathetic response, usually found in people in high-stress jobs, will undoubtedly make a person more susceptible to RSI conditions. The sympathetic response of adrenaline release and muscle tension is a predisposing factor to the fatigue of muscles, chronic stress and decreased immune function.[3]

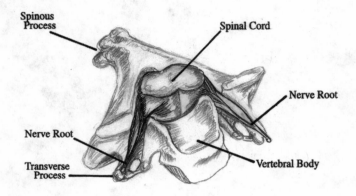

Figure 5: Cervical Vertebra, Spinal Cord and Nerve Root

Compression of the peripheral nerves may occur at various sites along the pathway to the arms. (This can also occur in the legs, but this book will not address that subject). In the following chapters, you will learn of the many "entrapment" sites in the neck, shoulder, arms and wrists. It is possible for the nerve to become trapped or compressed in more than one location at the same time. Multiple entrapment sites are common among RSI sufferers. Compression of the nerves in two locations is called a "double-crush" phenomena.

Research has shown that nerve impulses are drastically decreased if the nerve is compressed in more than one site.[4, 5] Here's an example. As a nerve passes through the spinal openings, it becomes compressed and irritated by tight neck muscles. This compression decreases its impulse flow by 40 to 50 percent. The nerve continues its travel downward to the wrist and encounters inflamed tendons and a small carpal tunnel. The nerve gets compressed more here, and it results in only 10 to 20 percent of the generated impulse reaching the fingertips. The resulting numbness and tingling sensations, as well as wrist pain, lead the person to perhaps wrongly assume that he has carpal tunnel syndrome.

I have found through clinical experience that there may be "triple" or even "quadruple" crush syndromes. The nerve gets compressed in multiple sites: for example, the spine, the thoracic outlet, the elbow and then the wrist. These cases are very challenging for the healthcare professional to treat. It takes great discernment by a doctor during the physical examination and history-taking to understand the location(s) of the nerve entrapment site(s). Be wary, therefore, of the healthcare professional who looks only at the two square inches above your carpal tunnel to diagnose and treat your RSI. The problem may not be the carpal tunnel at all!

THE FASCIA

The fascia connects all structures under the skin. It is a connective tissue that wraps around the muscles, tendons, nerves, blood vessels and bone. This congruous meshwork makes the shoulder, arm, forearm and hand a complex of interrelated tissues. Fascia that surrounds and encapsulates muscle is called myofascia. You will hear more about this later, when I discuss

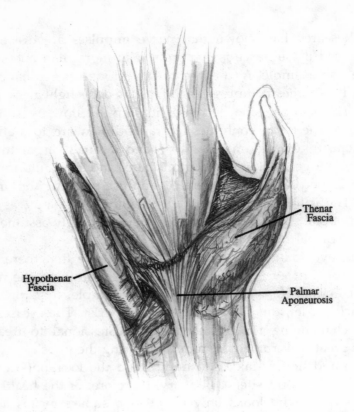

Figure 6: The Palmar Fascia

myofascial therapy. Fascia is constantly responding to stresses imposed upon the body. With overuse injuries, the fascia becomes constricted, loses its elasticity, and causes the contraction of muscles to be less efficient.[6] The muscles bind together, friction between them increases and a vicious cycle begins, as described in the Muscles section at the beginning of this chapter.

THE BURSA

A bursa is a fluid-filled sac that protects areas where tendons rub over bones. You can imagine a balloon-like structure that sits between the tendon and bone. The body is composed of 140 bursas surrounding all the joints. Inflammation of the bursas causes a deep, severe, continuous pain, that often aches whether the joint is moving or not. This pain is often accompanied by weakness of the surrounding muscles. Bursitis is usually secondary to other causative factors. Muscle imbalances and weaknesses, pre-existing degenerative changes in and around the joints near the bursa and calcific deposits adjacent to the bursa predispose it to an inflammatory event also known as bursitis.

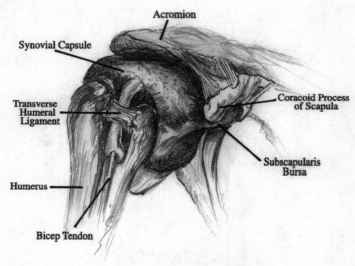

Figure 7: Bursa and Capsule of the Shoulder Joint

THE BLOOD VESSELS

RSIs may cause bleeding of the small capillaries and veins due to direct insult. This causes leakage of fluid to the surrounding areas outside the cells. An increase of pressure within the cells

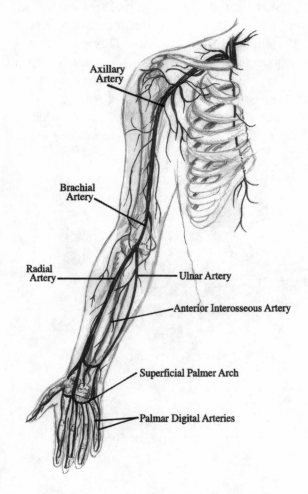

Figure 8: The Arterial Supply of Upper Extremity

results, and it causes a decrease of oxygen to the cell structures. Without oxygen, the cells die. Other cells surrounding the injured area leak fluid outward because of the pressure changes and can work only suboptimally.

Analysis of blood vessels through microscopic sampling indicates that the blood vessel walls thicken and narrow in regions of repetitive strain injury.[7] This is due to a number of factors, such as aggregation of particles in the blood, called platelets, and increased cell production in the blood vessel walls.

Compression of a nerve due to direct pressure or due to swollen tissues causes a decrease of blood flow to the nerve. This results in diminished oxygen to the nerve cells and subsequent degeneration of the fatty outer layer of the nerve, called myelin. Myelin allows for quick transmission of electrical impulses. The thinning of the myelin decreases the speed and distorts the nerve impulse. If decreased blood flow and nerve compression continue, the part of the nerve cells that transmits impulses to the tissues (the axon), will begin to degenerate also. Since a nerve is comprised of thousands of axons, symptoms are not noticed right away. After a long period of decreased blood flow, however, many axons will die, and nerve symptoms will appear. Axons regenerate very slowly, if at all. This is the reason why treatment for RSI conditions needs to be initiated as soon as complaints begin to develop. Lack of treatment and the onset of more severe nerve-related symptoms, such as numbness, can cause irreparable harm to the nerve cells, with long-term disability.

In the condition called Raynaud's syndrome, the blood vessels constrict and dilate inappropriately due to what is believed to be an overproductive sympathetic nervous system. See Chapter 7 for more information on this topic.

17

THE BONES

The bones playing an integral part in upper extremity RSIs are the following: the spinal bones described below, the first rib,

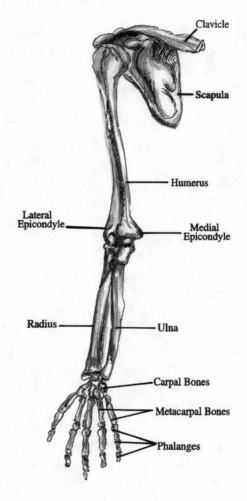

Figure 9: The Bones of the Upper Extremity

the clavicle (collarbone), the scapula (shoulder blade), the humerus (arm bone), the radius and ulna (forearm bones), the carpal bones (wrist bones) and the bones of the hand. Bones connecting with other bones have rounded or flattened surfaces at their farthest ends to form joints where the two bones meet. These joint surfaces are covered with a soft cartilage material that acts as a cushion to the bone and aids in the gliding of the joint. Wearing down of this cartilage is seen in arthritis and other degenerative conditions. The joints are surrounded by joint capsules, composed of a tough fibrous membrane on the outside and synovial membranes on the inside. The joint capsule prevents the joint from going beyond its normal range of motion and helps to lubricate the joint surface by secreting synovial fluid.

The Cervical Spine

As mentioned earlier, the cervical spine is an important factor in RSI conditions. Any abnormal state that affects the cervical spine will affect the nerve supply to the arms and hands. Such problems as spinal misalignments (subluxations), arthritis, hypermobility, bulging discs, degenerative joint disease, inflammatory conditions and spasmed muscles will cause abnormal stresses on the nervous system. Lower cervical subluxations are commonly detected in patients who have been previously diagnosed with carpal tunnel syndrome. Subluxations are misalignments of one spinal bone upon another, causing decreased joint motion, disc irritation and nerve irritation. Spinal adjustments or manipulations are performed by a doctor of chiropractic to correct subluxated spinal segments. These adjustments begin the healing process.

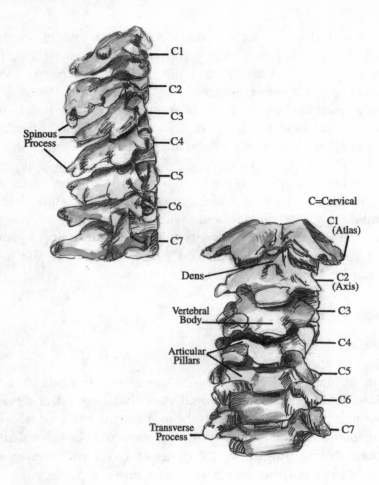

Figure 10: The Cervical Spine

THE BRAIN

Every function of the body and the way one feels pain is determined by what is happening in the brain. The brain not only

20

controls every situation in the body, it is the body. The body and brain are synonymous because of their interrelatedness. In some cases the brain attempts to control a situation but cannot, as in cases of pinched nerves and spinal cord damage. Everything experienced during an RSI, such as pain, tension and nausea, is due to thousands of nerve receptors from the affected parts relaying information to the brain and vice-versa. The overall response to this stimulation is determined by hundreds of different factors that make up an individual's persona. Some of these factors are past experiences with pain, previous traumas or abuse, emotions, anxieties, one's spirituality and so on. The list goes on indefinitely. This is not to say that all RSI patients need psychological work-ups. But it does emphasize the mind-body connection. The body and brain cannot be separated. What one thinks affects one's health. Here's an example. Think of someone who is depressed or has very low self-esteem. What does his or her posture look like? In most cases the posture is one of rounded shoulders, head looking down, increased curve of the upper back—all precursors for development of RSI conditions.

In summary, the repetitive strain injury is a multifactoral disease process. The person suffering from RSI must realize that it is a complicated dysfunction of a number of body tissues. The healthcare provider must rule in or rule out injury to all the structures mentioned above when deciding upon a diagnosis.

CHAPTER 2 _____

UNDERLYING HEALTH CONDITIONS THAT CAUSE OR MIMIC RSIS

In most cases, the diagnosis of a repetitive strain injury is straightforward and usually involves assessment of the musculoskeletal and nervous systems. In some cases, though, there are certain underlying disease states that increase the risks of repetitive strain injuries, and some can actually mimic the symptoms of RSIs. Let us look at each one individually to determine how a disease state can affect the body and how it can affect an RSI condition. If you find that some of the symptoms mentioned are similar to yours, please consult your healthcare provider. Further medical testing may be necessary to rule out these conditions.

DIABETES

Many people know something about the term diabetes, but are not familiar with its different forms. Here we will discuss diabetes mellitus, a very common disease in the industrialized world which is closely related to repetitive strain conditions.

Diabetes mellitus is broken down into two types: Type I (juvenile onset) and Type II (adult onset) diabetes. Both of these conditions can predispose one to repetitive strain injuries. The typical symptoms of someone suffering from diabetes are increased urination, increased thirst, increased hunger, rapid weight loss and overall fatigue.

Juvenile onset diabetes usually starts around the time of puberty as a result of a severe deficiency of insulin secretion from the pancreas. It is still unclear what causes this to happen. In most cases, supplemental insulin is required to make up for the insulin deficiency.

Adult onset diabetes generally occurs after the age of 40 and is commonly seen in obese or overweight individuals with poor nutrition. Insulin levels are decreased but at a higher rate than in Type I diabetes. A change of diet and an increase in exercise is generally sufficient to control Type II diabetes. I suggest that all diabetic patients read *The Zone* by Barry Sears, Ph.D. He offers an excellent explanation of the insulin reaction to certain foods we eat and helpful nutrition guidelines for Type II diabetics. I will talk more about nutrition in Chapter 11.

How Diabetes Affects RSI Conditions

In chronic cases of diabetes, there are three complications that may occur. The first is microvascular disease. This is a disease of the small blood vessels, especially of the eye and kidneys. The second is macrovascular disease, which affects the larger blood vessels, such as vessels that send blood to the heart (coronary arteries), to the brain (cerebral arteries) and to the peripheral muscles and tissues. Finally, neuropathies (damage to nerve cells) can develop, which cause changes in strength, sensation and internal organ function.[8]

Arteriosclerosis (hardening of the arteries) occurs in diabetics at a higher rate than in the general public. This is due to deposition of fats from the blood onto the walls of the blood vessels and is prevalent more frequently in those patients who suffer from frequent hyperglycemia. The narrowing of the blood vessels can lead to decreased flow of blood to the tissues. As we have already stated in Chapter 1, decreased blood flow to the muscles and ligaments makes the tissues highly susceptible to repetitive strain injuries.

Peripheral neuropathies (damaged nerves in the arms and legs) can mimic a repetitive strain injury. Diabetics may suffer from decreased sensation in the hands and feet which can be accompanied by "pins and needles" sensations. This can be a very painful condition and may cause sleep disturbances. The muscles in the hands can begin to atrophy with this condition. These types of problems tend to occur in both hands, or both feet, simultaneously. Therefore, the astute clinician should notice the pain pattern that has developed and key in to the possibility of a diabetic nerve condition. Usually, the patient has had diabetes for some time when these neuropathies occur. In some cases, there may be an RSI and a neuropathy due to diabetes, which makes treatment very challenging.

HYPOTHYROIDISM

Thyroid hormones affect the body's overall metabolic rate. Hypothyroidism is a condition in which the body is not secreting enough thyroid hormone. This results in such symptoms as fatigue, cold intolerance, muscle aches and joint aches. The skin can become scaly and dry, and hair loss is common.

Puffiness occurs in the face and around the eyes. Hypothyroidism can cause peripheral entrapment syndromes, such as carpal tunnel syndrome, due to increased fluid retention, therefore this disease needs to be ruled out with anyone suffering from CTS.

GOUT

Gout is a metabolic disorder due to elevated serum urate, a metabolite found in the bloodstream. It can lead to arthritic changes in the feet, fingers and wrists and predispose an individual to the development of carpal tunnel syndrome. Long-term gout can lead to deposition of a chalk-like substance called tophi. In some cases, tophi can deposit on the transverse carpal ligament and lead to compression of the median nerve, causing carpal tunnel syndrome.[9]

PREGNANCY AND OTHER FEMALE CONDITIONS

One of the most common symptoms of pregnancy is carpal tunnel syndrome. Mostly due to fluid retention, this problem tends to relieve itself once the pregnancy is over. Many doctors recommend vitamin B6 for pregnant women, which has shown some beneficial results. I recommend increasing water intake as well as careful monitoring of protein intake. Pregnant women need at least 80 to 100 grams of protein per day. Maintaining this level of protein prevents swelling and other disease states such as toxemia by modulating the blood's protein levels and maintaining proper water levels within the blood.[10]

BREASTFEEDING

Nursing moms continue to retain water following the birth due to milk production. It is important for women with an RSI to carefully choose a proper nursing position. Many times the mother will cradle the baby in her arms with the wrists bent and with the baby's weight supported by the hands and wrists. This will exacerbate any underlying carpal tunnel syndrome or wrist tendinitis. There are alternate ways of holding the baby. One method is called "the football hold," where the baby is positioned under the arm with head facing forward. The best position for RSI sufferers is the "side lying" position where the mother lays on her side with the baby next to her. In this position, there is no stress on the wrists whatsoever. Any woman experiencing difficulties nursing her baby should contact La Leche League International (1-800-LALECHE) which can refer her to a local support group.

MENSTRUATION

Women experiencing RSI complaints tend to notice a worsening of the condition during menstruation due to hormonal changes. This is most likely due to water retention along with increased peripheral nerve irritability.

ORAL CONTRACEPTIVES

"The pill" tends to cause fluid retention due to its hormonal effects which mimic a pregnant condition. This fluid retention can reduce the size of the tunnels where nerve compression can occur and lead to the neuropathies mentioned in Chapter 3.

ARTHRITIS

Osteoarthritis, rheumatoid and other arthritic conditions cause degenerative changes to the wrists and hands. Degeneration of the structures surrounding the carpal tunnel commonly seen in rheumatoid arthritis can irritate the median nerve due to inflammation and compression. Arthritic conditions in the spine can cause pinched nerves leading to an increased chance of developing RSI conditions. If these conditions are suspected, X-rays should be taken of the affected regions and blood work should be performed to verify the presence of the disease.

PREVIOUS TRAUMA

If you have had trauma to the wrist, such as a fracture from a fall, this could lead to CTS later on in life. Fractures of the elbow can make you more susceptible to ulnar nerve neuropathies. A history of shoulder dislocations increases the likelihood of posterior shoulder impingement and fibrosis, as well as thoracic outlet syndrome. Poorly set or poorly healed fractures can predispose you to RSIs as well. Car accidents are another important trauma to take into account. Whiplash injuries can alter the biomechanics of the neck and lead to accelerated degeneration of the cervical spine. Nerve compression may result as a cause of this process, leading to arm and hand complaints.

BODY WEIGHT

Statistics tell us that obesity in the United States is increasing. So many factors play a part in this, but the end result is an increase in repetitive strain injuries in obese people. Deposition of fatty material in the carpal tunnel and other tunnel areas causes increased pressure on the peripheral nerves and the resulting symptoms.

However, people with little muscle mass and who are very thin also have an increased chance of developing RSI conditions simply because the amount of muscle tissue is not adequate for the repetitive functions needed in the workplace or for a particular hobby.[11]

DRUG AND TOBACCO USE

Many drugs on the market can cause fluid retention. If you are currently taking medications for ailments other than RSI, consult with your doctor or go to the library and consult the *Physician's Desk Reference* or other drug reference books to check the drug's side effects. Sometimes, simply changing medications can eliminate some nerve-related disorders. Better yet, seek a holistic doctor who can decide what underlying condition is causing your ailment to develop in the first place. You may not need those medications!

Use of tobacco products such as cigarettes, cigars, pipes or chewing tobacco also causes arterial constriction because of the action of the potent chemical, nicotine. It also decreases oxygen to the tissues because of the increased amount of carbon monoxide in the bloodstream. This reduces the oxygen-binding capability of hemoglobin, the primary component of red blood cells.

PERNICIOUS ANEMIA

This kind of anemia, also known as megaloblastic anemia, is due to a B12 deficiency or folic acid deficiency. This deficiency results in impairment of DNA synthesis and enlarged blood cells. This condition is rare, since most meat-eating people store enough B12 in the liver to last for a few years. People who are susceptible to this disease process are vegetarians who eat no dairy or animal products, alcoholics, those who have a disease of the stomach or small intestine, pregnant women and those undergoing chemotherapy. The neurologic changes associated with pernicious anemia result initially from slow demyelination of the large peripheral nerve cells. Eventually, if untreated, the nerves of the spinal cord and the brain can be affected. The usual symptoms begin with pins and needles and/or numbness in the hands or feet (also known as paresthesias). The person suffering from this condition will begin to lose the perception of where a limb is in space. For example, he won't know if his toes are pointing up or down. It can effect the reflexes, strength, and may cause mild paralysis of the lower extremity.

LESS COMON CONDITIONS

The following conditions do not occur frequently, but they are important to mention. Acromegaly, renal dialysis, blood vessel lesions, lung and bone tumors, Paget's disease and less common metabolic disorders can cause symptoms that mimic those of a repetitive strain injury.

Your doctor should come up with a differential diagnosis when contemplating your particular condition. Differential diagnoses are a list of conditions that cause similar types of pain patterns. As you can see, there are some serious systemic diseases that can appear to be repetitive strain syndrome. Ask your doctor if there are any other conditions that he/she is considering when providing you with a diagnosis. Many of the conditions mentioned in this chapter can be ruled out by simple blood and urine tests. I recommend all RSI sufferers have these baseline tests performed after the initial examination to rule out any systemic disorders.

PART 2

THE GUIDE TO REPETITIVE STRAIN INJURIES

This section of the book will break down repetitive strain injuries according to the location of pain. For example, if you have pain in the forearm, refer to Chapter 5 (The Forearm). You can also look at the pain-locator chart on the following page to determine which chapters to read. Most chapters begin with a case study that gives an actual patient's account of the condition. (Names of the people involved in the case studies have been changed.) After the syndrome is explained in detail, an explanation of the patient's treatment program and the final result of the case follows at the end of the chapter.

Use this quick-reference pain-locator chart to help you determine which chapters relate to your symptoms. Please note that as you travel down toward the fingers, there are many more possibilities for the cause of pain. Therefore, you are referred to a greater num-

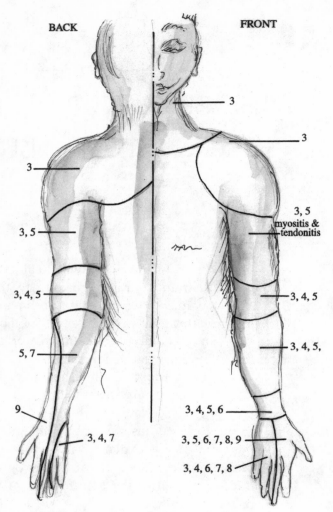

BACK   FRONT

3

3

3

3, 5

3, 5
myositis &
tendonitis

3, 4, 5

3, 4, 5

3, 4, 5,

5, 7

9

3, 4, 5, 6

3, 4, 7

3, 5, 6, 7, 8, 9

3, 4, 6, 7, 8

Figure 11: Pain Location with Chapter References

ber of chapters and possible RSIs relating to
your pain patterns.

If you are feeling mostly abnormal sensations in the upper extremity, shoulders or

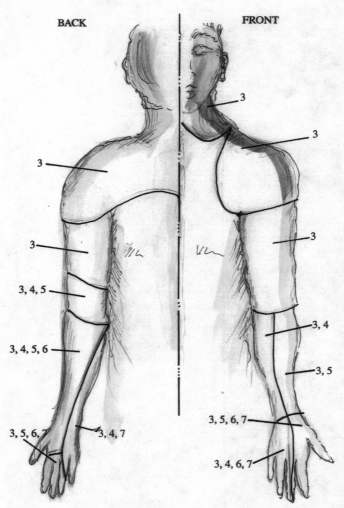

BACK

FRONT

3

3

3

3

3, 4, 5

3, 4

3, 4, 5, 6

3, 5

3, 5, 6, 7

3, 5, 6, 7

3, 4, 7

3, 4, 6, 7

Figure 12: Abnormal Sensations Chart & Chapter References

neck, or a combination of sensation changes with pain, use this chart to help you determine which chapters to read.

CHAPTER 3

THE NECK

CASE #1:
THE NECK AND UPPER BACK

Christine is a self-employed bookkeeper and manages accounts for a number of small businesses. This is her tenth year of business. Her work involves data entry and analysis of records for tax purposes. She finds herself leaning over the books for many hours throughout the day. She always notices a great deal of tension between her shoulders and stiffness in her neck, especially after a long day of working in front of the computer. The upper back pain can turn into burning pain when it is at its worst. Occasionally, the tightness will get so intense that she develops a severe headache that radiates from the back of the head to the front. She occasionally suffers from eye strain after a long day of staring at the computer monitor.

Discussion:

Christine is suffering from repetitive strain of the muscles attaching into the spine combined with a shortening of the mus-

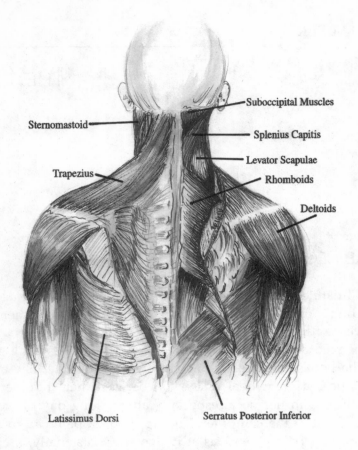

Figure 13: Muscles of the Neck and Upper Back

cles attaching into the anterior chest wall. The scenario described above is seen repeatedly in people who work at computers, in professions like architectural draftsmen, who lean over drawing tables, electronics workers who strain forward over a worktable while grasping small objects, and also in college students who spend long hours reading and studying, hunched over their books. Figure 13 shows the paraspinal muscles as they travel from the lower back up to the neck. These muscles maintain the spine in an erect posture. They work synergistically with the muscles of the chest and abdominal wall to keep you standing or sitting up. A prolonged hunched-over posture will strain the paraspinal muscles, causing them to pull unevenly on their attachments into the spinal bones. Spinal subluxations become prevalent as the strain continues.

Shortened and tightened chest muscles are a common result of a posture that requires repetitive forward bending. You can experience this after reading with your head looking down for a couple of hours. Anyone who attempts this posture knows the feeling of soreness and tightness in the neck after the reading is done. The muscles involved in this reaction are the neck flexor muscles, the pectoralis major and minor muscles, the abdominal muscles, and the intercostal muscles located between each rib. Tightening of the neck flexors leads to restricted range of motion of the neck and can result in chronic headaches due to irritation and swelling of the muscle insertions into the skull bones and trigger points located within the fatigued muscle belly.

Maintaining this poor posture for many years leads to spinal abnormalities, such as an increased thoracic (mid-back) curve, also known as hyperkyphosis in medical terminology. This is especially likely when poor posture is maintained during adolescent years when the bones are conforming and molding to the abnormal stresses. It is normal to have a gentle curve throughout the middle back, but an exaggeration of that curve is not normal. An increased thoracic curve compresses the anterior portion of the vertebrae along with the intervertebral disc, the spongy substance located between each vertebra. If the disc becomes inflamed due to this compression, then moderate to severe midback pain along with feelings of burning and numbness will soon follow. The increased thoracic curve may decrease the space available for the lungs to inflate because of the rounding and compression of the rib cage. Decreased lung capacity is a result. This in turn will lessen the amount of oxygen available to the body.

A forward tilt of the head is common in people with an increased curvature of the midback. This exerts a tremendous amount of downward pressure on the lower cervical nerve roots, thus predisposing the arms, forearms and hands to weakened nerve impulses, setting the stage for conditions such as carpal tunnel syndrome.

Computer users who round the lower back and sit in a slouched position are prone to another form of spinal stress. This position decreases the natural lumbar curve and leads to a decrease or straightening of the normal thoracic curve. This posture results in a flattened thoracic spine and is typically accompanied by rib irritation and neck soreness. This condition is also quite common among those who suffer from nerve-related complaints down the arms. It is common among these types of back pain sufferers to try to "pop" their backs by leaning back over the top of the chair. In most cases this attempt at self-manipulating does more harm than good and leads to more pain and irritation. To relieve this condition, a doctor of chiropractic uses specialized adjustments of the spine that normalize the spine/rib junction and relieves the pain between the shoulder blades that is so common to this syndrome. Part 5 focuses on rehabilitative exercises and describes strengthening techniques to lessen this kind of midback pain.

Treatment:

Upon postural examination, it was detected that Christine had an increase of the thoracic curvature along with a forward head carriage. Muscle spasm was evident along the entire paraspinal (along the spine) muscles in the neck and middle back, as well as in neck flexor muscles. Spinal joint irritation and subluxations were commonplace throughout this entire region. Chiropractic manipulation of the spine began on a three-time-per-week basis over the first two weeks. Interferential muscle stimulation, a form of electrical muscle stimulation that reduces muscle spasm and swelling, was implemented on each visit (See Chapter 13). Christine's treatments were reduced to two times per week for four weeks, then once per week for an additional four weeks. She was given instructions on proper sitting techniques and was advised to use a book rest to prop up her materials, thus decreasing the forward head tilt. She was given stretches for the chest and abdominal muscles. She also received massage therapy to aid in the healing of her tired back muscles. After four weeks, Christine began to respond favorably and was able to sit through her normal work day with little or no pain. She began a one-on-one stretching program with a personal trainer and has taken the steps to lead a more healthy lifestyle. Thus Christine's repetitive strain injury allowed her to increase her self-awareness, make changes in her work situation, and take charge of her health.

CASE #2:
THE SHOULDERS—THORACIC OUTLET SYNDROME

Janet is a professional violinist. Over the past two years, she has noted increasing pain in her left arm while playing the violin. This pain has increased to a point where it is becoming difficult for her to lift the instrument. She is becoming accustomed to the chronic neck soreness and stiffness that plague her on a daily basis. She states that her hand has been feeling cold while playing the instrument and that her neck is always sore after playing. Besides the neck pain, she is noticing pain in the front of her shoulder and in the elbow. Her neck pain radiates to the back of her shoulder. She experiences difficulty in turning her head when backing up her car. Tingling and numbness are increasing throughout her forearm and hand. When she tries to comb her hair with her left hand, her entire left forearm and hand go numb.

Discussion

This scenario typifies a case of thoracic outlet syndrome (TOS) combined with neck muscle strain. TOS is actually a generalized term that explains symptoms arising from nerve and/or blood vessel compression in four specific anatomical regions of the neck and shoulder. There may be only one site involved or up to all four sites may be involved. Each location of nerve and blood vessel compression should be termed a syndrome in itself since each one has its own specific diagnostic criteria and pain patterns.

The following syndromes all fall under the heading thoracic outlet syndrome: accessory cervical rib syndrome, scalene anticus syndrome, pectoralis minor syndrome, and costo-clavicular syndrome. These disorders will be analyzed individually, and the predisposing risk factors will be discussed. In general, the person suffering from TOS complains of pain that travels from the neck down to the arm. It may be associated with numbness or tingling sensations that spread over the entire

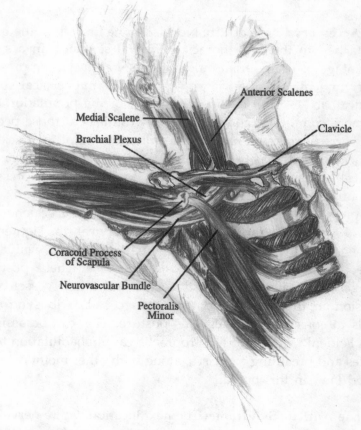

Figure 14: The Thoracic Outlet

hand. Many cases involve numbness and tingling of the ring and pinkie fingers and the inside of the forearm. Commonly, the person will complain of coldness in the arms or hands. This syndrome can occur in both arms at the same time. The pain may feel shooting, burning, aching or dull. Occasionally, weakness is involved in the arm, forearm or hand. It takes a well-educated diagnostician who is familiar with musculoskeletal pain patterns to discern among the four syndromes grouped under the heading TOS.

The Accessory Cervical Rib: Normally, the first rib of the body is attached to the first thoracic vertebral segment. In a small percentage of the population, an accessory rib will be present, protruding off one the lowest segments of the cervical spine. Cervical ribs are present in 0.5 percent of the population and are more common among females. Two-thirds of those people with cervical ribs will have them on both sides of the neck.[12, 13] Cervical ribs are easily detected by X-ray, but whether or not cervical ribs actually cause nerve or blood vessel compression is controversial. The common culprit is poor posture and drooping of the shoulders with irritation of the scalene and trapezius muscle attachments along the cervical rib. Tightening of the powerful latissimus dorsi muscle must be evaluated, since this can cause shoulder drooping also. These postural changes predicate the pinched nerves and blood vessel compression in the neck. Anyone with a cervical rib syndrome needs to consciously change his posture. This can be assisted with Feldenkrais sessions, chiropractic care, rehabilitation techniques and breathing exercises, along with other methods mentioned later in this book.

Scalene Anticus Syndrome: The next location where nerve and blood vessel compression may occur is where the plexus of

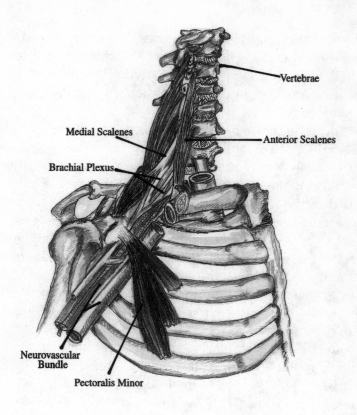

Figure 15: The Scalene Muscles and Thoracic Outlet

nerves pass between the anterior and medial scalene muscle groups. The scalene muscle groups have two actions: 1) lateral bending and rotation of the neck and 2) when contracted together simultaneously, elevation of the first rib to aid in respiration. These muscles are involved in the cough reflex to aid in elevating the rib cage. Also, asthma sufferers have chronic overuse of these muscles due to respiratory effort during attacks. Those people who use chest breathing rather than abdominal breathing (see page 248) will also tend to overuse the scalene muscles and increase their chances of developing TOS symptoms.

Office workers who hold the telephone between their ear and shoulder while typing or writing risk developing scalene anticus syndrome. This is due to the chronic contracture and shortening of the muscles due to overuse. Since the scalenes attach directly to the most lateral part of the vertebrae, the transverse processes (see Figure 10), contracture of these muscles will tug on the spine itself, causing misalignments and strain on the spinal joints. This leads to inflammation of the joints and the resulting dull neck pain that commonly accompanies scalene anticus syndrome. These inflamed and misaligned joints can lead to inflammation of the nerves as they exit the spine, thus worsening the condition. Realignment of the spine through spinal manipulation is imperative in this condition to allow for restored spinal mobility.

Anyone who spends a great deal of time on the telephone should obtain a headset. This frees up the arms and reduces strain on the neck musculature.

Costoclavicular Syndrome: Notice in the Figure 14 how the nerves and blood vessels must pass between the clavicle (collarbone) and the upper rib cage. Compression of this bundle may occur under a number of circumstances. This condition can result from "military posture," whereby the chest is protruded outward and the head is thrust backward. This posture compresses the clavicle (collarbone) against the ribs, leading to a squeezing of the nerves and blood vessels. People who wear backpacks are common sufferers of this syndrome due to the pressure of the straps on top of the shoulders and chest. Parents who wear baby or child backpacks are vulnerable for the same reason. Asthma and emphysema sufferers may develop costoclavicular syndrome due to changes in chest wall structure from the underlying disease state. Misalignments of the clavicle, upper thoracic vertebrae and ribs are common in this condition.

Pectoralis Minor Syndrome: As the neurovascular (nerves and blood vessels) bundle travels down to the arm, it must pass under the pectoralis minor muscle. The muscle is commonly strained and shortened in any person who performs repetitive forward motions of the arms, such as computer keyboarding, using a mouse, repetitive factory work, sporting activities such as tennis and playing musical instruments like the violin, viola and cello. The inexperienced body builder who overworks the chest and underworks the upper back musculature will be more apt to develop pectoralis minor syndrome. This is common in young men who want the "big chest" look and emphasize bench presses and incline presses in their workouts.

Chronic pectoralis minor contraction leads to rib pain in the upper chest. Inflammation of its attachment to the coracoid process of the shoulder blade (the little bony protrusion on the chest just below the collarbone, medial to the shoulder) can lead to inflammation and subsequent irritation of the short head of the biceps tendon and the coracobrachialis muscle which also attach to the coracoid process. (See detail in Figure 14.) This results in upper-arm soreness in conjunction with the symptoms of TOS, which complicates the diagnosis.

Abdominal vs. Chest Breathing:

People who primarily use the chest and neck muscles to breathe lose out in three ways. First, they cannot fully inflate

45

their lungs by just expanding the chest wall. Inspiration volume decreases with chest breathing, thus the tissues do not get the oxygen-rich blood needed for nourishment. Decreased oxygenation of the blood will amplify the effects of small blood vessel and nerve constriction, leading to quicker death of cells. Secondly, they overwork the neck muscles which aid in elevating the rib cage. This leads to susceptibility of developing scalene anticus syndrome. Finally, the diaphragm, the large muscle located circumferentially along the bottom of the rib cage that allows expansion of the lungs, does not contract fully. The rhythmical contraction of the diaphragm allows for a massage effect on the digestive organs, pumping blood and aiding digestion. Thus a restriction of this motion has deleterious effects on the entire abdominal contents. The diminished use of the diaphragm and the resulting poor muscle tone makes one more susceptible to hiatal hernia. This type of hernia is due to a widening of the opening where the esophagus passes through the diaphragm to enter into the stomach. This widening allows acidic stomach fluids to travel upwards from the stomach to the esophagus, leading to heartburn-type pain.

Diaphragmatic breathing increases the intake of air by the lungs. To discover if you are using abdominal breathing, place one hand on your abdomen and the other hand on your chest, and watch what happens to your hands as your breath normally for a minute or two. If you are using abdominal breathing, the hand on your abdomen will rise as you breath in and fall as you breath out. Very little will happen with the hand on your chest. If you are using chest breathing, the opposite will occur—the chest will rise higher than the abdomen upon inhaling.

If you find that you are chest breathing, you need to consciously begin to change this habit. In the beginning it will feel strange to allow your abdomen to expand when you breathe, but don't give up. Soon the breathing will begin to feel more natural and will involve less energy expenditure. This will relieve many neck and shoulder problems. For more information on breathing, see Chapter 25.

Evaluation and Treatment

Janet was videotaped while playing her violin. This helped to determine why her shoulder and neck were getting irritated. She was tightly holding her left arm towards the body while playing the violin. This caused tension in the shoulder. She also tightened the face and neck muscles while playing, producing an occasional grimace during the difficult measures. Some technique changes and modifications in playing style were recommended. Treatment began with physiotherapy modalities such as ultrasound, electrical muscle stimulation and ice to the neck and anterior shoulder region. I also performed a deep-tissue massage (myofascial release) to the forearm muscles to ease the tendinitis. Chiropractic spinal manipulation was performed on the entire spine to relieve nerve irritation. She was given stretching exercises at the onset of care to stretch the tightened chest muscles, forearm muscles and neck muscles. I also taught Janet some visualization techniques to aid in the healing process. She began responding to care in two to three weeks. We then began implementing exercise regimens to strengthen the upper back muscles and shoulder muscles. After six weeks of care and a total of 16 office visits, Janet was pain-free. She continues to come in for maintenance visits due to the stress of performing and the resulting neck tension.

CASE #3:
SHOULDER IMPINGEMENT SYNDROME

> Jennifer is a 45-year-old housewife and mother who began developing left shoulder pain about four months ago. She complained that the pain was deep and very achy and was affecting the entire shoulder area. She could not pinpoint a specific location of pain. Jennifer was having trouble moving her arm, especially above the head. She noticed the shoulder pain was affecting her daily activities, such as combing her hair, lifting her child and housecleaning. The pain was waking her up at night, and she found it difficult to find a comfortable position to sleep that did not irritate the shoulder. The shoulder pain seemed to be worsening daily. Jennifer smoked about a pack of cigarettes per day.

Discussion

Shoulder impingement syndrome is a condition where the tendons in the superior aspect of the shoulder joint become impinged or squeezed due to abnormal biomechanics, cumulative microtraumas or previous shoulder injury. The supraspinatus tendon and the long head of the biceps tendon are the affected structures due to their anatomical position just under the acromion, above the humeral head and within the space bounded by the coraco-acromial ligament. (See Figure 16.)

Repetitive actions involving raising the arm at shoulder height or above the head can precipitate this malady. Examples are an auto mechanic working at or above the head level or a hairstylist whose arms are raised in front throughout the day. Shoulder impingement is quite common as a result of sporting

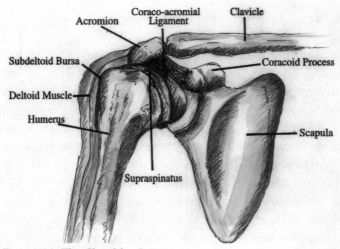

Figure 16: The Shoulder Joint

activities, such as tennis and other racquet sports, swimming and baseball pitching, which all involve raising the shoulder repeatedly.

Injury to the supraspinatus or biceps tendon can be a result of a number of factors. Repetitive trauma to the shoulder can lead to vascular impairment, thus decreasing blood flow to the tendons. Microtraumas of the tendon itself due to overuse are possible. There is also the possibility of tears within the "rotator cuff" muscles (the group of small muscles that rotate the shoulder) that lead to instability and abnormal biomechanics within the joint. Previous shoulder injuries, such as dislocations, sprains and acromioclavicular joint sprain (shoulder separation), can cause changes in the physical size of the acromion/shoulder joint complex and cause impingement on the tendons.[14]

49

Treatment

An examination was performed on Jennifer and it revealed pain upon shoulder motion in most of its ranges of motion, especially upon attempting to raise the arm to shoulder height. She could not bring the arm any higher than this, and my attempts to bring the arm above shoulder height, even through passive measures, elicited extreme pain. Muscle spasm was noted in the rotator cuff muscles, the anterior chest muscles, the trapezius and the neck muscles. Spinal exam revealed tenderness over the lower cervical spine as well as the upper cervical spine. X-rays of the shoulder were performed which revealed calcification of the supraspinatus tendon, a condition which can occur after long-term inflammation and irritation.

Treatment was started on a three-time-per-week schedule for three weeks, then twice per week for three weeks. Jennifer received low-amplitude ultrasound therapy to the shoulder, supraspinatous muscle and neck region. Chiropractic spinal adjustments were performed to normalize nerve flow to the shoulder region. Very gentle shoulder mobilization techniques, within the pain tolerance level of the patient were implemented at the beginning of treatment. As the shoulder pain lessened, more aggressive shoulder adjustments were used. Jennifer was given passive range-of-motion exercises at this time. Soft tissue massage of the anterior chest muscles, back muscles, and neck muscles was performed by a massage therapist one time per week. She also received microcurrent therapy for a short period of time.

After about two to three weeks of care, Jennifer began noticing improved shoulder mobility, lessened pain and better sleeping patterns. She was given shoulder rehabilitation exercises at this time which she complied with well. By the fourth week, the shoulder pain was less noticeable, and Jennifer was resuming her normal activities with little pain. An X-ray was taken after one month of treatment to determine the extent of calcification within the supraspinatus tendon. We were very happy to find that the X-ray showed a marked reduction of calcification; in fact, it was difficult to notice any calcification at all.

By six weeks, Jennifer was relatively pain-free except for some mild soreness during certain activities. Her treatment program was reduced to once weekly for four weeks. After this time she was prescribed a wellness program for the continued benefits of chiropractic care. Jennifer was also told about the harmful effects of smoking on her vascular and muscular systems, but, unfortunately, she ignored this information.

CHAPTER 4

THE ELBOW

CASE #4:
CUBITAL TUNNEL SYNDROME

Carol is a full-time hairstylist. Over the past several months, she has noticed some pain along the inner and outer edges of her right elbow and hand. Her condition worsens after a full day at the salon. The inner edge of her elbow is especially sore after a full day; in fact if she even taps it against an object, it causes a severe pain that radiates down to the hand. The past three weeks have been very trying, with recurring tingling and numbness in her ring and pinkie fingers on the palm side. Her grip is weakening and she is having trouble manipulating the scissors when cutting hair. The elbow pain is now constant and is affecting her sleep. She is very concerned that the injury may affect her career. Carol is physically active, works out daily, and enjoys martial arts. However, her martial arts activities further strain her arms and forearms as well as her knees and hips. She notices an increase of pain in her right elbow and hand during her workouts.

Discussion:

The ulnar nerve supplies sensation to the front and back of the ring and little fingers. It also provides motor control of the small hand muscles located in the palm on the pinkie side, the small interosseus muscles that control lateral movement of the fingers and two muscles that flex the thumb inward toward the pinkie. This nerve travels down from the spine and must pass through a small tunnel called the cubital tunnel. This tunnel is located just at and below the funny bone area on the inside of the elbow. (See Figure 17.) You can think of this tunnel as having four walls. The bottom wall consists of the flexor digitorum profundus muscle and the elbow joint capsule. The side walls consist of the two heads of the flexor carpi ulnaris muscle. A tough ligament forms the ceiling of this tunnel.

The ulnar nerve can become irritated at its location within the elbow for a number of reasons. Adhesions in the fascia and muscles can prevent the normal gliding of the nerve when the elbow is flexed. Inflammation in the surrounding tissues and in the nerve itself cause abnormalities in the nerve supply to the hand. Tugging and irritation of the nerve due to repetitive actions involving flexed elbows, such as violin playing and drumming, carpentry and assembly-line work damage the sensitive nerves inducing fibrosis and scarring.

A predisposing factor for cubital tunnel syndrome is seen in computer users who rest their wrists on a pad and repeatedly reach with the pinkie to hit the enter keys and tab keys while typing. Although this mainly involves the hand muscles which laterally deviate the pinkie, it also activates the lateral forearm muscles, specifically the flexor carpi ulnaris and flexor digitorum profundus and superficialis and the finger extensor muscles. Prolonged contraction of these muscles causes fatigue,

53

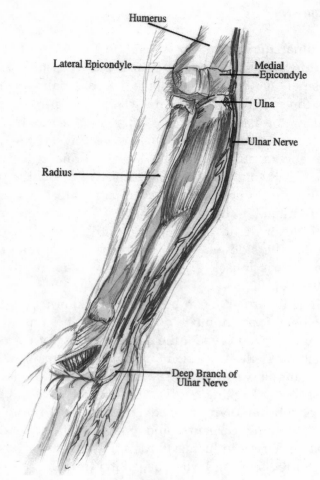

Figure 17: The Ulnar Nerve and Forearm

irritation and myofascial trigger points at their insertion into the elbow, thus setting the stage for cubital tunnel syndrome.

Another problem arises in anyone who rests upper body weight on the elbows. This is common in computer users, people seated at workbenches and those who sit for long periods with elbows bent and pressing into their chair's armrest. The pressure of the body weight upon the elbow leads to a structural derangement of the elbow joint along with inflammation. The bursa near the point of the elbow may become inflamed. Direct pressure of the ulnar nerve is also possible leading to pins and needles sensations in the fingers.

Finally, cubital tunnel syndrome can be a result of arthritis of the elbow joint. Arthritic and degenerative changes of the elbow joint may lead to small bone spurs which compress the ulnar nerve. If this is the cause of the symptoms, surgery may be needed to remove the spurs and decompress the nerve.[15]

Cubital tunnel syndrome leads to changes in sensation in the fingers; typically tingling or numbness develops in the ring and pinkie fingers. Pain is common along the inner part of the forearm, traveling down to the pinkie side of the hand. Prolonged ulnar nerve pressure leads to weakening of the muscles supplied by the nerve. Common problems that arise are difficulty in laterally deviating the pinkie, weakness in grip strength and clumsiness of the hand. It is common for cubital tunnel syndrome and medial epicondylitis (see next case study) to be present simultaneously. Continued untreated, ulnar nerve compression can cause muscle atrophy in the small muscles of the palm on the pinkie side and sensation loss to the fourth and fifth fingers.

Treatment

Examination of Carol revealed swelling and pain over the region of the cubital tunnel. Further inspection indicated lower cervical spine irritation with muscle spasm evident in the scalene muscles—the lateral neck flexors. The wrist flexors in the forearm were sore and inflamed. An evaluation of Carol's hairstyling technique revealed that she often used motions of the arms involving elevation of the elbows above the shoulders. She placed stress on the wrists by putting them in flexion while using the shears. Using a footstool helped to ease stress on her arms while performing her work. Carol's posture needed improving also. She stated that she had had a problem with her posture ever since she was a child. She sat with a hunched posture which caused a rounding of the shoulders and tightening of the chest muscles. Attempting to sit in a more upright posture seemed to hurt her back.

At the beginning of her treatment program, I restricted Carol's weight training for three weeks to give her arms a rest. She was performing strenuous workouts four to five times per week which did not allow the arms to heal fully. She was encouraged to continue aerobic activities and exercise routines for the lower body, abdominals and back muscles.

Carol's treatments included myofascial release to the wrist flexors and the muscles of the palm. Chiropractic manipulative techniques aided in relief of the lower neck tension, plus misalignments of the upper back and rib cage, and remedied a preexisting lower back condition. Ultrasound was used on the elbow to stimulate healing. After three weeks of care the patient was given rubber tubing exercises to begin toning the arms again. The arm pain and finger sensations began to ease during this time. After five weeks, she was instructed to begin using free weights to exercise the forearms and arms. After eight weeks of care, Carol only experienced sporadic arm soreness.

Carol's postural problems continued to cause recurrences of her arm and hand pain and weakness. It was suggested that she begin Feldenkrais classes to increase awareness of her deeply ingrained and harmful postural patterns. Carol continues on a wellness care program, and occasionally has recurring hand symptoms that are remedied by chiropractic treatments and deep tissue muscle work.

CASE #5:
LATERAL AND MEDIAL EPICONDYLITIS (TENNIS ELBOW AND GOLFER'S ELBOW)

Jack is an architect by trade and enjoys a rigorous game of racquetball following his stressful workday. He plays racquetball at least three times per week. Lately he has been feeling a great deal of soreness on the outside edge of his elbow. He has noticed that anytime he brings his racquet back in preparation to hit the ball he feels a deep ache in the elbow. He hasn't noticed any weakness in his arm or hand. His only pain arises when he attempts to contract the muscles in the forearm, notably the muscles that extend the hand. The forearm itself feels pretty good, but the elbow is quite painful to the touch. He notices that when he sleeps, the elbow pain occasionally will wake him up if he lays on it. He tries to lay on the other side, but letting the affected arm hang down also hurts the elbow. The elbow problem has begun to affect his work. Just holding on to his drawing pencil irritates the elbow, as does his computer work for designing floor plans and elevations. He was told by a number of his friends that a simple cortisone injection would take care of the problem, but Jack decided first to seek care from an alternative health provider who would look into the cause of the problem and use noninvasive methods to heal his arm. He decided that if he didn't see any results in a few weeks, then he would go for the cortisone.

Discussion

The epicondylar regions of the elbow are located just above the elbow joint, at the outermost edges. (See Figure 18a and 18b). Located on the outer lateral edge of the epicondyles are the tendon insertion points of the wrist and hand extensor muscles. Located on the inner medial edge of the epicondyles are the tendon insertion points of the wrist and hand flexor muscles. Lateral epicondylitis refers to inflammation of the lateral or outer edge where the extensor tendons arise. Medial epicondylitis refers to inflammation on the opposite side where the flexor tendons arise. Inflammation in these regions occurs because of repeated strain on the epicondyle. This strain can be due to a great number of factors. Lateral epicondylitis was termed "tennis elbow" because it was seen so commonly in tennis players due to repeated stress from swinging the racquet, especially the backhand swing, and the impact on the elbow when the ball hits the racket. That doesn't mean that only tennis players can suffer from this injury, just as "golfer's elbow" doesn't mean only golfers suffer from medial epicondylitis.

These conditions are common to anyone who repeatedly uses motions that rotate the hand back and forth (in medical terms, pronates and supinates), for example, a carpenter who uses a screwdriver repeatedly throughout the day. The repeated twisting motion of the elbow irritates the tendinous insertions. Another example is the assembly line worker who flips an item over hundreds of times daily, or a grocery checker whose hands rotate while scanning in merchandise. This condition is also seen in young children who want to learn how to throw "curve balls" at an early age. The twisting of the arm needed to throw the curve ball exerts extreme pressure on the epicondyles and leads to an inflammatory event. Any overuse

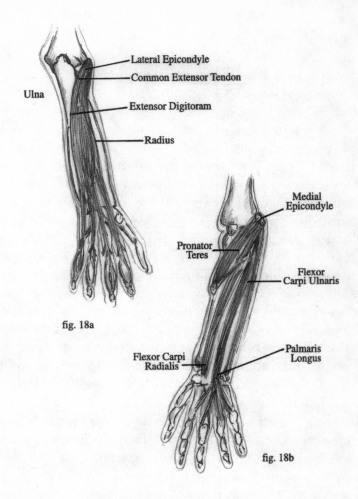

Lateral Epicondyle

Common Extensor Tendon

Extensor Digitoram

Ulna

Radius

fig. 18a

Medial
Epicondyle

Pronator
Teres

Flexor
Carpi Ulnaris

Palmaris
Longus

Flexor Carpi
Radialis

fig. 18b

Figure 18a-18b: The Elbow and its Muscular Attachments

of the hand and wrist flexor muscles or extensor muscles can irritate the epicondylar attachments.

Epicondylitis develops because the tendons attaching into the lower portion of the arm bone (humerus) cannot withstand the stress exerted upon them. They begin to pull from the bone's outer surface, called the *periosteum*. This sets up an inflammatory process and leads to the soreness upon movement so common with this disorder. Upon consistent strain the tendons begin to tear and degenerate. Blood flow becomes restricted to the worn-out structures, and weak scar tissue replaces the injured tissues. If left untreated, this can lead to chronic pain in the elbow.

Referred pain from the triceps muscle can mimic both medial and lateral epicondylitis.[16] Constant strain on the triceps (located on the back of the arm) from activities that call for arm and forearm extension, as in reaching overhead to paint a ceiling or hitting a nail with a hammer, can cause trigger points within the muscle belly. Trigger points are localized hyperirritated zones within muscle and fascia (similar to small areas of muscle spasm). They give rise to referred pain, meaning they can send pain to other areas of the body, usually in close proximity to the location of the trigger point. In this case, a trigger point within the triceps muscle can refer pain to the epicondyle, just above the elbow joint. Therefore, although pain is felt in the epicondyle, it actually arises from the triceps muscle. Trigger points with the pectoralis major muscle (the large anterior chest muscle) can refer pain to the medial elbow. This can mimic a medial epicondylitis. An astute clinician is able to discriminate between a true epicondylitis and referred pain in the epicondylar region.

Treatment

Jack was advised to quit racquetball playing for a month. He continued to do his drafting work during the initial treatment program, although his elbow did occasionally ache on the job. During that time, his arm was treated with chiropractic adjustments and the standard physical therapy modalities of ultra-sound and microcurrent electrical stimulation and ice therapy. He was given a tennis elbow brace, which aids in compressing the irritated tendons against the bone. This compression relieves the tugging on the periosteum from the tendon and allows the tendon-bone surface to heal. Bracing for any RSI condition should be implemented with caution. In some cases braces help tremendously, but sometimes they may cause an increase of pain. This may be a result of compression on the veins and lymphatic tissues, resulting in stagnation of the de-oxygenated blood in the extremities along with slowed lymph flow.

Each patient is tested for a week with the brace to determine its effectiveness. If signs of healing are seen, then we continue with the brace. In Jack's case, the brace did help, so we continued with it for the first four weeks. He was advised to wear the brace throughout the day when active, then to take it off at night. Jack received massage therapy to ease tense muscles in his neck, arms and forearms. Spinal, shoulder, elbow and wrist misalignments were corrected via chiropractic care. Once the swelling and pain subsided in his elbow after about three weeks of care, he was given exercises to rehabilitate his neck, arm and forearm muscles. After four weeks of care, he was allowed to resume his racquetball game. I advised him to return to play slowly and ice the arm following play. Jack was treated three times per week for the first three weeks, then twice per week for three weeks. After six weeks of care, his treatment program was reduced to once per week for four weeks, then it was reduced further to twice monthly. He maintains this schedule of treatment for wellness care. At eight weeks of care, Jack had no noticeable soreness in the elbow. He was very happy that he decided to forego the cortisone injections recommended by his friends.

CHAPTER 5

THE FOREARM

CASE #6:
TENDINITIS, MYOSITIS AND MYOFASCITIS

Janice is a full time data entry worker for a large insurance company. Management decided to redesign the employees' cubicles recently, thus altering the computer and keyboard arrangements Janice had become accustomed to over the years. Due to a lack of desk space in this new arrangement, Janice began to place the computer keyboard on her lap to have easier access to the books and paperwork on the desk in front of her. This rearrangement started irritating her arms almost immediately, but she ignored the discomfort at first. In time, it worsened and she began to notice nonstop pain on the top and bottom of the forearms, especially on the right side. Her arms felt tired and heavy, and her typing became sloppy. There was no tingling or numbness in her hands, but occasionally she would get a strange tingling feeling at the base of the thumb. She had a great deal of irritation in the right elbow and it was tender to the touch.

Discussion

Tendinitis is inflammation of the tendons (-itis = inflammation of). Tendon inflammation can occur anywhere in the body that is subject to repetitive strain. Tendons can also become inflamed when put under a sudden strain. In RSIs, the common locations of tendon irritation are the tendons attaching into the spine (scalene, SCM, and trapezius muscles), the front of the shoulder (the biceps tendon), the small tendons surrounding the shoulder joint (the rotator cuff), the posterior shoulder (triceps tendon, latissimus dorsi tendon), the elbow (wrist flexor and extensor tendons) and the tendons attaching into the hand and fingers. Tendinitis can develop into a very painful condition that can limit joint motion and thus cause pain upon initiation of movement of the limb. Tendons are spaghetti-like extensions of the muscles and attach directly into the inner layers of the bone. Under repetitive strain, microscopic tears at the muscle-tendon junction and the tendon-bone junction occur. This leads to the inflammation and pain common with the condition. Inflamed tendons are painful to the touch, and the pain can feel dull, achy and sometimes nauseating.

Tendinitis tends to be an overused diagnosis in repetitive strain injuries. Remember that tendons attach the muscles to bones; therefore, tendinitis can be found only in those areas where tendons are present. Some doctors will call any forearm pain tendinitis. Pain in the muscles is not tendinitis; it can be myositis or myofascitis as explained below, or possibly a strain. Tendinitis by itself will not give neurological symptoms such as tingling and numbness. It can cause weakness though, as we mentioned above. Therefore, the doctor who diagnoses such a condition must determine if the weakness is due to a neurological deficit or pain from tendon or muscle irritation. Most RSIs are a combination of factors including neurological involvement, tendon irritation and involvement of many other structures. If your doctor gives you a diagnosis of tendinitis and you are suffering from muscle aches, tingling or numbness, seek a second opinion.

Myositis is inflammation of the muscle. This frequently occurs in conjunction with tendinitis. For example, it is common to suffer from wrist flexor tendinitis along with wrist flexor myositis. The muscles become inflamed for the same reasons that tendons become inflamed. They respond to excessive stress by tearing and inflaming. When the fascia becomes involved in the inflammatory process, a condition known as myofascitis begins. The fascia, as previously explained, is a tough connective tissue that encases muscles along with all other structures within the body. Myofascitis indicates that an inflammatory process is affecting both muscle and the surrounding fascia. When this is the case, the small pebble-like swellings can be felt along the muscle fibers that are extremely sore and painful to the touch, and the muscles have a hardened feel to them.

Deep pressure and "myofascial release" techniques enable the muscles and fascia to heal properly.[17] Myofascial release technique is a deep tissue massage whereby the health provider performs slow stroking massages along the line of muscle fibers. This reduces the adhesions and "stickiness" of the inflamed tendons and muscles and allows increased fluidity of movement of the muscle. Myofascial release can be a painful procedure when the muscles and tendons are severely inflamed. The procedure is followed by ice therapy to reduce swelling and relieve the inflammatory response. Myofascial release technique is quite effective in the treatment of tendinitis, myositis, myofascitis, adhesions along tendons and muscles and some nervous compression syndromes.

Treatment

As a result of her keeping the keyboard on her lap, Janice was extending her wrists all day, which was irritating the forearm extensor tendons. She also was straining the outer pinkie muscles while reaching for the tab and return keys. This led to tightness and muscle spasm all the way up the pinkie (medial) side of the forearm.

Therefore, I gave her some basic ergonomic instruction regarding typing and sitting at a computer. I told her to keep the keyboard on top of the desk with her arms forming a 90° angle at the elbow and to raise or lower her seat height to attain this posture. To ease the burden of looking down at her paperwork, she was urged to obtain a bookstand to prop up her papers. This eased the strain on her neck from constantly looking down.

Treatment began with friction massage, a type of massage where the therapist rubs across the tendons to break up adhesions. Myofascial release technique was used on Janice's forearms. Pulsed ultrasound further facilitated her healing. Upon checking the lower cervical spine, it was found that the muscles attaching to the lower segments of the cervical spine were inflamed and in spasm. It was determined that Janice was suffering from some spinal sublaxations and would benefit from chiropractic spinal corrections to reduce nerve irritation to the arms. Janice was given stretching exercises for the neck, shoulder and arms to perform at home on a daily basis.

After three weeks of care at three times per week, Janice began to notice relief from her condition. At that time, she began rehabilitative exercises to strengthen her weakened forearms. At four weeks, we retested her grip strength with a dynamometer, (an instrument squeezed with the hand with maximum pressure for a few seconds. The clinician reads a meter which indicates the power of the grip.) Janice's strength increased by 10 percent in both hands after only four weeks of care. At four weeks, she still had some minor irritation at the posterior elbow area at the triceps muscle insertion point. More intensive massage and deep tissue work on the triceps muscle eased the pressure on her elbow. At eight weeks, Janice returned to her preinjured, pain-free state.

CASE #7:
PRONATOR TERES SYNDROME (PTS)

Frank, a carpenter specializing in cabinet making, is now in his 13th year of business. Over the past two months, he has noticed a deep soreness in his elbow and forearm that radiates pain down to his hand. After a long day, sometimes 12 hours on the job, he feels some tingling and numbness in his first three fingers. His wife told him that he has carpal tunnel syndrome since some of her co-workers suffer from the same complaints and were diagnosed with this common disorder. This is causing Frank great concern since he is self-employed and depends upon his work to support his family. Frank's work involves the use of many types of electric power tools along with manual equipment such as pliers, screwdrivers and hammers. He notices that when he uses a screwdriver, he feels an electric-shock sensation in the fingers. His thumb becomes achy, and rubbing it doesn't seem to help. It seems that any motion that involves twisting the forearm reproduces his pain. He also notices that after using a screwdriver, he has trouble gripping his drill and other power tools.

Discussion

The pronator teres muscle (see Figure 19) crosses the forearm to attach to the radius. Its action is to pronate the hand (turning the palm of the hand downward) and to flex the forearm. It has two heads or sites of origin. One head originates from the flexor muscle attachment into the medial epicondyle of the humerus; the other head originates from the uppermost portion of the ulna. Variations of these origins occur in a large portion of the population. Sometimes the head that attaches to the medial epicondyle is not muscle, but is composed of tendinous material instead. Recent medical studies indicate that these variations are the primary cause of compression of the median nerve, which must pass between the two heads of the pronator teres muscle.[18] This nerve supplies sensation to the first three fingers of the hand, muscle contraction to the forearm flexor muscles and some of the thumb muscles.

In most cases, PTS does not become apparent until a repetitive strain is exerted upon the tissues. This indicates that the repetitive strain is causing a wearing-down effect to these structures, leading to compression on the nerve. Therefore anatomical variations present in the arm musculature are not posing a problem until the insult of repetitive strain occurs. The repetitive strain causes fibrosis, scarring, inflammation and degeneration of the tissues, leading eventually to the compression of the median nerve.

The person suffering from PTS will feel an aching in the elbow, which may be difficult to localize because of the number of structures involved. Pronator teres muscle spasm causes derangement of the normal movement patterns in the joints connecting the radius, ulna and humerus. This derangement (or misalignment) initiates an inflammatory response within the elbow joints, causing generalized elbow pain and some-

67

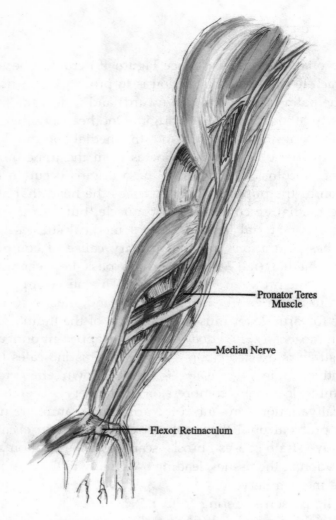

Figure 19: Pronator Teres Muscle and Median Nerve

times limitation of motion. Elbow joint misalignments may lead to irritation of the triceps muscle insertion at the tip of the elbow. This results in triceps tendinitis along with bursitis.

Compression of the median nerve from pronator teres syndrome produces symptoms that exactly replicate those of carpal tunnel syndrome. Pain and abnormal sensations in the first three fingers, weakness of grip strength and clumsiness of the hand are common with PTS. Misalignments of the elbow caused by PTS can instigate misalignment of the radius, ulna and the joints between those two forearm bones and the small carpal bones of the wrist. Therefore wrist pain may be secondary to the PTS. Muscle spasm of the pronator teres causes referred pain down the forearm to the thumb pad.[19] Therefore many people, including doctors, think they are suffering from carpal tunnel syndrome when they have pain in the arm and hand, when the cause is actually further up the arm. It is distressing to think how many carpal tunnel surgeries are unnecessarily performed each year because of a missed diagnosis of pronator teres syndrome.

How can one distinguish between the two syndromes? Carpal tunnel syndrome usually does not affect the elbow joints. So if elbow pain accompanies carpal tunnel related symptoms, make sure to have the structures in and around the elbow checked for irritation, inflammation, misalignments and any other abnormalities. PTS usually occurs with activity and does not cause pain while at rest.

The distinguishing sign of PTS is pain upon palpating the origin, muscle belly and insertion of the pronator teres muscle, along with the recreation of the median nerve symptoms when the pronator teres muscle belly is deeply compressed. Pronating the forearm against resistance also recreates the pain. Nerve conduction studies differentiate the two syndromes when the diagnosis is particularly difficult.

Treatment

Frank arrived in my office showing the signs of decreased grip strength in his right hand along with pain and swelling along the entire forearm musculature. Deep pressure in the upper arm over the pronator teres muscle recreated the sharp pain into his hand. The elbow joint was mildly inflamed, and tension was apparent along the radius and ulna down to the wrist. Tests for carpal tunnel syndrome showed no indication of the disease. Resisted pronation recreated the symptoms, which led to the diagnosis of PTS. No electrodiagnostic studies were performed since the exam findings proved the existence of the disease.

Treatment began with ultrasound to the upper forearm area. Deep tissue massage and deep goading of the origin and insertion of the pronator teres muscle was instituted. Active isolated stretching—a technique that contracts the opposing muscles (in this case the supinator muscles, the muscles that turn the palm upward)—was undertaken to achieve the stretch response in the relaxed pronator teres muscle. This stretching regimen is particularly useful for this condition, since it avoids any further irritation of the median nerve due to contraction of the pronator teres muscle. Manipulative techniques were implemented to the radius, ulna, humerus and carpal bones to normalize the alignment of those structures. Lower cervical spinal adjustments were performed to normalize spinal motion and nerve flow to the extremities. I advised Frank to avoid the repeated twisting of his arm for at least one month. This was simple to do in his job since he had screwdriver bits for his drill, which he made much better use of. Frank was treated three times per week for two weeks, then twice per week for four weeks. He was taught isometric exercises for the arm, which he performed from the fourth week of his treatment program until the seventh week. At that time we started fore-arm strengthening work with free weights. After six weeks of care, he still had some soreness in the elbow, but the median nerve irritation was gone. We continued treating him twice per week for three more weeks, then once per week for four weeks. After approximately three months, Frank had full use of his arm without any pain in the elbow or hand.

RADIAL TUNNEL SYNDROME

The radial tunnel is formed by the encasement of the radial nerve within the supinator muscle just below the elbow joint. The deep branch of the radial nerve passes through the supina-tor muscle on its way to supply motor impulses to a majority of the forearm extensor muscles, namely the extensor carpi ulnaris, extensor digiti minimi, extensor digitorum, abductor pollicis longus, extensor pollicus longus and brevis and exten-sor indices muscles. It also carries sensation from the wrist joints and the muscles mentioned above to the brain.

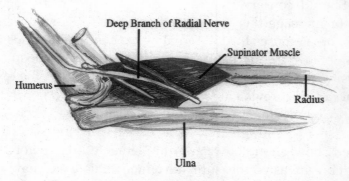

Figure 20: The Radial Tunnel

71

Compression of the radial nerve can occur if the supinator muscle goes into spasm due to activities that repetitively rotate the hand. This leads to the development myofascial trigger points, fibrosis and scarring. As the radial nerve enters the supinator muscle, it must pass over the anterior capsule of the joint connecting the radius and humerus bones together. Fibers of the supinator that attach into the anterior capsule may compress the nerve slightly at this point.[20]

Symptoms of radial tunnel syndrome can mimic tennis elbow syndrome. Deep aching pain of the elbow area just below the joint is common when trigger points are active in the supinator muscle. Entrapment of the nerve by the supinator can lead to muscle weakness of the extensor muscles, which cause weakness upon extension of the hand, fingers and thumb along with sensory changes from the wrist up to the posterior forearm.[21]

People at risk for radial tunnel syndrome are carpenters, bank tellers, grocery checkers, assembly line workers and people in any other profession that involves repetitive turning and rotation of the hands.

Should conservative care, such as chiropractic, acupuncture or massage therapy, not be effective in alleviating symptoms, other causes for the radial nerve compression need to be considered. Fibrotic bands in front of the joint capsule compressing the nerve, compression of the nerve from the extensor carpi radialis brevis tendon and even compression of the nerve due to blood vessels located in the same space can lead to radial nerve entrapment.[22] The conservative measures mentioned above should always be implemented first before initiating more invasive measures to remedy this condition.

CHAPTER 6

THE WRIST

CASE # 8:
CARPAL TUNNEL SYNDROME

Rita is a manager for a large computer repair business. She began experiencing carpal-tunnel-syndrome-type complaints about one year ago. She was advised by her physician to use ice packs on her wrists and take anti-inflammatory drugs when the symptoms flared up. She was given a wrist brace to wear throughout the day and night. After six months of this program of care she saw no relief and was having trouble with upset stomachs from the medication. The doctor advised her to take some over-the-counter medication to help ease the stomach pain. Wary of taking more medication, Rita searched the Internet for information on repetitive strain injuries, and came across a few of my postings for those suffering from complaints similar to hers. (See Resources for Internet mailing lists and web sites regarding RSIs). This prompted her to contact my office for an appointment.

Rita complained of burning pain in the right palm with numbness and tingling sensations in the thumb, index and middle fingers. She stated that the pain traveled up to her elbow and often would keep her awake at night. She had had previous bouts of low back pain, but she stated that they were not related to this injury. Over the past six months, Rita experienced clumsiness with her right hand and was always dropping items. She worked at a computer all day long and was sure that the computer was the reason for her pain. She reluctantly stated that her left hand was now giving her some trouble, too. Her doctor sent her for an electromyelogram (EMG) and a nerve conduction study (NCV) which showed positive results for median nerve compression in the right wrist only.

A Health Care Dilemma

Carpal tunnel syndrome (CTS) is evolving into the buzzword of the nineties. Millions of dollars in worker's compensation claims are paid every year for treatment of this disorder, and millions more are paid in disability benefits. The amount of lost work productivity due to this condition is staggering. One would assume that after all of the treatments given for carpal tunnel syndrome by M.D.s, physical therapists, chiropractors, acupuncturists and other health practitioners, there would be a standard of care by now, but there isn't. If you speak to 10 different health practitioners about their treatment for carpal tunnel syndrome, you will most likely hear 10 different approaches. For example, the chiropractor says, "Adjust the spine." The M.D. says, "Try physical therapy, take these drugs and if that doesn't work you will need surgery." The physical therapist says, "Let's perform an ergonomic study, then use ultrasound, rehabilitation and other therapies." The Feldenkrais instructor says, "You have to retrain your body's movements to overcome this injury." The massage therapist says,

"Relieve the muscle spasms and the tension in the fascia, and the syndrome will subside."

So who is right? Standing alone, no one is right, but together everyone is. Let me explain. RSI sufferers, especially carpal tunnel syndrome sufferers, need a team approach for healing their injuries. I firmly believe that no single healing discipline can completely handle all of the components needed to treat a patient with carpal tunnel syndrome—or any repetitive strain injury, for that matter. Those patients fortunate enough to receive a team approach to healing their CTS do better on the whole. This is because of the nature and complexity of CTS. The following chart lists the many factors involved in the diagnosis, treatment and rehabilitation of CTS.

FACTORS INVOLVED IN DIAGNOSIS, TREATMENT AND REHABILITATION OF CTS

Understanding of ergonomics

Sex, age, weight of patient

Patient's stress level

Emotional and psychological status

Medications taken

Preexisting conditions

Doctor's specialty

Familiarity of doctor with RSI complaints

Rehabilitation knowledge

Knowledge of exercise regimens

Underlying systemic disease states

Referral for diagnostic studies

Nutritional analysis of patient

Manipulation and adjustive techniques

Extent of injury
Personality of patient and doctor

Patient's hobbies

Patient's occupation

Investigation of previous traumas

Patient's attitude towards employer

Diagnostic ability of doctor

Massage therapy techniques

Knowledge of stretching

Knowledge of worker's compensation system

Ability to refer for second opinion

Good relationship with other health providers

Herbal/nutritional remedies to aid in healing

Physical therapy techniques

This list is far from complete as far as all the intricacies involved in the treatment of a CTS patient are concerned, but it does give you an idea of how complex the process is for the healthcare provider. It is rare to find one provider who is educated about all of these factors. Through this list you can understand why a team approach is critical in the treatment of carpal tunnel syndrome.

Providing a correct diagnosis of carpal tunnel system is a major obstacle. The reason for this is that many doctors, when hearing the telltale signs of CTS, automatically zoom into the two-cubic-inch area of the carpal tunnel, located in the wrist. The rest of the body is often disregarded and considered unimportant. My experience indicates that the CTS disease process is due to a combination of events occurring along the entire upper extremity and may even involve the middle (thoracic) and lower (lumbar) spines as well. Nutritional deficiencies and other subclinical disease states are often present simultaneously with CTS. There may be pinched nerves in the neck, thoracic outlet syndrome, pronator teres syndrome, or myofascial syndrome instigating the symptoms in the wrist. All of these syndromes may even be present at the same time! This explains why so many CTS surgeries provide little relief or lead to worsened symptoms months or years later. The body is not addressed as a whole. Therefore the preexisting factors causing CTS, neglected or ignored by the doctor before the surgery, continue to provoke CTS following the surgery. For this reason, the provider who looks at the health of the whole body is more likely to be successful in treating CTS complaints. It also explains why a team approach of alternative health care providers is more effective in discovering the underlying causes of carpal tunnel syndrome.

The Eight Causes of CTS

Figure 21 shows the location of the carpal tunnel, and Figure 22 shows a cross section of the carpal tunnel. Notice on Figure

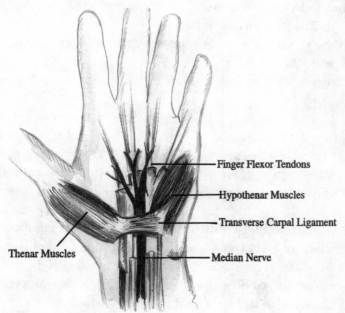

Finger Flexor Tendons

Hypothenar Muscles

Transverse Carpal Ligament

Thenar Muscles

Median Nerve

Figure 21: The Median Nerve

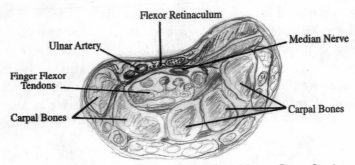

Figure 22: Median Nerve Cross Section

22 how the median nerve and flexor tendons, along with an artery and vein, traverse through the small tunnel within the wrist. The carpal bones form a U-shaped tunnel. The bones on either end of this "U" are connected by a tough unyielding ligament known as the flexor retinaculum or transverse carpal ligament. The symptoms of true CTS occur due to the compression of the median nerve as it passes through this tunnel. Many other conditions may mimic CTS.

Compression of the median nerve is due to a number of factors.

1. The first cause of CTS, and probably the most prevalent is inflammation of the flexor tendons. The hand flexor tendons may become inflamed due to overuse. Any occupation or hobby in which the hand is contracted in a constant flexed position or which involves constant movement of the hand from extension to flexion (such as with grocery checkers) makes the tendon susceptible to injury. The flexor tendons are surrounded by a synovial sheath or wrapping where they pass under the flexor retinaculum. Inside this sheath is the substance called synovium, the lubricant that aids movement of the tendons within the sheath. Inflammation of the tendon leads to enlargement of the tendon/sheath complex due to overproduction of synovium as well as a degradation of the synovium itself. The synovium transforms into a sticky, viscous compound. This leads to increased friction of the tendon/sheath complex, which instigates more inflammation. The irritation of the tendon and sheath is known as tenosynovitis. If left untreated, a condition called "trigger finger" or stenosing tenosynovitis can result. (See Chapter 8.) The enlargement of the tendon-sheath complex exerts pressure upon the median nerve in the uncompromising tunnel, causing the symptoms of carpal tunnel syndrome.

2. The second factor involved in causing carpal tunnel syndrome is misalignment of the carpal bones. As shown in Figure 22, if the carpal bones become misaligned, the transverse carpal ligament becomes taut, narrowing the carpal tunnel. Compression of the contents of the carpal tunnel ensues, including the median nerve. Misalignment of the radius and ulna, the two forearm bones, can lead to the carpal bones' misalignment. In cases of CTS, it is common to find the distal ends (the ends closest to the wrist) of the radius and ulna slightly spread apart from each other, causing stress to the interosseous membrane, the tough ligament that joins the two forearm bones together. Combined with this spreading of the bones are weakness, irritation and myofascial trigger points in the pronator quadratus muscle. This muscle is responsible, along with the pronator teres muscle, for turning the palm of the hand downwards (pronation). The bone spreading is slight, but it has a major affect on the carpal tunnel. The radius and ulna are connected to the carpal bones by ligaments, the radial collateral and ulnar collateral ligaments, respectively. Spreading of the radius and ulna leads to tugging and misalignment of the carpal bones and the misalignments mentioned above.

The radius and ulna become misaligned and spread apart from compressive forces translating through the wrist up into the arm. This can happen from weightlifting with barbells when the weight is repeatedly forced into the wrist and arms in those who perform benching exercises and inclines. Pushing activities involving extension of the wrist and pushing with the palm also can lead to this condition. Any sufferer of carpal tunnel syndrome will tell you how difficult it is to push a grocery cart. This phenomenon is the cause. Chiropractors suffer from CTS because of the compressive forces up the arm from performing spinal adjustments. (I know of a number of chiropractors who had to change their techniques and adjustment style because of carpal tunnel syndrome.) Mail handlers who push large mail carts are susceptible to this forearm problem also. Anyone involved with pushing heavy objects with the hands can be affected by this condition.

3. A third factor in causing carpal tunnel syndrome is a combined myofascial syndrome with carpal bone misalignments. If the forearm and hand muscles which attach into the carpal bones are suffering from myofascial syndromes (see Chapter 5), they will tighten and shorten, thus pulling on their attachments into the carpals. To be specific, the muscles susceptible to this are the flexor *carpi ulnaris* and abductor *digiti minimi*, which both attach into the pisiform bone, and the muscles involved in thumb movement which attach into the carpal bones. Myofascial syndromes in these muscles cause misalignments of the carpals leading to the series of events stated above.

4. Any occupation that involves direct compression upon the carpal tunnel itself may cause CTS. The major culprit here is the use of a computer mouse. Most people will rest their wrists on the mouse pad and extend the hand and fingers to click the button. This posture puts direct pressure on the area of the carpal tunnel. A prolonged posture such as this will lead to nerve compression. Of course, the same goes for anyone who rests their wrists on a computer mouse pad or table top.

5. Any occupation involving vibration may cause CTS. Laborers using jackhammers, chainsaws, buffers or grinders subject their wrists to excessive vibration. Studies indicate that vibration inhibits blood flow to the nerve tissue and other tissues in the hand. Researchers put this repetitive strain injury into its own classification. (See Hand-Arm Vibration Syndrome in Chapter 7.) This syndrome can lead to a condition called Raynaud's disease.

6. Environmental temperature may cause CTS, and people who work in cold environments are much more susceptible. The cold temperature causes constriction of blood vessels, thus decreasing the blood flow to the tissues. Thus people who put ice packs on their arms and hands while working at a computer or other repetitive task are at risk. The decreased blood flow to the tissues because of the ice pack will predispose them to increased injury if they attempt to perform repetitive movements while using the ice pack. Use ice only during rest, not during activity.

7. Underlying changes in the carpal bone structure, such as previous wrist fractures which have caused changes to the size and shape of one or more carpal bones, hypertophic (enlargement) changes of the carpal bones due to imposed stresses over a long period of time and callus formations in and around the bones from healing fractures may also lead to CTS. Changes to the bones because of pathological processes, such as tumors, must also be considered.

8. Last but not least, spinal subluxations or misalignments of the lower cervical spine can cause swelling in and around the nerves traveling to the hand. The pinched nerves cause irritation of the muscles and tissues they supply throughout the arm, making the subluxation a primary causative factor in the development of carpal tunnel syndrome. The irritated tissues cause abnormal tensions in the forearm, predisposing the person to developing CTS complaints.

The Median Nerve

The common thread among all of these causes is that they all lead to median nerve dysfunction. Decreased blood flow to the nerve is the first event that takes place due to compressive forces. This is what causes the pins and needles sensations in the fingers. When the nerve becomes hypoxic (lacking blood flow), the brain perceives distorted signals which feel like pins and needles. This affects the outer layer of the nerve first. If the pressure is released at this point, the nerve will heal fully and the abnormal sensations will go away.

If decreased blood supply continues, the outer layers of the nerve, called the myelin, will break down and degenerate. This leaves the inner layer of nerve (the axon) unprotected. Without the myelin, the nerves cannot conduct electricity very quickly, thus the speed of the impulse decreases. Nerve conduction velocity tests detect changes in the speed of nerve impulses. Remember though, that the median nerve is comprised of thousands of axons, therefore it takes a considerable amount of prolonged compression and decreased blood flow to affect the overall nerve function. Myelin can regenerate, so at this stage there is still hope. If the compression is relieved, the nerve can heal.

If the process is left unchecked, the axon will die. This leads to numbness of the skin and atrophy of the muscles supplied by the median nerve. Luckily, our amazing bodies do have the ability to regenerate some of the less affected cells, even some of the degenerated cells, depending upon the health of the nerve cells and myelin further up the arm.

The success of a treatment program for CTS is dependent upon the stage of the carpal tunnel syndrome present, the time span of median nerve compression and the extent of nerve cell death. Those suffering from the beginning stages of CTS with occasional mild symptoms have a good chance of recovering fully if the proper treatment is given immediately. Those suffering from middle stages of CTS, with constant, unremitting symptoms and positive orthopedic and neurological tests still have a good chance of recovery since the nerves do have the ability to heal. However, those at end-stage CTS, with nerve damage, muscle atrophy and sensation loss, have a much smaller chance of recovery because of the extent of nerve axon degeneration.

The Symptoms of CTS

CTS gives a specific pain pattern due to the median nerve supply to the palm side of the hand. The most common presentation is tingling or numbness in the thumb, index and middle fingers, along with pain in the wrist and sometimes the forearm. More severe cases cause atrophy of the muscles at the base of the thumb, which as a group are called the thenar muscles. It is common for symptoms to wake the sufferer from sleep. Clumsiness and difficulty in holding objects, such as cups, jars or paper, can make life extremely difficult. Pain can travel from the wrist upwards to the elbow. (As stated earlier, if this is the case, the healthcare provider should determine if there is a problem higher up the arm causing nerve irritation.) The CTS sufferer will often complain of weakness in the hands along with a heavy feeling in the forearm. There may be increased sensitivity in the affected hand because of the irritated nerve endings. Thus, just a slight banging of the hand on a door can cause shooting pain in the fingers and arm.

The median nerve usually does not supply nerve impulses to the pinkie and may only affect the medial portion of the ring finger. Therefore, if symptoms involve just the ring or pinkie, a case of cubital tunnel syndrome, thoracic outlet syndrome or Guyon's canal syndrome should be considered. Also, if the tingling and numbness is affecting all of the fingers of the hand, there may be a combined nerve irritation of median and ulnar nerves or the problem may stem from the cervical spine or thoracic outlet.

Diagnosis

A healthcare provider should be able to diagnose a case of carpal tunnel syndrome without using expensive procedures such as a nerve conduction study or MRI. A good history from the patient along with an in-depth examination is suitable for a diagnosis. The doctor may order neurological studies, X-rays (neck, wrist or hand), blood work or even an MRI, to confirm the diagnosis or to rule out other disease states. However, these tests should not be used to make the diagnosis. Those doctors who begin with these expensive procedures are probably not familiar with RSI complaints, and their CTS patients should consider seeking care elsewhere.

Do not let a positive test finding of CTS automatically lead you to surgery. For example, a number of patients have been treated in my office through conservative measures even though they were diagnosed with a positive nerve conduction velocity test (NCV) showing median nerve damage. Yet after six weeks of care, they experienced healing and decreased symptoms. The problem with NCV tests is that they are very subjective—in other words, the outcome of the test is determined by the skill of the examiner. It is always best for the doctor to correlate the symptoms, extent of illness, exam findings, neurological findings and diagnostic findings to determine if alternative methods can be effective in each particular case. Sometimes surgery is needed, but not unless there is extensive nerve damage or an emergency situation where the nerve has been severely damaged in a short period of time. Otherwise, a conservative approach is best for healing CTS.

Treatment

An examination of Rita revealed signs of median nerve irritation in the wrist along with forearm muscle spasm, elbow joint irritation and medial epicondylitis, pronator teres muscle spasm and lower neck subluxation. She was suffering from a number of conditions that manifested themselves as carpal tunnel syndrome complaints. Treatment began with ultrasound and deep tissue myofascial release techniques to the forearm, palm and neck muscles. Spinal, elbow and wrist manipulations were performed to correct the subluxations present. The patient found the myofascial techniques quite painful at the beginning of care, but they began to ease as progress was made. A videotape of Rita's workspace and of her at work at her computer was made to detect ergonomic conditions that might affect her hands and arms. She use two different keyboards for her job. One was located directly in front of her, and the other was off to the side. When she used the keyboard off to the side, she would twist her body while not making any compensations in her seated position. This caused stress on her shoulder and torso. She would also need to extend her right arm forward to reach the keyboard. Recommendations were made to correct the ergonomic situation to relieve stress on the neck, shoulder and forearm.

At the onset of treatments, healing was slow, although Rita did enjoy better range of motion in her neck along with decreased stiffness and soreness. She was given a logbook to register her day-to-day complaints, changes in symptoms, eating habits and medications. After about four to six weeks we began to see improvements in the hands and forearm. The tingling and numbness she complained of began to disappear. At eight weeks, she could work a full day and began to notice some abnormal sensations only toward the end of the day.

Rita was taught stretching and exercise routines to perform at home and at work. She stated the stretching helped immensely with the forearm and wrist pain. After 10 weeks of care, Rita no longer had wrist pain, numbness or tingling. She continues to have some elbow soreness occasionally due to some persistent bad habits she has found very difficult to break, such as leaning on her elbows while typing.

AUTHOR'S NOTE: This case illustrates how Rita's initial diagnosis of "carpal tunnel syndrome" was actually a myriad of complaints stemming from the neck all the way down to the wrist. I believe that hundreds, if not many thousands, of CTS cases are misdiagnosed each year, just as this one was originally. We can only guess at the number of unnecessary surgeries for CTS that are performed each year as a result of such misdiagnoses.

CASE # 9:
GUYON'S (ULNAR) TUNNEL SYNDROME

Jim, an avid 60-year-old bicyclist, is retired. He has been involved with the local bicycling club and partakes in all of the events throughout the year, including century rides (100 miles). Over a one-year period, he began noticing numbness in the fourth and fifth fingers of his left hand and sometimes on the right as well. He states that he only notices the numbness when riding the bicycle, and it only happens about a half hour into his ride. Once the ride is completed, his symptoms go away after an hour or so. He doesn't have any constant symptoms but, when they are present, he has to constantly change his grip on the bicycle handle to ease them. He seeks treatment because the symptoms are affecting his enjoyment of bicycling.

Discussion

Guyon's tunnel is located on the palm side of the wrist, towards the pinkie side. It is formed by two bones, the hammate, which has an appendage called the "hook" of the hammate, and the small pisiform bone, which serves as an attachment site for the *flexor carpi ulnaris* along with many wrist ligaments. Between these two small bones travels the deep branch of the ulnar nerve providing sensory function to the fourth and fifth fingers and motor control to the small intrinsic hand muscles. This nerve is encased in this tunnel by a ligamentous covering. Therefore, any alteration of the bony compartment can deleteriously affect the delicate nerve. There are a number of conditions that can compress this nerve. One is direct compression,

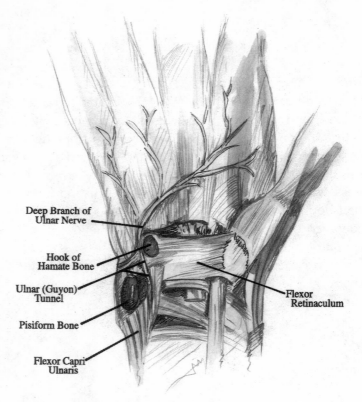

Deep Branch of
Ulnar Nerve

Hook of
Hamate Bone

Ulnar (Guyon)
Tunnel

Pisiform Bone

Flexor Capri
Ulnaris

Flexor
Retinaculum

Figure 23: The Ulnar (Guyon's) Tunnel

as in this case of the bicyclist. Another is vibrational compression, as in anyone who uses equipment such as jackhammers, buffers and grinders. It may also occur in combination with forearm tendinitis, medial epicondylitis and especially flexor tendinitis affecting the flexor *carpi ulnaris* muscle. Since the pisiform bone is an attachment for the flexor *carpi ulnaris*, any abnormal tugging because of muscle tension can irritate this branch of the ulnar nerve. Other less common conditions that can cause nerve entrapment in Guyon's tunnel are bone tumors, arthritic conditons and gout.[23]

Treatment

We analyzed Jim's bicycle riding posture and found that he rode with a great deal of his upper body weight coming down on his extended wrists, thus forcing stress directly upon Guyon's tunnel. I recommended some changes in grip, riding posture and seat height to help alleviate the strain on the wrist. I also advised him to buy spongy hand grips for the bicycle. Examination revealed tenderness over Guyon's tunnel, and restriction of mobility of the hammate, pisiform and scaphoid bones, along with misaligned radius and ulna bones. No inflamed tissues could be found in the forearm muscle groups, elbow or shoulder. Some mild irritation of the lower cervical spine was palpated and noted by the patient. Because of the patient's riding style, he often extended his head to look forward. This posture was irritating his neck. Chiropractic spinal manipulation was performed to the neck area, and extremity joint manipulation was performed to the wrist bones mentioned as well as the radius and ulna. No physical therapy modalities were necessary for the treatment of this condition. The patient received chiropractic treatments over a two-month period of time. The condition diminished, but occasionally returned upon extended biking. The patient maintains a maintenance program of care to alleviate occasional flare-ups of his condition.

CHAPTER 7

THE HAND

HAND-ARM VIBRATION SYNDROME

It is important to distinguish hand-arm vibration (HAV) syndrome from carpal tunnel syndrome, since they have similar pain patterns. HAV is suffered by people who work with tools or objects that involve vibration, such as buffers, grinders, sanders and jackhammers. This is one of the distinguishing differences between HAV and CTS. Consistent subjection of the hands to vibration leads to circulatory and neurological changes. The sufferer may complain of tingling and numbness in all or some of the fingers due to involvement of both the median and ulnar nerves. Muscle weakness may occur with prolonged nerve irritation. The hand may become pale or white due to a decrease of blood flow, leading to a condition known as Raynaud's disease. The HAV sufferer usually does not complain of sleep disturbances as does the CTS patient. Muscle aches, along with pain up the arm is common in HAV.[24]

Since the symptoms of HAV are similar to CTS, the patient's occupational and medical histories are important in deciding upon a correct diagnosis. The key factors to look for are the inclusion of vibration in daily tasks along with vascular changes, which are not typical with carpal tunnel syndrome. Occasionally, HAV and CTS may occur simultaneously, making the treatment difficult. The source of repetitive strain as well as the source of vibration needs to be discovered.

CASE #10:
REFLEX SYMPATHETIC DYSTROPHY (RSD): RAYNAUD'S DISEASE
The author thanks Dr. Robert Wright, La.C., Ph.D. for the contribution of this case study.

Sharon C. is a 47-year-old female flight attendant who suffered from gradual onset of tendinitis in the left thumb and wrist over a one year period. This was a work-related injury, precipitated by continually pushing a beverage cart while in flight. The cart weighed several hundred pounds. Sharon would have to clutch the cart tightly while it shifted in flight for up to 30 minutes at a time. Eventually her pain increased and she could no longer push the cart at all or lift objects over 15 or 20 pounds without severe and constant pain.

Reconstructive surgery was performed on her left hand. One week after the surgery she began noticing redness, hot sensations in the hand, marked swelling and local tenderness throughout the whole wrist and extending halfway up the forearm. These episodes would often be precipitated by moving quickly from warm to cold environments. Sharon wore gloves to try to minimize the daily episodes. She complained that if she held her hand down for any extended period the swelling and redness would begin; therefore she occasionally carried her gloved hand in an elevated position. She smoked half a pack of cigarettes a day.

Discussion

RSD is thought to be caused by an overactive sympathetic nervous system. An exact cause is still not certain. The sympathetic nervous system controls the body's reaction to stressful events and leads to the "fight or flight" reaction. The sympathetic system is responsible for increased heart rate, increased air intake by the lungs, muscle excitability and decreased blood flow to the skin and organs. (This explains why you have cold hands when you are under stress.)

There are many other names for RSD including causalgia, neurodystrophy, shoulder-hand syndrome, traumatic vasospasm, and Raynaud's disease or phenomenon. It is termed Raynaud's disease when there is no precipitating injury or crisis that instigated the symptoms. Raynaud's phenomena refers to an RSD that is secondary to another factor, like a recent fracture, surgery, scarring or contusion.

RSD can be caused by a number of events. The first is trauma, such as a recent car accident, bad fall, broken bone, dislocation or crush of a finger or toe. Surgical excision of ganglias, surgical procedures of the extremities, damage to peripheral blood vessels due to injections, or tight castings may also cause RSDs. Neurological disorders affecting the spinal cord or peripheral nerves, as in hand-arm vibration syndrome, make the sufferer more susceptible to RSD. Previous infection of the extremity is another causative factor as are certain vascular diseases, such as periarthritis nodosa and arteriosclosis. Finally, musculoskeletal disorders, such as repetitive strain injuries, increase the chances of developing RSD.

RSD causes a constant severe burning pain in the hands and/or feet. Other less common structures involved are the tongue, ears, nose and nipples. It typically develops after subjecting the body to a hot or cold environment. Increased emotional stress can stimulate the reaction as well. The RSD reaction can be broken down into three stages. The first (acute) stage is accompanied by burning and aching pain, swelling and muscle spasm of the affected parts. The skin tends to be warm, dry and has a red coloration. Later in the first stage, the skin can become cold, sweaty and blueish in color due to decreased blood flow to the skin. The second (dystrophic) stage is characterized by increased burning and aching along with an increased perception of pain from even the slightest pressure on the skin. The nails can become brittle, and the skin feels cool and looks pale. Joint movement becomes limited. Finally, the third (atrophic) stage is characterized by tight, glossy skin which looks bluish and feels cold. Atrophy of the subcutaneous tissues and muscles occur.[25]

Treatment for RSD should begin with chiropractic, acupuncture and herbal treatments. Chiropractic adjustments of the upper thoracic spine will normalize the sympathetic nerve flow to the hands, while lower cervical adjustments will allow for proper nerve function in the muscles and tissues of the arm and hand. Acupuncture, as mentioned below, affects the microcirculation in and around the affected tissues. Herbs and homeopathic remedies will help the body boost its healing capabilities.

Medical approaches to RSD include sympathetic nerve blocks, a procedure in which the stellate ganglion, a cluster of sympathetic nerves located in the lower neck, is injected with an anesthetic. The effects are usually temporary and may lead to complications such as injections into the blood vessels, blocking (anesthetizing) the wrong nerves, most commonly the recurrent laryngeal, the brachial plexus or the phrenic nerve. On rare occasions the spinal cord itself can be blocked. A more severe complication is the development of a pneumothorax due to penetration of lung tissue with the needle.[26] Pain medications are often prescribed, including analgesics, antidepressants and narcotics, all having serious side effects, with no long-term approach to curing the ailment. The medical approach to this condition is still in its infancy, thus the person suffering from RSD should look seriously at the alternative health care system to remedy this disease process.

Treatment

Sharon's physical exam revealed local tenderness at the site of surgery. The hand appeared pale and cold to the touch, the thumb's range of motion was limited in all directions and all fingers were severely limited in flexion.

Acupuncture with moxa therapy along with herbal therapy as support were performed on Sharon's first visit, then twice a week thereafter for two months and then once a week for two months. At this point Sharon regained full range of motion without pain or any RSD symptoms whatsoever.

This case presented as a severe deficiency of qi and yang of the lung and kidney channels. Points were used to build the flow to these channels to increase the energy. The lung channel flows through the point of pain. Herbal and moxa therapy were used to support the qi yang.

Acupuncture works through the central nervous system to adjust peripheral nerve and microcirculation response. It also stimulates the release of cortisol and endorphins to help with pain and inflammation at the local site. In Sharon's case, moxa therapy was used at the site of her operation to increase local circulation with heat and speed healing. We used points at the site of pain and at the C5-6 nerve root to normalize the conduction along the nerve pathway and also treated points on the whole body to support her general condition.

CHAPTER 8

THE FINGERS

TRIGGER FINGER

Trigger finger is a difficult condition to treat conservatively. Once a tendon and its sheath reach the end stages of thickening and scarring to develop trigger finger, it is usually too late for conservative care. In most cases, corticosteroid injections and surgery are needed to release the thickened tendon from its sheath.

Finger movement is facilitated by spaghetti-like tendons that extend from the muscles in the forearms to various attachment points along the front and back of the fingers. Along their route to the fingers, these tendons must pass under bands of tough fibrous material called retinaculums. Retinaculums help guide tendons to their insertion points, and act as retaining bands and fulcrums that keep the tendons in close proximity to the bones of the hand. The tendons become surrounded by fluid-filled protective sheaths as they pass under a retinaculum. This sheath prevents friction from developing between the tendon and the retinaculum.

With overuse of a tendon from such activities as computer use, playing musical instruments and hobbies such as cro-

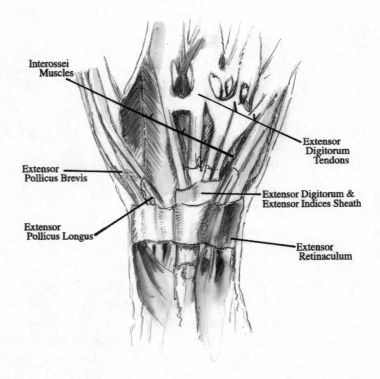

Interossei
Muscles

Extensor
Digitorum
Tendons

Extensor
Pollicus Brevis

Extensor Digitorum &
Extensor Indices Sheath

Extensor
Pollicus Longus

Extensor
Retinaculum

Figure 24: Tendons Passing Under Retinaculum

cheting and firing pistols or rifles, its sheath may become in-flamed and the contents will thicken. This compresses the tendon as it passes through the sheath. Because of this constriction, it begins to swell. The tendon swelling tends to occur just before it passes through the sheath and retinaculum. In most cases, this condition involves the flexor tendons of the hand. When they become inflamed and enlarged, they have difficulty passing through the swollen sheath and under the retinaculum.

The person suffering from this condition will notice that when attempting to straighten the affected fingers from a flexed position, one or more fingers will get caught up or stuck. Then he or she will have to physically straighten the finger with the opposite hand. This procedure can be painful enough to bring the individual to tears. When straightened, the finger may audibly snap. This occurs when the thickened tendon squeezes through the tunnel of swollen sheath.

Treatment of this condition should begin as soon as the person begins to feel pain in the hands or fingers. If treated early on, conservative measures will be effective to bring the inflammation down and normalize tendon movement. Conservative measures would include physical therapy modalities, such as pulsed ultrasound and microcurrent, acupuncture to stimulate healing and microcirculation, chiropractic manipulation, myofascial release work for the affected musculature and nutritional support, such as adding proteolytic enzymes to the diet.

If the condition has progressed to the point where the finger cannot straighten, conservative measures should be used for a period of two weeks. If no relief is noticed in that time frame then more invasive measures need to be taken, such as corticosteroid injection and possibly surgery to cut open the sheath thereby giving the tendon more space to glide.

Several studies have reported a higher incidence of the development of trigger finger, carpal tunnel syndrome and tenosynovitis in diabetics. The use of corticosteroids in this population has not been very successful in remedying these conditions, with only a 50 percent success rate.[27] Diabetics tend to have multiple digits involved. In these cases it is important to use conservative care initially, such as massage therapy, chiropractic and acupuncture, since most medically cared for individuals will inevitably be led to surgical intervention.

CHAPTER 9

THE THUMB

STENOSING TENOSYNOVITIS OR DEQUERVAIN'S SYNDROME

Barbara is an administrative assistant for a lighting fixture company. She has right arm and neck complaints which have been occurring over the past three years. She states that over the past six months, the symptoms have worsened. Barbara works at least six hours per day at the computer keyboard and also answers phones, uses an adding machine, copy machine and printers. All of these items are situated in and around her work station. Increased stress worsens her condition. Barbara also has trouble opening jars, shifting gears in her car and using a can opener. Besides pain she has tingling and numbness in her hand. She is experiencing an increase of sensitivity in her hand and fingertips. Barbara's pain is most severe at the end of a workday, and occasionally wakes her up at night. She suffers from headaches at least two to three times per week, and occasionally, her neck and shoulder muscles will ache.

Barbara began a treatment and rehabilitation program

for an upper extremity RSI in our clinic and did quite well. In her first few weeks as a patient her symptoms, although not totally relieved, lessened and became bearable. After four months of care in our office and very good progress, she suffered a major setback due to an injury while grocery shopping. While attempting to transfer paper grocery bags from a shopping cart into the trunk of her car, she felt a tremendous strain in the right wrist and thumb. Almost immediately she noticed an increase of pain and swelling in the wrist and forearm. Over the next week, she began having difficulty bending her thumb inward. Attempts to do so caused excruciating pain in her forearm, just above the thumb. Besides this, her wrist also hurt. The thumb and wrist area hurt throughout the day and woke her up at night.

Discussion

Notice in Figure 25 the three tendons situated towards the back of the hand that attach into the thumb. These tendons perform different actions and together they make up what is called "the anatomical snuffbox." The extensor pollicus longus makes up the posterior border of the snuff box. The word pollicus refers to the thumb, and longus indicates that this is the longer tendon whose muscle insertion travels farther up the arm in contrast to the extensor pollicus brevis, which is a shorter tendon. The action of these two muscles and tendons is to extend the thumb. Finally, notice the abductor pollicus longus, whose action is to laterally deviate the thumb away from the other fingers. The medical term for this action is abduction. DeQuervain's disease affects the common sheath that wraps around the extensor pollicus brevis and the abductor

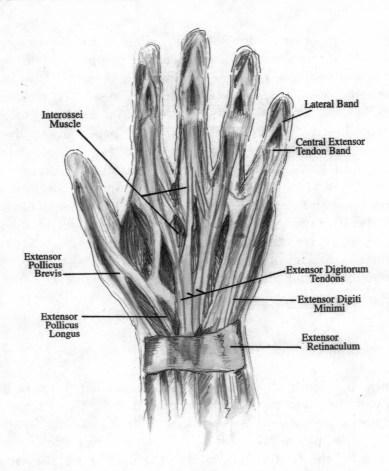

Figure 25: Tendons of the Thumb

pollicus longus tendons as they pass under the retinaculum. The retinaculum helps guide the tendon to its insertion point. Under the retinaculum, the tendon is encapsulated by a sheath similar to the way a sausage is wrapped in a casing. Within the sheath is the clear synovial fluid that aids in helping the tendon glide and as a lubricant.

Let's analyze the term stenosing tenosynovitis. Stenosing refers to a narrowing of the sheath or canal; teno refers to inflammation of the tendon and synovitis refers to an increased production of synovial fluid due to irritation of the structures involved. Stenosing tenosynovitis is a narrowing of the tendon sheath due to tendon inflammation and thickening and increase synovial fluid production due to a trauma or repetitive strain or friction of the tissues.

The sufferer of DeQuervain's disease usually feels intense pain in the wrist that radiates to the thumb and upward to the forearm. Moving the thumb, especially inward toward the other fingers, is difficult to impossible without severe pain. When the tendon/sheath structure is severely inflamed, the sufferer cannot move the thumb at all and any slight pressure on the area below the thumb causes immediate pain.

Traditional medical treatment for DeQuervain's disease is cortisone injection into the sheath and surgery to cut the common sheath to relieve pressure. As you will see below, more conservative alternative measures were successful in treating Barbara's case.

Treatment

Before reinjuring herself, Barbara was being treated twice monthly on a chiropractic maintenance program. Her previous neck and arm condition had stabilized, and she was enjoying the benefits of regular wellness care. On the visit following her new wrist injury, she was put on a three-time-per-week treatment program once again to immediately counteract the inflammatory and fibrosis process. We began treating her wrist and thumb with pulsed ultrasound in a warm water bath. Pulsed ultrasound was used to prevent further swelling. Pulsing the waves provides an on-off-on cycle that imparts very little heat to the tissues while at the same time providing the chemical and cellular benefits of the ultrasound. Performing the ultrasound under water prevents the ultrasound waves from harming the bones which are close to the skin's surface in the wrist area.

Deep tissue massage techniques were instituted over the retinaculum and inflamed tendons. At first, this was quite painful for Barbara. She was instructed to follow the therapy with icing to prevent further swelling. Along with work on the thumb and wrist region, myofascial work was performed on the forearm, arm and neck musculature, which showed increased tension following the new injury. Chiropractic spinal adjustments were performed to the spine with each treatment. Each visit showed decreased pain in the thumb region and, after four weeks of care, Barbara had only minor complaints of thumb irritation. She continued her treatments on a reduced schedule of one time per week and, after eight weeks, had no noticeable pain in the tendons of her thumb. She is once again back on a wellness program for the continued benefits of regular chiropractic care.

PART 3

WHAT TO DO IF YOU
EXPERIENCE THE SYMPTOMS
OF A REPETITIVE STRAIN INJURY

CHAPTER 10

First Aid For RSIs

If you have symptoms that resemble those of the repetitive strain injuries mentioned earlier in this book, there are prevention techniques you can implement right away to prevent worsening of your condition. RSIs need immediate attention and quick action. Lack of awareness and indifference toward your condition will lead to worsening of the symptoms and, if left untreated, long-term disability and chronic pain may develop.

In general, it is a good idea to seek an opinion from your healthcare provider as soon as possible if you experience any symptoms resembling those of a repetitive strain injury. The steps mentioned below may or may not eradicate your symptoms. They are meant to help you understand why your symptoms are developing and aid in your treatment program. See Chapter 12 for the RSI warning signals. If you find you are experiencing the warning signals, begin a treatment program for your injuries as soon as possible. If you are currently under medical care or a holistic treatment program for any condition, it is always prudent to consult with your healthcare provider before initiating the suggestions mentioned below.

#1. Drink plenty of water!

Muscles are composed mostly of water. If your body is suffering from chronic dehydration (a long-term deficiency of water intake) the muscles cannot function properly. Adhesions between muscles are likely to occur. Decreased water intake predisposes you to myofascial syndromes, muscle soreness and tendon irritation. Your muscles will fatigue faster, with dehydration also causing them to feel tired and heavy. Adequate water intake is almost always overlooked in books and articles relating to RSI prevention.

How do you know if you are dehydrated? There's a simple test you can do yourself. Grab (pinch) some skin on the back of your hand to make it fold up. Then let it go. Your skin should quickly rebound to its normal position (in less than a second). If you find that your skin is slowly returning, or simply seems stuck in the pinched position, you are suffering from dehydration. The body does not give you good indicators of dehydration, therefore you must make a habit of drinking fresh pure water throughout the day to replenish the water you lose through perspiration and excretion.

The following factors make one susceptible to dehydration:

- Working in a warm environment.
- Physical exercise.
- Any job that involves strenuous work, such as lifting, pulling, walking and so on.
- Drinking caffeinated liquids, such as soft drinks, coffee, teas. Caffeine increases urination, thus releasing water and minerals from your body.
- Alcohol intake increases urination due to a hormonal change in the kidneys. Two or more alcoholic drinks should be followed by an increased intake of water the

next day—at least one 8 oz. glass of water per hour during your waking moments. Besides its toxic effects on the internal organs, heavier, chronic use of alcohol (two or three drinks per evening or more), leads to dehydration of the tissues and increases your chance of developing an RSI.

- Medications may cause dehydration. Check with your pharmacist or doctor and read the literature about the side effects of any drugs you are taking.

I recommend that my patients drink a glass (8–12 ounces) of water at least every other hour, if not every hour. The more the better. I have had a number of RSI patients who noticed a beneficial change in symptoms within two to three days of increasing water intake and avoiding the substances mentioned above.

Make sure you drink natural spring water or water that has been purified. In some areas, the tap water can do more harm than good because of the sediments, heavy metals, fluoridation, chlorination and all the other harmful chemicals that come through a faucet. Invest in a water purification system if access to a better water supply is not possible.

#2: Take frequent breaks.

Taking frequent breaks may be the simplest yet most important aspect of on-the-job RSI reduction. Until management understands the importance of this single strategy, RSI conditions will continue to increase at an epidemic proportion. Taking a break has many meanings. Most people think that a break means a trip to the water cooler or talking to a friend on the telephone. My interpretation of a break is this: a 5-to-10 minute interruption of your normal work duties filled in with a short stretching program and self-massage of the shoulders arms and hands. This might be called a "health maintenance break" to influence employers and management to begin implementing this important part of the work day. Breaks should be taken at least once per hour, and preferably every 45 minutes. If active symptoms of an RSI are present, breaks should be more frequent, at least one every 20 to 30 minutes.

#3: Rest your arms and hands as much as possible.

The best thing you can do when beginning to feel the tell-tale symptoms of an RSI is to rest your hands, arms and body. Many people do not have the luxury of doing this since most RSIs are due to work-related conditions and sick leave may not be an option. If you do have that option though, take advantage of it. You will be better off with a few days off from work to rest your body than trying to work through the pain and increasing the chance of further injury. See if you can alter your work schedule in order to give your body more rest during the day. If you have an understanding employer, let him/ her know about your symptoms in order to arrive at a solution that is good for both of you. This scenario may not be an option for those who fear losing their job if they disclose the fact that they are injured. These individuals must take the responsibility to improve their job environment and lifestyle and take more time for rest.

#4: Use ice to reduce swelling and pain.

Applying an ice pack is a simple measure which can relieve a great deal of muscle pain, joint inflammation and tendon irritation. For the RSI sufferer, ice therapy is critical during times of early inflammation and during the onset of symptoms. Remember that ice offers only temporary relief for a much more serious problem. If using ice becomes necessary often during the day, consider consulting a competent healthcare provider. Do not attempt to perform repetitive tasks with an ice pack on the injured area. This will decrease blood flow to an already injured tissue. Further damage to the tissues may ensue.

Ice therapy should be used no more than 20 minutes per session. After this period of time, it will make matters worse. A good scenario is 20 minutes on, then 30 minutes off. This process can be repeated a number of times without causing harm to the tissues. Be careful to protect your skin by placing a thin towel between the ice pack and the skin's surface. Ice packs can damage the skin if used improperly. When using ice, there is a typical sensation change. Initially, the application of ice will initiate a cold sensation, then a burning sensation, followed by aching, then by dull pain and then finally anesthesia (loss of sensation). The anesthetic affect of ice therapy is an excellent way to control a localized pain response due to inflammation.

What about heat?

The use of heat therapy, such as from a heating pad, water bottle or other source should not be used if there are inflamed or swollen tissues. This will further inflame the area and worsen the pain. If the area above the sore muscles or tendons in the arm or neck feels warm to the touch, then they are most likely inflamed. Heat should be avoided at the onset of a repetitive strain injury. As an RSI enters the chronic stage (approximately one month or more after the initial symptoms), heat can slowly be introduced as part of your treatment arsenal. Moist heat is preferred because it keeps the tissues hydrated. Avoid using a dry heating pad, which leads to dehydration of the tissues and actually increases your chance of developing RSI complaints. It may feel good when you apply it, but the next day an increase of symptoms will result because of the dehydrating effect.

Alternating heat and ice is effective in the chronic stage of injury. This produces a pumping mechanism of the blood in response to the temperature change and its affects on the capillaries and blood vessels. Apply moist heat for 20 minutes. As with ice, remember to put a thin towel between your skin and the heat for protection. After the 20 minutes of heat, allow your body about 20 minutes to rest and then apply ice for 20 minutes. I would recommend stretching the arms and back after the heating process to reduce tension and increase flexibility. If your body is prone to swelling, finish the alternating heat/ice sessions with ice.

#5: Increase your self-awareness of predisposing factors and work conditions.

There are many factors that influence the development of an RSI condition. Someone developing an RSI needs to immediately inspect the work station involved, whether it be a meat cutter's production line or a secretary's desk. If the company offers ergonomic evaluations, take advantage of one quickly. If the company does not offer this service, then you will need to perform one yourself. Tuning in to your body's response to different stressors is a good way to start. Make a list of activities you perform throughout the day and their affect on your body. Does holding the phone to your ear irritate your neck?

Does holding a meat cleaver cause your wrists to hurt? Does bringing your arm above your head to paint ceilings cause numbness in your arms? Is the chair you're sitting in irritate your back? Investigate all of the circumstances that may instigate your present symptoms and consider alternatives. If you cannot find alternatives or simply are not aware of the alternatives available, urge your employer to seek counsel with professionals who specialize in ergonomic evaluation. It is much cheaper for an employer to have an erogonomic evaluation performed than to pay worker's compensation benefits for a repetitive strain injury. Begin the process of prevention. Do not hope that the next person will do it for you. Your body is at risk.

#6: Keep a logbook of your RSI complaints

I urge my patients to begin a daily logbook of their activities, symptoms and dietary intake. Note when you felt pain, tension or cramping of the muscles; tingling, numbing or any other abnormal sensation; and what you think led to that episode. Note any medications taken that day, and what frequency. Note your dietary intake and whether you think it was adequate. Note your water intake and whether you sufficiently met your body's needs. Note any exercises or stretches performed during the day and whether you feel they helped ease the symptoms. This whole process begins to tune the RSI sufferer into the mechanisms of injury and into the body's functioning.

Your particular diary can be as short or as long as desired, but make an attempt to include all of the topics mentioned earlier for a complete breakdown of your daily activities.

SAMPLE LOG ENTRY:

Monday, February 18: *Difficult time sleeping last night—hand went numb and woke me up. I might have slept on my arm. Had to take some ibuprofen in the morning for the pain, some improvement afterwards. Worked eight hours today, but took breaks every 30 minutes and stretched hands, this felt great. Drank six glasses of water today— need to get up to eight! Numbness in hand worsened toward end of workday. (Might be due to deadline on Mr. Robertson's file—spent last two hours typing at computer). Meals today: Bagel and cream cheese for breakfast, tuna sandwich for lunch, chicken sandwich at McDonald's for dinner (bad idea). Had some crackers for snacks. (Need more protein at breakfast.) Overall, was not too bad a day. Saw chiropractor and massage therapist today, felt some improvement after treatment.*

#7: Don't become an "anti-inflammatory junkie"

Some people ingest anti-inflammatory drugs like they were candy. I've heard of one person who kept such a drug easily accessible in a large bowl so she could grab three or four at a time without needing to open the bottle! Anti-inflammatories are powerful drugs. Just because you can buy them over the counter does not mean they are harmless. Long-term use predisposes one to kidney and liver damage, suppression of the immune system and suppression of the body's natural inflammatory response, an essential part of its defense mechanism. An anti-inflammatory drug is not going to solve your RSI condition. It will simply decrease inflammation temporarily. Unless you determine the root cause of your condition and take measures to alleviate stressors affecting your body, it will be impossible to overcome RSI symptoms—whether from a bad work station, an assembly line that requires fine motor control of the fingers, grasping on to a meat cleaver too tightly or a pinched nerve in your neck. The biggest problem I see in my office is that ibuprofen is the primary form of treatment prescribed for RSI patients by their primary care medical physicians. The following prescription has been repeated too many times: "Take 600 mg. of ibuprofen two to three times daily and wear this wrist brace." For the RSI sufferer, this advice is a great disservice; in fact it is downright negligent for a doctor to ignore the cause of an RSI and deal only with its symptoms. Drugs will not heal it.

Anti-inflammatories are just one of the many drugs dispensed for RSI conditions by medical professionals. Before they consulted me, my patients have been given arsenals of medications—from muscle relaxants, narcotics and sleeping pills to potent steroidal injections and medications—to combat RSI pain. The medical community is quick to dispense the drugs but not quick enough to warn of the contraindications (situations where the drug may harmfully interact with other conditions in the body) and the side effects, which often are worse than the condition they were meant to treat. If your medical practitioner is about to prescribe medications, be sure to ask why they are being prescribed, how they will affect your RSI condition and what side effects to expect while taking them. Make sure you know the pros and cons before ingesting a handful of pills. In most cases, the pills simply mask your RSI condition. This may even worsen your RSI condition since medicated individuals will continue to use the injured extremity because of the lack of pain response. The theory that "if it doesn't hurt then it must be healed" doesn't fit with an RSI condition. I have included below a sampling of three drugs that are typically used to combat the pain and muscle soreness of repetitive strain injuries. Their benefits and side effects are also listed.

113

DRUGS COMMONLY PRESCRIBED FOR RSI CONDITIONS[28]

Drug	Type of Drug	Effects	Side Effects
Ibuprofen	Nonsteroidal anti-inflammatories	Relieves inflammation, swelling, stiffness, joint pains	Stomach pain and cramping, hives, nausea, indigestion, trouble breathing, liver and kidney malfunction, ringing in the ears
Flexeril	Cyclobenzaprine	Muscle relaxant, helps relieve pain from sprains and strains	Blurred vision, drowsiness, confusion, mental depression, mood changes, ringing in the ears, dizziness, dryness of the mouth
Cortisone	Steroidal anti-inflammatories, corticosteroids	Decreases inflammation	Demineralization of bone, weakening of tendons and ligaments, stomach pain, skin conditions, nausea, unusual bruising of skin, weight gain, nervousness, restlessness, headaches, vomiting, weakness

#8: Avoid working in cold environments.

Placing yourself into a cold working environment with an RSI condition is equivalent to playing Russian roulette. A cold environment will decrease blood flow to the extremities, thus restricting the supply of important nutrients and oxygen to the already irritated tendons and muscles.

Musicians work in these environments regularly. They may play a concert in a cold damp church or outdoors on a cool autumn afternoon. Many musicians will wear gloves with the fingertips cut off to provide warmth to the hands without sacrificing dexterity for the fingertips. This is a good idea for any RSI sufferer who is subjected to a cold work environment.

Keeping your arms and hands warm is important in preventing RSI flare-ups. Invest in a portable heater if you have to. Don't wait for your employer to supply it. Remember, your body is at risk, so take action immediately.

#9: Locate gadgets that will make using your hands easier.

With the ever-increasing awareness of RSI conditions, companies are now coming out with many products to make the workplace safer and "ergonomically correct." For computer users, ergonomic mice, keyboards, chairs and work stations are available to ease the strain on hands and arms. If you use fine motor skills of the fingers, maybe a rubberized fingertip purchased from a local stationary store may help you. Rubber grips for many types of items are available, such as for jars, pens, pencils, etc. These grips can ease a tightened grasp on a pen or make opening a jar a bit easier. There has been a surge of products touting themselves as "ergonomic" because of the increasing market for them. Always research the product first and decide whether it is really suited to help your condition.

115

#10: Temporarily avoid hobbies and sports that can make your condition worse

Hobbies such as knitting and crocheting are prime instigators of RSIs. Gardening can irritate your hands and arms as well as your back. Creating artwork, such as painting, airbrushing and pencil drawings, requires tightening muscles of the hand, and the shoulders and neck. Sports can cause and/or worsen an RSI condition. For example, tennis, golf, baseball, softball, racquetball, badminton and bowling commonly irritate the arm. Therefore, temporarily discontinue a sporting activity involving repetitive use of the upper extremity if you have RSI symptoms. Keep in mind that this is not a complete stoppage of the hobby or sport, just a temporary time-off to give your body rest. I urge my patients to continue with sports that involve aerobic exercise. This would include using a treadmill, running, bicycling, swimming and aerobics classes. Maintaining an exercise regimen is important to increase oxygenation of the blood and to increase blood flow to the arms and legs. Exercise causes muscle contractions, which help to pump swelling out of the muscles and tissues and stimulate lymphatic drainage from the areas of complaint. Exercise also decreases depression, a common malady among RSI sufferers.

#11: Examine your diet and start making healthful changes.

This is a great time to begin eating better. If you are suffering from an RSI condition, chances are your nutritional intake is not up to par. Begin to invest some time and money into learning how to eat well. See the next chapter.

#12: Avoid cigarettes and other tobacco products

Using nicotine, whether through cigarette, cigar or pipe smoking or chewing tobacco, increases muscular tension and possibly causes back pain. Nicotine negatively affects blood vessels, causing decreased blood flow to the muscles. In addition, the increased amount of carbon monoxide due to cigarette smoking decreases oxygenation of the blood. Therefore, besides decreasing overall blood supply to the muscles, the blood that does get to them is poorly oxygenated, thus starving the muscles and tissues of life-giving oxygen.

#13: Join a support group

You will be amazed at how many people have symptoms just like yours. Every major city and metropolitan area has RSI support groups. This is a great way to exchange information about your particular condition, learn about doctors and therapists in your area who are adept at handling RSIs and make new friends as a bonus. If your area does not have a support group, then search the Internet for RSI-related sites. A listing of World Wide Web sites which are informative and helpful to the RSI sufferer can be found in the Resource Section. There is a wide variety of mailing lists and newsgroups on the Internet dedicated to the subject of RSIs. These offer a wealth of information on all aspects of RSI conditions, from specific complaints and symptom relief to worker's compensation issues. You can even sign on to RSI mailing lists from other countries. Remember though, that excessive computer use may exacerbate your RSI condition, so don't spend three or four hours surfing the net or sending e-mail messages without a break.

117

CHAPTER 11

NUTRITIONAL GUIDELINES

It is rare to find a book about repetitive strain injuries that mentions even one word about the importance of good nutrition, yet the role of nutrition in the development and healing of RSIs could fill an entire book.

Every cell of the body relies upon proper nutrition to grow, divide and function, and whether or not your cells are optimally nourished depends upon the foods you eat. If you eat food with poor nutritional value, your cells cannot grow, function or divide well. Eat the proper foods, and they will. Cells inside your body are constantly growing and dying. It is estimated that muscle cells are completely replaced with new muscle cells every six months. The state of health of the newly-replaced cells depends upon a combination of factors, including your nutrition, a properly functioning nervous system and genetics.

We can control two of these factors—nutrition and nervous system function. Nervous system function, for example, can be corrected and maintained through such disciplines as acupuncture and chiropractic care. As explained in *The Body Electric* by Robert Becker, M.D., the peripheral nervous system (the nerves going to your arms and legs) consists of growth

118

factors, critical to the development of new tissues.[29] Therefore, new cells developing within your body rely upon a healthy nervous system, which in turn is dependent upon good nutrition from the vitamins, minerals and other substances necessary for nerve conduction. No matter what type of cell—nerve, heart, muscle, brain or intestinal—all depend on dietary nourishment to assure a normal healthy life span.

How does this relate to repetitive strain injuries? Cells affected by a repetitive strain condition can become hypoxic, or devoid of oxygen, due to swelling in the surrounding tissues and a decreased blood flow from squeezed capillaries. In these conditions the cells will die off and need to be replaced. The new cells' health depends upon your nutritional status. Nutrition has also been linked to the frequency and severity of the inflammatory response. For these reasons, changing your diet can help heal RSI conditions.

CREATING AN OPTIMAL DIET FOR HEALING RSIS

The six nutritional components of the diet; carbohydrates, proteins, fats, vitamins, minerals and water must be balanced in every meal you eat. Overindulgence in one or more of the components and a lack of others will cause your body to function suboptimally. Each meal should contain about 30 percent of its calories from protein, about 30 percent from healthy fats, and 40 percent from complex carbohydrates.[30] The goal is to achieve balance of all these nutrients through your daily meals, emphasizing the foods that help the body to heal and optimize energy levels.

The importance of fats

The percentage of fats needed in each meal may sound high, but essential fatty acids and unsaturated fats play an important role in your body, especially in the brain, nervous system and cellular function. Don't worry: eating the right fats will not automatically make you fat! However, I am not suggesting that you overindulge in animal foods loaded with saturated fats which might lead to an increased cholesterol level. I am suggesting that the RSI sufferer not limit monounsaturated or polyunsaturated fat intake. These fats will actually be beneficial to you.

Twenty to thirty percent of every meal's calories should be composed of monounsaturated fats. Good examples of these are fish, sesame or sunflower seeds, flaxseed oil, avocado, almonds, olive oil, olives, natural peanut or almond butter, macadamia nuts, and mayonnaise. These rules are especially important not only for RSI sufferers who have a very thin body frame and have a difficult time holding on to fats, but also for overweight or obese RSI sufferers who are making attempts to lose weight.

When to eat

During the waking hours, our bodies need food about every four hours to maintain adequate blood glucose levels. Remember that brain and nervous system function utilize most of the glucose in our bloodstream. Therefore, if you are suffering from a nerve-related RSI condition, make sure that you don't go too long between meals, since nerve and muscle function will diminish slightly under low glucose levels, thus aggravating your condition. To keep the body's energy level at an even keel, eat breakfast from 6 to 8 a.m., lunch at 12 or 1 p.m., a snack at 4 p.m., dinner at 6 or 7 p.m. and finally a snack at about 9 or 10 p.m. If more than four hours lapse between meals because of a busy work schedule, be sure to keep snacks on hand balanced with protein, carbohydrates and fats.

Essential fatty acids (EFAs) are very important for RSI sufferers. These substances alter the prostaglandin concentrations in your body to decrease the inflammatory response. Common sources of EFAs are borage oil, black currant seed oil and evening primrose oil. Another great way of obtaining EFAs are from consuming cold water fish, such as salmon and mackerel.

What to eat

Anyone suffering from a repetitive strain injury has to seriously look at their diet to determine where the strengths and weaknesses are. I encourage my patients to include their daily intake of food in their logbook. This forces them to think more about the foods they are eating and at the same time gives the health care provider insight into their nutritional status.

The simplest approach is to only eat foods that have not been processed. That means whole foods such as vegetables, fruits, whole grain breads, grains, nuts, seeds, cereals, meats, fish and poultry. Red meats such as hamburgers and steak may increase your inflammatory response, so I don't recommend them during an active RSI. If possible, buy foods that are pesticide-free, hormone-free and organic. Health food stores and more and more supermarkets carry these products.

Hormonal responses from foods

The quality, quantity and combination of foods you eat are important factors producing a beneficial nutritional and hormonal balance. Foods produce a hormonal response when eaten. The two major hormones involved are insulin and glucagon.[31] Insulin takes sugars from the blood and deposits them into the cells. Glucagon does the opposite. These two hormones are always balancing the body's needs of glucose.

Insulin activates the production of a substance called arachidonic acid which is a precursor to hormones called eicosanoids. Prostaglandins are members of the eicosanoid family. Some of the many forms of prostaglandins are good for the body, while some are bad. Arachidonic acid initiates production of the "bad" eicosanoids, the enemy for RSI sufferers. They prolong the inflammatory response, promote constriction of blood vessels, increase the transmission of pain, and depress the immune response. Therefore, inhibiting a large insulin response to the foods we eat is imperative.[32]

How do we decrease the insulin response? The first thing needed is smaller, more frequent meals. Most Americans eat much more than necessary. Large intake of food promotes increased secretion of insulin into the bloodstream to counteract the huge influx of carbohydrates. (Think how you feel after that big Thanksgiving dinner—that is insulin working in full force). In fact, our diets would be better with five or six small meals eaten more frequently throughout the day than with the standard fare of three meals per day. This promotes a more steady intake of nutrients and prevents the ups and downs most people feel throughout the day because of insulin surges and blood glucose fluctuations.

The second way to decrease insulin levels is to reduce the high percentage of carbohydrates in our meals. One nutritional school of thought believes that high-carbohydrate, low-fat diets are the best way to reduce cholesterol and weight, and to stay healthy. However, in *The Zone Diet* Barry Sears explains the detrimental effect of high carbohydrates and subsequent elevated insulin production. Dr. Sears suggests a protein to carbo-hydrate ration of .75 at every meal (which translates into three parts protein to four parts carbohydrate). This ratio has been found to reduce blood insulin levels, and increase glucagon levels. The protein-to-carbohydrate ratio should be followed in every meal and snack, whether just a few crackers and cheese, or an entire dinner. I recommend reading Dr. Sears' book to learn how to follow this diet more specifically.

PLANNING YOUR DIET

Meats and Poultry

When choosing meat products, avoid fatty, marbled meats since these are loaded with saturated fats. Purchase the leanest meats possible. It is best to focus on fish, with some poultry, if desired, during an active RSI. Red meat may aggravate your inflammatory condition.

Choose poultry and meat that is free of hormones and antibiotics, whenever possible. We do not know the long term effects of these additives on human health.[33]

Vegetarian Diets

Most vegetarians are more knowledgeable about their food se-lections and choices. The biggest obstacle with a vegetarian diet is maintaining good protein intake with every meal, and obtaining adequate B12 intake. Since protein should make up about 30 percent of each meal (whether vegetarian or non-vegetarian), the vegetarian must choose non-meat sources of protein to make up this requirement. Tofu, dried legumes, egg, soy-based products, nuts and seeds are good choices. Dairy also contains protein, but excess saturated fat can be a problem. Make sure to eat a wide variety of protein to get an adequate amount of all the essential amino acids in your diet.

Vegans (vegetarians who do not eat eggs or dairy products) risk a B12 deficiency, since it is found only in animal products, and is necessary for normal human function. Also, vegans, as well as other vegetarians, can suffer from mineral depletion due to the phytic acid present in whole grains, which can deplete mineral stores of calcium, copper, chromium, vanadium, lithium and zinc.[34] Supplementation is sometimes necessary to prevent anemia and other nervous system disorders. Vegetarians with RSIs should consider consulting with a registered dietician or nutritionist for a diet analysis. You may be lacking protein or other important factors which are predisposing you to repetitive injuries.

THE IMPORTANCE OF ADEQUATE WATER INTAKE

Dehydration will decrease the performance level of the entire body. Muscle function decreases 20–30 percent when dehydrated.[35] Thus, those suffering from RSI conditions cannot afford to be dehydrated. An already taxed muscle due to repetitive strain will experience a sharp decline in function when faced with dehydration. Dehydration can result from a number of causes. Exercise, sweating due to high temperatures or heavy work activities and increased urine output due to caffeine or alcohol intake all lead to decreased water levels.

If you are experiencing a large amount of fluid loss due to intense exercise routines (lasting one hour or longer) or if illness is causing prolonged vomiting and/or diarrhea, consider using a product that contains salts, minerals and sugars

HEALING FOODS FOR RSIs

Whole Grains
- Wheat, corn, buckwheat, rye, millet, rice, quinoa, barley
- Whole grain breads, cereals, pancakes, muffins, waffles
- Brown rice, basmati rice, couscous
- Wheat germ, bran, psyllium

Legumes, Nuts, and Seeds
- Soybeans and soy products; soy milk, tofu, miso, tempeh
- Legumes such as black-eyed peas, navy beans, lentils, chick-peas, lima beans, pinto beans
- Sesame, pumpkin, sunflower seeds
- Macadamia nuts, almonds, chestnuts, walnuts

Vegetables
- Green leafy vegetables such as spinach, lettuce, collard greens, mustard greens, kale, watercress, Brussels sprouts, parsley turnip greens, broccoli
- Cauliflower, Yams, carrots, onions, garlic, cabbage, winter squash

All vegetables are good! Each as many as possible.

Vegetable oils: use extra virgin, cold pressed olive oil

Fruits
- All forms of fresh fruit. Include citrus for vitamin C.
- Dried fruits: figs, raisins, dates, apricots, prunes

Dairy
- Skim or low-fat milk
- Cheeses (use sparingly due to high saturated fat content)

Animal Protein
Fish—especially cold water fish: salmon, mackerel, sardines
Chicken, turkey, pork
Eggs

125

along with water. A good example of this is Gatorade. Drinking large amounts of pure water in these extreme circumstances will result in the cells getting flooded with water while loosing their normal minerals and nutrients. This can effectively shut down cellular function. Replacing the lost nutrients is important in these circumstances. Six to eight glasses of water per day is recommended for maintenance of normal water levels.

FOODS TO AVOID

There are a number of foods that must be avoided while combating an RSI condition. The main foods to avoid are those that will cause a release of the bad prostaglandins within your body. These include red meats such as hamburger and steak, and processed meats such as ham, corned beef, bacon, salami, sausage, hot dogs and bologna which are loaded with saturated fats, harmful nitrites, sodium and cholesterol. Avoid liver and other organ meats. These too contain large amounts of cholesterol and saturated fats and will throw off your prostaglandin levels. Avoid palm, corn and safflower oil, butter, lard, hard cheeses, ice cream and whipped cream. Avoid margarine and other hydrogenated vegetable oils that contain harmful transfatty acids.

Avoid all white flour products, such as white bread, muffins, biscuits, sweet rolls, waffles, pancakes and bagels. These have little nutritional value compared to whole wheat products.

Alcohol should be consumed in very small amounts, if at all. If you feel the need to drink an alcoholic beverage, red wine is your best choice because of its beneficial circulatory effects. Consuming more than two alcoholic beverages daily will worsen your RSI condition. Alcohol causes dehydration—the enemy for RSI sufferers, and also is destructive to a number of bodily organs, especially the liver.

Refined sugar products should be avoided as well. These include all forms of candy, sugared cereals, soft drinks, many baked goods such as pastries and muffins and table sugar. Refined sugar has a detrimental effect on your adrenal glands, blood sugar levels, insulin levels, brain function and immune function. Besides its bad qualities, sugar offers "empty calories" with no nutritional benefit.

Avoid any products that contain "high-fructose corn syrup." If you stroll down the aisle of a grocery store and look at labels, you will be amazed at how many products contain high-fructose corn syrup. Many RSI sufferers who avoid high-fructose corn syrup have noticed a rapid decrease in their RSI symptoms. If you feel a craving for a sugary product, drink some herbal tea with natural honey. Honey actually contains vitamins (B complex, C, D, and E) along with some amino acids, so it is not an "empty calorie" sweetener.

Avoid artificial sweeteners such as saccharine and Nutrisweet. The harmful affects of saccharine are well documented, and aspartame (Nutrisweet) has been shown clinically to cause arthritis and joint pains, seizures, chronic fatigue, vision damage, tingling in the extremities, anxiety attacks, depression and memory loss.

Caffeine should be avoided as well. Caffeine is found in coffee, tea, soda, cocoa products and chocolate. Caffeine stimulates muscle tension, may lead to anxiety and sleeplessness, and can cause a flare-up of RSI symptoms.

FASTING AND SEVERELY REDUCED CALORIE DIETS

The RSI sufferer should not engage in fasting, severely reduced calorie diets or liquid diets. These diets may lead to protein breakdown for glucose production and the protein will most likely come from the muscles, the worst case scenario for RSI sufferers. It is very important that RSI patients maintain an optimal intake of all the nutrients to afford the body the building blocks needed to grow, heal and strengthen tissue.

IMPORTANT VITAMINS, MINERALS AND OTHER NUTRIENTS

Vitamin C. It is important to increase the intake of vitamin C which is crucial for soft tissue healing. Increase your consumption of citrus fruits and green leafy vegetables. Natural sources of vitamins are always preferred to the synthetic pill forms. If you feel you are not getting at least five fruits and vegetables in your daily diet, take supplemental vitamin C as an insurance policy to maintain adequate levels. One to three grams (1000 to 3000 mg) per day of vitamin C usually can be tolerated easily. This vitamin has an easy way of telling you when you're consuming too much—it causes diarrhea and abdominal complaints at high levels.

The B-Complex Vitamins. Many sufferers of carpal tunnel syndrome and other RSI maladies are advised to take vitamin B6. This compound has shown some beneficial results with carpal tunnel syndrome, but the benefits are not consistent for everyone. Some people find it very effective, while others see no change in the condition. B6 is important for preventing muscle cramps, improving nerve function, and maintaining body fluid levels. It has been found effective not only for carpal tunnel syndrome, but also for relieving fluid retention in pre-menstrual syndrome. Since the vitamin is water-soluble, it is safe to take on a daily basis without worry of overdose. I recommend a B-complex vitamin to increase the intake of all the B vitamins, due to their important role in nervous system functioning.

Minerals. I believe that a large majority of repetitive injury sufferers develop their conditions due to a depletion of both major and trace minerals. The continued depletion of our nation's soils of trace minerals, and the ever-increasing trend toward fast foods have combined to foster a mineral deficient population.

When contemplating mineral supplementation, look for minerals in the "colloidal" form. Colloidal minerals are absorbed at a rate of up to 95 percent, compared to "chelated" minerals which are absorbed at approximately 50 percent. I have found the "Soaring Eagle" brand of colloidal minerals to be quite effective in combating mineral depletion. This product contains 72 minerals needed for normal human functioning. For information on ordering, see the Resources.

Calcium and Magnesium. Adequate calcium levels need to be maintained in anyone complaining of repetitive strain injuries. Calcium is important for muscle and nerve function. Deficiencies can lead to problems with muscle cramps and impaired nerve conduction. Calcium along with magnesium and vitamin D is a good combination, and is found in every health food store.

The best food sources of calcium are tofu, dried figs, broccoli, many forms of beans, collard greens and low- or non-fat milk. Optimum daily intake of calcium is approximately 800 mg per day for adults, increasing to 1200 mg in pregnant women, and up to 1500 mg per day in postmenopausal women.

Magnesium is the fourth most abundant mineral in the body. About 200 to 300 mg per day should be ingested through the diet. Magnesium serves as a coenzyme for about 80 percent of the enzymes in the body. The best sources are sea vegetables, sesame seeds, figs, whole grains, green leafy vegetables, fish and meat.

Vitamin D is naturally found in the skin, and is activated by sunlight. About 400 IU per day is recommended. Vitamin D is found in large quantities in halibut, salmon, mackerel and bluefish.

Manganese. According to Dr. Joel Wallach, author of *Rare Earths, Forbidden Cures,* a manganese deficiency is a primary factor in the development of repetitive motion disorders. Manganese is important for activating enzyme systems, glucose metabolism, and is a constituent of metalloenzymes. It helps reduce fatigue, and improves memory. The RDA is 2 to 5 mg per day for adults. Whole grain cereals and green vegetables are the best sources for this mineral. Tea is an excellent source as well.

Zinc. Zinc is necessary for the healing of cells and the development of new cells. It aids enzymes in digestion and metabolism and is an essential part of more than 100 enzymes involved in digestion, metabolism, reproduction and wound healing. It is also very important for prostate gland function. Zinc is found in high levels in fish, meats, poultry and whole grains. Alcohol, high calcium diets and diuretics can lower zinc levels. 20 to 30 mg per day is recommended.

Antioxidants. Antioxidants, such as selenium, vitamin E, vitamin C, betacarotene, coenzyme Q10, bioflavonoids, zinc, copper and manganese all help to reduce the body of free radicals. Free radicals form from various metabolic reactions in the body and are destructive to the tissues.

Selenium can be found naturally in fish, sea vegetables, wheat germ, garlic, onions, chicken, broccoli, whole grain breads, rice, pasta and cereals. Fifty to 200 mcg per day is recommended. Selenium has also been shown to be a powerful anticancer agent.

Vitamin E is important to prevent the breakdown of unsaturated fatty acids into free radicals. Vitamin E's correlation with reducing heart disease is well documented. Daily intake should be maintained between 200 and 400 IU. The best sources for this vitamin are wheat germ oil and peanut oil, along with green leafy vegetables, nuts, seeds and dried beans.

Vitamin C improves immune system function and is a powerful antioxidant. It is necessary for tissue growth and repair. People under psychological and/or emotional stress lose their stores of vitamin C, therefore supplementation via food or pill is very important in this group. Some of the best food sources of vitamin C are papaya, orange juice, guava, broccoli and Brussels sprouts.

Betacarotene is a yellowish compound found in vegetables that have a yellow, orange or dark green coloring. Carrot juice is an excellent source of this substance; there are 11,500 IU in just three and one-half ounces of carrot juice. Betacarotene is actually a precursor to vitamin A. Its benefits include immune enhancement, protection against the common cold, protection against environmental pollutants and aiding in the development of healthy bones, tissues and hair. I would recommend approximately 10,000 IU to 15,000 IU of betacarotene per day.

Coenzyme Q10 is another powerful antioxidant found in high concentrations in organs, and especially the heart. It is deficient in most patients with cardiovascular disease. CoQ10 stabilizes the cell membranes, and functions as a free radical scavenger. The best sources of coenzyme Q10 are beef and pork, along with lesser quantities in mackerel, salmon, sardines, eggs, broccoli, wheat germ and spinach. Between 100 and 150 mg of coenzyme Q10 is recommended daily.

Proteolytic Enzymes. These enzymes are important for reducing the inflammatory response. Some plant enzymes are commonly used for this purpose, such as papain from papaya and bromelin from pineapples. Also, animal enzymes such as pepsin, trypsin, rennin and pancreatin are also proteolytic.

Superoxide dismutase (SOD) is an enzyme produced in the body to reduce the rate of cell destruction and helps to revitalize the cell. It does this by removing superoxide, another type of free radical. Many health food stores carry this product, but be sure it is enteric coated to bypass the digestive enzymes in the stomach. The best natural sources of SOD are barley grass, broccoli, Brussels sprouts and cabbage.

Cartilage Growth Factors. Any RSI sufferer who complains of joint aches and pains, or has preexisting osteoarthritis, can benefit from cartilage growth factors, such as glucosamine sulfate, chondroitan sulfate and shark cartilage. Scientific studies and clinical evidence show that these natural compounds initiate cartilage growth and healing in degenerative conditions. For further information on these compounds, read *The Arthritis Cure* by Jason Theodosakis.

HERBAL SUPPLEMENTS

Warning: Herbs are potent substances having a wide range of effects upon the body. They are natural medicines derived

OPTIMAL NUTRITION FOR HEALING RSIs

- *Eat a wide variety of natural whole foods.*
- *Maintain adequate water intake, at least 8 glasses or 64 oz per day.*
- *Supplement the diet with vitamins and minerals where necessary.*
- *Eat smaller amounts of food every three or four hours to maintain glucose levels and lower insulin levels.*
- *Make green leafy vegetables and other forms of vegetables a part of every meal.*
- *Plan every meal for approximately 30 percent protein, 30 percent fat, and 40 percent carbohydrate.*
- *Reduce harmful saturated fats and non-nutritious processed and junk foods*
- *Avoid caffeinated products and excessive alcohol intake.*
- *Eat at least two different types of fruit daily (preferably four).*
- *Avoid all processed foods and meats.*

from plants. Treat them as you would treat a prescription medicine. Always seek advice from your natural health care professional before using herbs, preferably a provider who is familiar with herbs and utilizes specialized or applied kinesiology to individually test you for your body's needs. Use caution when combining herbs. Implement herbs slowly into your diet, one at a time. This will help you determine how your body is reacting to each individual herb.

The following table of herbs is a starting point for the RSI sufferer. It includes some of the better known herbs which show benefits for nerve, inflammatory and muscle conditions. Anyone interested in herbal therapy should consult an herbalist or naturopath. See the Resource section for books about herbs.

HELPFUL HERBS FOR RSI CONDITIONS

Alfalfa	Aids in arthritic conditions, cleanses the kidneys and removes toxins from the body. Used to neutralize acids and is an excellent blood purifier and blood thinner. Has been found to improve appetite and aid in the assimilation of protein, calcium and other nutrients. An excellent source of minerals, chlorophyll and vitamins.
Capsicum (cayenne)	Used as a catalyst to aid other herb functions. Helpful for increasing circulation, relieving nerve disorders when combined with lobelia, relieving rheumatism and arthritis.
Celery seed	Good for reducing muscle spasm, relieving arthritis symptoms, reducing blood pressure.
Chamomile	An excellent cleanser and toner of the digestive tract. Aids in calming the nerves and has antispasmodic properties. Commonly found in tea preparations.
Chickweed	The fresh leaves can be used as a poultice for inflammation.
Garlic	A natural antibiotic used to combat infection and strengthen blood vessels. Useful for a large number of disorders. Has an overall cleansing property for the body.
Gingko biloba	Enhances circulatory function. An essential herb for RSI sufferers.
Ginseng	Used for stress relief. Strengthens the adrenal glands, provides energy and enhances immune function.
Goldenseal	A great anti-inflammatory; helpful for diabetes, colds, glandular swelling and gum disease. Enhances functioning capacity of many organ systems.

Hops	Used as a sedative, relaxant. Eases muscle tension and relaxes nervous tension.
Kelp	Helpful to restore sensory nerve function. Aids in brain function and the central nervous system. A great source of minerals and vitamins.
Lobelia	Used to subdue muscle spasm. When combined with capsicum, is useful for nerve disorders.
Passionflower	Mild narcotic properties; for diarrhea and dysentery, neuralgia, sleeplessness and dysmenorrhea.
Rose hips	Used for stress relief. Often seen in vitamin C preparations.
Skullcap	Useful in nervous system disorders. Helpful in decreasing pain, muscle aches, cramping and muscle spasms. May help as a sleep aid.
Valerian root	Good for reducing muscle spasms. Has a calming and relaxing affect, therefore good in combating anxiety and sleep disorders. Take in the evening, since it may cause drowsiness.

Also helpful for RSI conditions are herbal preparations found in health food stores labeled "nerve disorders," "stress" or "joint disorders." Homeopathic combination formulas are also available with similar labels—"calming," "nervousness" or "Injuries." Again, it is always best to check with a healthcare provider familiar with these preparations to determine which one would be best for your particular condition. Chapter 18 provides you with more information on homeopathy and homeopathic remedies.

CHAPTER 12

WHEN to SEE A HEALTHCARE PROVIDER

Most doctors would say that any symptoms that seem to indicate a repetitive strain injury should be treated immediately because of their potential for worsening. In most cases, if symptoms are present, the tissues are already undergoing damage. If you have attempted all of the self-help recommendations in this book without success in relieving your symptoms, then a trip to your healthcare provider is imperative. The following table indicates when diagnosis and treatment become necessary.

WHEN TO SEE A HEALTHCARE PROVIDER

Changes in nutrition, ergonomics, and activities do not help symptoms.

Condition continues for more than two weeks.

Symptoms begin to worsen.

Feelings of tingling or numbness anywhere.

Increased sensation of coldness in arms and hands.

Activitites of daily living become affected by symptoms.

Increased fatigue is felt in the muscles.

Loss of coordination of the hands and fingers.

You begin to be clumsy with your hands.

Decreased strength of the muscles.

Sensation of heaviness in the extremities.

Constant muscle twitching in the hands or arms combined with pain.

Loss of function of extremity.

Symptoms are leading to depression or are affecting your emotional state.

HOW TO CHOOSE A HEALTHCARE PROVIDER

This is the hardest decision the RSI sufferer has to make. Contact an RSI support group in your area to learn which healthcare providers are obtaining good results with their cases. Since you are reading this book, you already have an interest in alternative medicine, therefore I have included in the following chapters a sampling of some natural health disciplines showing great benefits for RSI patients. Read through the disciplines to discover which one or combination of providers sound right for you.

It is good to first locate a primary healthcare provider who works in partnership with other health professionals experienced in treating RSIs. As stated earlier, RSI problems need a multidisciplinary approach for healing. It may take a combined effort of two, three or even more healthcare providers to achieve optimum results.

Examples of primary healthcare providers are doctors of

137

chiropractic, acupuncturists, doctors of Oriental medicine, medical doctors, osteopathic doctors and, in some states, naturopathic and homeopathic doctors. These doctors are your portal of entry into the healthcare system. They can refer you to other healthcare providers when needed, such as physical therapists, Feldenkreis instructors, etc. The key is to find one who is experienced with RSIs and is knowledgeable and willing to work with alternative health providers.

The best route for finding a good doctor is to seek a referral from someone who has had treatment already and has seen good results. If you have access to the Internet, there are a number of mailing lists and news groups you can subscribe to at no cost. This is a great medium for finding a doctor in your area who has helped others. In the Resource section, I have included the addresses and instructions on how to sign on to these groups. You can even search for "repetitive strain injuries" and other related subjects on on-line search engines. (See Resources for examples). There you can get an entire listing of doctors, products and research areas on the World Wide Web that can be helpful to your condition.

If you have a worker's compensation claim, chances are you will be sent by your employer to the company doctor. In most cases this is an M.D. who may or may not be familiar with RSI conditions (In most cases, not). It is important that injured employees immediately learn their rights in regards to receiving adequate health care. In California, for example, if the employee is not happy with the doctor chosen by the employer, the employee can demand a change of physician. Check with your library or bookstore to locate books about the worker's compensation system in your state. The system is complex and difficult to understand for most people. Your primary care physician should be knowledgeable about worker's compensation issues and provide guidance for you.

How to prepare for your first appointment

Before your initial visit with your healthcare provider, get a pen and paper and take an inventory of your current health status. It is easier to remember your health history when you have time to think about it. Many people leave out important bits of information when they feel rushed filling out forms in the health provider's office. This prepared information will offer your healthcare provider an excellent introduction to your overall health status and shorten the question/answer period known as the consultation. However, don't present the doctor with a mountain of paperwork—it will most likely not be read. Try to be concise.

1. List the symptoms you are currently experiencing and any symptoms you have experienced over the past few months that correlate to this injury. List any other health complaints that may or may not be related to your RSI.
2. List any previous traumas such as falls, auto accidents, motorcycle accidents, blows to the head or body, broken bones, abuse, etc. These are very important for the doctor to know about. They may be a predisposing factor to your condition.
3. List any surgeries you have had, no matter how big or small.
4. If you are taking any medications, vitamins, and/or minerals, list them as well, and the reason for taking each one.
5. If you have seen other doctors or health care providers for this RSI condition, list them and state what therapies

were used and their overall effectiveness. Make note of any therapies you felt made your condition worse.

6. List any daily activities that have been affected by your condition, such as getting dressed, combing your hair, taking care of a child, etc.

7. List your work duties, and what duties bring on your pain. Be precise. Figure in the number of minutes or hours for the pain to arise while working. Also list how long it takes for the pain to be relieved during or after work, and what you needed to do or use to relieve the pain.

After your initial consultation and exam, how do you feel about this health provider?

This is an important question to ask yourself. Did your provider seem interested in your health? Did he look you in the eye? Did he respond quickly to your questions or did he try to avoid some questioning? Do you feel he spent an adequate amount of time discussing your condition and performing the initial exam? I have come across many patients who stated their doctor spent no more than 5 or 10 minutes with them at their initial exam. There is no way a doctor can examine your RSI condition in less than 15 to 20 minutes—and longer is definitely better. A complete exam includes range of motion testing, orthopedic and neurological testing, motor strength testing, checking vital signs, checking the tone of the upper extremity and spinal muscles for swelling and spasm, checking the spinal joints, checking posture, etc. In complex cases, expect to spend 45 minutes to an hour with the doctor for a complete history-taking and physical exam.

An important question to ask yourself is this: Did the doctor seem concerned about your health and well-being? Remember that this person will determine your healthcare for the many months of treatment ahead. If you have a work injury, this doctor will determine whether you receive an optimum treatment plan, your disability status and work modifications and will determine whether you are going to be relegated to drugs and surgery or natural, conservative healthcare. If you don't feel comfortable with the doctor or healthcare provider, then speak to him/her about your feelings and concerns and if necessary look for another provider. Remember, it's your health, not the doctor's at stake here. Choose a provider you have confidence in, one you feel personally attuned to, and one that is upbeat and excited about his work.

If you are considering a change of physician for the treatment of your RSI or if this is the first physician you are seeing, consider setting up a consultation first—without the examination. Many doctors will not charge for a 10-to-15 minute consultation. (Be wary of those who do—if you have to pay just to speak with them for a few minutes, then consider what the rest of your care will be like.) Consider your healthcare provider as your employee. Make the initial 15-minute consultation your interview for the position of "personal healthcare provider." You are paying for this doctor's services, treat him or her the same way you would treat anyone in a fee-for-service arrangement. Expect the best service, treatment and respect from your caregiver and if you don't get it, then fire the individual! The doctor-patient relationship is an important bond that can foster hope, improved health and a positive healing environment. Choose wisely.

PART 4

THE ALTERNATIVE HEALING
THERAPIES

The following chapters will familiarize the reader with the many forms of alternative or natural health care available for RSI conditions. Mostly mainstream therapies that show good benefits for RSIs are included. There are literally hundreds of other alternative health disciplines, some better than others. If you are interested in learning more about alternative healing techniques, visit your local bookstore or library. There are many books written on this subject. I have included some good examples in the Resource Section.

CHAPTER 13

CHIROPRACTIC HEALTHCARE

Chiropractic healthcare is actually an ancient form of healing. Its origins in the Untied States are attributed to the works of D.D. Palmer in the late 1800s. The Palmer family developed the first chiropractic college, Palmer College of Chiropractic in Davenport, Iowa, which is still in existence today. Currently, there are 20 chiropractic colleges throughout the United States, Canada and Australia. Today, chiropractors are the second largest group of health providers in the U.S., and chiropractic is the largest growing healthcare profession in the world.

WHAT IS CHIROPRACTIC HEALTH CARE?

Doctors of chiropractic (D.C.) are licensed in every state of the U.S. and are considered primary healthcare providers. Diagnostic skills needed for recognizing all disease states within the body are learned during chiropractic schooling. The doctor of chiropractic can order any testing procedure needed to aid in the diagnosis, such as MRIs, CAT scans, blood tests, EKGs, ultrasounds, etc. Many chiropractors develop good working relationships with medical doctors and other healthcare providers.

The philosophy of chiropractic is based upon the fact that spinal subluxations (misalignments) cause joint and nerve irritation. These irritated nerves send improper or aberrant impulses to the organs they provide information to. The organ can be any bodily tissue, such as muscle, blood vessel, heart, lungs, arms and legs. Since every organ of the body has a nerve supply, any organ can be seriously affected by spinal misalignments.

Nerves are the body's electrical wiring system. They carry impulses from the brain to create changes in organs and carry impulses from organs back to the brain to relay sensory information. A nerve impulse going to a muscle, for example, causes the muscle to contract. A nerve impulse going to the small intestine may increase its motility, thus making digestion better. A nerve impulse to the adrenal glands might stimulate hormonal production, while an impulse to the bladder causes one to urinate. It goes the other way also—nerve cells on the skin send impulses to the brain to indicate sensation. Nerve receptors in the joints tell the brain when they are stressed or relaxed. Finally, nerve receptors in the internal organs relay information to the brain as well. The body's function is dependent upon proper nerve balance.

Chiropractic philosophy is based upon maintaining this proper nerve balance through spinal and extremity joint adjustments. Many disease states within the body can be created by a dysfunctioning nervous system. In muscles, nerve irritation leads to an increase of muscle tension, trigger points and spasm. In organs, weakened nerve impulses may instigate such conditions as constipation, incontinence and asthma. A weakened nervous system is a primary contributing factor to such conditions as carpal tunnel syndrome, cubital tunnel syndrome and thoracic outlet syndrome.

Spinal and extremity (i.e., elbow, wrist) adjustments are

the primary forms of a chiropractor's treatment. Many chiropractors also use physical therapy modalities, rehabilitation techniques and nutritional advice to further aid in recovery from all forms of ailments. Some states allow chiropractors to perform only spinal manipulation, while others offer more options for the doctor of chiropractic's treatment program. Check with your state's chiropractic licensing board for further information on chiropractic scope of practice.

What Is a Doctor of Chiropractic's Training?

Most chiropractic colleges now recommend a Bachelor of Science undergraduate degree before entering the rigorous four-year chiropractic program. The chiropractic curriculum includes studies in basic sciences, clinical sciences, spinal and extremity joint adjusting, nutrition, X-ray diagnosis, and rehabilitation. The basic science background of a chiropractor is quite similar to that of a medical doctor. In fact, chiropractors receive 2,887 hours of basic sciences, while medical doctors receive 2,756 hours. So the education is quite substantial. Chiropractic students complete a one-year internship that occurs during the last year of schooling. When doctors of chiropractic graduate from chiropractic college, they must pass state board examinations to receive licensure to practice.

WHY SHOULD I GO TO A CHIROPRACTOR FOR AN RSI?

Since chiropractors are primary health care providers and they specialize in the diagnosis, treatment and rehabilitation of musculoskeletal conditions, they are an excellent portal of entry into the healthcare system for a repetitive strain injury. Chiropractors look at symptoms as the result of nervous system and body imbalance, so when you seek care from a chiropractor for your RSI complaint, expect to be examined as a whole being—not just a person with an arm or wrist problem. A chiropractic examination for an RSI condition should include a complete analysis of posture, ergonomics, biomechanics, nutritional status and structure. This examination provides the patient with an excellent overview of why the condition is occurring and an evaluation of the overall health of the patient's nervous system. It should also offer guidelines to prevent further injury.

After the initial examination, the chiropractor begins the treatment program. It is common in the initial intensive care phase of treatment to see the chiropractor two to three times per week. This frequency may last one to two months, then typically is reduced to twice weekly, then tapers off to one time weekly when symptoms are resolved. During this time, the doctor of chiropractic may refer you to other alternative health providers, such as an acupuncturist, nutritionist or massage therapist. This is an important aspect of your healing program, since successful treatment for RSI conditions requires a team approach.

Compared to traditional allopathic medicine, chiropractic care is quite reasonable. Most doctors of chiropractic charge around $50 to $75 for the initial examination, then charge anywhere from $30 to $50 per treatment. The dollar amount varies from rural to urban areas. There may be additional costs such as X-rays, and other therapies. Considering that an examination and diagnostic study (without treatment) at a neurologist's office runs about $500 to $750, chiropractic health care is quite reasonable. For $500, you can receive a month of chiropractic treatments.

Most chiropractors accept insurance payments. A large majority of offices will contact your insurance company for you to determine your benefits, and will bill your insurance company for you. With the growing trend towards HMO coverage though, more and more chiropractic offices are requesting direct payments due to the restrictions imposed by and reduced payments from the HMO carriers. Before making an appointment, ask your potential chiropractor whether his or her office accepts your particular insurance plan.

HOW TO CHOOSE A CHIROPRACTOR

Choosing the right doctor is quite challenging. The following are some questions to ask a doctor of chiropractic to understand more fully their areas of expertise, and if they will be able to help you with your RSI complaints.

1. What is the doctor's experience with RSI complaints and what is his success rate? Nothing could be better than a doctor who has had many years experience working with RSI patients. Obviously, these chiropractors know what to look for. The doctor should offer at least an 80 percent success rate for RSI cases. If the doctor states he has 100 percent success with his patients, he may not be telling the whole truth.

2. How many years has the doctor been in practice? This allows the prospective patient to further understand the doctor's competency for treating patients. Make sure that the doctor gives you the number of years of active practice.

3. What is the doctor's chiropractic philosophy on healing? This question will allow you to understand the chiropractor's approach to your treatment program. Some chiropractors offer a "straight" approach and adjust the spine only for all health conditions, while others offer a "mixed" approach and adjust the spine, extremities, perform therapies, rehabilitation, etc. as part of their treatment program. If your chiropractor uses a straight approach, make sure he/she is able to refer you for physical therapy, rehabilitation and other ancillary services to aid in the healing of your condition.

4. What is the chiropractor's treatment method? Within the chiropractic community, there are close to 50 different forms of treatment methods. The most common methods are called "diversified" and "Gonstead." These are standard manipulative forms of treatments. Some chiropractors use nonforce methods such as Dynamic Nonforce Technique (DNFT) and Network Chiropractic. Applied Kinesiology is a form of chiropractic treatment that involves spinal and extremity joint adjustments along with muscle and nutritional testing. A doctor who is well-versed in Applied Kinesiology (AK) along with rehabilitation may be very helpful for your RSI condition.

It is important to understand that different methods exist since you may have one type of treatment with chiropractor A on the west side of town, then go to chiropractor B on the east side of town and receive a totally different form of treatment. For RSI conditions, I recommend a chiropractor who performs standard manipulative techniques on the entire spine and extremities and offers myofascial release techniques, therapy and rehabilitation services.

5. Does the doctor refer RSI patients to other alternative health care providers? As stated earlier, a team approach is the best method for battling an RSI problem. Check if your chiropractor offers other ancillary services in his clinic, such as acupuncture and massage therapy. If not, does he regularly refer his patients for these treatment modalities? Be wary of a chiropractor who thinks his treatments are the one and only cure for your RSI complaints.

6. Has the chiropractor undergone postgraduate training in specialty areas? Once a chiropractor receives his license to practice, he can continue his education by attending postgraduate courses in many different specialty areas. Some examples of these are neurology, orthopedics, sports injuries, nutrition, radiology and rehabilitation. Postgraduate courses in these specialties are rigorous 100- to 300-hour programs that further the doctor's diagnostic and treatment skills. Anyone with RSI problems should seek a doctor with higher levels of postgraduate education. I would recommend a doctor with a sports injury, rehabilitation, and/or orthopedics background.

7. Is the doctor familiar with the worker's compensation system? If your RSI problem is due to a work injury, it is critical that you have treatment performed by a chiropractor familiar with handling worker's compensation claims. Determine how many years the doctor has dealt with work injuries and if he is familiar with all laws pertaining to treatment and disability for worker's compensation.

8. How long is a typical office visit? Most chiropractors who treat RSI complaints spend at least 10 to 15 minutes or more one-on-one with the patient. The patient may receive an additional 15 to 20 minutes of therapies, sometimes performed by office staff. If you find yourself in and out of the chiropractic office in five minutes, you are most likely not receiving the full extent of care needed to overcome an RSI complaint. The only scenario where this might be effective is when the chiropractor has referred you to other alternative health providers for therapy in conjunction with the chiropractic care. The three- to five-minute office visit is fine for a patient on wellness or maintenance care, but not for a challenging case of repetitive strain injury.

These questions will aid you in choosing the right doctor of chiropractic to help you overcome your RSI condition. Finally, ask yourself if this doctor feels right for you. Do your personalities mesh well? Is the doctor spending enough time answering your questions? Do you feel rushed in the clinic? Does the office staff greet you kindly and with respect? These are items to consider when making that important choice of health care providers.

CHAPTER 14

ACUPUNCTURE AND TRADITIONAL CHINESE MEDICINE (TCM)
by Robert C. Wright Ph.D., L.Ac., DNBAO

The birth of Chinese medicine dates back approximately 4,000 years. Archaeological evidence suggests that as early as the neolithic period, stone needles were used for medical purposes. In the 1970s, many new discoveries of artifacts deepened our knowledge of medical practice in ancient imperial China.

THE SCIENTIFIC BASIS FOR THE TREATMENT OF RSIS WITH ACUPUNCTURE

For 50 years, acupuncture and Chinese medicine have been investigated from the standpoint of Western scientific method. Acupuncture normalizes the electrical energy of the body. The ancient theory says that the life-force energy called Qi (chee) flows through pathways that connect all the tissues and organs of the body. There are 12 main meridians that convey this force throughout the body and enable organs to function. Disease results when the flow of energy is disrupted or disturbed. The principle of therapy is to increase or diminish the flow of energy to a given organ or tissue in order to restore the normal functional balance to it so that healing is encouraged. Recent investigation has confirmed many of the ancient principles on which acupuncture is based.

Acupuncture, or the insertion of micro-thin sterile needles into the body at precise locations works through nerve reflex action which is transmitted through nerve pathways. It harnesses the electrical energy and programs it to regulate the energy flow to a tissue or organ. Worldwide efforts have identified as many as 27 known physiological mechanisms of acupuncture therapy. The known neurological effects of acupuncture can be explained through the neuro-gate theory in which the insertion of needles at particular points blocks nerve synapses. This very minor traumatic irritation of local tissue allows nerves that are excessively stimulated to cease firing and rest. It is one mechanism useful for the treatment of pain and muscle spasm. Acupuncture also causes the release of natural pain relievers (endorphins) and an anti-inflammatory hormone (cortisol) into the bloodstream. Acupuncture has profound effects upon the central nervous system, causing dilation of capillaries surrounding injured tissues. This aids in cell respiration, which is so important for healing.

Modern acupuncturists rely both on scientific and traditional theory to formulate treatment protocols. In China, a special branch of traditional Chinese medicine developed called orthotraumatology which focuses on the treatment of physical injury and includes acupuncture, herbal therapy, medical acupressure and special rehabilitation exercises. Acupuncture has a distinct advantage in very inflamed or chronic conditions because of its analgesic and circulation-enhancing effects. It is often more useful when medications are ineffective, contraindicated or when a more natural, completely safe and effective means is sought to help the condition. In RSIs, it is an effective adjunct to other therapies as well and can be easily combined with biomedical techniques, medication, chiropractic, osteopathy and as an extremely useful aid to postsurgical recovery, if that becomes necessary.

THE EXAMINATION AND TREATMENT

It is significant that TCM developed a different empirical system than that of the West. Consequently, because TCM has a different view of physiology, it may not approach a problem in the same way as a practitioner who uses only the Western tradition pathophysiological model of disease. Modern acupuncturists use both models to diagnose and treat illness. They complement rather than conflict with one another. In RSI in particular, they would perform the standard orthopedic tests and diagnostic procedures including any necessary radiological or laboratory work if indicated. However, because of the unique perspective of TCM analysis, additional information acquired from the pulse, tongue and analysis of the general condition of the body and affected tissue would also provide useful treatment guidelines.

The examination of pulse and tongue are prominent features of an acupuncturist's physical examination and reveal many useful additional clues about the general health of the patient. The pulse quality as well as its rate gives much useful information about the nature of disease and the relative balance of the body and organ function to the fully trained practitioner. Many of the seemingly exotic and unusual terms about excess and deficiency, the elements, dampness, wind and fire that you might hear about actually have precise physiological meaning and technical significance to fully trained practitioners. Coupled with modern medicine, TCM affords a more comprehensive look at the energetic and pathophysiological processes than either system could alone.

The TCM diagnosis can be useful for the treatment of carpal tunnel syndrome or some other conditions resulting from an RSI by giving us information from the body about the relative chronicity of a problem. This is determined by evaluating the body and its energetic response to the condition. For example, determining whether an individual is more hot (inflammatory) or cold (chronic) would influence choice of a treatment plan. Sometimes the pulse can provide more information than either merely inspecting the affected area for inflammation or inquiring about the length of the disease to determine the stage of an illness. Like laboratory findings, pulse diagnosis can offer another window into the workings of metabolic processes.

The insertion of very thin presterilized disposable needles is the accepted method for acupuncture therapy. The needles are composed of hair-thin surgical wire from 30 to 38 gauge with a filiform (pencil-like) tip that spreads rather than cuts tissue. A hypodermic needle, which can be 14 to 24 gauge (the higher the gauge the thinner the needle), is more than twice as thick and has a hollow portion and a cutting edge. This thickness is necessary to deliver medication either to veins or muscles. Acupuncture needle therapy in many cases is almost pain-free. Any small amount of discomfort experienced is usually right at the beginning of the insertion and lasts only a few seconds. Many times the patient doesn't feel the insertion at all. Most people adjust quickly to the experience and the session becomes a pleasant and relaxing experience as the body's immune-enhancing, pain-relieving and anti-inflammatory resources are mobilized and channeled to heal the condition.

Electrical stimulation of the needle (which is experienced as a faint tapping sensation) is often combined with the therapy to increase the effect. Often other traditional modalities are combined with needle therapy, like moxabustion, which is the use of a compressed and then lighted herb stick to gently warm acupuncture points and help injured tissue. Cupping and the use of herbal liniments and patches are sometimes used to stimulate circulation on the affected site. Licensed practitioners may use other modern methods and combine them with the needle treatment.

In seeking help from a specialist in Chinese medicine, make sure that he or she is fully qualified and licensed as an acupuncturist in your state. There is both national and state certification which requires a minimum of training and expertise in acupuncture training specifically. Contact the American Association of Acupuncture and Oriental Medicine in Washington D.C. to find a practitioner trained and board certified in your local area.

CHAPTER 15

MASSAGE THERAPY

Massage therapy is a form of healing that dates back to ancient times. In Eastern civilizations, massage is taught to children at a young age and is considered a standard form of therapy within the household. In Western cultures, it is regaining popularity as an alternative approach to healing and as a stress relief technique. As with many other natural health disciplines, massage therapy lost favor with the rise of the medical establishment in the mid-20th century. But this hands-on discipline is enjoying a great resurgence of popularity as modern cultures begin searching for more conservative, enjoyable methods of healing. It is now common for many medical doctors to refer their patients to massage therapists for relaxation and bodywork.

Massage therapy is a generalized term. A massage therapist can offer many different forms of hands-on healing or energy techniques, such as Reiki, that may not involve laying on of hands at all. The overall goal of massage is to promote relaxation of the muscles and the client, thus enhancing the client's health. Other benefits are an increase of blood flow, increase of lymph flow, and possibly an increase or decrease in blood pressure, depending upon the style of massage.

For the RSI sufferer, massage is one of the mandatory forms of healing needed for an effective treatment program. When performed by an experienced therapist, massage therapy can reduce or alleviate the muscle and tendon aches and pains that often accompany an RSI. Stroking techniques such as petrissage, a firm friction-like stroking, and kneading of the muscles, fascia and tendons can induce blood flow into tired, achy muscles that have been subjected to repetitive strain. Gentle stroking techniques, such as effleurage, stimulate circulation as the therapist strokes towards the heart and encourages total relaxation of the subject. Massage can even be stimulatory, through such techniques as tapotement, a rhythmic tapping with cupped hands upon the muscles, or vibration massage, which instills a shaking or pulsating movement to the muscles.

The type of massage you receive is based upon the massage therapist's knowledge and experience. Some states require massage therapists to be licensed before they can lay hands on people, whereas some states still have little control over the practice of massage. If you are experiencing an RSI, always ask about the schooling of your potential massage therapist. Some schools offer a 100-hour program, while others offer 750 to 1,000-hour programs. Always consider the therapist's schooling along with the therapist's reputation before making the decision to begin sessions. When contemplating a massage therapist for an RSI consider employing a therapist who has a professional relationship with other health providers and may even have an office located within a health clinic or center. This scenario will, in most cases, indicate that the therapist is well-qualified. Also, consider massage therapists who are members of national organizations, such as the American Massage Therapy Association (AMTA).

Some massage therapists specialize in certain forms of massage, while others offer many varieties and customize massage to the client's goals. A good example of this is the massage therapist who performs rolfing, which is a specific technique implemented over a 10-week period of time to lengthen and restore mobility to the body's major muscle groups. On the other hand, a therapist may offer Swedish massage, a more relaxing stroking-type therapy, combined with other methods, such as trigger point therapy and myofascial release therapy. Always seek information on the forms of massage therapy offered by the therapist and the length of a typical session.

Massage sessions are usually offered in time frames of half-hour, hour, 90 minute or two hours. The most common is the hour massage, which allows the therapist to work all of the major muscle groups of the body. Massages lasting longer than one hour are wonderful, but make sure you have someone to drive you home from the therapist's office. You will feel almost sedated.

One of the biggest concerns among potential massage therapy clients is whether or not they will need to remove their clothing to have a massage. This is especially true for those clients who may not feel comfortable with their bodies. Some forms of massage can be performed through clothing, but it is always best to have hand-to-skin contact to ensure the best results. A good therapist will keep all areas not being massaged covered with blankets, sheets or towels while the massage is in progress. The areas being massaged will be exposed, but all other body parts surrounding the exposed area should be covered to maintain the modesty (and warmth) of the client. If, for any reason, you do not feel comfortable with the therapist or the therapist's techniques during a massage, immediately explain your apprehensions and discontinue the session if necessary. It is better to be up-front with the therapist and enjoy a relaxing experience than to leave the therapist's office with distaste and ingratitude because of an uncomfortable session.

For the RSI patient, seek a massage therapist who offers gentle stroking massage for relaxation along with deep tissue massage for breaking up adhesions within the scarred myofascial tissue. A good massage therapy session should concentrate on the injured areas for at least half of the session, while at the same time allowing relaxation to release the tension and stress in other regions of the body induced by the RSI.

It is important to drink plenty of water after a massage session to flush away the toxins emitted from the tissues. Before you leave the therapist's office, be sure to drink at least six to eight ounces of water and continue that amount hourly for the next few hours. This will reduce any residual soreness you may feel from deep tissue work and myofascial work.

CHAPTER 16

PHYSICAL THERAPISTS AND
PHYSICAL THERAPIES

The use of physical therapy modalities is an important component in the healing of RSI conditions. Many healing disciplines such as chiropractic, acupuncture, physical therapy, osteopathic medicine and physiatry use various forms of physical therapy as a standard part of a treatment program.

THE PHYSICAL THERAPIST

A physical therapist (P.T.) is a person who has completed a college-level program to become state-licensed to practice physical therapy. When licensed, P.T.s can use physical therapy modalities within their treatment program for various injuries. Physical therapists may specialize in various forms of rehabilitation from treatment of stroke or burn victims to musculoskeletal injuries. Before you choose a physical therapist, make sure he or she is experienced in the rehabilitation of repetitive strain injuries. Physical therapists have marginal diagnostic training and are not primary healthcare providers;

therefore the diagnosis of your RSI condition should come from an experienced chiropractor, acupuncturist or medical doctor.

Physical therapists use a number of strategies in the treatment of RSI conditions such as ultrasound, contrast baths and electrical muscle stimulation. Their rehabilitation programs may include pool therapy, rubber tubing exercises, free weight exercises and exercise on the weight machines typical of health clubs. They may even offer ergonomic evaluations. Some therapists use advanced rehabilitative procedures, such as proprioception skills, wobble board exercises and exercise ball programs.

Because a team approach is essential in healing RSI injuries, do not rely on the physical therapist alone. It is best to undergo combined treatment programs with a complementary group of providers who work well together. This may be difficult if your M.D. is not open to alternative therapies, but be persistent in your quest for health. If you are seeking treatment from a physical therapist, locate one who is familiar with other disciplines and can work well with other alternative health providers. Be wary of any physical therapist who wants to manipulate your spine. Physical therapists receive no formal training in spinal manipulation, nor are they licensed to perform spinal manipulation. It takes years of education and learning to be proficient at this art form. Depend on a skilled chiropractor for spinal and extremity joint adjustments or manipulations.

THE PHYSICAL THERAPIES

Ultrasound

Ultrasound is one of the most common forms of physical therapy modalities used for the treatment of repetitive strain injuries. This is because of its ability to warm the tissues below the skin's surface. It also increases cellular respiration and blood flow and initiates chemical changes that promote healing of the tissues. Because of the mircromassaging effect of the high-frequency sound waves, ultrasound is helpful in softening and reducing scar tissue. It increases the permeability of cellular membranes, allowing disbursement of fluids. Ultrasound is actually the application of very high-frequency sound waves that penetrate the skin via a conducting gel. Natural conducting gels include proteolytic enzymes and herbal formulas to aid in the healing process. The use of healing gels along with ultrasound is called "phonophoresis." Some therapists use a hydrocortisone gel for its anti-inflammatory effects. However, the use of cortisone is not advisable because of its side effects.

When ultrasound is correctly used there should be no sensations of heat. The sound "head" (the small hand-held portion of the ultrasound machine), should be in constant motion to avoid overheating the tissues. If you do feel heat, then the machine is set too high, or the sound head has been in the same place too long and there's a good chance your tissues are going to get irritated. The heat sensation is actually detected by nerve receptors along the sensitive outer surface of the bone called the periosteum. When the ultrasound machine is set too high, there is a possibility of burning this portion of the bone.

Electrical Muscle Stimulation

There are many forms of electrical muscle stimulation. These therapies are used to reduce muscle spasm, provide pain relief, disperse inflammation and aid in nervous system relaxation; they are also used in electro-acupuncture. The most common forms of muscle stimulation used in doctors' and physical therapists' offices are microcurrent stimulation, galvanic stimulation, interferential stimulation and transcutaneous electrical nerve stimulation (TENS).

Although all muscle stimulation devices use electrical current to affect tissue change, their underlying bioelectric properties are quite different. For example, TENS is typically used as a pain-control measure in cases of acute and chronic pain. It provides only symptomatic relief, offering few long-term benefits. Microcurrent therapy, on the other hand, has been found to initiate healing within the cellular tissues; it is quite effective for treatment of soft tissue injuries, such as myofascitis, tendinitis, sprains, strains and synovitis. It is effective in wound healing and fracture healing also. Interferential and galvanic currents allow for nerve stimulation and muscle contraction. These therapies are effective in pumping out swelling from tissues, sedating nerve tissue and relaxing muscles so they are a good adjunct in a complete treatment program. As with ultrasound, sometimes chemicals are used in conjunction with the electrical muscle stimulation. The electrical properties of the electrodes propel the chemicals through the skin into the tissues. This process is called "iontophoresis." Commonly used substances are zinc, copper, chloride and procaine.

Cold Therapy

The use of ice or other cold-producing techniques has a number of purposes. It causes vasoconstriction (a narrowing of the arteries and veins near the skin), anesthesia (numbing), relieves muscle spasm and inhibits swelling. When ice is used, there is a characteristic response, as noted earlier. The person first feels the cold sensation, then burning, then aching, then pain, then finally anesthesia. All of these sensations occur over a 15- to 20-minute time frame. Typical methods of applying cold therapy are through ice packs, vapocoolant sprays such as flourimethane (only found in doctors' offices) and ice massage. Many patients find that a bag of frozen peas makes an excellent ice pack that can be reused time after time. Ice massage is performed by applying either ice cubes in a cloth or paper cups previously frozen with water directly over the muscle or tendon. If you decide to use this technique, consult with your health care provider first. If done improperly, it can irritate and even injure your skin. Remember, never attempt to perform repetitive tasks with ice on an injured area.

The RSI sufferer should make cold therapy a standard treatment program when flare-ups occur in the condition. It is inexpensive, works directly on the problem area (unlike medications), and can easily be kept handy near your desk or workplace. When using ice, apply for no more than 20-minute time periods. A 20-minute-on, 20-minute-off protocol is effective for pain relief and reduction of swelling.

Heat Therapy

Heat is used to soothe irritated muscles, relax irritated nerve endings and promote circulation to an injured area. The use of heat promotes sweating, which in itself is good for expelling toxins that build up below the skin's surface. Many people like the overall calming affect of heat.

However, heat can be harmful for certain conditions. Never apply heat on a fresh injury like a sprain or strain within the initial 24 to 48 hours. With cumulative injuries where frequent attacks of inflammation and muscle pain are occurring, heat is not recommended. The heat may feel good temporarily, but will result in increased pain due to nerve irritation and increased swelling. It's also best to avoid heat if you have vascular problems, are pregnant, have low blood pressure or have sensory deficiencies.

Heat is applied therapeutically in many ways, such as in moist heating pads or hydrocollator packs, dry heating pads, water bottles, hot wet towels, diathermy, paraffin baths and infrared heat. Patients with muscle aches and pains do well with moist heat. Moist heat can be achieved through hydrocollator packs, which are canvas bags filled with a silica and gel mixture that absorbs water. The absorbed heated water radiates heat outward through the skin into the muscle tissue. These packs can be found at most drugstores. Avoid dry electric heating pads since they will dry out the muscle, leading to irritation hours after the application. They also emit high amounts of harmful electromagnetic radiation.

Diathermy is a physical therapy found in some medical, chiropractic and physical therapy clinics. It has to be administered by a trained professional. A paraffin bath is a form of heat therapy applied via melted paraffin wax directly onto the hand or elbow. The affected area is dipped into the wax four or five times, building layer upon layer of warm wax over the skin. After the applications, the hand is wrapped in a cloth or bag, and the heat is allowed to penetrate through the skin for a period of 15 to 20 minutes. These treatments are very affective for arthritic conditions of the hands and for muscle cramping and aches. Paraffin wax treatments can be found in many physical therapy clinics, chiropractic offices and massage therapy offices.

Heat applications should last no more than 20 minutes. If the tissues are heated longer than this, there is a chance of increased fluid buildup and swelling. A 20-minute application followed by a 30-minute rest period is generally a good program.

Contrast Baths

Contrast baths use alternating heat and cold therapy. Two buckets are used: one filled with very cold water, the other with warm water. If the affected area is already inflamed, begin with cold water, alternating with warm, and finishing with cold. Finishing with the cold water bath will constrict the blood vessels to prevent swelling. If the purpose is muscle relaxation, begin and end with the warm water. Contrast baths cause a pumping of blood in and out of the tissues. This is an effective way to reduce swelling while at the same time bringing fresh blood flow to an area to promote healing.

OCCUPATIONAL THERAPY

Many people undergoing treatment programs for repetitive strain injuries are assigned to an occupational therapist. Occupational therapists are state-licensed providers who teach patients how to perform critical daily activities such as dressing, grooming and bathing. If these activities are not an issue or if they have been mastered, other daily activities that may be giving the RSI sufferer difficulties, such as maintaining employment while injured or caring for the family are addressed. The occupational therapist may also help evaluate the patient's work conditions, such as erognomics, work environment or time management. In many cases they are a valuable asset to the injured worker's arsenal of health care providers.

CHAPTER 17

NATUROPATHIC HEALTHCARE

Naturopathy is in essence a conglomeration of all current natural healing methods. Its origins stem from ancient Egyptian and Greek healers. The term "naturopathy" was coined in the 20th century by a German homeopath named John Scheel, who emphasized the importance of natural forms of treatment. The roots of organized naturopathy began with the works of Sebastian Kneipp, who in the late 1800s and early 1900s developed a hydrotherapy system for healing. One of Kneipp's students, Benedict Lust, emigrated to the United States and founded the American School of Naturopathy in New York. A large following quickly developed, and the naturopathic movement began in the United States. Although the powerful pharmaceutical and medical industries tried to eradicate naturopathy in the 1940s and '50s, (just as they also attempted to eradicate chiropractic in the 1960s and '70s), the ideology of the profession held on and is once again gaining great popularity.

The key principle in the philosophy of naturopathy is that the body has an inborn ability to heal itself and can be guided to heal more quickly through the use of natural measures, such as a balanced diet, exercise, herbs, structural alignment, water baths, etc. There are six main beliefs within the naturopathic profession:

1. **The healing power of nature.** The body has an inborn ability to heal itself. The naturopath should provide the needed ingredients to enhance the body's healing abilities.

2. **Treat the whole person.** Each person is made up of genetic, physical, mental, spiritual, emotional and environmental factors. The functioning of the human being is the result of a meshwork of these factors that may enhance or hinder health. The doctor's job is to identify any factor that may be unbalanced and use whatever therapy or treatment is needed to normalize these issues.

3. **Treat the cause rather than the effect.** Symptoms are warning signals to the body that one or more of its systems is unbalanced. The cause of the illness must be addressed, not the symptoms. The cause may be stress from work, a trauma, an irritated digestive system, a pinched nerve or a combination of factors. The doctor has to identify these causes and should treat them through natural methods.

4. **First, do no harm.** The doctor should aid in healing, not hinder it or cause further harm.

5. **Prevention is the cure.** The doctor has to offer the patient choices to yield a healthier lifestyle. The patient must accept the fact that he is responsible for his own health and understand that by changing bad habits to good ones, illness can be prevented from occurring in the first place.

6. **The physician is a teacher.** The doctor should educate

patients on wellness, healthy lifestyles and prevention techniques to keep the body working at its best.

Naturopathic schooling includes studies of basic sciences, such as anatomy, physiology and biochemistry. A wide range of therapeutic modalities are taught to the naturopathic student such as clinical nutrition, herbal medicine, homeopathy, acupuncture, physical medicine, hydrotherapy, iridology, emotional stress release, physical therapy, manipulation, guided imagery, counseling and even some minor surgical procedures. In states that recognize naturopathy, they are considered primary healthcare physicians.

There are currently 12 states that license naturopaths— Alaska, Arizona, Connecticut, Florida, Hawaii, Maine, Montana, New Hampshire, Oregon, Utah, Vermont and Washington. Idaho recognizes naturopathic practitioners without imposing a state standard. In all these states, the naturopath can refer the patient to other health providers and order testing procedures, such as X-rays, diagnostic studies and blood work. In the remainder of the states, there are certain restrictions that naturopathic practitioners must adhere to. An unlicensed practitioner may not diagnose, cure, prescribe or treat disease. Naturopaths in these states can assess, measure, determine or evaluate a condition in order to alleviate, improve, balance or normalize a problem or imbalance.

NATUROPATHY FOR RSIs

Many people choose to visit the naturopath for an RSI condition because of the naturopath's arsenal of natural healing techniques. Naturopaths may specialize in one or more of the many natural healing techniques mentioned above. It is unlikely a naturopath will offer all the techniques mentioned, since one person usually cannot be an expert in every aspect of natural medicine. In most cases a naturopath would refer a patient to an experienced chiropractor for manipulation or to an experienced acupuncturist for acupuncture.

One of naturopathy's many strong points is the implementation of herbal remedies, homeopathic remedies, flower essences and emotional stress relief techniques to initiate healing. Many RSI conditions stem from not only structural imbalance, but also emotional and stress imbalance. Implementing the correct herbal or homeopathic formulas can eradicate these imbalances and further the body's healing abilities.

SPECIALIZED KINESIOLOGY

Some naturopaths use a technique called "specialized kinesiology" which is a form of muscle testing originally developed by a chiropractor. This technique should not be confused with "applied kinesiology" (A.K.) used within the chiropractic profession, which differs in the type of muscle testing used and the assessment and treatment. Specialized kinesiology, when performed by an experienced practitioner, can quickly detect many emotional, structural, spiritual and nutritional imbalances. Imbalances can be detected even at the subclinical (before symptoms develop) level.

On the nutritional level, specialized kinesiology can end the possible confusion that occurs when entering a health food store. The naturopath can recommend specific herbs or supplements needed by the body for a specific condition or a deeper core issue. On the emotional level, there are methods such as "Golden Light Healing" or "Three-in-One Concepts" that work well at clearing out deeply held emotional blocks. In some cases, deep emotional issues can manifest themselves as musculoskeletal disorders. The mind and body can use RSI symptoms as an outlet for psychological and emotional stress. Using specialized kinesiology, emotional imbalances can be identified without the need to dig up trauma consciously as is typically done in standard psychotherapy. Once identified, these emotional charges can be cleared via energy balancing techniques, aromas, flower essences or other vibrational techniques such as color and sound. This type of work often makes a subtle, yet profound difference in the overall health of the client.

CHOOSING A NATUROPATH

Once you have made the decision to visit a naturopath for your RSI condition, it is advisable to set up a consultation before beginning any treatment. Some questions you may want to ask are:

1. What is the naturopath's education?
2. Is the naturopath familiar with repetitive strain injuries?
3. What forms of therapies does the doctor most commonly use (i.e. herbs, homeopathics, emotional stress relief, acupuncture, etc.)?
4. How many years has he or she been in practice?
5. How does the naturopath assess a client's/patient's health problems?
6. What is the doctor's philosophy of healing?
7. Does he or she often refer clients to other natural health disciplines for a team approach to RSI treatment, such as chiropractic or acupuncture? What disciplines does the naturopath commonly refer to?

Since naturopathy is an extremely personal technique and may involve the treatment of difficult structural and emotional issues, it is good to find a doctor that you feel very comfortable with and one you can connect with. Seek a naturopath who has a health care team approach to healing your RSI.

CHAPTER 18

HOMEOPATHY

Homeopathy was developed by a physician named Samuel Hahnemann in the late 1700s and early 1800s. He coined the term homeopathy from two Greek roots, "homoios" meaning similar, and "pathos" meaning suffering. Although he was the first to fully study this discipline, its use dates back centuries to the time of Hippocrates. Mr. Hahnemann began his research with Peruvian bark in 1789. This herb was used at the time for healing malaria. While other researchers believed Peruvian bark was helpful because of its bitter and astringent properties, Hahnemann thought differently. He experimented on himself with small doses, gradually increasing the dosage to find out that when taken in large doses the substance mimicked malaria-like symptoms.

This discovery led Hahnemann to propose the "law of similars." This law states that like cures like; a substance in minute quantities will heal the body, whereas the same substance in large quantities will cause symptoms. A good example would be an allergen such as ragweed. In homeopathy, a person who suffers from allergic reactions to ragweed would be given minute doses of the same substance (the remedy). Administering minute quantities of the offending substance stimulates the body's defenses and immune system to over-come harmful allergic reactions. At such a small quantity, the body can easily handle the reaction without symptoms and is stimulated to initiate a healing process. Once the body has learned to overcome the allergic reaction on this minute scale, it can then learn to overcome the reaction on a larger scale, such as when walking through a field of ragweed.

Homeopathic remedies are made from substances within nature, such as plants, herbs, animal products and minerals, and can be found in the form of pills, granules, liquids and ointments. Homeopathic remedies are entirely safe to the human being. The active substance is in such small quantities that no adverse side effects can occur. Homeopathic remedies undergo a process called "potentization" through a series of dilutions. For example, one part of a substance will be diluted in 99 parts water or ethyl alcohol and then stirred to suspend the substance within the solution. This combined product is then diluted once again by adding one part of the previous solution to 99 parts distilled water and stirring again. This process is repeated a number of times, depending upon the strength or dosage needed for the patient. The strengths are measured as 3, 6, 9, 12, 30, 200, 1,000, 10,000, 50,000 or 100,000, with each number representing the amount of times the sub-stance undergoes the dilution process. Most chemists argue that the higher dilutions could not possibly have any molecules of the substance left in the solution. But homeopaths argue that it may not be the substance itself that is causing the bodily reaction, but the essence or energy of the substance left in the dilution. And, in actuality, it has been found through clinical trials that the higher dilutions provide longer and deeper heal-ing. The essence of the remedy is responsible for the profound response on the emotional, mental and physical being. Deep-seated problems can be cured with the correct remedy. Remedies are said to increase the vital force of the patient. Science does not have all the answers to this phenomenon.

Homeopathic remedies fall into one or more of three categories: acute, chronic and constitutional. Each category of remedy is given specifically for the associated stage of illness. For example, an acute remedy would be given for a bad cold or sore throat, while a chronic remedy would be given for a long-standing condition such as asthma, colitis or ulcers. Constitutional remedies offer long-term rebuilding and strengthening properties once the acute or chronic condition is healed.

The classical homeopathic doctor takes an in-depth history of the complaint to understand fully the symptoms suffered by the patient. He will look at all aspects of the disease state including physical, emotional and mental disturbances. With the help of a homeopathic "materia medica" and perhaps a computer data base, the homeopath then chooses one specific remedy which matches this particular patient's symptoms.

A nonclassical homeopath will simply look at the symptoms and advise a remedy for them. This is a less stringent approach, and is often used by healthcare providers who simply want to incorporate the benefits of homeopathic remedies in their practice. The results may not be as good as a classical homeopath's results because of the lack of attention to deeper issues and the patient's physical and psychological makeup. In these cases, over-the-counter remedies available in health food stores are typically prescribed, such as remedies labeled "earache," "migraine," "muscle strain" or "arthritis pain."

Since there is no governing body for homeopathic doctors, it is important to seek information on a provider's years of experience and whether the provider uses classical or nonclassical forms of homeopathy. Check on the homeopath's educational background. Did he or she attend a recognized school of homeopathy, or are they self-taught? You may want to ask for references from other patients. Many primary healthcare physicians, such as chiropractors, medical doctors, osteopaths, acupuncturists and even veterinarians, may recommend homeopathic remedies along with their standard treatment protocols, although it usually is a nonclassical form of homeopathy.

HEALING WITH HOMEOPATHY

The amount of time for healing disease with homeopathic remedies depends upon the chronicity of the symptoms. More acute symptoms, such as a flu or virus, will abate quickly, while chronic conditions such as asthma and headaches may take longer to heal. In most cases, the symptoms which develop later on in the illness will disappear first, while the earlier symptoms will ease up further into the treatment program. It's similar to peeling away an onion skin, where the outer layers are the physical symptoms, and as you get closer and closer to the core, the deeper symptoms and deeper reasons for the symptoms such as emotional or psychological issues, are cured.

Homeopathy works best with chronic health problems and some acute health problems. Long-standing problems such as headaches, musculoskeletal disorders, digestive disorders, heart conditions, high blood pressure and hormonal disturbances do very well with homeopathy. More acute conditions, such as infections and broken bones may need Western medical approaches, but the body's vital force can be boosted by the use of homeopathic remedies during these acute conditions.

Can homeopathy help a RSI condition?

It may or may not. There's no documentation or studies that indicate homeopathy is effective for repetitive strain injuries, but over the years and centuries it has effectively helped many musculoskeletal conditions and healed underlying emotional issues. Since some patients with RSIs do have underlying emotional or stress issues, homeopathic remedies may prove useful. The use of a classical homeopath is recommended to obtain the best possible result from your treatment. Homeopathy is an excellent treatment regimen to add to your arsenal against repetitive strain injury. In conjunction with other health disciplines, it can be quite effective in providing relief from the injury as well as increasing your body's vital force.

CHAPTER 19

SOMATIC EDUCATION TECHNIQUES

This chapter explains four of the best types of somatic education readily available to the RSI sufferer. All somatic education sessions have one thing in common: they offer a method of releasing unwanted muscular tension and ways of making muscular movements more efficient and graceful. If these techniques interest you, you can learn more by reading the books listed in the Resources.

THE FELDENKRAIS METHOD

The Feldenkrais method was developed by Moshe Feldenkrais (1904–1984). He was born in Poland and relocated at a young age to Palestine, where he worked as a laborer and cartographer. He then moved on to Paris and worked in the Joliet-Curie lab as an engineer after receiving a D.Sc. in physics and engineering. During this time he was very active in sports, enjoying martial arts, gymnastics and soccer.

Due to an old knee injury, he developed great difficulty in walking and was advised by his doctors to undergo surgery. Moshe's interest in the biological and medical sciences intensified. He decided against the surgery and began experimenting with ways to use gentle easy movements of his legs to increase his agility and endurance. His wife was a pediatrician, which allowed Moshe to analyze the movement of infants in their early development. He began integrating these movements into his own rehabilitation program.

Through his new awareness of biomechanics and movement along with his expertise in judo, Moshe Feldenkrais learned how to walk again without the pain he had previously suffered. He developed his knowledge base into a technique called the Feldenkrais method. He began teaching classes he would later call "awareness through movement" to groups of people who suffered from many forms of musculoskeletal complaints. He also began doing individualized sessions with people called "functional integration." These two types of sessions are practiced today through certified Feldenkrais practitioners.

The Feldenkrais Method is based upon the fact that muscle movements are learned habits, involving both conscious and subconscious thoughts. When walking down the street, one does not consciously think about how to walk, where to place one's foot or how high to raise the hip while bringing one foot in front of the other. These are learned traits that develop from the first to second year of life onwards. The Feldenkrais method modifies the fundamental movements that guide your daily activities, enhancing self-awareness. The method encourages fluid easy movements instead of harsh, restrictive and painful ones.

Many people under stress, or who may have a musculoskeletal complaint such as an RSI, develop abnormal movement patterns and muscle tension patterns. The person with chronic lower back pain will begin to walk and breathe differently. The person with a repetitive strain injury may not be aware of the constant chest tension while working, or the elevated shoulders due to stress. The Feldenkrais method aids in the awareness of these detrimental changes and allows for more relaxed, less stressed and more efficient movements.

Awareness through Movement

The first of the two Feldenkrais methods sessions, awareness through movement, is a group session in which students usually begin by lying on their backs. They are led through a mental scan of the body, beginning the self-awareness training. The students are then given verbal sequences of carefully engineered movements that begin retraining the body's motion patterns. These slow, gentle movements can be performed by most people, even those with marked stiffness and pain. The instructor will ask the students to become aware of trunk or limb movements as the exercises are repeated. Eventually, students become aware of their own patterns of movements. Once this self-realization occurs, changes can be made to correct faulty movement patterns. Awareness through movement sessions are also available on tape for those who do not have instructors in their area. See Resources.

Functional Integration

This Feldenkrais method is a hands-on, one-on-one session in which the instructor gently guides the student's body in slow, gradual movements. The clothed student lies horizontally during these sessions. As the instructor obtains information from the student's body about subconscious muscle movement patterns, he or she guides and moves the student's extremities and detects reactions to the imposed movements. As the instructor begins to understand the complicated movement patterns of the student, he can offer less stressful alternatives. Functional integration is based upon neuromuscular organization and behavioral patterns that can go undetected in a typical structural approach to healing such as physical therapy. Its main goal is to increase the body's efficiency in movements. The instructor does not impose any healing effect upon the student. Through this technique students learn more about themselves and increase overall body awareness.

THE ALEXANDER TECHNIQUE

The Alexander technique was developed by Frederick Matthias Alexander (1869–1955) whose livelihood was acting and Shakespearean oratory. Alexander developed laryngitis after many years of performing. He began watching himself in the mirror while speaking and noticed that he was extending his head and compressing his neck and spine. He started making changes in his posture to reduce muscular tension and began experiencing relief of his throat condition. After this experience, he began a hands-on teaching method of muscular retraining and performed this work, the Alexander technique, on such famous clients as Aldous Huxley and George Bernard Shaw.

Teachers of the Alexander method will observe their students' muscle movement patterns, especially upon the motions of standing, sitting and walking. The Alexander teacher maintains hands-on contact with the student's clothed body to register normal and abnormal muscle contractions during these movements. The student is given verbal instructions on movements to avoid and is encouraged on movements to preserve. Directions are given to relax muscles, emphasizing the head, neck and torso muscle groups. Alexander's goal was to maximize the length of the spine through proper alignment of the head, neck and torso. He called this dynamic change "primary control." The student learns to control muscles or sets of muscles through conscious acts of will while learning to avoid harmful and energy-wasting habits of muscle movement. Students also learn an awareness of their bodies and their positions during typical daily activities such as walking, standing and sitting. As with Feldenkrais, the main purpose of the Alexander technique is to rid the body of faulty postures and unnaturally overworked, tensed muscles.

Alexander lessons can be private or in a group session. Many teachers prefer the one-on-one approach due to the nature of the technique. Lessons last between 30 and 45 minutes and are usually repeated weekly during a two- to three-month period. The Alexander technique has been shown to improve such conditions as high blood pressure, asthma, depression, breathing difficulties and insomnia. It aids in mental alertness, movements for dance and theater, voice control and overall poise.

HELLERWORK

Hellerwork was designed in 1979 by Joseph Heller, the first president of the Rolf Institute. This system of muscle education and structural reintegration is patterned after rolfing. Mr. Heller developed this system of bodywork to address the physical, structural, psychological, emotional and energetic qualities of the body. The method aids in the relief of chronic muscle strain, stiffness and poor flexibility.

The series of 11 structured sessions, each about 90 minutes long, emphasize movement awareness through touch, verbal clues and motion. A more fluid pattern of movement is formulated for daily activities such as walking, standing, sitting, bending, reaching and running. The goal is to reduce stress on the musculature and create a more efficient body.

Hellerwork is beneficial to anyone suffering from muscular and structural imbalances. There are over 300 Hellerwork practitioners throughout the United States. See Resources.

TRAGER

The Trager approach was developed by Milton Trager, M.D. in 1927 with the goal of releasing deep-seated physical and mental patterns within the musculature. His technique involves a series of touches and movements to release muscular tension. Dr. Trager believed that muscle tension, stiffness and pain were the results of unconscious mental processes due to such events as accidents, illnesses, psychological or emotional trauma and poor postural habits.

The Trager instructor engages the client in gentle rhythmical movements allowing for the development of new sensory patterns between the brain and muscles and offering deep relaxation as well. The practitioner will attempt to create a safe and loving atmosphere and will instill gentle rocking motions to stimulate the client's cerebral activity. The sessions increase physical mobility and mental clarity and often bring the student into a deeply relaxed, almost meditative state. Many students will notice a feeling of inner peace, contentment and happiness during and after a session.

Dr. Trager developed a series of free-flowing dance-like maneuvers which he titled "Mentastics" (meaning mental gymnastics). The student is instructed to perform these exercises outside of the classroom to reinforce the changes made during the sessions.

Tragerwork is used to help many muscular conditions such as backache, poor posture and more serious conditions such as polio, multiple sclerosis and muscular dystrophy. It has aided people suffering from migraines, high blood pressure, nerve-related conditions and asthma. Many athletes partake in the sessions to increase their agility and to learn more graceful, less strenuous movements.

CHAPTER 20

BIOFEEDBACK

Biofeedback is a method of training the body to alter vital functions through the mind/body connection. Heart rate, muscular tension, breathing rate, etc., can be measured through the use of a monitoring device fitted with noninvasive electrodes that are placed on the skin. This device helps the person undergoing biofeedback learn to make conscious changes in his/her body, thus aiding in reducing stress, headaches, and neck, shoulder and arm tension in RSI sufferers; as well as enhancing pain control and relieving TMJ dysfunctions and sleep disorders.

In a typical biofeedback session, the electrodes placed on the person compile data on muscle tension, brain waves, heart rate, skin conductivity and skin temperature. The data retrieved enters a computer for analysis of the subject's bodily functions. The person is then instructed to begin relaxing specific regions or structures of the body through various techniques. Usually, he or she will hear "beeps" or see flashes relating to whatever organ is being tested at that moment. For example, to reduce the heart rate and thus relieve tension, the subject will hear one beep per heartbeat. Through relaxation techniques, the subject is taught to lower the heartbeat and will hear a coinciding slowing of the beeping noise as an affirmation of the relaxation. Once the subject becomes familiar with the technique, the biofeedback practitioner will give relaxation lessons to be performed at home.

The biofeedback machine does not directly impact on the subjects body; it is not "treating" any condition. It is simply registering biological processes within the subject's body through sensitive sensors on the skin's surface. Therefore, this technique should only be used by RSI sufferers who are seriously motivated to make changes within their body. Learning to take control of one's body may take great effort and time, especially for those people who are not tuned in to the body's functioning or feel like their bodies are out of control. Biofeedback is a method that involves work and training, and the amount of effort one puts into it correlates to the amount of benefit received.

BIOFEEDBACK FOR RSIS

Biofeedback is quite effective for the RSI sufferer. Since many cases of RSI involve habitual tension of muscle groups, techniques are needed to make the patient more aware of abnormal muscle stress patterns. Biofeedback, through the use of EMG studies, can teach the patient to change muscle tension, reduce muscle activity, and even strengthen weak muscle groups. The ability to change muscle tension in the neck, arm and hands through this method is a great benefit for anyone with a repetitive strain injury.

Because of the ability to detect skin temperature measurements through biofeedback, it is quite effective in teaching the patient to increase blood flow to an extremity. This is important in the healing process of an RSI, and is crucial to the RSI

189

or Raynaud's disease sufferer who may experience coldness in the hands or who works long hours performing repetitive activities. The ability to increase blood flow through a conscious effort can prevent many disabling RSIs, and also can speed the healing process of many RSI conditions.

Biofeedback is not a medical treatment. It is a process of learning and retraining to overcome symptoms which feel uncontrollable. Biofeedback students begin to understand that they can control many of their bodily functions and take renewed responsibility for their health and RSI conditions.

Since the success of biofeedback lessons depends in part upon the experience of the practitioner, always inquire into the teaching techniques and years in practice of a biofeedback practitioner before beginning any sessions for your RSI condition. It is always a good idea to ask where the practitioner was certified and whether he or she has used biofeedback on clients with similar conditions to yours. Also find out the practitioner's success rate with RSI conditions.

CHAPTER 21

GUIDED IMAGERY

Guided imagery is one of the many mind/body techniques experiencing great popularity in the 1990s. The fact that the brain controls all bodily functions is not new to science. What is new is the growing popularity of imagery and visualization techniques for overcoming many states of illness. Imagery is the use of the mind to conjure up pleasant thoughts, sensations, feelings and emotions for the purpose of making changes in one's physical state.

The average person uses imagery on a daily basis without even realizing it. Sometimes the imagery is good and sometimes it is not so good. Think about the last time you worried about a problem. This is a form of imagery. What happened to your body? The usual consequences are increased heart rate and blood pressure, muscle tension and emotional changes such as anger or sadness. In this scenario, the mind imagined a distressing event which led to a physiological change for the worse.

On the other hand, imagery can initiate positive mental, emotional and physical changes. Imagine laying on a pristine white sandy beach on a beautifully warm afternoon with your loved one beside you massaging your back. You hear the waves gently crashing against the shore. You smell the salty air. Sounds good, doesn't it? Just reading this may have initiated a positive response in your body. Unless you hate sandy beaches.

GUIDED IMAGERY AND PHYSICAL PAIN

Guided Imagery is a beneficial tool for overcoming chronic pain conditions such as those that accompany repetitive strain injuries because it teaches the subject to imagine more constructive, positive associations to healing. For example, you may use imaging techniques to visualize a flow of bright green energy passing down through the nerves entering into your weak and achy forearm muscles and hands. The green energy is bringing with it nutrients and your vital life force to instill healing in the tissues. Along with this energy comes increased blood flow. You can imagine the white blood cells engulfing the dead and dying tissues and cleaning up the injured area. You may even think of the white cells as an army coming in to fight the enemy. The red blood cells are infiltrating all of the healthy tissues, diffusing life-giving oxygen wherever they go. You can visualize the tired cells in your forearm "breathing" in this oxygen and revitalizing themselves. These imaging techniques are much more beneficial than the self-doubt and helpless depression that often accompanies chronic RSI pain.

GUIDED IMAGERY AND EMOTIONAL CONFLICTS

Guided imagery is an excellent method of exploring deeply held emotional conflicts using positive associations and visualizations. Everyone experiencing pain has an emotional component associated with it. The emotional association depends upon past experiences with pain starting as an infant and continuing through adulthood. Sometimes pain can be a result of unresolved emotional conflict. Some people hold emotional issues deep within, not willing to express them in constructive ways. These deep-seated emotional conflicts can express themselves in conditions such as irritable bowel syndrome, Crohn's disease, repetitive strain injuries, migraines, etc. Using imaging techniques, such sufferers can begin accessing the deeper roots of the pain and begin to understand more about themselves and their feelings. See Chapter 17 for more information about resolving emotional conflicts.

IMAGERY FOR RSIS

Imagery techniques can be used as an adjunct to a person's RSI treatment protocol. They are quite useful, especially if difficult procedures are undertaken, such as surgeries or invasive tests. But even in noninvasive procedures such as chiropractic care, the use of imagery in conjunction with treatment is a powerful tool for healing.

The chiropractic patient can use imagery to imagine the act of receiving a chiropractic spinal adjustment as flipping the switch in a fuse box, restoring the vital energy to the affected structures. The massage therapy client can imagine the deep stroking massage techniques whisking away old dying cells, restoring life and energy to the remaining cells and flushing the area with oxygen-rich blood. The acupuncture patient can imagine the needles affecting the small nerve receptors and creating a flow of energy between the needles. This imagery empowers the patient to take an active part in the treatment program instead of simply laying on the table and letting the treatment happen. The human imagination is an incredible tool when used wisely.

Guided imagery is an effective tool for many health conditions besides RSIs and can be used by the healthy individual to maximize the body's performance. Some conditions which benefit from guided imagery are: high blood pressure, cancer, anxiety, depression, acute injuries such as broken bones, sprains and strains, allergies, menstrual irregularities, immune system-related disorders such as AIDS and digestive system problems. Nonmedical conditions, such as pregnancy and birth, benefit tremendously from imagery techniques. This list is not comprehensive, for all disorders can be lessened or alleviated through implementing the powerful approach of this mind/body technique.

INTERACTIVE IMAGERY

Health professionals trained and certified to perform interactive guided imagery can work with a client to understand many aspects of the client's health through imagery techniques. One institution that trains individuals in interactive guided imagery is The Academy for Guided Imagery, located in Mill Valley, CA. You should always ask about the practitioner's background and education in this field when considering sessions in guided imagery.

These sessions usually last about one hour with about 30 minutes of that hour concentrating on the imagery process. The imagery instructor will begin by taking a history of the client's complaints. He or she will then determine what imagery techniques or relaxation techniques the client may be comfortable with or has had previous experience with. With this information, the instructor begins a session with some easy relaxation exercises. Once the client has entered a more relaxed state of mind, the imagery process can begin.

For the RSI sufferer, the imagery process can take a number of different forms. Pain reduction techniques can be implemented to allow the mind to control and reduce the amount of perceived pain. One example is the anesthesia technique whereby the client is given instructions to imagine the affected body parts becoming anesthetized to reduce pain. The instructor can begin the session with a scale from 0 to 10 indicating pain level, and compare it to pain level at the end of the session. Combining relaxation techniques with the anesthesia technique has a profound affect on pain relief.

Another interactive imagery technique used is called the "symptom dialogue" technique, whereby the client is instructed to "talk" to the symptoms as if they could respond. This helps bring to the surface some deeper issues that might be hindering the recovery of the RSI condition. For example, the client may say, "My elbow feels as if there's a knife in it." The instructor can than begin asking questions about the knife and what the client thinks about the knife. This is an excellent method of utilizing the brain's healing capacity to overcome physical ailments.

Guided imagery is an excellent adjunct to a physical treatment and rehabilitation program. As with all therapeutic disciplines, it does not address all issues of healing by itself, but it can be a powerful method to aid in the recovery of an RSI condition when combined with other natural health disciplines.

CHAPTER 22

MEDITATION

The use of meditation to affect human physiology has been practiced for thousands of years. It is the simplest method of self-examination and self-control available to us and can easily be used by anyone at any time. Its roots stem from ancient civilizations that used meditation as part of religious and healing ceremonies. It has since evolved into an accepted form of personal healing offering a wide range of benefits for many types of conditions. This discipline is slowly gaining more acceptance in Western cultures and is undergoing scientific investigation due to its many physiological benefits.

Meditation comes in many forms. Two of the major types, mindfulness meditation and concentrative meditation, will be discussed here. Mindfulness meditation allows the subject to become aware of all the senses during the meditation time. The person begins tuning in to his or her body and surroundings. All sounds, feelings, images, thoughts, sensations and ideas are registered in the mind. The meditator does not judge these mental impressions, but simply lets them happen. The purpose of these exercises is to become more aware of moment-to-moment activities during one's daily life, instead of focusing on distant and usually negative future events or previous events. The technique develops an inner peace and hope that can get one through even the toughest of times.

In concentrative meditation the mediator focuses on a specific sound (mantra), an image or breathing. The subject finds a quiet location empty of all other noises and interferences and begins concentrating on his or her breathing. The concentration on breathing takes the person's focus away from all external stresses. The goal is to achieve a slow, deep and regular breathing pattern during the exercise.

The deeply relaxed state of meditation can lower blood pressure, decrease heart and breathing rate as well as decrease cortisol (the stress hormone) in the blood. For the RSI sufferer, the decreased cortisol level is of special significance because of its role in the inflammatory process. Meditation is helpful for people with stressful lives and for people dealing with chronic pain syndromes and chronic illnesses.

CHAPTER 23

T'AI CHI AND YOGA

T'ai chi is a martial art used in the West for its gentle exercise and movements. In the East, it was developed as a self-defense strategy. The art consists of a series of graceful movements called forms that may range from 18 different positions or stances to over 100 positions. Although this technique is not physically demanding, it does involve complex motions that take time to master.

The movements of t'ai chi are a balance of opposites. The Taoist principle of yin and yang is emphasized with each technique. For example to go up, you must first slide downward. To move to the right, you must first slightly lean to the left. All the movements involve circles, spirals and arches, and because of this, the person develops a great sense of balance and coordination. The body maintains constant motion in t'ai chi, with weight being transferred from one leg to another in an uninterrupted fashion. Rigidity and static postures lead to strain and imbalance; therefore they are avoided in this martial art. When done correctly, t'ai chi can be considered a form of meditation.

Many of the names of t'ai chi movements come from nature, such as "waving hands in clouds," "snake creeps in the grass" and "white crane spreading its wings." Along with movements, correct breathing patterns are important. A good student of this art will use deep, slow abdominal breathing while performing the movements, again showing the similarity of t'ai chi to meditation.

T'ai chi can be performed with a partner. This is a technique called "push hands." The partners diagonally face each other with the back of one wrist and forearm against the partner's. One partner begins to slowly move and the other partner reacts by gently yielding or shifting in response to the movement. Circular patterns develop which enhance equilibrium, increase alertness and ease psychological reactions to change.

T'AI CHI FOR RSI CONDITIONS

Due to the gentle flowing movement patterns of t'ai chi, in most cases it is not injurious to RSI sufferers except for those who may be experiencing acute distress or those who are experiencing nerve irritation due to nerve tractioning conditions. The use of t'ai chi with these conditions may worsen them due to the stretching of the nerves in some of the t'ai chi forms. In most cases, though, t'ai chi is a good method for developing muscle tone and flexibility.

The art is also an excellent method for turning inward to discover one's self. It develops balance and stability. RSI sufferers begin to realize that the hands and arms are extensions of their bodies, not external, distant painful structures. The gentle arm movements allow for increased lymphatic flow. T'ai chi teaches the body to relax while at the same time maintaining alertness. Sharpened mental clarity is often achieved as a result of the meditative state. T'ai chi can help relieve spinal conditions, stress-related conditions, hypertension and arthritis.

YOGA

Yoga has been enjoyed for centuries as an excellent form of relaxation and stress reduction. It has been shown to normalize blood glucose levels and increase HDL levels. It also relieves the symptoms of arthritis, chronic fatigue and heart conditions. Yoga benefits the entire muscular system due to its stretching and toning of the muscles and increases the mobility of the joints. Breathing patterns used in yoga help to increase oxygenation of the tissues, and provide renewed energy to the body as a whole. In some yoga techniques, meditation is an integral part of the exercise. As mentioned earlier, this in itself is beneficial for many bodily functions.

If you are considering yoga as part of your overall treatment regimen, make sure to seek a yoga instructor who is certified. Tell the instructor about your RSI complaints, so that you can avoid postures that stress the arms and hands. If certain postures cause hand, forearm or arm pain, discontinue them immediately and consult with the instructor.

Yoga can be practiced three or more times per week. The more you perform yoga exercises, the more benefits you will receive. Not only will more difficult postures become easier, but you will also begin to feel a better sense of self. Yoga can also cultivate a sense of self-love and self-acceptance, both of which are important for overcoming an RSI.

PART 5

REHABILITATION

These last few chapters deal with physical rehabilitative and preventive techniques for the person who wants to avoid repetitive strain injuries
as well as the person who may be suffering from
an RSI. The following chapters provide a wide
range of therapeutic stretches and exercises to
benefit all RSI conditions. It is always wise to consult with a health professional before trying any
of these exercises. These chapters are structured
in a sequence of easiest to hardest, beginning
with passive movements, then passive stretches
building to active stretches. The chapter on exercise begins with breathing exercises followed by
the simplest of exercises, the isometrics, then
moves on to resistive exercises with rubber tubing, then weight training and equipment training. Steps to increase aerobic capacity are offered
in Chapter 27. My goal is to help heal the RSI sufferer with a low-cost, easy-to-learn training program. This chapter may also benefit healthcare
providers looking for a good rehabilitative program for their patients.

Caution: Some RSI conditions will worsen with an exercise routine that is begun too soon. If you feel weaker, fatigued or notice increased neurological complaints during any of these exercises, discontinue them immediately. **Do not** exercise through pain. You will only worsen your condition. Always consult your physician first before performing any of these exercise routines.

CHAPTER 24

STRETCHING TECHNIQUES

The purpose of stretching is to:

- Relax tightened restrictive muscles and improve flexibility of relaxed muscles.
- Improve range of motion.
- Relax the mind as well as the body (when performed correctly).
- Help prevent and rehabilitate muscular injuries such as strains.
- Improve circulation.
- Allow the tissue remolding process to occur after an injury in the correct stress patterns, leading to stronger tissues. Without stretching, the body may develop weak, haphazard patterns of healing as seen in scar tissue formation.

HOW TO STRETCH

Stretching must be performed in a precise manner to prove effective. It can be done almost anywhere—in a chair, standing at a table, watching television, etc. The following are some tips to enable you to perform stretches safely and effectively.

1. Don't ever bounce the body while stretching. Years ago, in grammar and high school gym classes, instructors used to teach their students to perform standing leg stretches by reaching for the floor, then come up a second and then reaching down again. Current thinking is against this method of stretching. It is now felt that prolonged, gentle stretches are much more effective than the bouncing type. So when you stretch, slowly reach until you feel a gentle stretching and hold that position for about 10 to 15 seconds.

2. You should not feel pain upon stretching nor should you feel like the muscle is so stretched it might tear. Stretch the muscle just to the point where you feel there's a gentle tugging. If you stretch too far, the brain will reflexively attempt to contract the muscle back to its original position to prevent the muscle from tearing or straining. This is counterproductive to the stretch and can actually cause further tension following the stretch. When patients complain that after stretching for half an hour they feel just as "tight" as before this is usually the reason.

3. Stretch in a warm environment, with warmed muscles. Cold muscles are less pliable and more apt to be injured. You may even want to use a 15-minute warm water bath to aid in preparing the muscles for stretching. The environment you stretch in also has an effect on the success of the exercises. A cold room is not an optimum environment in which to stretch. Choose a warm location, if possible, to aid the muscles in achieving the best stretch.

4. In passive stretching, hold the stretch about 10 to 15 seconds on each side, repeating the sequence three times. Active stretching will be explained in more detail later on.

5. Stretching can be performed on a daily basis, even for those patients who are in inflamed stages of an RSI, as long as it is done properly. For people with more chronic cases, stretching can be performed two or more times per day. The goal is to instill more elasticity and pliability to the muscles. Therefore, the more stretching you do, the better the muscles should respond.

6. Use your body's natural abdominal breathing to aid in the stretch. Before you stretch, take a deep cleansing breath inward. As you stretch, slowly exhale and gently allow the muscles to elongate. Use the full exhalation as your way of determining the time allowance for each stretch. For example, implement a slow exhalation of about 10 seconds long as you stretch. Then relax a bit as you inhale, and again reach into the stretch as you exhale.

Warning Signals to Stop Stretching

1. Increase of pain
2. Muscle weakness
3. Increase of numbness or tingling
4. Sensation of increased coldness of extremity

If you feel any of these warning signs, then discontinue the stretching. Either your body is not ready for the stretching or you are not performing the stretch correctly. Contact your health provider for assistance.

PASSIVE AND ACTIVE STRETCHING

There are many theories about stretching, but there are no real standards as to which form of stretching is the most effective for repetitive strain conditions. Both passive and active stretching techniques have pros and cons.

In passive stretching the muscles are stretched without muscle contraction of the target muscle or its antagonistic muscles during the stretching activity. This is the kind of stretching most people are familiar with. Active stretching involves contraction of the antagonistic muscle to reflexively induce a stretch response in the target muscle. Antagonistic muscles are those that directly oppose the action of the target muscle; for example, stretching the back of the thigh would involve contraction of the front of the thigh.

I recommend passive stretching exercises for the RSI sufferer who is in an acute or subacute condition; in other words the condition is in a moderate or severely inflamed state, or it may be undergoing a flare-up with active symptoms. Active stretching exercises are recommended for those patients who are in the chronic stage of RSI conditions or are in rehabilitation where remission of symptoms is nearing. Since active stretches involve muscle contraction, they can be detrimental to the acute case because rest is most important. In the stretching exercises that follow, use this advice to determine which regimen to use. Passive stretching exercises are for inflamed muscles, flare-ups of conditions and pain as well as for chronic conditions. Active exercises are for chronic stages of conditions with little inflammation and pain in the tissues.

THE PASSIVE STRETCHING EXERCISE REGIMEN

Neck stretches

With all of the neck stretches, beware of any feeling of lightheadedness, nausea or dizziness. If you feel any of these abnormal sensations, discontinue the stretch immediately and consult with your health provider. In neck flexion (#1), gently roll the chin towards the chest, while gently tugging the top of the head forward with your hand. You should feel a stretch in the back of the neck. In neck extension (#2), arch your neck backward while gently pushing the forehead with your fingertips. In neck side-bending (#3) stretch the muscles on one side of the neck by gently tugging the neck toward the opposite side with your hand. You can assist this procedure by holding on to a stationary object with the resting hand. While attempting rotation (#4) be careful not to place too much pressure on the jaw. Use a broad contact over the entire lower face area to prevent stress on the temperomandibular joint (TMJ). Finally, on combined rotation and lateral flexion, perform this exercise similarly to lateral flexion but rotate the head in small increments to stretch different muscle bands along the front, side and back of the neck.

To achieve optimum stretching in the neck, incorporate the different range of motions as in the following pictures. It is best to avoid circular neck motions because they do not produce an effective stretch; in fact they may be injurious to a preexisting neck injury or condition. The stretches shown above are good for TOS cases where scalene muscle spasm is the cause. Be sure not to contract the muscles when stretching.

#1: Neck flexion

#2: Neck extension

#3: Neck side-bending

#4: Neck rotation

#5: Combined neck rotation and lateral flexion

Jaw Stretches

These stretches will aid in relaxing the small jaw muscles. Yes, the jaw can be involved in many RSI injuries, especially for musicians who place instruments against the mouth, such as woodwind and brass players and violinists and violists who jut the instrument up against the chin or jaw. These exercises are good for people who need to talk frequently throughout the day, such as telephone operators or salesmen. If you have (or think you have) a TMJ dysfunction, ask your doctor whether these stretches are suitable for your condition. The closed and side-to-side stretches do involve muscle contractions, but I've included them here as an addition to the passive stretching routine, since the jaw muscles are very difficult to isolate through passive stretches.

#6: Open jaw stretch

Stretch the mouth open and gently tug the chin downward to stretch the muscles that open the jaw.

#7: Closed jaw stretch/ contraction

Although this stretch does involve some active muscle contraction, it is added here to present an overall stretching routine for the head, neck and upper extremity. While attempting to close the jaw, use a gentle downward force on the chin with your hand to prevent closure. Use only about 30 to 40 percent of your total force. The purpose of this stretch is to contract the muscles that close the jaw, thus fatiguing them temporarily. Follow this with jaw exercise #6 to aid in the stretch.

#8: Side-to-side jaw stretch-contraction

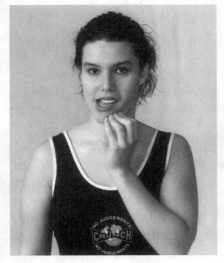

#9: Side-to-side jaw stretch

Place one hand on the side of your jaw, and attempt to push your jaw sideways into the hand. Again, use only a small amount of your total power. After the contraction, gently push the jaw to the opposite side to initiate the stretch. Perform on both sides.

Upper Back Stretches

The upper back is an important region to stretch, especially in computer operators, people working over work benches or tables, assembly-line workers, students and in any other occupation that involves repetitively leaning forward. Occupations that require leaning back, such as painters and auto mechanics can also benefit from these stretches.

#10: Forward
  body curl
  stretch

Curl your body forward while seated or on the floor and gently tug on your neck to assist the upper back stretch. Attempt to bring the head between or below the knees.

#11: Shoulder
  blade stretch

Grab on to a door frame or any stationary object at arm's height. Lean back and rotate your opposite shoulder towards the door frame so you feel a stretch across the shoulder blade region over to the spine.

213

#12: Shoulder blade squeeze

Contract the muscles in the upper back so the shoulder blades will squeeze together. This is great for the person who sits at a desk job and notices tightness in the upper back. If you feel a persistent ache in the upper back which does not subside with the contraction, consider chiropractic spinal care to relieve the possible spinal misalignments.

Shoulder Stretches

#13: Pectoralis stretch, arm horizontal

#14: Pectoralis stretch, arm vertical

#15: Pectoralis stretch, arm downward

Situate yourself next to a door frame and grasp the frame while leaning forward with your body. You should feel a stretching in the anterior chest muscles. Alternate pointing the thumb up and rotating the hand so the thumb points downward to affect different muscle groups. This exercise is very important for anyone performing work directly in front of them. The anterior chest muscles can tighten and lead to many maladies such as TOS, tendinitis, upper back pain and hand complaints.

#16: Arm reaching overhead to opposite shoulder blade

Reach the hand so it touches the opposite shoulder area. This stretches the muscles in the underarm area, as well as the triceps. You can gently tug on the elbow with the opposite hand to stretch the triceps more and pull the elbow away from the shoulder until you feel a stretch in the back of your arm.

#17: Arm reaching under to opposite shoulder blade.

Attempt to touch the spine with your thumb, and slowly climb up the spine to increase your shoulder range of motions of internal rotation and extension.

#18: Arms overhead stretch

Again, find a door frame (check for stability) and allow your body to hang forward so some of your weight is distributed to the arms. You should feel the stretch in the back of the arms and underarms.

Forearm Stretches

#19: Arm straight with wrist
      flexion

#20: Arm flexed, wrist
      flexion

With the wrist bent forward, straighten the arm. Pull the wrist downward so you feel a stretch in the muscles on top of the arm. Do not press downward on the wrist too firmly, especially if you are suffering from CTS. If your CTS is active, you may want to experiment gently with this exercise to determine if it irritates your condition. This exercise can also be performed with the arm in a 90 degree bent position, as in stretch #20. Sufferers of Cubital Tunnel Syndrome should perform the straight arm stretch instead of the bent arm stretch since the straight arm does not tug on the ulnar nerve.

#21: Arm straight, hand
        extended

#22: Arm bent, hand
        extended

This stretch affects the wrist
flexors. The same cautions
apply as above.

#23: Forearm pronation

While laying on the floor with the arm stretched out to the side, gently roll the arm counterclockwise so the thumb goes underneath and toward the head. Keep the fingers pointed straight and away from your body. Be very careful with this stretch. You do not want to force the elbow beyond its normal range of motion and you do not want to stress the wrist joints.

#24: Forearm supination

Continue laying on the floor and now rotate the hand clockwise so the pinkie finger rotates towards the ceiling. Again, show care in performing this stretch. This stretch is very important for people who keep their hands constantly pointing downward and pronated, such as computer and mouse users. The pronator muscles will shorten over time, causing the arm to have difficulty performing supination and leading to decreased external rotation of the forearm.

Wrist Stretches

#25: Radial deviation

The muscles on the inside of the arm tend to be overused in computer users, knitters and meat cutters. This stretch helps to elongate those tired muscles. With the arm outstretched and the palm facing downward, pull the hand toward your body as shown above. It is difficult to stretch these muscles, so try various positions to obtain the optimum stretch.

#26: Ulnar deviation

This stretch helps to elongate the thumb muscles and tendons. Place the thumb under the fingers and stretch the thumb away from the outstretched arm. If you feel moderate to severe pain when performing this stretch, then seek care from a health practitioner. You may be suffering from tendinitis or tenosynovitis. You should feel a slight stretching along the outside of the forearm.

Hand Stretches

#27: Finger extension

Stretch the fingers out-ward as far as you can and with the other hand gently push the fingers into extension. This stretches the finger flexor muscles and tendons.

#28: Finger lateral deviation

The small intrinsic muscles of the hand are responsible for many RSI complaints. This stretch helps to reduce the ten-sion in this region. You need to stretch the fingers two at a time. Start with the thumb and index finger. With the opposite hand stretch apart the two fingers.

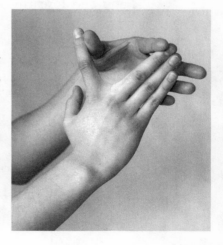

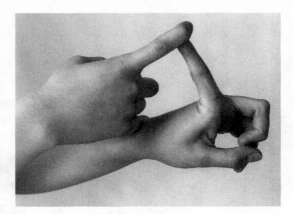

#29: Single finger extension and flexion

Take each finger and extend it backward until you feel a slight stretch in the palm and forearm. Take the same finger and bend it forward while gently tugging on it to obtain a stretch in the back of the hand and forearm.

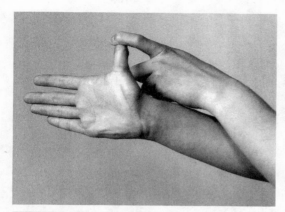

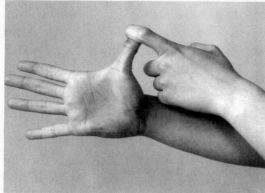

#30, 31, 32: Thumb extension, abduction and flexion

Gently stretch the thumb in its different ranges of motion as show above.

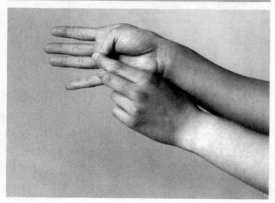

227

ACTIVE STRETCHING TECHNIQUES

Active stretches should be reserved only for mildly inflamed or chronic conditions that are nearing the rehabilitation and strengthening stage. These exercises involve short bursts of muscle contractions; therefore, they should not be performed in acute, moderately and/or severely inflamed conditions.

Active stretches are effective because they implement both a muscle contraction of the "antagonist" muscle, which reflexively causes a temporary relaxation response in the target muscle group and a stretch of the "agonist" muscle. For example, an active stretch of the triceps muscle (the muscle on the back of your arm) would include contraction of the biceps (front of the arm) while stretching the triceps at the same time. So this technique takes stretching one step further. It is a combination of standard stretching mentioned in the last chapter along with muscle contraction of the opposing muscle groups.

Active stretches are performed in short 2-second contractions of the antagonistic muscle groups. To use the example above, we would contract the biceps for 2 seconds, while at the same time stretching the triceps. The muscles are allowed to rest for 2 more seconds, then the contraction and stretch begins again. This contract-rest-contract cycle continues for 8 to 10 repetitions per muscle group. It may seem like a lot of work, but the entire process takes less than one minute per muscle group (10 repetitions of 2-second contractions and 2-second relaxation periods = 40 seconds). The theory behind the 2-second contraction is that the brain will not inhibit the stretching of the muscle in this short period of time, whereas in longer stretches, the brain may respond by tightening the muscle group in response to the strain. So the end product is a more efficiently stretched muscle and, at the same time, there is the added benefit of toning the opposing muscle group. As

228

with passive stretching, do not begin bouncing back and forth between contraction and stretching or use momentum to perform the movement for you. Each stretch should be a well-defined, calculated event.

Active stretches can increase their effectiveness with the assistance of a friend or personal trainer. The trainer can enhance the stretching by adding a small amount of force to help stretch the muscle while you contract the antagonist muscle group. See the examples below.

I do not recommend active stretching of the TMJ or jaw joint muscles because of the delicate nature of the jaw joint. Those unfamiliar with the technique may damage it or injure the biomechanics of the jaw.

Some Active Stretches

#33: Active stretch of the neck extensors

As you can see, this picture resembles passive stretch #1 in the previous section. But notice that the subject is contracting the neck muscles in front of her neck while at the same time stretching the muscles (the neck extensors) in the back of her neck. Again, this muscle stretch and contraction is for only 2 seconds, followed by a 2-second rest. Use the same technique for the neck flexors, rotators and neck side-bending muscles.

#34: Active stretch of the biceps

The subject is extending the arm back, contracting the triceps, while at the same time stretching the biceps.

#35: Active stretch of the
triceps

The subject is raising the hand
overhead, stretching the triceps and contracting the biceps simultaneously.

#36: Active stretch
of the wrist
flexors

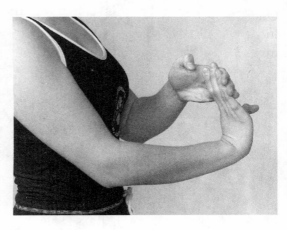

The subject is stretch-
ing the hand into
extension thus stretch-
ing the wrist flexor
muscles, while con-
tracting the wrist
extensors.

232

#37: Active stretch of the wrist
     extensors

The subject is flexing the hand and
contracting the wrist flexor muscles,
while simultaneously stretching the
wrist extensors. These stretches can
be used for individual fingers as well.

Once you get the overall idea of how they work, you can
incorporate active stretching into all of your passive stretching routines.

CHAPTER 25

MUSCLE REHABILITATION

Muscle strengthening techniques are typically performed as the patient's symptoms are subsiding and are almost gone and no flare-ups or neurological symptoms are noted by the patient over a one-month period. Also, the patient should be nearing normal range of motion in the affected body part before starting muscle rehabilitation. Patients with limited range of motion in a joint or joints need to be placed on specialized rehabilitation programs, which are beyond the scope of this book.

Experience has shown that exercise programs begun too soon are not effective for RSIs and in some cases cause flare-ups of the RSI symptoms. Always check with a healthcare provider before starting any of these exercises.

Patients undergoing rehabilitation will start off with simple muscle toning techniques called isometric exercises, along with an analysis of their breathing methods. If there is no increase of neurological or musculoskeletal symptoms during the isometrics, then the patient begins with easy resistive exercises utilizing rubber tubing. Rubber tubing comes in different grades of thickness, offering increasing levels of resistance. Once patients master the rubber tubing, again showing no signs of increased symptoms, they graduate to free weight exercise programs, using dumbbells. Free weights involve a more cognitive approach to training since the brain has to contract muscles as well as balance them in movement to achieve the desired goals. I prefer free weight exercises versus the weight machines seen in gyms because of the increased potential they afford for muscle development and strengthening. Once patients reach the free weight rehabilitation stage, they are usually pain-free, or very close to becoming pain-free. I add to the free weight training the use of fast-repetition, short-arc tubing exercises to enhance neurological activity in the muscles. When needed, the patient undergoes proprioceptive training of the postural muscles, along with leg, knee and foot stabilization.

Each of the techniques mentioned above (breathing exercises, isometrics, resistive, free weights and fast-repetition short-arc tubing exercises and proprioceptive training) will be explained in more detail later in this chapter. First, we will look at some basic concepts of muscle building and exercise.

BASIC CONCEPTS IN REHABILITATION

To understand how to strengthen and rehabilitate muscles there are a few concepts that need to be learned. It is important to understand the theory behind resistive and weight training to perform the exercises efficiently and effectively and without injuring yourself.

1. Threshold. A muscle's threshold is the amount of force that muscle can create at 70 percent of its maximum capacity. For example, a patient performs a biceps curl using free weights. Weights are added to determine the maximum strength for that particular muscle group. For this person it is 25 pounds. Once the weight goes over 25 pounds, the person cannot complete the biceps curl. The threshold of this muscle, then, would be about 20 pounds. The muscle's threshold determines the weight needed to build muscle strength.

2. Overload. The person must go above the threshold (overload) to begin causing hypertrophy (enlargement) of the muscle cells. In the scenario above, if the person performs biceps curls with 15-pound dumbbells, no increase of muscle strength is achieved, while if that person begins an exercise program lifting 20 pounds, and increases to 25, then the muscle will respond by strengthening and enlarging.

3. Reversibility. As the saying goes, "If you don't use it, you lose it." Muscles have the characteristic of reversibility. They can increase in size in response to increased forces, but they can decrease in size when not used. This is one of the dilemmas with any treatment program and one of the main reasons why splints are so controversial. With an active RSI, rest is imperative, but only to a degree. Continued rest with no activity leads to muscle atrophy (shrinking). For this reason, I do not recommend long-term bracing or splinting for RSIs due to the atrophic effect upon the muscles in and around the splinted area. The last thing an RSI sufferer needs is shrinking muscles! Relative rest, along with simple exercises is a way to maintain muscle mass while at the same time offering rest to the injured body part.

Exercising the opposite uninjured limb has been shown to have a strengthening effect on the muscles of the injured side. This is called "crossover" training and is commonly used with people who are casted for fractures or have immobilized joints for any reason. They are given exercises for the opposite healthy side, which helps to maintain muscle mass on the casted or splinted side.

4. "Repetitions" vs. "Sets." A person on a weight-training or resistive-training exercise program will be given a number of repetitions and sets to perform for each exercise prescribed. Repetitions refer to the number of movements for a single period of time for a particular exercise. For example, someone performs eight repetitions of biceps curls with a 20-pound dumbbell. The number of sets refers to the amount of times those repetitions (eight in this case) are repeated for each muscle group. In this case, the person performs three sets of eight repetitions each. Therefore, he has performed 24 total repetitions of biceps curls. (3×8). Usually a one-minute rest period is common between each set of exercises.

The number of repetitions you can perform with a given weight is a good way to determine your muscle's threshold. Typically, you can perform 8 to 10 repetitions with a weight that reaches or just surpasses your muscle's threshold. At 10 repetitions, you should feel very tired and the muscle will give that "burn" feel. If you find you can perform 15 repetitions with no problem, then you are not reaching your threshold. The weight would be too light if you want an increase of muscle strength. On the other hand, if you can only do five reps, then you have completely surpassed the threshold and are probably using too much weight for this particular rehabilitation goal. (Some power lifters and body builders do perform these types of exercises, but their goals are different than those of a person rehabilitating from an injury.)

5. Overall goal of the rehabilitation program. Before beginning rehabilitation exercises, the doctor and/or personal trainer and the patient need to decide upon the overall goal of the program. The goals of a rehab program for an Olympic athlete with a knee strain will be completely different from the rehabilitation goals of an architect with carpal tunnel syndrome. The goals of the architect will be different from the rehabilitation goals of an injured dockworker who frequently lifts objects heavier than 100 pounds. Sporting activities enjoyed by the patient need to be considered in the program as well. For example, the architect with carpal tunnel syndrome might play competitive volleyball on the weekends. A good rehabilitation program for this individual would therefore consider job duties, the patient's personal goals, sports-related goals, whether the patient typically performs repetitive tasks or heavy-lifting tasks (or both) and the patient's aerobic capacity. Aerobic exercise is discussed in the next chapter.

Phase 1: Breathing Exercises

Breathing exercises are probably one of the most overlooked but most important aspects in reconditioning and body retraining for an RSI. As mentioned in Chapter 3, there are two forms of breathing, abdominal breathing and chest breathing. Some people use a combined form of the two. Clinical evidence shows me that many people with stressful, deadline-type jobs typically use chest breathing. This stresses muscles in the neck, upper back and chest, and clamps down on the neurovascular bundle traveling from the neck to the hands. Therefore, the first exercises given to RSI patients are breathing exercises to change the harmful patterns developed over the years. The breathing exercises mentioned here are adapted from the excellent book *The Tao of Natural Breathing* by Dennis Lewis.

Breathing Exercise #1:

Lay relaxed on a bed or the floor and place one hand on your chest and the other on your abdomen. With each inhalation, feel where the movement is occurring. Normally, your abdomen should be rising with inhalation and falling with expiration. Very little movement should occur in your head, neck or upper chest area. The diaphragmatic movement actually massages the digestive system, lungs and heart, pumping blood in and out of these organs. If you feel you are moving your upper chest too much or you are contracting your neck muscles, concentrate on letting go in these areas to allow all the movement to occur in your abdomen. Make believe you have a balloon in your abdomen that expands as you breath in and deflates as you breath out.

Breathing Exercise #2:

This is a self-awareness exercise that allows you to understand the impact of proper breathing on the functioning of the digestive system. While laying down or seated, place both of your hands toward each other on the lower rib cage, so the fingertips meet. Notice what happens as you breath. Are the ribs expanding? Do you feel the powerful diaphragm muscle moving under your hands? Hold each of the following positions for five minutes and concentrate on your body's movements. Are you using abdominal breathing or chest breathing? Next, place your hands over your belly button, which overlies the small intestines. Feel the movement of the small intestines as you inhale and exhale. Once this is done, put your hands just below the right hand border of the rib cage. The liver is situated here. Feel the movement occurring while you breath. Your diaphragm is massaging the liver. Move your hands over to the left side now, so they are situated over the stomach and pancreas. Perceive any movements, sensations, and sounds under your hands as you investigate your body's response to breathing. Finally, put both hands just above your large pelvic

239

bone, one on each side, so they lay over the large intestines. What happens as you take relaxed breaths in and out?

This exercise can be a self-awareness training as well as a visualization exercise. Many people under stress have restricted diaphragmatic movement, causing decreased oxygenation of the blood, a decreased amount of oxygen to the tissues, and an increased adrenaline response because of all of these detrimental effects. The adrenaline response leads to increased muscle tension, chest tightness, fear, anxiety and a perpetuation of chronic RSI symptoms. This breathing exercise can stop that vicious cycle by allowing better control over the body and an increase of parasympathetic action, such as increased digestion, blood flow to extremities and relaxation.

Phase 2: Isometric Exercises

Isometric means "same length." Thus, the goal of these exercises is to contract a muscle while keeping the muscle at the same length and preventing motion of the joints. For example, an isometric exercise for the neck flexors would be one where the person places his hands on the front of the head and pushes the head into the hands. No movement occurs in the neck while the muscles are contracting.

The goal of isometric exercises is to tone the muscle groups involved without inducing movement in the joints. Increase of muscle mass and strength usually does not occur with isometric exercises, but this is an excellent starting point to discover whether an RSI sufferer is ready to begin the rehabilitation process. If isometric exercises cause flare-ups or a recurrence of pain, then the doctor needs to reevaluate the treatment and rehabilitation program.

240

#38: Isometric exercise of the lateral neck flexors

In photo #38 above, notice how the subject is pushing her head sideways against her hand to contract the lateral flexors of the neck. In photo #39, the subject is isometrically contracting the shoulder external rotators, abductors and extensors by pushing against a wall. In photo #40, the subject is pushing her arm outward against a wall, isometrically contracting the triceps muscle in the back of the arm. (This can be done on a table or other horizontal surface also.) In photo #41, the subject is isometrically contracting the wrist flexors against the wall.

Every muscle group can be isometrically contracted. The RSI sufferer can progress from the neck downwards to the fingers, using isometric contractions for each muscle group along the way. The isometrics are prescribed in my clinic for a time period of approximately two to three weeks. If they are handled well by the patient, we move on to the next category of resistive exercises.

#39: Isometric exercise for shoulder abduction/external rotation

#40: Isometric exercise for the triceps

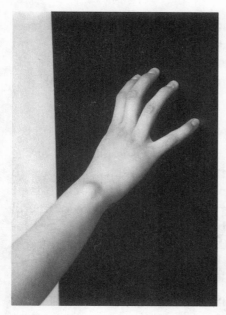

#41: Isometric exercise of the
wrist flexors

Phase 3: Resistive Exercises

Once the person has mastered isometrics with no recurrence
of symptoms, then it is time to move on to resistive exercises.
Resistive exercises allow for muscle contraction in gentle arcs
of movement against progressive resistance. The exercises also
induce joint motion. The further the tubing is stretched, the
more resistance it provides to the muscles. Since tubing comes
in different thicknesses and strengths, the type used for each
particular condition can be tailored to one's muscle build.

There is an excellent product on the market that is very
helpful in hand and forearm resistive strengthening. Sid May-
cock, D.C. developed a wrist exerciser that is showing great
promise for rehabilitation of RSI injuries, evidenced by the recommendations from members of the SOREHAND Internet
mailing list. It is called The Wristiciser® and can be found via

the Wristiciser® website that is included in the Resource section. This product can facilitate 26 therapeutic exercises and comes in a small carrying case which is easily portable. Its convenience and reputation earn its mention in this book.

Tubing exercises:

Here are examples of resistive tubing exercises for some of the major muscle groups involved in RSI conditions. It is best to have your particular resistive exercise program tailored to your specific body build and RSI condition. Therefore, I recommend that these exercises be prescribed by a health professional familiar with rehabilitation and exercise physiology. In most cases exercises are prescribed by a physical therapist, chiropractor, acupuncturist, exercise physiologist, occupational therapist and occasionally by a medical doctor. Always ask about your provider's background in rehabilitation before beginning your strengthening program.

#42: Tubing exercise for the shoulder adductors

The subject is elevating the arm away from the body against the resistance of the tubing. This exercise can be done to the side, to the front and to the rear to affect all the shoulder abductor, flexor and extensor muscles. These exercises are good for overall shoulder stability.

245

#43: Tubing exercise for shoulder adductors

The subject is bringing the straightened arm across the body. This is helpful for toning the pectoralis and some of the rotator cuff muscles.

#44: Tubing exercise for shoulder internal rotators

With the elbow flexed and the tubing attached to a stationary object, rotate the forearm inward to the chest. This exercise specifically tones the pectoralis major muscle and the internal rotators of the rotator cuff.

246

#45: Tubing exercise for shoulder external rotators

Again, with the elbow flexed rotate the forearm away from the body. This exercise strengthens the external rotators of the rotator cuff muscles.

#46: Tubing exercise for arm extensors

Extend the arm (at the shoulder, not at the elbow) against resistance. Bring the arm forward and use resistance exercises for the arm flexors as well. Keep the arm straight at all times during these exercises. The arm flexion and extension exercises are important for overall toning following an RSI injury.

247

#47: Tubing exercise for wrist flexors

With the tubing held down by your foot, flex the wrist against the resistance. This exercise is very important for patients who have experienced tendinitis and myostitis in the forearm, especially medial epicondylitis.

#48: Tubing exercise for wrist extensors

Continue holding the tubing in place with the foot and now extend the wrist against resistance. Exercising the wrist extensors is important for patients who suffered from lateral epicondylitis, forearm tendinitis and myositis.

#49: Tubing exercise for hand pronators

While holding one end of the tubing with one hand, place the tubing in the opposite hand, the end of the tubing in the palm towards the pinkie side. Rotate the hand downward so resistance occurs. These exercises are very important for patients with forearm RSI conditions. These exercises are meant to strengthen the small forearm pronator muscles.

#50: Tubing exercise for hand supinators

Place the tubing so the end of it is in the palm towards the thumb and wrap it around your hand so resistance occurs upon rotating the palm of the hand upwards. Exercising the supinators is one of the first exercises I give to my patients with RSIs. Almost all patients with carpal tunnel syndrome or other RSIs involving the hand or wrist have a weak supinator muscle. Most patients are used to keeping the hand palm side down (especially computer users) in a pronated position. The supinators become weak and stretched. Toning them is an important part of the rehabilitation process.

Phase 4: Free-weight Exercises

Once the patient has advanced to higher levels of resistance-tubing exercises, she is instructed to begin free-weight exercises with low-weight dumbbells. Dumbbells as light as three pounds are effective in some patients for forearm strengthening. Again, these exercises need to be tailored to the patient's body frame and weight training experience by an experienced athletic trainer, physical therapist or doctor. Below are some examples of free weight exercises.

#51: Shoulder fly exercises

Shoulder fly exercises are excellent for increasing strength of the upper back, lower neck and posterior arm region.

251

#52 Arm flexors

Raise the straightened arm upwards in front of you.

#53 Forearm extensors.

The extensors are important to strengthen in those people who type, use a mouse or are involved in sporting events such as tennis, badminton or bowling.

5: Fast-repetition, Short-arc Tubing Exercises

To further rehabilitate the muscles and increase neurological input, a series of fast-repetition, short-arc exercises are pre-scribed, targeting muscle groups primarily affected by the RSI. These exercises are very important when recovering from a neurological deficit since they consciously increase the brain's neurologic control over the muscle groups and enhance nerve firing to the muscles. The patient is instructed to perform re-petitive muscle contractions as fast as possible for a 10-second period of time against the resistance of the rubber tubing. The contractions occur only over a very short arc of motion—about 30 degrees. This arc can increase as the patient improves his technique. In most cases, the person feels quite clumsy when attempting this procedure, especially after suffering an RSI, but within one to two week's time, a marked improvement is often noted in speed and movement. This indicates better control of the muscle's function by the brain. As the person improves at this technique, heavier tubing is used, and larger arcs of move-ment are incorporated into the program.

Other Rehabilitative Protocols

Depending upon the patient's history, other rehabilitation tech-niques can be used to allow for a complete recovery of both the RSI condition, and other underlying musculoskeletal condi-tions. One technique often used in our clinic is proprioceptive retraining. Proprioceptors are nerve endings that detect where the limb or torso is situated in space. For example, they allow your brain to recognize if you are bending versus standing or if your arm is by your side or held out in front of you. Retrain-ing the proprioceptors is a powerful method of stabilizing and

#54: Wobble board exercise.

increasing efficiency of the postural muscles such as the back extensors and the hip flexors. Proprioceptive retraining can be performed via a "wobble board," which is a flat circular piece of wood or plastic that wobbles due to its uneven bottom surface (See photo #54). The patient stands on this board and learns to control his body's reactions to the uneven movements. Another good device is a large inflatable gym ball (See photo #55) which is used for exercises leading to trunk stabilization, strengthening of the upper back, abdomen, legs and torso.

For persons with access to fitness centers and gyms, there

#55: Gym ball exercise

are hundreds of different forms of exercise equipment. Some are better than others. Do not blindly begin a self-designed exercise program if you have an RSI condition (unless you are fully trained in rehabilitation). It is always best to ask your healthcare practitioner about specific exercises and equipment to use in a gym setting. If your doctor is not educated about rehabilitation, talk to a certified personal trainer at your gym. (Always ask a trainer about his/her credentials and experience. Some "trainers" working in gyms do not have a great deal of rehabilitation education.) Ask the trainer to speak to your doctor or health care provider to allow him to understand the extent of injuries involved and the rehabilitation goals for that specific time period. The trainer may be better suited to help you than the doctor, especially if the doctor has no background in rehabilitation and/or sports injuries.

Rehabilitation for an RSI condition is challenging to the health care provider. There is no one-size-fits-all rehabilitation program for all RSI sufferers. Because the extent of tissue damage and multiple structure involvement, each program has to be tailored specifically for the patient's condition. The goal of this chapter is not to provide the RSI patient with a comprehensive program designed to heal all wounds. The goal is to show the patient, doctor or therapist how to begin an effective rehabilitation process for retraining of muscles, tendons and other structures affected by an RSI injury.

CHAPTER 26

AEROBIC EXERCISE

Maintaining good aerobic fitness before, during and after a repetitive strain injury cannot be emphasized enough. Aerobic exercise increases blood supply to the muscles, tendons and ligaments, increases metabolic rate, allows for pumping and drainage of stagnant lymphatic tissues and gives one a sense of accomplishment. Aerobic exercise also helps to relieve depression, provides a higher sense of self-worth and induces weight loss.

A sedentary lifestyle and an RSI are a terrible mix. A downward spiral can develop whereby the pain of the RSI causes depression, leading to inactivity and an unwillingness to exercise. This in turn leads to poor circulation and stagnant lymphatic tissues, resulting in increased RSI problems. This downward spiral can be put to an end quickly with a little willpower and a desire to make changes to your body via an aerobic exercise program. The best part about aerobic exercise for RSI sufferers is that in most of them you don't need to use your hands.

When most people hear the word "aerobic" they picture a group of people exercising in an aerobics class. Although this is one form of aerobic exercise, it is not the only form.

Aerobic exercise simply means raising the heartbeat up to a level about 60 percent to 80 percent of its maximum for at least 20 minutes or more by exercising the major muscle groups. This increases cellular activity and induces aerobic respiration within the cells. Recent literature shows aerobic exercise induces a hormonal response, reducing insulin levels and increasing glucagon levels.[36]

It is important to think about what type of activities you enjoy doing before considering an aerobic exercise plan. Do you enjoy bike riding, fast walking, jogging, skipping rope, rowing, aerobic classes or swimming? All of these exercises develop aerobic respiration within the cells. Bicycle riding and swimming may be more difficult for the RSI sufferer because of the use of the hands and upper extremities during the exercise. Aerobic classes are an excellent form of exercise since most of them include some stretching beforehand along with a cool-down period following the intensive workout. You have the added benefit of meeting people and making new friends. If you belong to a gym, then the bicycling, rowing, walking and running can be simulated by the use of exercise bikes, rowing machines and treadmills. These are excellent alternatives to allow you to reach aerobic levels of fitness.

Fast walking and jogging are excellent forms of aerobic workouts for the RSI sufferer since these exercises stimulate muscular activity throughout the body, and can be performed without use of the hands. I use the word "fast" with walking since to achieve an aerobic exercise level you need to quicken the pace of the walk. Slow walks are good for the mind and help to work muscles as well as the heart, but taking a stroll does not reach the level of aerobic exercise we are attempting to achieve. For some RSI sufferers who are out of shape, a slow walk may be the starting point. Slowly increase the length and speed of the walk as you get into better shape.

How often do you need to perform aerobic exercise? The benefits of aerobic exercise mentioned earlier occur with each exercise session but also continue for an hour or more after the exercise. Therefore, the more you perform aerobic exercises, the more of the beneficial results you will achieve. If you are just beginning an aerobic workout routine, do it three to four times per week, allowing rest days in between for muscle healing. Each aerobic workout should last at least 20 minutes to induce the desired metabolic changes.

As you become stronger (and healthier), consider aerobic workouts five days per week, each one 45 to 60 minutes in length. Remember that you don't have to do only one aerobic exercise for this time period: you can jog for 20 minutes, ride an exercise bike for 20 minutes, then walk for 10 minutes. Be creative!

For people battling with obesity, "aerobics" may seem like a dirty word. For obese patients, it is important to decide upon a game plan that looks toward the future to determine overall aerobic exercise goals. With this in mind, it is helpful to begin a step-by-step process that may mean walking five minutes five times per week for the first two weeks, then building to 10, and so on. Obese people have much more weight to move, therefore their hearts are going to be working harder even with less strenuous exercise. They may not need to perform fast, prolonged muscle movements as in aerobic classes to achieve the recommended heart rate. In many cases, once the obesity is controlled and reduced, their correlating RSI symptoms will subside due to lessen fat surrounding the tissues.

Anaerobic Exercise

Anaerobic exercise occurs when a muscle's need for energy goes beyond what the aerobic energy cycle can supply. For

259

example, this occurs when performing sprints, weight lifting and sudden bursts of power from any muscle group. Anaerobic exercise has benefits also. The main benefit with anaerobic exercise is building muscle mass. High intensity anaerobic exercise causes the body to secrete human growth hormone, a powerful substance that initiates muscle healing and growth.

One of the byproducts of anaerobic exercise is lactic acid production. Lactic acid buildup in the muscles causes soreness a day or two after a hard workout. The RSI sufferer with an active acute condition wants to avoid lactic acid production since it will simply cause more pain and discomfort in the affected regions. For this reason, anaerobic exercise in an acute stage of RSIs is not recommended.

An overall body conditioning workout combining the two disciplines of aerobic and anaerobic training is the ultimate goal for the RSI sufferer. The aerobic exercise brings oxygen into the tissues while anaerobic exercise increases muscle strength. In the inflamed stage of RSIs, aerobic exercise is more important. Then, as the symptoms subside, adding some anaerobic exercise such as weight training will help the muscles regain their strength.

REFERENCES

1. Michael Leahy, D.C., 1995. "Improved Treatments for Carpal Tunnel and Related Syndromes," *Chiropractic Sports Medicine* 9(1): 6–9.
2. Steven Roy and Richard Irvin, *Sports Medicine: Prevention, Evaluation, Management, and Rehabilitation*, (Englewood Cliffs, N.J., Prentice Hall, Inc., 1983), pp. 127–128.
3. Hans Selye, *Stress Without Distress*, (New York, Harper and Row, 1974) pp. 27–51.
4. R.L. Simpson and S.A. Fern, "Multiple Compression Neuropathies and the Double Crush Syndrome," *Orthop Clin North Am*, Apr 1996, 27(2): 381–388.
5. Kurt Mariano, Mark McDougle, and Gary Tanksley, "Double Crush Syndrome: Chiropractic Care of an Entrapment Neuropathy," *J Manipulative Physiol Ther*, May 1991, 14(4): 262–265.
6. Sharon Butler, *Conquering Carpal Tunnel Syndrome and Other Repetitive Strain Injuries*, (Oakland, CA, New Harbinger Publications, 1996), pp. 5–7.
7. Marko Pecina and Ivan Bojanic, *Overuse Injuries of the Musculoskeletal System*, (Boca Raton, FL, CRC Press, 1993), pp. 9–14.
8. Thomas Andreoli, Charles Carpenter, Fred Plum, and Lloyd Smith, *Cecil's Essentials of Medicine*, (Philadelphia, W.B. Saunders Company, 1986), pp. 484–485.
9. C.Y. Tsai, C.L. Yu, and S.T. Tsai, "Bilateral carpal tunnel syndrome secondary to tophaceous compression of the median nerves," *Scand J Rheumatol*, 1996, 25(2): 107–108.

10. Marie Krause and L. Kathleen Mahon, *Food Nutrition and Diet Therapy*, (Philadelphia, W.B. Saunders & Co., 1984), p. 245.
11. Emil Pascarelli and Deborah Quilter, *Repetitive Strain Injury: A Computer User's Guide*, (New York, John Wiley & Sons, 1994), p. 33.
12. Terry Yochum and Lindsay Row, *Essentials of Skeletal Radiology*, Volume 1, (Baltimore, Williams and Wilkens, 1987), pp. 109–110.
13. R.C. Schafer, D.C., *Clinical Biomechanics, Musculoskeletal Actions and Reactions*, (Baltimore, Williams & Wilkens, 1983), p. 327.
14. Roy and Irvin op. cit., pp. 184–185
15. H. Kurosawa, K. Nakashita, H. Hankashita, and S. Sasaki, "Pathogenesis and treatment of cubital tunnel syndrome caused by osteoarthritis of the elbow joint," *J Shoulder Elbow Surg*, Jan-Feb 1995 4(1): 30–34.
16. Janet Travell and David Simons, *Myofascial Pain and Dysfunction: The Trigger Point Manual*, (Baltimore, Williams and Wilkens, 1983), pp. 462–472.
17. Michael Leahy and Lewis Mock, "Altered Biomechanics of the shoulder and the subscapularis," *Chiropractic Sports Medicine*, 1991, 5(3): 62–66.
18. Pecina and Bojanic, op.cit., pp. 61–62.
19. Travell and Simons, op.cit., p. 533.
20. Ibid, p. 516.
21. Ibid, p. 516.
22. Ibid, p. 516.
23. C.Y. Tsai, C.L. Yu, and S.T. Tsai, "Bilateral carpal tunnel syndrome secondary to tophaceous compression of the median nerves," *Scand J Rheumatol*, 1996, 25(2): 107–108.
24. Robert G. Schwartz and Stuart M. Weinstein, "Getting a hand on cumulative trauma disorders," *Patient Care*, Feb 15, 1996, 30(3): 113–118.
25. John H. Eisele, M.D., "Reflex Sympathetic Dystrophy," *QME Quarterly*, 1997, 1(2): 3–15.
26. Ibid, p. 10.
27. S.M. Griggs, et al., "Treatment of trigger finger in patients with diabetes mellitus," *J Hand Surg*, 1995 Sep., 20(5): 787–789.

28. James W Long, M.D., and James J. Rybachi, Pharm. D., *The Essential Guide to Prescription Drugs*, (New York, Harper Perennial Books, 1995).
29. Robert Becker and Gary Selden, *The Body Electric*, (New York, William Morrow, 1985), pp. 52–65.
30. Barry Sears, Ph.D., *Enter The Zone*, (New York, Regan Books/ Harper Collins, 1995), p. 72.
31. Ibid, pp. 24–31.
32. Ibid, pp. 32–39.
33. Joel D. Wallach, D.V.M., N.D., *Rare Earths: Forbidden Cures*, (Bonita, CA, Double Happiness Publishing Company, 1996) p. 373.
34. Helen A. Guthrie, *Introductory Nutrition*, (St. Louis, Time Mirror, 1986), p. 195.
35. Sears, *op.cit.*, pp. 59–60.
36. Wallach, Joel, D., D.V.M., N.D., *Rare Earths: Forbidden Cures*, (Bonita, CA, Double Happiness Publishing Company, 1996) p. 373.

RESOURCES

RESOURCES ON THE INTERNET

The following World Wide Web pages offer a tremendous wealth of knowledge and information on all aspects of repetitive strain injuries, ergonomics, labor and other work-related issues. The Internet addresses were up-to-date as of publication of this book. Because of the frequent changes made in web pages, some of the addresses may change by the time you read this information. Use the search engines mentioned to perform your own search of repetitive strain injury information.

Repetitive Strain Injuries: Web Pages

Computer-related repetitive strain injuries page:
    http://www.engr.unl.edu/ee/eeshop/rsi.html
RSI-UK (United Kingdom) home page:
    http://www.demon.co.uk/rsi/
Typing Injury Archives:
    http://alumni.caltech.edu/~dank/typing-archive.html
    http://www.tifaq.com
Amara's RSI page:
    http://www.best.com/~agraps/aboutme/rsi.html

264

CTD News:
> http://ctdnews.com

Carpal Tunnel Syndrome:
> http://www.sechrest.com/mmg/cts/ctsintro.html

Cumulative Trauma Disorders:
> Products, Information, etc. through IMPACC USA:
> http://www.impaccusa.com/impacch.html

Richard Donkin's RSI page:
> http://www.netcomuk.uk/~ishbeld/index/html
> http://hNww.netaxs.com/~iris/cts/welcome.html

Occupational Overuse Syndrome:
> http://www.comp.vuw.ac.nz/General/OOS/

The Los Angeles RSI support group:
> http://www.geocities.com/hotsprings/1702/

Deborah Quilter's Web Page:
> http://www.users.interport.net/~webdeb/

RSI and VDT radiation issues:
> http://scitsc.wln.ac.uk/~c9584315/rsi.html

REPETITIVE STRAIN INJURIES IN MUSICIANS
> http://www.engr.unl.edu.eeshop/music.html
> http://www.jamesonchiro.com/ (the author's home page)

Canadian Network for Health in the Arts:
> http://web.indirect.com/~cnha

Performing Arts Medicine Associations:
> http://www.artsmed.org

International Arts Medicine Association (IAMA):
> http://members.aol.com/iamaorg/index.html

Performing Arts Medicine at Ithaca College:
> http://www.ithaca.edu/hshp/pt/pt1/

Hazards of Piano Playing:
> ftp.centrum.is/pub/sen/MusicMedicine.txt

British Performing Arts Medical Trust:
> http://www.cygnet.co.uk/BPAMT/

WWW Virtual Library:
    Classical Music Department: http://www.gprep.pvt.k12.md.us/
    classical/ click on "performance"

Musculoskeletal Problems in Musicians
http://gopher.tmn.com:70/0/Artswire/csa/arthazards/performing/
    musicians

RSI Internet Mailing Lists

Mailing lists allow you to exchange messages back and forth between health professionals and people who are experiencing RSIs. I highly recommend the SOREHAND mailing list to anyone suffering from RSIs. There is no fee to belong to an Internet mailing list.

SOREHAND:
email address: listserv@ucsfvm.ucsf.edu
    to send message:
    Subscribe SOREHAND <your name>
RSI-UK email address:
    listserver@tictac.demon.co.uk
    to send message:
    Subscribe RSI-UK <your name>

RSI Internet Newsgroups

Internet Newsgroups are discussion areas you can visit offering a compilation of messages posted by people around the world. There is no fee for participating in a newsgroup. There are two newsgroups related to repetitive strain injuries:

Misc.health.injuries.rsi.misc
Misc.health.injuries.rsi.moderated

Ergonomic Issues

University of Virginia Ergonomics Policy:
  http://poe.acc.virginia.edu/~kka2u/.ergo.html
Berkeley/UCSF Ergonomics Masters and Doctoral Program:
  http://www.me.berkeley.edu
Cornell Ergonomics Web Page:
  http://ergo.human.cornell.edu
Michigan State University's Ergonomics Research Lab.:
  http://ihes1.ergo.msu.edu/
Ergonomic Engineering Inc. (Ergonomic issues, regulations, rsi issues,
  workplace design)
  http://www.ergo.engin.com/

Human Factors and Ergonomics

Crew System Ergonomics Information Analysis Center:
  http://cseriac.udri.udayton.edu
Comp.human factors, frequently asked questions:
  http://www.dgp.toronto.edu/people/ematias/faq/
  contents.html
Biomechanics worldwide:
  http://dragon.acadiau.ca/~pbaudin/biomch.html
Human Factors of Ergonomics Society:
  http://hfes.org/
Human Factors/Ergonomics at the University of Toronto:
  http://www.ie.utoronto.ca/IE/HF/summary.html
Institute for Ergonomics and Man-Machine Systems:
  http://hvwwifa.kf.tu-berlin.de/e_ifa_home.html

Labor Issues

Bureau of Labor Statistics:
>   http://stats.bls.gov/safety.htm

Canadian Centre for Occupational Health and Safety:
>   http://www.ccohs.ca/

Job Stress Web Site:
>   http://www.workhealth.org

Job Strain:
>   http://www.workhealth.org/strain/hpjs.htm

LaborNet:
>   computer communications, news, information, and resources for a democratic labor movement:
>   http://www.igc. apc.org/labornet/

NIOSH:
>   http://www.cdc.gov/niosh/homepage.html

Occupational Safety and Health Administration:
>   http://www.osha.gov

OSHWEB:
>   Metaindex to Ergonomics/Human Factors
>   http://turva.me.tut.fi/cgi-bin/wilma/erghf

U.S. Dept. of Labor Statistical Database: (with links to Bureau of labor statistics)
>   http://www.dol.gov/dol/asp/public/dollabdata/labdata.htm

Worker's Compensation Issues

California Worker's Compensation Law:
>   http://www.geocities.com/Paris/1676/wc.html

Department of Industrial Relations:
>   http://www.dir.ca.gov

Links to Worker's Compensation related web sites:
>   http://www.wcb.bc.ca/resmat/websites.htm

National Council of Compensation Issues:
    http://ncci.com
National Center for Injury Prevention and Control:
    www.cdc.gov/ncipc/ncipchm.htm
Work related issues:
    http://www.geocities.com

Alternative Health Care Sites

Chiropractic Health Care
American Chiropractic Association "Chiro On Line"
    http://www.amerchiro.org
Chiroweb:
    http://www.chiroweb.com
Chiroaccess:
    http://www.chiroaccess.com
International Chiropracters Assn.:
    http://www.chiropractic.org
Network Chiropractic:
    http://network-chiropractic.net/netright.html
World Chiropractic Alliance:
    http://www.choicemail.com/worldchiropractic/
Dr. Jameson's web site:
    http://www.jamesonchiro.com

Acupuncture and Traditional Chinese Medicine
Acupuncture history:
    http://www.rhemamed.com/acuhis.htm
Acupuncture information and practitioners:
    http://www.Acupuncture.com

Foundation for Traditional Chinese Medicine:
http://www.demon.co.uk/acupuncture/index.html

FELDENKRAIS TECHNIQUE
The Feldenkrais Guild:
http://www.feldenkrais.com
Ralph Strauss' web site:
http://www.somatic.com
Phillipe LeBlond's site:
http://www.axess.com/feld/

ALEXANDER TECHNIQUE
Rick Rickover's site:
http://www.shrameksvideo.com/alextech/
Society of Alexander Teachers:
http://www.pavilion.co.uk/stat/
Jeff Haas site:
http://www.life.uiuc.edu/jeff/alextech.html

BIOFEEDBACK
Association for Applied Psychophysiology and Biofeedback:
http://www.aapb.org/index.htm

COLLOIDAL MINERALS
For more information on purchasing Soaring Eagle colloidal minerals,
contact Dr. Jameson at chiro4u@aol.com.

GUIDED IMAGERY
Academy for Guided Imagery:
http://www.healthy.net/agi/

HELLERWORK
http://www.hellerwork.com/

Homeopathy
Homeopathy home page with links:
http://www.dungeon.com/~cam/homeo.html

Massage
Information page:
http://www.sw3d.com/MASSAGETHERAPY
Home of Reflexology:
http://www.reflexology.org/
Shiatsu:
http://www.tip.nl/users/t283083/e-index.htm
Therapeutic Massage:
http://www.doubleclickd.com/theramassage.htm
Touch for Health:
http://www.lovinglife.org

Nutrition Web Pages
Arbor Nutrition Guide - links to web related nutrition sites:
http://www.arbor.com
Fast Food Finder:
http://www.olen.com/food
International Food and Information Council:
http://ificinfo.org
USDA Food and Nutrition Guide:
http://www.nal.usda.gov/fnic/software/software.html
The Zone Diet:
http://www.eicotech.com/

Physical Therapy
Physical Therapy:
The Web Space http://www.ualberta.ca/~jdo.ree/rus.html
World of Physical Therapy:
http://ucsw.byu.edu/ucs/ucf/physther/pthome.htm

ROLFING
Information page:
   http://www.rolf.org

T'AI CHI
T'ai Chi page:
   http://lifematters.com/taijin.html
T'ai Chi Chuan with Ron Perfetti:
   http://www.maui.net/~taichi4u/taichi.html

Therapeutic Devices

The Wristiciser:
   http://www.wristiciser.com

Internet Search Engines:

Use these search engines to find more information about RSIs and related topics.
Yahoo:
   http://www.yahoo.com
Altavista:
   http://altavista.digital.com
WebCrawler:
   http://www.webcrawler.com
Excite:
   http://www.excite.com

REFERENCE BOOKS

This purpose of this appendix is to let the reader know what's on the bookshelves regarding repetitive strain injuries, stretching, alternative health care and other health-related topics. Please visit your bookstore or library to become better educated about RSIs.

Carpal Tunnel Syndrome and RSIs

Butler, Sharon J., *Conquering Carpal Tunnel Syndrome and Other Repetitive Strain Injuries*, (Oakland, CA, New Harbinger Publications, 1996).

Montgomery, Kate, *Carpal Tunnel Syndrome, Prevention and Treatment, A Nonsurgical, Drug-free Approach*, (Sports Touch Publishing, 1992).

Pascarelli and Quilter, *Repetitive Strain Injury, A Computer User's Guide*, (New York, John Wiley and Sons, 1994).

Pinsky, Mark A., *The Carpal Tunnel Syndrome Book: Preventing and Treating CTS, Tendinitis and Related Cumulative Trauma Disorders*, (New York, Warner Books, 1993.

Pecina and Bojanic, *Overuse Injuries of the Musculoskeletal System*, (Boca Ration, FL, CRC Press, 1993).

Ergonomics

Schaffer and Cross, *ErgoWise: A Personal Guide to Making Your Workspace Comfortable and Safe*, (AMACON, 1996).

Musicians' RSI Information:

Lieberman, Julie L., *You Are Your Instrument*, (New York, Huiksi Music, 1991).

Norris, Richard, M.D., *The Musician's Survival Manual: A Guide to Preventing and Treating Injuries in Instrumentalists*, ICSOM, (Through MMB Music, Saint Louis, MO) 1993.

Sander, Gyorgy, *Motion, Sound, and Expression*, (New York, Shermer Books, 1981).

Sataloff, Brandfenbrener, Lederman, eds., *Textbook of Performing Arts Medicine*, (New York Raven Press, 1990).

Alternative Health Care

Collinge, William, M.P.H., *The American Holistic Health Association Complete Guide to Alternative Medicine*, (New York, Warner Books, 1996).

Marti, James, *The Alternative Health and Medicine Encyclopedia*, (Detroit, Visible Ink Press, 1995).

Morton, Mary and Michael, *Five Steps to Selecting the Best Alternative Medicine: A Guide to Complementary and Integrative Health Care*, (Novato, CA, New World Library, 1996).

Guiness, Alma E., editor, *The Reader's Digest Family Guide to Natural Medicine*, (New York, Reader's Digest, 1993).

Null, Gary, *Healing Your Body Naturally: Alternative Treatments to Illness*, (N.Y., Seven Stories Press, 1992).

Shealy, Norman, M.D., editor, *The Complete Family Guide to Alternative Medicine: An Illustrated Encyclopedia of Natural Healing*, (Element Books, 1996).

Acupuncture

Cohen, Misha Ruth, O.M.D., L.Ac., *The Chinese Way of Healing.* (N.Y., Perigee Books, 1996).

Firebrace and Hill, *Acupuncture: How It Works, How It Cures*, (New Canaan, CT, Keats Publishing, 1994).

Mole, Peter, *Acupuncture: Energy Balancing for Body, Mind, and Spirit,* (Element Books, 1992).

Reid, Daniel, *Traditional Chinese Medicine,* (Boston, MA, Shambala Books, 1996).

Breathing Techniques

Lewis, Dennis, *The Tao of Natural Breathing,* (San Francisco, Mountain Wind Publishing, 1997).

Chiropractic

Cohen, Don, D.C., *An Introduction to Craniosacral Therapy,* (Berkeley, CA, North Atlantic Books, 1997).

Epstein, Donald, D.C., *The 12 Stages of Healing: A Network Approach to Wellness,* (New World Library, 1994).

McGill, Leonard, D.C., *The Chiropractor's Health Book,* (Crown Publishers, 1997).

Rondberg, Terry A., D.C., *Chiropractic First,* (Chandler, A.Z., The Chiropractic Journal, 1996).

Homeopathy

Cummings, Steven and Ullman, Dana: *Everybody's Guide to Homeopathic Medicine,* (New York, Tarcher/Putnam Books, 1997).

Garion-Hutchings, Nigel and Susan: *The New Concise Guide to Homeopathy,* (Element Books, 1996).

Jacobs, Wayne, B., M.D.: *Healing With Homeopathy, The Complete Guide,* (New York, Warner Books, 1996).

Imagery

Epstein, Gerald, M.D.: *Healing Visualizations, Creating Health Through Imagery,* (New York, Bantam Books, 1989).

Naparstek, Belleruth: *Staying Well with Guided Imagery,* (New York, Warner Books, 1994).

Herbology

McIntyre, Anne: *Herbs for Common Ailments,* (New York, Simon & Schuster, 1992).

Mindell, Earl: *Earl Mindell's Herb Bible,* (New York, Simon & Schuster, 1992).

Massage Therapy/Bodywork

Shen, Peijian: *Massage For Pain Relief: A Step-by-Step Guide,* (London, Gaia Books Limited, 1996).

Maxwell-Hudson, Clare: *The Complete Book of Massage,* (New York, Random House, 1988).

Maxwell-Hudson, Clare: *Aromatherapy Massage,* (DK Publishing, 1994).

Carter Mildred, *Healing Yourself with Foot Reflexology,* (Englewood Cliffs, New Jersey, Prentice Hall, 1997).

Thompson: *The Shiatsu Manual,* (New York, Sterling Publishing, 1994).

Macrae, Janet: *Therapeutic Touch, A Practical Guide,* (New York, Alfred Knopf, 1987).

Nutrition

Barnard, Neal, M.D.: *Eat Right, Live Longer* (New York, Crown Paperbacks, 1995).

Sinatra, Stephen, M.D.: *Optimum Health,* (New York, Bantam Books, 1997).

Somatic Education

Brennen, Richard: *The Alexander Technique Manual,* (Boston, MA, Journey Editions, 1996).

Feldenkrais, Moshe: *The Elusive Obvious,* (Self-published, 1981).

Feldenkrais, Moshe: *Awareness Through Movement,* (New York, HarperCollins, 1977).

Leibowitz and Connington: *The Alexander Technique,* (New York, HarperCollins, 1990).

Stretching

Anderson, Bob: *Stretching,* (Bolinas, CA, Shelter Publications, 1980).

Anderson, Bob: *Stretching at Your Computer or Desk,* (Bolinas, CA, Shelter Publications, 1997).

Warton, Jim and Phil: *The Wharton's Stretch Book: Active Isolated Stretching,* (New York, Times Books, 1996).

Computer Ergonomic Software

ErgoSentry, Manufactured by Magnitude™. This software runs in the background while you're working at the computer. It monitors your working patterns and offers pop-up windows that alert you when breaks are needed. It offers advice on computer ergonomic set-up, posture, and informs the user of repetitive injuries. Web address: http://www.magnitude. com, email address: MAGLLC@AOL.COM

ErgoStar, The Personal Computer Ergonomic Adjustment System, manufactured by the Starfield Group, Inc. Web address: www. ergostar.com, email: starfield@ergostar.com

This ergonomic program is an excellent starting point to set up your work station properly. The program takes you through a step-by-step process of tailoring the work station to your body's dimensions.

Index

INDEX

CANOEING MAP

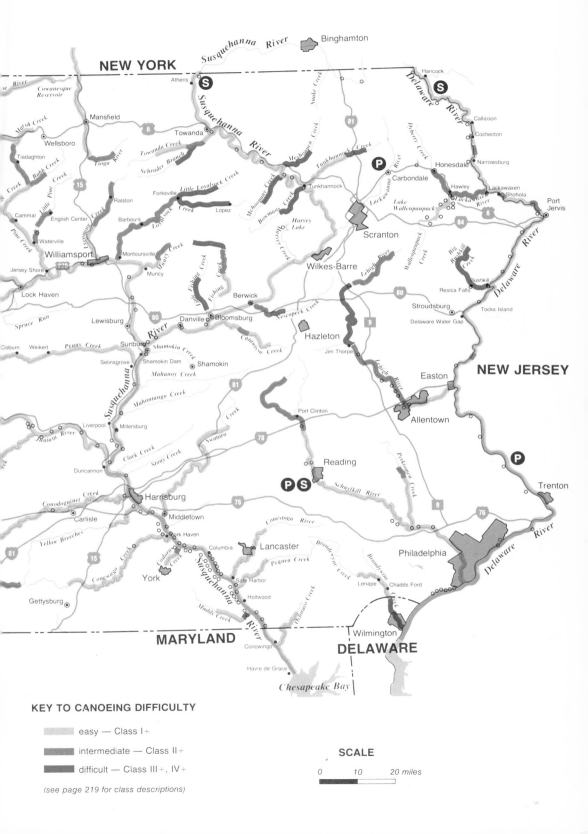

KEY TO CANOEING DIFFICULTY

easy — Class I+

intermediate — Class II+

difficult — Class III+, IV+

(see page 219 for class descriptions)

SCALE

0   10   20 miles

Rivers of Pennsylvania

Rivers
of
Pennsylvania

Tim Palmer

 Keystone Books

The Pennsylvania State University Press
University Park and London

Frontispiece: A mountain tributary to Schrader Branch, Towanda Creek

Parts of several chapters originally appeared in
Wilderness Camping, Trout, Pennsylvania Angler, and
River World

Library of Congress Cataloging in Publication Data

Palmer, Tim.
Rivers of Pennsylvania

(Keystone books)
Includes bibliography.
1. Rivers—Pennsylvania. I. Title.
GB1225.P4P33   917.48'09'693   79-15378
ISBN 0-271-00226-3 cloth
ISBN 0-271-00246-8 paper

Designed by Glenn Ruby and Chris van Dyck
Printed in the United States of America

for Cindy, who always heard the river's singing

Contents

Acknowledgments

My thanks to many river people: Cindy Palmer, Bob McCullough, Jim McClure, Ed McCarthy, Pete Fletcher, Jerry Walls, Helen Wilhelm, Art Davis, Red Arnold, Ken Sink, John Oliver, Walt Lyon, Bob Cortez, Gerry Lacy, John Sweet, Jerry Miller, Bill Parsons, George Reese, Bob Butler, Cass Chestnut, Bob Banks, Howard Brown and others. Although most photos were taken by me, four are by John Lazenby of Moretown, Vermont, and the historical photos were provided by the Lycoming County Historical Museum. Much of the black and white photo printing was done by Vannucci Photos and Mark Anderman of Williamsport.

Maps at the front and back of the book were prepared by Bob Texter and Chris van Dyck. Base map information was compiled from the *Official Map of Pennsylvania (1977)* prepared by the Pennsylvania Department of Transportation and the *Stream Map of Pennsylvania (1965)* prepared by Howard Wm. Higbee. *Canoeing Map* details were obtained from *Canoeing Guide to Western Pennsylvania and Northern West Virginia* by the Pittsburgh Council of American Youth Hostels, Inc., and from *Appalachian Waters 1: The Delaware and Its Tributaries* and *Appalachian Waters 3: The Susquehanna River and Its Tributaries* by Walter E. Burmeister. Public access, fishery, and acid mine drainage details on the *Fishing Map* were provided by the Pennsylvania Fish Commission.

Introduction: Penn's Rivers

Pennsylvania is a land of rivers and streams, 45,000 miles of them flowing toward the Chesapeake Bay, Delaware estuary, Great Lakes, and Gulf of Mexico. These waters brought European explorers into wilderness of the Indian's land, and later the continent was settled by people who drifted down the Ohio on keelboats. Today, streams twist and foam as they descend rocky, wooded slopes of the Appalachian Plateau. They wind through farmlands in a pastoral way, then roll slowly around cities and lowlands. Adding their increasing volume to one another, they grow in power. The rivers have distinction and importance of many kinds:

95 percent of our domestic water supply comes from rivers and streams. Water of one major river is used seven times before it reaches the sea.

Streams of the north central highlands are the wildest, least developed between New York and Chicago.

In southwestern Pennsylvania, the Youghiogheny provides more whitewater recreation than any other river in the nation.

Pittsburgh is America's busiest inland port. The Ohio River carries more commerce than the Panama Canal.

Legislation in 1978 designated the upper and middle Delaware as a National Scenic and Recreational River. Five other streams are being considered for federal protection.

The Lehigh River, Pine Creek, and the Susquehanna's West Branch have gorges of 1000-foot depth. They are scenic and recreational highlights of the Appalachians.

Bordering the Schuylkill River, Fairmount Park is the country's largest urban greenspace.

Wildlife thrive along many streams. Some of the finest fishing in the East is here. Commercial fishermen of the Chesapeake are dependent on the quality of Susquehanna water.

Other specialties go unrecognized. This book will discuss many of them.

How does one begin to view the vast complex of Pennsylvania waters? We can generalize and see differences between the north and south. Many northern rivers plunge from rapids to pools, crowded by steep slopes of

Opposite: Loyalsock Creek, below route 220, near the Haystacks

hemlock, hardwoods, and pine. Wildness and small towns are both found along the shorelines. While the origin, the paths, and the appearance of many streams are similar, they also reveal unending variety. In the south, some rivers are steep, wild, and rocky, but most form a meandering boundary of fields and communities. Waters become sluggish with dams or vile with waste. Each stream changes constantly, with every bend opening onto a new scene. Each valley is different from the last.

The Susquehanna, Pine Creek, Loyalsock, Moshannon, Juniata, Allegheny, Clarion, Youghiogheny, Lehigh, and Delaware—these rivers have been given separate chapters in this book. Short sketches describe other important waterways: French and Tionesta creeks are well known in western parts of the state. The Casselman has wild whitewater, though acid mine drainage has destroyed its life. The First Fork of the Sinnemahoning attracts crowds of anglers, while the scenic Bennett and Driftwood branches of the same stream are excellent for canoeing. Penns Creek and the Lackawaxen are favorites of trout fishermen, and expert whitewater runners meet Wills Creek, Stony Creek, and the Slippery Rock. The Schuylkill's lower reaches are a rowing center of the nation. In the southeast, the Brandywine flows through gentle, open landscape that faces development pressure. Johnstown's Conemaugh is notorious for floods. The Monongahela is much-used and polluted; the Ohio is a giant in size and industry.

In one book it is impossible to deal with all the waterways of Pennsylvania or with all aspects of their character and use. *Rivers of Pennsylvania* emphasizes the scenic, less-developed rivers of our state. These are the streams most suitable for recreation, and because of their high quality, environmental degradation would represent a great loss. Most chapters focus upon issues of importance, such as scenic river designation, acid mine drainage, recreational use, dam construction, and water pollution.

The overall organization of the book is by major river basins: first the Susquehanna, the largest in Pennsylvania; next the Ohio; and finally the Delaware. Although streams feeding the Potomac, Genesee, and Lake Erie basins also run through small parts of the Keystone State, these waterways are not discussed except for a short sketch of the Potomac's Wills Creek. This follows the sketch of the Ohio basin's Casselman River, which shares the same mountain source near the Mason-Dixon Line.*

As a prologue to other chapters, "The Natural River" describes riverine evolution before people intervened. A concluding chapter, "The Future of Pennsylvania Rivers," summarizes the challenges of environmental protection. Following the formal chapters, a section headed "Information for River People" presents guidelines for safe and satisfying recreational experiences.

---

*A table headed "Major Stream Basins of Pennsylvania" at the back of the book lists all the state's streams with watersheds of one hundred square miles or more, grouped under the five basins.

The Susquehanna Basin

The Susquehanna is our country's largest river basin on the Atlantic coast, and the West Branch is one of the least developed streams of its size in the East. Twenty-four miles of river wind between Karthaus and Keating in a deeply incised valley with mountains that rise 800 and 1,000 feet from the shore. The Susquehanna is many rivers in one. A ten-day voyage will take the canoeist through coal country, a wild canyon, small towns, fertile farmland, the state capital, hydroelectric dams, and finally the coastal plain and Chesapeake Bay. The waterway bisects three major regions of the state: the rugged Appalachian Plateau, the picturesque Ridge and Valley Province, and the rolling Piedmont.

Pine Creek, attracting thousands of fishermen and canoeists, is known for its scenery of mountains and gorges. The "Grand Canyon of Pennsylvania" has been a popular tourist stop for half a century. More than other streams, this one has been the focus of protection activities. The efforts of residents, preservationists, and various levels of government have been intense, sometimes successful, and always instructive in showing the complexity of approaches to river protection—some that have worked and some that have not.

Twenty-five more miles to the east, the Loyalsock empties into the widening West Branch near Williamsport. No river has the dual excellence of this one—superb trout fishing along chilling pools and hemlock-shaded

Photo courtesy of Lycoming County Historical Museum

West Branch of the Susquehanna near Williamsport, 1900-1910

banks, and unsurpassed kayaking or canoeing in the upper reaches. Eastern whitewater championships have been held here, and the annual races at Worlds End State Park attract thousands of contestants and visitors. For those who aren't expert with a paddle, this river offers hiking along the banks, with rapids, cliffs, glacial boulders, and aged timber as highlights.

Moshannon Creek enters the Susquehanna's West Branch above Karthaus, after a tumultuous pitch that is a favorite among whitewater canoeists of central Pennsylvania. Ironically, acid pollution is partly responsible for wild Moshannon shorelines—without game fish, there has been very little pressure for access roads and cabin developments. A proposed dam at Keating would flood the Moshannon, the West Branch Canyon, and two other streams that have been recommended for consideration in the Pennsylvania State Scenic Rivers System.

From the sandstone ridges and limestone valleys of south central Pennsylvania, the Juniata flows slowly eastward. Natural chemistry of the water and reduced pollution have made the Juniata remarkably productive for stream life. Shellfish seem to cover the bottom in places, and crayfish can often be found under large rocks. Great blue herons, green herons, kingfishers, mergansers, and other waterfowl thrive, as do bass and muskellunge and people fishing for them. The food chain and ecosystem of a freshwater stream can be seen here more easily than other places because

Photo courtesy of Lycoming County Historical Museum

Log rafts at the Hepburn Street Dam, Williamsport, 1900

Photo courtesy of Lycoming County Historical Museum

The Hiawatha, near Williamsport, about 1900

aquatic life is so evident. Not all of the Juniata is healthy, though. Wastes from a paper mill radically affect the river's upper reaches; however, improvements in water quality have made the Juniata famous as a "comeback" stream, one where abatement of pollution has made a difference.

Several of Pennsylvania's rivers were critical to the history of our country. William Penn settled the lower Delaware, and at the Ohio River's origin, Fort Duquesne, or Fort Pitt, was an important frontier outpost of the French and Indian War. Canal systems paralleled many large waterways. The history of the upper Susquehanna is especially interesting, for it was by this river that Pennsylvania's great but unknown explorer, Etienne Brulé, crossed the state in 1615 and 1616. One hundred fifty years later, the valley housed a core of pioneering settlements, and here the Iroquois Nations tried to reclaim their lands during the Revolutionary War.

The Ohio Basin

The Ohio is the state's second largest river basin. Here the broad and well-known Allegheny captures and carries most of the rainfall from northwestern Pennsylvania. Scenic reaches from Buckaloons to Oil City and from Franklin to Emlenton are very popular, serving as an unspoiled recreation area for the industrialized regions of Pittsburgh, Erie, and eastern Ohio.

Above the town of Warren lies Kinzua Dam and a thirty-mile-long reservoir that was built in 1967, displacing people of the Seneca Nation of Indians. Efforts of the Western Pennsylvania Conservancy, state government, and the United States Forest Service have been effective in protecting some of the Allegheny islands and shorelines below Warren. The lower river is dammed for commercial river traffic, and shorelines are often developed. Valued because of their scarcity, some open spaces are being protected and opened for public access to the water.

The Clarion is one of the Allegheny's largest tributaries, wild and scenic as it penetrates the mountains. Below Portland Mills and again below Cooksburg, there are no paralleling roads or railroads, only rhododendron-lined banks that rise sharply to steep slopes. The Allegheny National Forest, state forests, game lands, and parks adjoin the river, one-fourth of the shoreline being in public ownership. The lower twenty miles includes one of the wildest sections, though it shows clear evidence of problems. Acid mine drainage is severe in this reach, as it is on many tributaries. Piney Dam impounds the river for twelve miles near the town of Clarion, and a new dam that would inundate thirty miles of river has been proposed at St. Petersburg, five miles above the Allegheny. Sewage and industrial wastes have severely polluted the stream; however, recent years have brought improvements in nearly all aspects of water quality. A 1971 report of the Federal Bureau of Outdoor Recreation recommended that the Clarion not be designated in the National Wild and Scenic Rivers System, but suggested that it be reconsidered when water quality improves.

Southwestern Pennsylvania has the incomparable Youghiogheny, the finest of the whitewater streams. With a rare combination of clarity, wildness, challenging rapids, and accessibility, this is one of the most floated rivers in the world. One hundred thousand rafters, canoeists, and kayakers splash through Youghiogheny turbulence each year. The contrast of dark forests and brilliant churning water cannot be found elsewhere in the state. Outfitters serve masses of people with astonishing safety: there have been no drownings among guided groups. River running is a new phenomenon, and in the last ten years, this sport, and a state park, have transformed the quiet mountain town of Ohiopyle to a busy recreation center.

Opposite: Sunrise, Susquehanna above New Buffalo

The Delaware Basin

In the east, the Delaware basin incorporates unusual variety. Wildwater pours from the Pocono plateau, and much of it falls toward the sea by way of the Lehigh River. Below Walters Dam, rafters and kayakers converge on the third weekend of each month as extra water is released from the impoundment, guaranteeing a rapid journey through a spectacular gorge to the town of Jim Thorpe. Fishermen also like the Lehigh, and boater-angler conflicts are becoming common here, as they are on some other rivers. The Lehigh is being considered for inclusion in Pennsylvania's Scenic Rivers System.

A master of rivers, the Delaware is outstanding in many ways. Its history involves some of the earliest settlers on the continent, and its estuary is a major seaport. Above Trenton, the river's ecosystem is one of diversity and vigor, with fish, birds, mammals, and plant life to fascinate the naturalist. The Delaware has more recreational use than many other rivers combined, as a nature-starved urban population flocks to the upper reaches which became Pennsylvania's first National River in 1978. Headwaters provide drinking water to New York City.

Growing Importance of Rivers

In the past people have relied upon waterways as a means of transportation and as a source of water, fish, or power. The added importance of rivers in the future cannot be overestimated. A movement is under way that represents a definite and complex trend. Though there has been no clear focus, it involves rivers as the center of many approaches in recreational activity, environmental protection, and land-use planning. Several features of the trend are apparent:

Emphasis has been given to wild, scenic, and recreational river programs at the national and at some state levels. In the past eight years, eighty-three streams of the United States have been nominated for or included in a national system, and twenty-seven states have begun scenic-river programs of their own.*

The Clean Streams Act of Pennsylvania and the Federal Water Pollution Control Act have been effective instruments toward elimination of pollution. Much remains to be done.

---

*A table at the back of the book lists the streams recommended for study by the Scenic Rivers Task Force, Pennsylvania Department of Environmental Resources. Streams are located by basin and by county.

High construction costs, resistance to land acquisition, and expenses of facility operation mean less likelihood of major new park developments. Recreation will become more common in "open systems" that involve a mixture of public and private land with an emphasis on natural area appeal—conditions that are found along many rivers.

Due to a scarcity of suitable sites, high costs, social-environmental impacts, and a frequent surplus of reservoir recreation areas, fewer dams are likely to be built in the future. Rivers, rather than man-made lakes, will answer many of our water-related needs. Counter to this trend is the water-resource development philosophy of some public agencies, concern for electric power production, local pressures for flood control, and the possibility of future water shortages.

Nearly every community has a stream flowing past it. Leisure-time opportunities can be available close to home, without traveling great distances.

Rivers as a means of recreational travel are increasing greatly in popularity. People are discovering that a whole network of wilderness "highways" can be explored.

Flood-plain management is recognized in many areas as a priority concern that can economically lead to decreased flood damages and to open space protection of stream frontage. In the larger sense, a "natural systems approach" toward land-use planning, which recognizes ecological and social values of the riverine environment, is being instituted in many places.

The future poses many questions about the rivers of Pennsylvania—questions that will involve the welfare of people who live there, the concerns of visitors who enjoy the waters, and the interest of those who simply admire a river and its life. Problems are present. Pollution and flood-plain development threaten the valuable qualities of many waterways. Downstream needs for water supply, flood control, and electric power generation will lead to more pressure for dams. With many conflicting goals for our streams, we need various means to meet a variety of objectives. In making difficult decisions regarding the future of Pennsylvania rivers, an understanding of the resource is important. It is hoped that this book will help us toward a better knowledge of our rivers and their meaning in our lives.

Page 10: Brandywine Creek above Lenape

Page 11: Lehigh River above Oxbow Bend

The Natural River

Where forests, farms, and towns can now be seen, waters once gleamed as a mirror through the day, or at night, the wind-tossed waves reflected the brilliance of a full moon. Today's highlands of northern Pennsylvania were a vast sea of prehistoric water, while the human race was yet unborn.

These waters of 400 million years ago were surrounded by higher ground, and the continuing cycle of evaporation, condensation, and rainfall brought another continuing but markedly slower cycle to the region now known as the Appalachian Plateau. This was the unending flow of silt and sand from land to the water. For eons it continued, layer upon layer of earth settling beneath currents and waves, burdening the floor of the ancient Pennsylvanian sea. Under the added pressure of this mighty deposit, the inner earth became heated, accumulating energy for a process of massive change.

Pressure within the earth at last reached a cataclysmic level, and the planet's crusted surface could sustain no more. The upheaval began, and once again, the earth that had been water-borne, as minute particles of soil, returned toward the sky and the open air from which it came. Underwater

West Branch Susquehanna below Montoursville

depths gave way, in this upheaval of 200 million years ago, and the northern sea of the Appalachians slowly flowed from its rising floor, channeling new routes to a lower level as waters receded. The land rose higher and higher; subterranean pressure was unceasing in its release of energy. A cycle had been completed: mountains to the sea and then to high plateau again. Evidence of the plateau can be seen from hundreds of overlooks across northern Pennsylvania—high ridges that are almost level and uniform in their elevation.

Change is unending, and the flattened mass of the Appalachian Plateau began to age. Soils of earlier erosion had consolidated into rock under waters that screened out the daylight; now the process reversed itself, as the hard surface loosened and softened into soil that could support a host of plant life in the millenia that lay ahead. Prehistoric rains pounded new clay from shale and sand from stone, and waters rinsed away the lightest fragments, carrying them downward on a new journey to a distant ocean. Forces of water wore upon the highlands, just as they do today.

In this way the rivers of northern Pennsylvania were born. From an almost indeterminate slope, they began their descent across the plateau, weaving most often from north to south. We think of rivers as beginning where the highest rainfall lands and following a well-defined route to the sea; instead, the channels and stream valleys evolved from the lowest point upward. Where a rill or drainage course formed, waters constantly washed soil away to make the channel deeper. As they did so, the water-carving action would also extend upstream, with floods and heavy runoff plucking particles of earth from headwater regions and rinsing them downward. The most erodible upland soils and rocks were the first to become dislodged, and the network of streams advanced upward following a crooked route of least resistance. Thus the many-fingered paths of the Delaware, Susquehanna, and Allegheny penetrated a plateau, and sculptured artwork of rivers infiltrated all corners of the highlands.

In later years people would gaze up in wonder at rugged slopes rising from the canyon of the Susquehanna's West Branch and other places. From the river, the depth of the eroded trough makes the plateau *seem* like a range of pointed or folded peaks. In fact, valleys were carved out rather than the mountains built up.

Rivers sway from side to side, sometimes pounding a shoreline or rocky cliff, but usually rolling over the stream bed and gently slicking the earth at its edge. Dislocated soil is carried downstream, leaving clean riverstone and bedrock behind. While the lightest silt does not hesitate on its journey to the Gulf of Mexico, the Delaware estuary, or the Chesapeake Bay, larger particles of earth do. They settle wherever the water slows, at quiet pools or on the inside of great bends, brown fragments swirling in eddies at the edge of a rapid current. Sand and gravel bars are thus formed, and islands appear where the current pursues two routes downhill.

Page 14: Clarion River at Cook Forest

Page 15: Loyalsock Creek above Barbours

During floods, the washing of soil is accelerated a thousand times or even ten thousand times. Then the rivers sweep land away in a process that has continued since the rising of the plateau, a process that created the scenic grandeur of northern Pennsylvania valleys and gorges. When the high flow overtops its banks, muddied waters become ponded on the flood plain, and the grains of suspended soil settle once again to the ground. Countless times this has been repeated, leaving broad and flat expanses of flood-borne silt, finely textured and rich in fertility. This is the lush agricultural plain of nearly all large rivers.

No process of building occurs without the destruction of something else, and so, while flood plains are being developed in one place, they are disappearing in others—the river turns upon lands it created, washing them into the current again, to be redeposited elsewhere downstream. The waterway continually changes its course. Belatedly, people have realized this as homes crash into the channel of a raging flood, the wandering current having undermined a cinder-block foundation. The river leaves its ancient channels only temporarily.

As the rivers worked deep into the plateau of northern Pennsylvania, higher lands crumbled and weathered into a surface that could hold moisture between fine particles. When the moisture froze, its volume expanded, bursting and further fracturing the earthen crust. Life took hold as lichens grasped onto stone. The process of birth and growth developed in a spartan but nourishing environment. Death and decay followed; life was breeding on life, and the surface of the plateau took on a darker, softer complexion. Roots and humus of new ages settled and tangled with finer particles of soil, and a cycle of increased fertility and greater growth began. This pattern was to continue uninterrupted until a disastrous stripping of vegetation left the soil bare. In 1880 the towering trees of centuries were cut for cities and railroad ties of a growing America, and the humus of ages was seared or destroyed by fires that raged over millions of acres on the Appalachian Plateau.

When the first Europeans set foot on the American Continent and began to clear and plow their way inland from the sea, a wilderness engulfed northern Pennsylvania. Then as now, the dominant features were rivers, which bound the region together in a branching pattern of life. Columns of conifers grew interspaced with giant hardwoods—ash, maple, beech, oak, basswood, poplar, and others. With enclosing shade, small streams seldom heated beyond the groundwater temperature of fifty-five degrees. Soil was a matted duff, full of decomposing vegetation and forest-floor organisms. It held water like a sponge, retaining the snowmelt and rains, then releasing pure water slowly. As a result, a mature pine log could float the length of Pine Creek during the summer. Today, without the softer, absorbing forest floor of the past, water speeds to the Chesapeake much faster, leaving a rocky stream bed in the dryness of August.

At the water's edge three distinct ecosystems existed. The deepest shade and quiet shelter of the forest met the sunlight of the flood plain and the aquatic life of flowing water. Tangled, impenetrable masses of willow, witch hazel, and birch thrived along the banks. They were a full-course meal for the beaver, but the aspen that grew in the sunshine was its favorite. Swallows nested in the eroding sand banks, and mallards ate from the shallows, while herons waded in open flats of warm, ponded water. Mergansers dove in deeper pools, with the osprey and eagle competing for cold and warm water fishes. Like the salmon of New England, shad migrated to headwaters each year, their backs rolling to the surface as they powerfully pushed their way upward on a journey for survival of their species—something that hasn't happened on many streams since the first Susquehanna dam was built. Elk roamed in herds along some northern rivers. They lumbered to a wild shoreline in the evening, their darkened skins and bleached antlers majestic on the glistening riffles, a sight no one sees today.

Page 18: Lower Moshannon Creek
Page 19: Moshannon Creek below route 53

Log jam, West Branch of the Susquehanna at Curwensville, 1900

Beyond the gravel bars grew the yellow birch, crowded together with their peeling papery skins and newer branches showing red tips in the sun. Then came the sycamores, giants of the riverine ecosystem. They had trunks of two, three, and four feet across, roots probing into the water beneath the alluvial soil, and branches of white, tan, and olive designs where old bark would peel and fall, showing a new and different surface beneath.

At the edge of water and land, forest and brush, most dramas of the wilderness were played. While primeval shade was welcome cover, the river's edge meant food. Not only was the slapping-tailed beaver attracted to the tender shoots and brushy landscape, but the muskrat built its home of sticks and mud here. Mink passed silently through wooded sections, and otter sneaked and slid along deep pools. Animals that preferred the forest came to the edge intermittently. On a log that protruded into the current, a raccoon would crouch to moisten its food each night. The bobcat was found, and occasionally the lynx, for these streams carry a dual identity, one of the north and one of the south.

Plant life reflects both these elements. Red pine can be found here, a northern tree. Virginia pines, native to a warmer land, stand in scattered groups. The sugar maple, hemlock, and beech that characterize New England forests do well on cooler slopes and northern exposure, while the oak and hickory forests that are the mainstay of the Virginia and Carolina Appalachians are also very common. You can find a sassafras in the sun and a balsam fir in secluded shade of a high bog.

The climatic differences that cause the diverse blending of plant life are accentuated by the steep descent from plateau to river bottom—a pattern of topography that is prevalent on many north central rivers, like the Sinnemahoning, Pine Creek, and Loyalsock. While frigid air and northerly winter winds bite and rage on the heights, valleys of five hundred or one thousand feet below lie in comparative mildness. Another effect of the elevation differences is a lowland fog and morning mist occurring almost daily in the summertime. Unable to rise and unable to diffuse itself, moisture-laden air shrouds the narrow valleys until a higher sun can penetrate.

The north central highlands

A picture of these untouched rivers could not be painted today. The vast wilderness that thrived on itself cannot be imagined by people who have seen only a woodlot of virgin timber. Some parks have fortunately been preserved so we may see the forest heritage of Pennsylvania, but they stand more as popular museums, only hints of the immense wilds and forever-winding waters that once flourished here. Primitive and rugged high country of some western states has been preserved, but it cannot compare to the fertile richness of the darkened forest floor and the gently glimmering brilliance of northern Pennsylvania rivers only two hundred years ago.

A character is left, however, and wherever rivers flow free we can see a part of these earlier waterways. Because of their scarcity, the wildest reaches have become invaluable as samples and relics of the riverine environment that Indians joined and that early explorers and settlers faced.

The rivers of Pennsylvania include these reminders and more. Their shorelines are now traveled by railroads. Coal formed in ancient ages is mined from the plateau. Communities stand on flood plains and high banks. Dams have put an end to some parts of the rivers, flattening their flow for miles. What is a river of Pennsylvania like today? Let's take a look.

Opposite: Bear Run, tributary to Pine Creek

The Susquehanna Basin

A River Voyage:
The Susquehanna and Its West Branch

Through a mist not yet touched by early sunlight, we began the journey. The world ahead of us lay obscured; it seemed two-dimensional, with depth missing. We listened to the rush of flowing water, then peered into grayness that seemed prehistoric, like artists' drawings of the first day that amphibian creatures became reptiles and stepped forth onto a steaming rocky landscape. Water swirled and the air grew patchy, so that we could see through voids to a wooded shoreline of dripping hemlocks and shining rhododendron. Rivers are mysterious, but never more so than in fog. Each stroke of the paddle, each instant of movement brought another discovery, a rock to miss, a merganser moving away from us. Distant scenes gradually became recognizable, like an image through binoculars that are slowly being focused.

On this trip there were four of us, in two canoes, my wife Cindy and I in one, Bob and Marna Banks in the other. This wasn't my first journey down the West Branch of the Susquehanna, but somehow, the experience always seems new. For a while, I thought the feeling was caused by seeing different things and by paddling alternate routes. The changing seasons, weather, and wildlife make each cruise unique. Later I realized that the water itself, so foreign to our landlocked lives, makes every voyage new and exciting. Some of us can swim across the English Channel or the Susquehanna River, but we are still land creatures. Though water is common to us, it is mysterious, ephemeral, evaporating into the sky, then falling again out of nowhere. The greatest thrill is the motion. On land, only *we* move, but on rivers, we move *and* our highway moves. To deal with both-as-one is an art. Those who travel rivers often use the phrase "reading the water." It means to know what the stream is doing and what it will do to *you*. And so, during those first few minutes, the solid tie to land is broken and the tenuous relationship to water is established. Ready or not, travel begins as the current clutches its new partner, and we are off on a journey to the sea.

Opposite: Sterling Run in the West Branch Canyon

Canoeing on the upper West Branch

This river is one of four in northern Pennsylvania that have sufficient flow for a summer voyage. All are worth traveling, but the upper West Branch is a favorite. Unlike the Delaware and Allegheny, both branches of the Susquehanna can easily be followed to salt water. This ambition is complicated by days of polluted tidal flow on the Delaware and by 2,000 miles of flat and dirty current below the Allegheny. Mountains of the West Branch are continuously higher and the shoreline is wilder than nearly any river of its size in Pennsylvania. Sometimes the midsummer flow is too sparse for rockless canoeing, but this time we had high and fast water from our starting point below Shawville.

At Moshannon Falls the pace of the river became swift. I thought of the time near Rolling Stone when we met an adventuresome crew who asked, "What happens if you go over the falls?" Cindy explained that if you go over the falls you won't know it, that in fact it's only a small rapids. We splashed our way through, the spray of the river feeling good now that the morning was warm. Below the "falls" the West Branch is joined by Moshannon Creek, a turbulent stream whose bed is stained deep orange from years of acid mine drainage but which still holds values of scenery, wildness, and challenging rapids.

Another hour of drifting took us to Karthaus, a typical Pennsylvania coal town. Deep miners went to stripping long ago, scraping the hills for veins near the top. Coal dust and ordinary dust have left their mark on the village and countryside. Still we are glad to be here, for Karthaus is at the head of the West Branch Canyon, a section of the river with vast complexes of ridge lines, ravines, and shadows. Forming a rugged gorge, layers of forested mountains are seemingly set one upon another as winding waters unfold view after towering view. The pools were as clear as fine crystal, but there were no game fish because of the low pH from acid-bearing shales at the mines. It would be like expecting a trout to live in a cup of coffee.

At Buttermilk Rapids, Cindy and I drew our canoe into swirls and back channels just for the fun of it, while Bob and Marna followed, cutting behind one rock and then around another, always plotting to go somewhere just a little more exciting than the Susquehanna would normally send us. By now it was early afternoon, so at the cool, shaded mouth of Sterling Run, we stopped for lunch and felt like staying a week.

It was sheer summer pleasure as we swam and drifted, Cindy and I in our 16½-foot Mad River canoe and Bob and Marna in a 17-foot Grumman that we borrowed from Ed McCarthy, who outfits and guides canoeists and rafters through Pine Creek Canyon. Earlier in the year I had paddled my smaller 13-foot canoe next to weather-beaten, canyon-molded Ed, age sixty-seven. I told him of our plans for a long journey to the Chesapeake. Interrupting me with his usual enthusiasm, Ed said, "Tim, take this craft; she's a doll in heavy waters. You can load five hundred pounds with room for a Strauss waltz, and a mighty headwind won't send you back to Williamsport, Jersey Shore, Lock Haven." A wrinkled smile broke across his suntanned face. "In your small boat, you'd run as scared as a pregnant fox!" McCarthy himself is unrepeatable and inseparable from the twenty-three miles of water he calls home. His wary stare downstream, his forceful paddle in the muddy crosscurrents of swollen springtime floods, and his mad exuberance on a day when the sun shines set him apart as a personality in a time when most people seem pretty much the same.

Like the canyon that Ed runs, this section of river is an outstanding example of Appalachian water. Spruce Run, Burns Run, Yost Run, and a dozen others fall off the mountainsides, unspoiled by rusted signs of acid mine drainage that are so prevalent in the upper basins of many central and western Pennsylvania streams. Valley walls enclose you in a world shared only with friends and a railroad, and good camp sites are plentiful.

The height of mountains increases as you follow the river north from Karthaus. Rocky cliffs hang above Bougher Run, and Twin Hollows form a complex backdrop. Scenery is most spectacular near Yost Run, where ridge lines are 900 feet above, and the gentle current of the river weaves against one shoreline, then the other, an ageless but changing pattern as waters of the highlands fall to the sea. This is the site of the proposed Keating Dam, a project identified by the Army Corps of Engineers in 1934. In 1977 it was reevaluated, but not recommended for construction. With political pressure, however, the project could threaten to permanently flood the West Branch Canyon.

Burnt hashbrowns and overdone eggs tasted delicious in the morning. When you're camping and therefore hungry, you don't even notice, except that the food is a little blacker than it ought to be. A slight stiffness from yesterday and from the chill air of a restful night made us ready for a hot cup of coffee or tea and the savory, smoky taste of anything that will fit in the frying pan. When I eat finely prepared food, I often reflect a little and wish I could enjoy it as much as I enjoy burnt potatoes on a riverbank.

Our expedition of four plus dogs slipped into the water, drifted a moment, then felt the grip of the current. The character of the West Branch changes dramatically at Keating where the Sinnemahoning joins to form a larger river that bends eastward. Renovo marks yet a greater difference. Strip mines, roads, and cabins we had seen, but here the first sizable town of the voyage meets the stream, stark and unpolished. The confines of rugged mountain and narrow valley push buildings to the edge.

Hyner Mountain has a high and curiously capped summit overlooking the West Branch Valley, and on a gravel beach within sight of the peak we

West Branch Susquehanna below Renovo

stopped for lunch. The first canoe of the day came in sight around an upstream bend; looking closely, we saw it carried three boys, probably high school age or so. All three pulled hard on their paddles, forcing the fifteen-foot overloaded boat to surge, then sink. The gunwales or sides of the canoe would rock as the load shifted this way, then that, each time narrowly escaping the river. The three canoeists, wearing swimming trunks, shouted hello. We were soon behind them, drifting into McCloskey Island riffles, one of the better rapids on that part of the Susquehanna. As if in slow motion replay, the canoe shipped one wave over the side, then another. In rapid succession, despite desperate squirming, the boys fell out as the craft rolled. It was no tragedy, so my first concern was to get some good pictures.

"Pull up there where those life jackets are floating, Bob," I shouted. As he deftly swung across the whitewater, snatching stray life jackets from the waves and returning them, I shot film. Cindy backpaddled effectively, keeping our boat in flatter waters. At the instant of lost balance, when the canoe had capsized, I caught a glimpse of beer cans flashing in the sun and then gone to the waves. Rendezvousing with Bob and Marna below the island, I saw them again—on the bottom of their canoe.

"My conscience just wouldn't let me give them back," Bob said, pointing to the two six-packs. "Without all that extra weight they'd have made it through that riff, and next time they're just liable to drown."

Finding a place to sleep that night was a problem. Between Hyner and Lock Haven, the river offers few sites. With the road to the south and railroad to the north, we had our choice of cars, trains, or cabins. Choosing none of them, I scouted a few likely looking areas, only to find a maze of eight-foot-high undergrowth and poison ivy—a sweating haven for mosquitoes. By unexplainable luck, Bob struck upon a spot used by other campers. There we beached, cooked, and enjoyed the sunset.

Early in the still mist of Saturday morning, our canoes rippled quietly through the two-mile pool of Lock Haven Dam where motorboats were docked along the river's edge. We moved forward with caution, as one must when nearing water-over-the-top impoundments. The trouble is that very little can be seen or heard from above. Structures are invisible. A smooth sheet of water slips over the breast of the dam with no riffle but with alarming velocity and force. An anarchy of eddies and whirlpools froth and foam below, all of which are screened from the boater's view. A roar uncommon to the Susquehanna drowns out voices below the dam, but above and on the approach, the sound of falling waters is a muted and seemingly distant warning. After portaging the dam, we began a forty-mile section that parallels Bald Eagle Mountain, the northernmost of high central Pennsylvania ridges.

Even though the water above Lock Haven had an acid content from coal mining that rendered the river unfit for most fish, it was still remarkably clear. The channel would run dark and blue, a submerged paddle blade showing wooden grain in distinct detail. Then, suddenly and soundlessly, the yellow-brown volume of Bald Eagle Creek met the larger stream. It was the end of clear water for the voyage. We could see the silt and waste-laden current along the southern shore, and at the mix line where Bald Eagle met West Branch, it was like pouring cream into coffee. Mud clung together in lacy fingers, penetrating the river, then flowed downhill in a mildly agitated mixture, soon diffusing throughout the water. Though the river was of much greater volume than the creek, the color of suspended earth soon took over the entire waterway with little apparent mutation or dilution. We remembered the thunder and lightning that had driven us off the river on the second night, and the ominous storm clouds that billowed in the southern sky that evening. The Bald Eagle basin had been hit by a summer storm, and now we saw the results. Much of the limestone valley is farmland, a major source of silt in heavy rains, and extensive highway construction was under way for the "Susquehanna Beltway," involving both sides and the stream bed of Fishing Creek, a major tributary.

Worse than mud, Kepone and Mirex have been found in the fish of Spring Creek, another Bald Eagle tributary that flows past State College and through Bellefonte. Caught near the Ruetgers-Nease Chemical Company, the fish showed concentrations of toxic chemicals exceeding United States Food and Drug Administration safety levels. Spring Creek is regarded as one of our better trout streams, and many anglers have been to Fisherman's Paradise, near Bellefonte. The Fish Commission has posted the area most-affected by Ruetgers-Nease, warning people not to eat the fish. The Department of Environmental Resources is suing the company to clean up their old waste lagoons, which are percolating into groundwater and the creek. Bulk dumping of Kepone into Virginia's James River brought public outrage in the mid 1970s, when it was learned that the chemical's caustic effects may last for one hundred years or more, contaminating Chesapeake Bay seafood whenever rough waters stir the poisoned sludge from the James River bed.

After stopping for supplies in Jersey Shore, we fell into a new rhythm of paddling that quickly took us to the Crane Island riffles. For the first time since above Lock Haven, the West Branch narrowed into a swift and tumbling chute. Now, carrying the additional loads of Bald Eagle Creek, Pine Creek, and many lesser streams, the river rolled with a new force. A quiet but relentless pressure engulfed us as the great volume of swollen and muddied waters pushed from behind, swept underneath, and crested in three-foot rollers at both sides.

In dramatic contrast, the riffle ends at the Williamsport stillwater. Impounded by the low dam eleven miles downstream, the Susquehanna quickly settles to a flattened surface. Now that stillness was broken by the sound of motorboats, waterskiers, houseboats, and fishingboats. They

West Branch Susquehanna below Jersey Shore

ripped, roared, putt-putted, and choked. Some gave us the courtesy of slowing or keeping a distance to reduce their wake, and some didn't. We passed the first proliferation of riverfront trailers—mostly replacements from flood destruction in 1972. Many were bought with so-called disaster relief funds—money intended for needy flood victims but also used to put new weekend trailers back on the flood plain where they will be damaged again.

Crawling like ants over the Linden railroad bridge, boys were scaling the stone pier, sitting on a side rail, and climbing iron trusses to the very top. After staring for long moments into the waves, they would leap to enthralling dives from the steel girders. Standing by as backstage actors, silhouetted against the late afternoon sun, younger kids watched and awaited more courage.

Squatter's Island, as it is called, is a long and slender haven of wildness in the city of Williamsport. Here we landed and found a welcoming sign of the Department of Environmental Resources, saying that overnight camping was permitted. Amid ancient remains of stone cribbing that held the 1880 log boom of Williamsport in place, the island had been covered with squatter shacks of canvas or wooden construction. The Hurricane Agnes flood of 1972 swept them all away, and the Department has prohibited development on the state-owned land. It's now a paradise for the modern-day Huck Finn—an excitement of aged willows with rope swings, grapevines, forest, and wildflowers. But Huck wasn't there, and we had the place

Diving from the Linden railroad bridge

to ourselves. Ghostly remains of a trailer lay with one end on the ground and the other wedged high between two trees, its savagely battered hulk pointing to the sky. Amid solitude, songbirds, and low evening sunlight, this former home served as a torn reminder of a river's force.

The next day at seven o'clock, in a sullen mist, we beached and unloaded for portage around the Williamsport Dam. Water was high and swirling below the spillway. We carried around the newly repaired impoundment, stopping long enough to see an angler pull in and gently return a ten-inch bass. The Susquehanna at Williamsport has been making a healthy come-back since the last major acid slug from the Barnes and Tucker mine in 1970. Walleye fishing is excellent, and brown trout have been caught. To chance the chaos of water below the dam would have likely ended in swamped and overturned canoes, so knee deep we waded the boats through a maze of boulders, willows, and snagged driftwood that is usually above water.

Loyalsock Creek entered the river over a broad, sweeping gravel bar at Montoursville. Its crystal clear, shining northern waters met the yellowed current from the south and west. We stared down at gravel five feet below, then plunged headlong into the last clean tributary of notable size on the entire river. All the others were moribund in comparison, lacking the chilling exuberance of that beautiful stream.

The Susquehanna between Montoursville and Muncy has many distinctive features. Leaving the Loyalsock, we knifed our canoes through a riffle, barely fitting between rocks in a small chute. Nothing has been built in the eight-mile section except one cabin and the railroad. Among large rivers, this is one of the most significant undeveloped reaches in Pennsylvania. I thought of a trip we took in April when we saw four ospreys, four mergansers, three wood ducks, two scaups, two grebes, and a ring-billed gull. They were just passing through, headed north, but we also saw the kingfisher, the great blue heron, six mallards, three deer, one muskrat, and a host of more common wildlife that live along the river year round.

Always there are riffles at the islands—Birch, Racetrack, King, and Brock, and water levels continually change them. In high flows, large waves roll through the main channel to the south of the islands, while remote and tree-lined passages to the north may be open for the cautious canoeist. Lower water means the small passages are closed. Rocks and logs become

West Branch Susquehanna at Loyalsock Creek

The West Branch below Montoursville

obstacles that were buried before. We took the south side of Racetrack Island, picking our way with special care through a channel that was riddled with stumps and drowned sycamore trees. If caution is used, it doesn't take a great deal of experience to float the wild reach, but even for those who have piloted hundreds of miles, the size of the Susquehanna gives its own exciting sensation. It's a lot of water for those who are accustomed to smaller streams.

This was our day of big mileage. Paddling at a steady pace, we comfortably passed Muncy at noon, Montgomery at 1:30, then Watsontown, Milton, and Lewisburg in turn. Between the twin bridges of Interstate 80 swam a gang of kids, dwarfed by monolithic structures of concrete and steel. Their shouts were drowned out by truck traffic over the bridge, and I thought, "Somehow, something's gone from the old swimming hole." Lewisburg's church spires are traditional landmarks, marking the approach to that town from far upstream. We stopped there at suppertime, relaxed in the borough's park atop a high bank, and cooked dinner on a public fireplace.

Blue Mountain glowed in the sunset as we neared Northumberland and Sunbury. A golden sky behind us reflected soft, mellow ripples for a soothing and relaxing forty-fifth mile of the day. That was our fifth night out, and suddenly it was a different river where we slept, as the West Branch met the Main Branch. We had a feeling for the changes, the rhythm, the life of northern Pennsylvania waters. With their beauty we found ugliness, with wildness, civilization, and with peacefulness, we'd found excitement, an energetic happiness. Sunburnt and weathered, we felt as though we belonged. We couldn't imagine doing anything else tomorrow but pulling a canoe down a massive and widening river. A wary eye downstream was now second nature, and a long sweep of the paddle—one every other second—had grown to be a habit and a love. It was as though we could go on forever to a new sunrise, a different land to see, and always a new day to explore. Mountain rivers have haunted me since. The bend that splashes or shimmers out of sight is the one where life goes on all the rivers of Pennsylvania.

The Susquehanna at the Penns Creek confluence

Just as a wild, disordered topography marks the Susquehanna valley in its northern and western reaches, so do the graceful, picturesque ridges of central Pennsylvania leave an image of their own. Bald Eagle was the first of the central mountains and one of the most classic in the state. Beginning far to the west, the borderline ridge looms over the river for forty miles and ends at Muncy. Borderline, I say, because this mountain marks the start of the Ridge and Valley Region, a series of high, scenic ridges interspersed with rolling, fertile valleys of limestone farms and meadows. Blue Mountain at Sunbury, Little Mountain below Selinsgrove, Hooflander at Dalmatia, Mahantango at Liverpool, Berry at Millersburg, Peters Cove at Duncannon, Second Mountain at Dauphin, and another Blue Mountain at Harrisburg—all are landmarks to the heartland of Pennsylvania. Unlike the continual folding and winding of the highlands, these are singular and shapely, standing alone to be admired from a distance. South of those peaks we would bisect the gentle and rolling piedmont, and finally, below the Conowingo Dam would be coastal plain and tidewater.

We rose early from beneath the railroad bridge where we'd slept. Nightmares of freight trains didn't compare to the grisly scene of water we faced. As we approached the night before, we sensed a change, but now, in the hazy reflection of dawn, we saw the nauseating brown-yellow chunks of foam and unusually thick particles of solids. Outdoing Bald Eagle Creek, the upper Susquehanna, or North Branch, waters assumed distinction as the ugliest of the trip. Like Bald Eagle, the North Branch experienced heavy rains several days before, which caused the water to look worse than usual.

The first order of business was to move ourselves to the western side of the river, into better-looking water. The two Susquehanna branches remained discrete to Harrisburg and beyond—over fifty miles. Dark brown waters of the North Branch flowed down the eastern side, and lighter waters of the West Branch stayed along that shore.

For our third portage, we landed our canoes next to the Sunbury Fabridam, an inflated fabric dam. State park personnel were scuba diving for missing park property, thought to have been thrown into the river by vandals. Neither the divers nor the crowd of catfish, carp, and bass fishermen had any luck.

With a deep-pitched resonance and a belch of smoke, a new kind of landmark appeared: the electric power plant. The Pennsylvania Power and Light Company's facility at Shamokin Dam was the first of many; we'd see them again at Three Mile Island, York Haven, Brunner Island, Safe Harbor, Holtwood, Peach Bottom, and Conowingo (Maryland). They would become the dominant feature of the river below Harrisburg; this one was just a forerunner.

That afternoon was a squelcher. Sunburnt and sweaty, we pulled the canoes onto a grassy beach at Liverpool. With Eli on his leash, we headed to the corner store for a good chilling milkshake. This small-town namesake

Susquehanna below Sunbury

of Liverpool, England, held an interest greater than its size. In the slow pace of a summer afternoon, porches were full of oldtimers sitting, staying out of indoor heat and outdoor work. Not everyone was as lucky, though; one man spent the day tearing the roof off an old, weathered barn. The cashier at the grocery store talked of a Harrisburger who wanted to come north to Liverpool, "to get away from it." The Good Samaritan Hotel remains from long ago, when canal passengers would spend the night on their way to Sunbury or Williamsport. Curiously, Liverpool is a one-sided town; the west side of the main street is full of houses, the east side nearly vacant. The canal filled the space on the river, or eastern side, and now Highways 11 and 15 carry a different kind of traffic over the same route. Mahantango Mountain stands in rugged prominence across the wide and rocky Susquehanna from the town, and downstream is the steeple of a Millersburg church. I hesitated only a moment or so to take a picture of the Liverpool Bank, but during that time an off-duty clerk stopped his car to find out "just what my business was, anyway." Small town protectiveness soon changed to friendliness as we talked about the river.

Swinging our canoes to Millersburg across wide, shallow flats, we found the real riverfront town. With no road or railroad interrupting its view to the water, the hamlet had an integrity and oneness with the Susquehanna. The riverfront park at the Fish Commission's access area was a community center. A gang of shouting children ran on the wet, slick surface of a log and leaped into the current. They seemed to care nothing about an eddy

Millersburg Ferry

Bob Banks, Susquehanna River below Millersburg

of yellow foam and blackened refuse behind their plankway. Neither sudsed-up water nor the raucous play of the kids disturbed the flock of ducks, which swam just beyond the splashing divers. Townspeople came to the riverfront to walk or to sit and watch, while river people like us wandered up the street to buy another late-afternoon refreshment. Across the waters the sternwheel ferryboat pushed its way toward us, water rising at its wake to catch the flash of 6:00 P.M. sunlight. As the ferry drew closer, watchers on shore took closer looks, shaded their eyes with cupped hands, and smiled at the pilot's adeptness as he swung the ferry to dock. Jack Dillman owns and runs the fleet of two boats, one being an old "coal digger" and the other a new custom-built model. Only four sternwheel ferryboats remain in the country. Dillman's career as a riverman began when he was eight.

"The current you can see, but wind is the worst since you can't tell what it'll do. Northeast always makes for trouble. If we get blown on the rocks, usually I can get it off myself, but sometimes four or five of us get out there up to our waists to pry her off." But groundings are scarce, and Jack has never had serious trouble.

Having to move on and make camp before dark, we paddled toward the shadow of Berry Mountain. An evening sun cast its golden light over the river, and as swirls and eddies gleamed with the sun's warmth, the sound of whitewater grew in a slow crescendo. "The best water of the trip is just ahead," Bob said, and we swung the canoes to the right, narrowly missing a

Photo by John Lazenby

Rockville Railroad Bridge, Susquehanna River above Harrisburg

submerged rock. I took the camera and began shooting pictures of the action that was all around us. Unlike most Susquehanna riffles, this one didn't quickly end but continued plunging on and on.

We spent the night on an island and left in fog early Tuesday. From Clarks Ferry Bridge and the mouth of the Juniata, there was just enough whitewater to keep us alert. Above the massive Rockville railroad bridge, the whole world suddenly began to froth around us. With a few excited strokes we saved ourselves, but we had nearly lost control in one of the sudden and steeply dropping outcrops that cross the river. The story of a Renovo native came to mind. In 1917 the river adventurer canoed from home to Harrisburg, then capsized in rocky waters. Having lost most of his gear, he ended up catching the next train going upriver.

Shielded from Harrisburg by the trees of McCormick Island, we drifted silently within twenty-five feet of a dozen Canada geese. Our lunch stop was on the western side of an island—"Poison Ivy Paradise," we called it. You couldn't step out of the boat without stepping in the itchy stuff. Like Squatter's Island in Williamsport, those city-owned islands were vacant of campers, children fishing, one-day runaways, and rowboat adventurers. They must be around, but where?

The dam in Harrisburg sinks a boater every now and then, its drop be-ing nearly invisible from waters above. Not paying attention, we soon were within a paddle's throw of the spillway. Making a sharp turn, we headed for the eastern shore, where the spillway is reduced to an incline. At lower

Harrisburg, from the Susquehanna River

levels it could be negotiated, but now it promised a bath in stinking water. Tying ropes to bow and stern, we carefully walked the canoes through the chute, avoiding the labor of another unloading and reloading operation. At the lower end of the capital city, sewage and other wastes drove us to the western shore and into cleaner waters.

A sultry and humid haze added little to the next twelve miles of paddling—a reach that was the least scenic of the trip and in fact the only stretch of continued ugliness in the whole river. Lower Harrisburg, Steelton, and Olmstead Airport covered the eastern shore with industry, earthen fill, and junked wreckage. We passed the Three Mile Island nuclear power plant, which was still under construction. In many ways, that was a turning point of the voyage. There would be good water ahead, and we'd even see another osprey, but the squalor of the river that afternoon was a bitter illness from which we would never really recover. There were no more Sterling Runs for drinking water, no more Loyalsocks for chilling swims, no more picturesque Mahantango Mountains, no more Liverpools or Millersburg Ferries, and not even very many more islands creating remote back channels. Mostly there would be power plants with monolithic profiles, transmission lines sweeping toward distant homes and factories, and dams impounding the river into flatwater of half-day cruises.

Hill Island, just below Middletown, is distinguished as the only hill island in the river, reaching 230 feet above the water's edge. We shot the rapids around the west side and entered the headwaters of York Haven Dam.

Photo by John Lazenby

Three-Mile Island nuclear plant (1977), Susquehanna River at Goldsboro

The impoundment is built at the site of Conewago Falls (not to be confused with Conowingo), which used to be a series of steep rapids, dropping
twenty-three feet in three-fourths of a mile. For nearly two miles the
breastwork of the structure extends *up and down* the Susquehanna while
crossing it. We docked at the hydroelectric power plant, and meeting a
maintenance crew, I asked, "Where's the best place to carry canoes
around?"

The Metropolitan Edison employee cocked his hard hat, thought, and
then pointed. "Go across the walkway, down the tracks, past the power
plant. Get onto a service road, and then down below, you'll see the river."
We started thinking of two loads each for gear, wishing we'd made the trip
seventy-three years ago when we could have shot Conewago Falls and
taken our chances on a cold spill. "Wait a minute," he said. "A while back,
some canoes came through, and we picked them up with a crane and carried them around the dam. Go see the superintendent, and he'll tell you
what we can do."

Twenty minutes later, we paddled up to a loading dock, fastened straps
around the boats, and watched Don Leakway and his friendly crew swing
our canoes out of the water and onto a flatbed truck. We unloaded below
the dam and set out again for the Chesapeake. It turned out that law required the utility to portage canoes—the dam blocks the river, so they carry
us around. All the other power companies did the same thing.

It was noon when we pulled our canoes onto the beach at Columbia. A

Penn Central crew took advantage of the setting, having lunch and a few hands of poker. One tall railroader intercepted me as I went back to the canoe for my maps, and we ended up telling the men of our trip. "Everybody used to canoe on the river," one said, "but more people have motorboats now."

Hard on our backs was a northwesterly wind as we drifted into Lake Clarke—the impoundment of Safe Harbor Dam. The river broadened to an immense width and spaciousness. Sailboats darted with the wind, then tacked and cut a ragged groove in choppy waters. The dam was soon ahead, while an ominous and blackening sky caught up from the rear. Amid a mountain of accumulated driftwood, tin cans, and dead fish, we tried to beach the canoes, having to haul them over the trash for lack of any other landing area. Cold raindrops the size of green peas came with thunderclaps and flashes. Derelict cranes and an endless array of scrap metal surrounded us, offering the perfect lightning target. The place was no "safe harbor" to us, so we were interested in getting out of there, quick. We'd just started the long walk to the power plant office to ask for our portage, when a uniformed guard drove up. One thing led to another, and we ended up under a shelter along Conestoga Creek for the night. The plant supervisor wanted us off the river and away from the plant for safety and so offered special permission for us to spend the night in the company's park nearby.

Settling into a quiet nighttime rain, the storm passed, and a brilliant morning welcomed us for our last day on the Susquehanna. By 11:00 A.M. we beached at Holtwood Dam. Water flows over the top of Holtwood, making it a hazard to river travelers in the past. Billboards now warn approaching boaters, and a shield has been constructed to keep unsuspecting tourists from getting too close. A few years ago, a couple on their first date raced two other speedboats to the dam, and not watching the water ahead, they sailed over the sixty-foot wall of concrete. Miraculously landing rightside up, they reached for nearby life jackets and swam away without an injury. The boat sank, but the couple later got married. As the local media put it, "They're going to take another chance."

The afternoon was a wild one. Our course through expansive Conowingo Dam included the stiffest paddling, highest winds, and most turbulent waters of the journey. Two, three, and then four-foot high waves rolled beneath us, our boats pitching, surfing, and bobbing like corks. Luckily the wind was still behind us, otherwise we would have been forced in. Not wanting to be far from an emergency landing, we clung to the western shore. A stiffness and exhaustion moved up my back and into my shoulder as we pushed around the exposed and windiest point of land where Peach Bottom nuclear plant is built on rock and earthen fill. We found a rhythm for surfing; power strokes would send the canoes skimming down the breaking crest of a wave for an exhilarating instant, then back into the trough we'd go.

Holtwood Dam, the lower Susquehanna

Relief came with Glenn Cove, the marina where we landed and telephoned for portage around Conowingo Dam. A utility truck came in an hour or so, hauling us to a relaunching area. Conowingo is on the "fall line," or that point where tides and upstream travel end. In 1608 John Smith sailed to Conowingo Falls, but no further.

In an early evening stillness, we entered the final phase of our journey. The Susquehanna current took its last plunge downward; low rapids would swirl for only another mile. Seagulls and sailboats thrived on a flatter arm of the Atlantic Ocean ahead. Two hundred and forty-five miles of river had brought us to elevation zero. In much the same way that we had loaded and embarked at Karthaus, Lock Haven, and Williamsport, we cast off the Maryland shore, only now for the last time, to see the end of central Pennsylvania water. Two railroad bridges and the monumental highway crossings of Interstate 95 and U.S. Route 40 stole that last final breath of peacefulness that might have gone with the broadening of river into bay. Instead they accented the difference, making it possible for an old riverfront local to respond to a question by saying, "Yep, right there, the last bridge, that's where the Susquehanna River ends and the Chesapeake Bay begins."

We could see the end below and the bay with its different world of water beyond the river's flow. Salt water mixes with fresh, forming a different ecosystem and a way of life unlike any we had seen on the Susquehanna. Yachts and beaches, tides and endless waters—none of it is like the river, but none of it would be there without the river.

And so, with a certain completeness to our paddle stroke, with the fullness of nine days of sun and eight nights of listening to water as it passed our camp site in a continuous drop, and with visions of the Pennsylvania heartland forever in mind, we finished our cruise on that quiet evening.

The variety of scenes and the differences between them drove us to get on the river and ride it to the sea. A chilling taste of Sterling Run in the West Branch Canyon, the rapids at Millersburg, a sultry afternoon's heat at Steelton, and the orange-blanketed sky at the Chesapeake vitalized our lives again. Seeing the river world around us gave a sense of discovery that many of us enjoyed only when we were younger.

We know the river best when we see it firsthand. Draining the waters of our lands, the river gives us, and all the places we know, a timeless continuity. In the past it brought logs, rafts, canal boats, and settlers. It brought shad runs, before dams blocked the migrating fish's journey to spawning beds. It brought floods, in 1889, 1936, 1946, and 1972. Today it brings over three million people a year to its edge for recreation.

The next time we make the trip, will we still have the wild West Branch Canyon? Will bass and walleye be thriving at Williamsport, or will an acid slug poison the river as before? On those long stretches of water where you see nothing but islands and mountains—how many more power plants, bridges, and industries will we see instead? Change is unavoidable, but changes on the Susquehanna may show a different kind of progress. The next time we go down to the Chesapeake, or the next time you do, a wilderness might remain—not through neglect but because people want to keep it that way. You might see a trout darting above Lock Haven, and the orange stain of mining might have faded from the rocks. Bald Eagle Creek might run without the suffocating load of silt that we saw. Instead of a tangled web of power lines, maybe a lighter hand will have put new lines where they won't be seen. Maybe the trailers will be above the flood plain, leaving low shores for high waters.

At our fifth camp site, we had looked at the dark brown river and thought of an early canoeist quenching his thirst with Susquehanna water. That day was long ago, and it won't come again in our lifetime, but we just might be able to swim without wading through foam, like the children in Millersburg. Yes, we'll look forward to going another time, and maybe a wilder, more scenic, less polluted Susquehanna will carry us to the sea. But for you, go now, because you might never see it this good again.

Protection for the Waters of Pine Creek

More than any other stream of northern Pennsylvania, Pine Creek has received the attention it deserves. Too much, some people would say. "With all those reports and studies you could paper the creek from Galeton to the Susquehanna River," a resident of the area remarked at a public meeting in 1976. Some fruitless efforts have been undertaken along with other necessary and productive ones—enough that the case of "Tiadaghton"* has been a valuable experiment in what works and what doesn't.

October 2, 1968
Most of the talk at the time dealt with Hubert Humphrey and Richard Nixon. One or the other would soon be elected President. News articles included nothing about rivers: "Hanoi Aides Reject Humphrey's Plan"; "House Ethics Panel Will Study Votes Cast for Absent Members"; "Gallup Poll Finds Many Traditionally Democratic Voting Groups Are Switching to Nixon"; "Vassar Going Coed; Plans Williams Link." In an action that attracted no headlines, Lyndon Baines Johnson signed the National Wild and Scenic Rivers Act into law. The absence of theatrics and excitement was understandable. Five years earlier, in 1963, a study of the Interior and Agriculture departments included the seeds of a National Rivers System. Groups like the Wilderness Society pushed the program, and Representative John Saylor of Johnstown, Pennsylvania, sponsored legislation. Most people agreed that the idea was a good one. It had the support of conservation interests, yet it didn't raise strenuous objections from groups involved in dams or river development, since the law posed few major threats to foreseeable water resource projects. The secretaries of Interior and Agriculture recommended the bill, saying, "We have enjoyed wild rivers as have our forebears for generations. Our descendants deserve the same opportunity." The Act states:

> It is hereby declared to be the policy of the United States that certain selected rivers of the Nation which, with their immediate environments, possess outstandingly remarkable scenic, recreational, geologic, fish and wildlife, historic, cultural, or other similar values, shall be preserved in free-flowing condition, and that they and their immediate environments shall be protected for the benefit and enjoyment of present and future generations. The Congress declares that the established national policy of dam and other construction at appropriate sections of the rivers of the United States needs to be complemented by a policy that would preserve other selected rivers or sections thereof

---

*An Indian word meaning "river of pines." There is a controversy over the location of the true Tiadaghton. Some evidence suggests that the Indians' Tiadaghton was Lycoming Creek and that white men moved the name further west to "stretch" the treaty agreement.

Pine Creek below the village of Blackwell

in their free-flowing condition to protect the water quality of such rivers and to fulfill other vital national conservation purposes.

The force of the Act was apparent:

The Federal Power Commission shall not license the construction of any dam, water conduit, reservoir powerhouse, transmission line, or other project works . . . on any river . . . which is hereafter designated for inclusion in that system, and no department or agency of the United States shall assist by loan, grant, license, or otherwise the construction of any water resources project that would have a direct and adverse effect on the values for which the river was established.

In other words, no dams.

Eight rivers were granted such protection on October 2, 1968, and twenty-seven others were identified as possible National Rivers, their status to be determined by Congress or the Secretary of Interior after study was completed. Pine Creek was one of those twenty-seven, along with the Clarion, lower Allegheny, upper Delaware, and Youghiogheny of Pennsylvania. The upper West Branch of the Susquehanna narrowly missed inclusion.

Four years later, the national study began. Since the end of the logging era in 1909, the creek had been a popular fishing stream, and over the years millions of tourists viewed the "Grand Canyon of Pennsylvania" from overlooks near Wellsboro. Now Pine Creek was considered nationally significant, and this distinction gave rise to interests and actions of importance.

August 18, 1969

On those hot summer days the flies hover and swarm, and it's hard to keep them out of your eyes. In a routine he had followed for thirty-five years, the forestry professor cleaned his pipe and lit it again, cherry-scented smoke driving the worst pesky bugs away. This was at least the hundredth time that he untied an old wooden canoe from his car roof and carried it to the edge of Pine Creek. He patiently loaded the craft with gear, and in the slow, deliberate manner that takes hold after one's fiftieth season, he pushed the red canoe away from Sugar Island, leaving his car near the site where John English and his family built the first homestead in the valley two hundred years before.

Many times Fletcher had sensed a difference in Pine Creek, but as everything changes to people who live long enough and look hard enough, he didn't give it much thought. Today was different. A blanket of algae completely covered the creek bottom, unlike anything the forester had seen in the fifty-four years that he had visited the family camp site. "The water's low and the temperature's high. But this comes from more than natural causes." He continued to reason while he paddled. When the canoe scraped the stone beach at Fletcher Camp, his idea had formed.

"A total water study is needed," he decided, "one that can identify the cause of overfertilization in Pine Creek, one that would reach to the headwaters." The upstream towns of Wellsboro and Galeton were scarcely regarded as part of the same creek—they were so different from the valley, and the seventeen-mile-long canyon separated them. "It should be done," he concluded, "before our problem becomes too big to solve." He always liked the idea of using research to *do* something.

It wasn't long until Fletcher's students were scouting, wading, sampling, testing, and recording at a score of stations along the creek. Coliform pollution counts were plotted and graphed, and when preliminary results were in, the professor was ready to talk. He left a troubled group at the Wellsboro Rotary Club with charts that showed pollution from their community exceptionally high, depressing the life of the stream for miles. His data alarmed conservationists and fishermen, precipitating formation of a Pine Creek Watershed Association, whose first task was to gain improved treatment by upstream towns.

The brilliant algae bloom of August was the result of voluminous quantities of silt that had washed downstream from a highway construction project fifty miles away. As is often the case, the initial impetus for the water-quality research turned out to be one of the less significant findings. Little did Dr. Peter W. Fletcher know that a water-quality study would go so far. The concern that it raised, coupled with inclusion of Pine Creek in the National Wild and Scenic Rivers Act, served to spawn efforts on a diversity of fronts and to involve growing numbers of people. Fletcher promoted this idea: "When Pine Creek is evaluated for Scenic River designation, we should make sure that it qualifies." Unanticipated by the professor but arising from his study, many actions followed: a crack-down on industrial pollution, new orders for Wellsboro and Galeton to upgrade their treatment of waste, inspection of on-site sewage facilities, public acquisition of prime open-space lands, designation of state Wild and Natural Areas, and a host of other projects aimed at a quality environment along Pine Creek. Problems were not to be neglected.

February 23, 1972
"I'd like to call this meeting to order." In a small, overheated conference room in Williamsport, sixty-seven people were crowded elbow-to-elbow. "I'd like to thank you all for coming; it's good to see so many people who are interested in Pine Creek." Walter Lyon, director of the Pennsylvania Bureau of Water Quality Management, began the meeting on a note of cooperation that would become characteristic. The Pine Creek Task Force worked through effective leadership.

It also worked because of the people who attended. As soon as the chairman introduced himself, everybody else did likewise. An incredible array of interests were represented. One room held township officials, industrialists, strip-mine interests, municipal sewer authority directors, environmentalists, county planners, university professors, and the whole spectrum of state agencies—the many bureaus of the Department of Environmental Resources (DER), the Department of Transportation, Fish Commission, Game Commission, and others. They all came in response to an invitation by the Secretary of DER, Dr. Maurice Goddard.

The formation of the Task Force was a climax of protection activities up to that date. Dr. Goddard had been flooded by requests and complaints, the variety and complexity of which, he decided, warranted a special organization to be headed by one of the Department's chief administrators. "Finally we can sit down face to face and discuss the problems of Pine Creek," responded Trout Unlimited representative Bob McCullough, a man who initiated many protection programs, devoting years of effort to this stream and others. "A lot of these state agencies don't know what the others are doing, let alone the different counties," he added. When criticized that the new group was just another forum for discussion, McCullough responded, "Talking isn't necessarily *bad*. Things are going to happen, you wait and see. Nobody likes to have an accusing finger pointed at them in meetings like this. If the Department agrees to do something, they'll be reluctant to return to the next meeting without having it done."

It was apparent from the February 21 session that something had changed, that a new thrust to correct pollution and other problems along Pine Creek had indeed begun. Early objectives were stated: to adopt water quality standards, to seek national designation, to establish good land-use management programs, and others. The chairman established six committees and appointed a chairman for each; these became the working groups reporting back to the Task Force at quarterly meetings. No one knew, how-

ever, of the diversity and depth that would mark their involvement in the
Task Force. Highway design standards, rural solid waste collection, dam
construction, flood-plain zoning, and myriad other issues would be
pursued.

April 18, 1972
"You, sir—do you know which end of a paddle to put in the water?" The
middle-aged balding office administrator to whom the question was directed looked around. His eyes were two big question marks.
    "Why, sure I do."
    "Good. Then you will go in my canoe." That is how outfitter, Pine Creek
native, canyon expert, and ace raconteur Ed McCarthy selects his partner.
"When you drive a car you steer from the front, and that's where you put
your best tires, but remember, a six-man Avon raft is not a car. You steer
from the back, and that's where your big stick should be. Show them,
George." George, the district forester, pushed his raft this way then that,
with a rudderlike sweep of his paddle. "Any man who does like George will
come back alive, I promise you."
    Then the suntanned riverman turned to a representative of the National
Park Service. "Sir, your rainpants will stay dry if you leave them rolled up,
but if you wear them, *you* will stay dry." He leaned toward the park representative. "In the canyon it will be as cold as the shady side of a banker's
heart. Wear 'em!"
    While ten people boarded rafts and six climbed into canoes, Ed
McCarthy extolled the virtues of the day. "Never will you see such a morning as this, gentlemen. The three greatest variables on the face of the earth
are water, weather, and people, and we've done exceptionally well on all
counts today."
    We began, not with a rush but into a sluggish current, paddling the final
half mile of Marsh Creek to its confluence with Pine. This was the long-
awaited beginning of the National Wild and Scenic River Study. Many actors were present for the drama. The federal Bureau of Outdoor Recreation (BOR) headed the team and would be in charge of preparing the
study report. The National Park Service and Forest Service were represented but made sure that their agencies didn't end up having anything to
do with Pine Creek, since none of the land is federally owned. Exceeding
the expectations of the Fish and Wildlife Service expert, a bald eagle
soared northward up the creek, no more than fifty feet over our heads.
The Army Corps of Engineers sent a biologist rather than an engineer.
Two park planners from the state selected a covered or decked canoe
rather than a raft, and paid for the increased maneuverability with leg
cramps caused by crowded seat compartments. Representatives for county
planning agencies were there, along with those of the Susquehanna River
Basin Commission and The Pennsylvania State University.
    We beached at Owassee, where the creek takes a tortuous bend to the

The Owassee Rapids, Pine Creek Canyon

east and water thunders through a narrow, rock-studded chute. "How did the canyon get here, anyway?" one of the federal officials asked.

"The glacier stopped at Ansonia," I began to explain, "where we started the trip. A moraine of sand and stone blocked the southern channel until lakewater covered the lands up above—"

"Then it all broke loose at once?" he interrupted.

"And carved the canyon when it did," I finished.

"That makes the geology outstanding enough," the official concluded, referring to the special qualities that a river should have if it's to be eligible for the National Rivers System.

Pine Creek was still carving the canyon as we floated on its high waters through the treacherous bend at Owassee, over rapids at Bear Run, and past high cliffs called Falling Springs, where cold water seeped from the mountain and splashed in a series of exhilarating cascades that ended in the swollen creek.

Later that afternoon the group met in the upstairs bunkroom of "Mallard," one of Ed's rental cabins.

"What do you think the classification ought to be?" the group leader asked.

"One thing's for sure—it can't be wild." With this statement nearly everyone agreed, since they knew the railroad paralleled the stream.

"The railroad's there, but it doesn't provide access to the creek," another person countered, "and this is about as wild as any large streams get in the northeast."

Canoes at the Owassee Rapids

"The shorelines can't have any development if it's to be classified as wild," answered Noll Granzo, the study leader. "Besides that, it can always be *managed* as a wild river, even if it's classified as recreational or scenic."

"Somewhere along the way things became more crowded. I don't know if the whole area could be scenic," the Forest Service representative said.

"One mile above Slate Run there are a lot more cabins," a local authority answered, "and then at Cammal—"

"Cammal!" interrupted a BOR official. "Cammal's where the power line is, isn't it? We must have looked at that butcher job for two miles!"

"But just below it is one of the best stretches of the whole creek," a younger man added. "The west shore from the power line to Jersey Mills is wild—no road or railroad. A lot of people stopped there at Solomon Run

Pine Creek Canyon near Bear Run

to drink water, and all of the public lands on that side are being designated a Natural Area by the state."

"Well, if it's going to be 'scenic' to Jersey Mills, shouldn't we just call the whole thing scenic?" a state man asked.

"That would have the most local support," the other answered. "Less likelihood of encouraging recreational development." And so "scenic" it was.

Later that spring, the Bureau of Outdoor Recreation conducted public meetings at Wellsboro and Jersey Shore. The study was delayed several times, and additional public meetings were held in 1975. The issue had

Pine Creek Canyon near Pine Island Run

Rafting through the Pine Creek Canyon

become exceedingly complex by that time, with passage of a State Scenic Rivers Act and with other activities of the Pennsylvania Department of Environmental Resources. The sessions became mired in questions regarding DER land acquisition and whether or not parcels at Tiadaghton village would be condemned. BOR officials announced that Pine Creek would qualify as a National Scenic River and that it should be administered by the state, meaning that the federal government would not be involved in acquisition, recreation development, regulation, or management.

Some months later, the Army Corps of Engineers selected Cammal as one of the six sites in the Susquehanna Basin for a hydroelectric dam analysis, thereby raising fears that hadn't existed before and support for national designation. The state Department of Environmental Resources opposed the dam and also opposed National Scenic River designation for reasons that were to become heatedly controversial.

February 2, 1973
Two Lycoming County planners walked into the cinder-block fire hall. You could hear the tension. The truck was parked outside to make room for thirty cold metal folding chairs, and a new furnace blew warmed-over air in too-small quantities, so that everybody left their dark winter coats on. "That's him, right there," a woman said, as the two men entered. While their arrival quieted some people, it caused as many others to say something to their neighbors.

"Quite a turnout here, fellas," one of the township supervisors said to the pair of guests. He smiled, but he knew this wasn't going to be pleasant. "How'd ya want to handle it?"

A few minutes later the meeting began. "These two fellas agreed to come up here today to talk about something that could affect all of us on Pine Creek," the chairman began. "Flood insurance."

"Zonin', you mean!" echoed a voice from the back. That was the extent of the introductions.

The planners attempted an explanation, but it didn't last long. "The idea is that the federal government will help pay the cost to insure development that already exists on the flood plain, but only if the township takes steps to see that flood damages won't get worse."

"It's zoning, isn't it?"

"The township would zone the flood plain in order to discourage construction of buildings that would be damaged during floods."

"Three years ago they were talking about zonin' up here, and I don't see that this is any different. We ran it out then and we'll run it out now." There was a chorus of agreement from the crowd, by this time obscured in a haze of cigar, cigarette, and pipe smoke. A few older Pine Creekers stood in the back and listened, their minds not made up. From the middle of the crowd, a whiskered man put up his hand and began talking at the same time.

Marsh Creek, a major Pine Creek tributary

"We had zoning in Williamsport and you couldn't even trim your trees."

"Sir, I don't know what you couldn't do in Williamsport, but for zoning to meet flood-insurance requirements, you don't need to be concerned about tree-trimming," the county man answered. The old Williamsporter looked at the flannel-shirted man next to him, and between chews on his tobacco, he said, "Won't even be able to prune those apple trees of yours."

Taking a subtler approach, a man in the front asked, "Taxes'll go up, won't they?"

"Taxes might go up, but not because of zoning," was the answer.

"Just wondered. Where I came from they had zoning, and then taxes went up." He went on to say that increased taxes resulted when public sewer lines were added to his old Bucks County neighborhood. The planner tried to explain that with the right kind of zoning in a rural area like Pine Creek, the people could make sure they'd never need sewer lines, but the Bucks County man's firsthand experience of tax increases had impressed the others.

"You say that state law requires us to zone everything in the township?" This man was one of the few who lived in the mountains, away from the valley. Everyone knew what was coming.

"The law says that if you zone, all of the township needs to be identified under one land-use classification or another, in order for all landowners to get equal treatment," came the answer, though in some ways it didn't make good sense.

"In other words, we have to live with regulations so that a few people can get insurance paid for." Since it was not a question, the officials didn't answer. "I say we've been takin' care of ourselves for years and we can keep on doin' so."

That did get a response. The other county planner mentioned that 1972 flood victims received $1.5 billion in relief, and that the federal government spends $1 billion per year for flood-control projects. "There are a lot of people here who collected taxpayers' money to recover from the flood."

The discussion went on for some time. Stubbornly, and with foresight, the township supervisors refused to take immediate action to reject the program but left it alive. "We've got to think about this," they said, and adjourned the meeting.

The flood insurance program began with the prospect of a better future: new flood-plain development would cease, while the program would recognize and help people who had already invested in property. But the implementation has been ragged with compromise, indecision, cost, and delay. Initial mapping prepared by consultants for the Federal Flood Insurance Administration, a division of the Department of Housing and Urban Development, was regularly, grossly inaccurate. Flood-plain restrictions and standards for compliance were set at a level that may not afford true protection to the homeowner or to the riverfront. New construction in the "flood fringe" zone is permitted if it is raised on earthen fill, but this displaces water and aggravates the neighbor's problems. No zoning whatever is required until FIA finishes their mapping, which can go on for years in some municipalities. Places like Lewis Township on Lycoming Creek belligerently rejected zoning, yet enjoy the benefits of flood insurance that is 48 percent subsidized by the general taxpayer. "Floodproofing" requirements increase the cost of construction, but can still result in widespread flood-plain development, where economic loss and disaster remain inevitable.

For all those shortcomings, the program still has merit, for it offers the incentive to zone—maybe enough incentive to convince people who wouldn't do it otherwise. It could be one of the most important measures of river protection all over the country, resulting in less flood damage, more open riverbanks, less water pollution, and more scenic streams. Both the state and federal wild and scenic river programs encourage zoning, but neither can require it. In Pennsylvania, the authority to zone lies solely with the township or county.

Despite the objections at the grim meeting on Pine Creek, a few weeks later the township passed a resolution agreeing with the flood insurance program. Those residents who wanted it had apparently convinced many of the others that it was a good thing. Other townships did likewise. For all the damage it created, the flood of 1972 left a clear impression on people's minds and, with some, a willingness to go about life a little differently in

Pine Creek above Cedar Run

Rowing across Pine Creek at Waterville

the future. Incentives were strengthened, as municipalities were required to participate in order for federally insured mortgages to be available. Some people now look at local land-use regulation as a way of protecting what they have, and the idea of restrictions on development of flood plains and steep slopes has some support. In 1972 only one township along the creek had zoning, but by 1975 nearly all of them were in the process of adopting regulations. If they are adequately administered, these local land-use management programs will represent a very large step toward protection of Pine Creek.

May 1975
The Pine Creek Valley Preservation Association was organized in early 1975. It represented an advance in the approach toward protecting the creek. For the first time an organization of valley residents and landowners existed, whose responsibility it was to speak for local people. Residents had always been involved in the Watershed Association (which became inactive in 1972), in the Task Force, and as individuals, but now there was a group of residents. While the basic objective of the Association is to "keep Pine Creek the way it is today," the motivation to organize came largely from a single event and the fear it brought that land would be condemned.

For a number of years, a program of land acquisition by the Pennsylvania Department of Environmental Resources had been going very well. That is, many local owners wanted to sell their land for open-space protection, the state had money to pay fair if not top prices, and everybody was pleased with the arrangements. A prime 500-acre tract with 1½ miles of creek frontage was one of the first to be bought; the Nature Conservancy acquired it and then resold it to the state. Its owner had been the most outspoken critic of government, and so it was said, "If they pleased Stu, they can probably please anybody." All in all, a few thousand acres of open space were added to the state forest through purchase of valley lands. Nearly half of the stream corridor is now in public ownership, which is one reason so much of the region has been protected.

The state then turned its attention to the canyon. Where Campbell Run had carved a notch and created a delta, a small village had grown in the logging days and was given the name Tiadaghton. For eight miles above and eight below, there are only a half-dozen cabins. A foully pitched mud and mountainstone road drops from the rim, providing access of a sort, and over the years, loggers' homes became hunting cabins or were left to rot. Partly due to a threat of commercial campground construction, partly due to the canyon's designation as a National Natural Landmark and a state Natural Area, and partly because Tiadaghton is the only developed area of the seventeen-mile-long reach, the Department of Environmental Resources decided that it should acquire the private parcels. To establish public ownership of the canyon seemed to be a worthwhile objective. Unfortunately, officials decided to send a letter to each owner rather than initiate the more personalized contact that had proven so successful to date. The letter included implications of condemnation:

> The purpose of this letter is to inform you that the Department proposes to acquire your property, leading to the consolidation in public ownership of the topographic feature known as the Pennsylvania Grand Canyon. . . . Upon acquisition of your property, the Department, as a condition of settlement, will permit you to continue your occupancy of the improvement on the property under the terms of a lease-back arrangement for a period of five (5) years.

This letter caused a reaction much akin to the spontaneous combustion of an overloaded hay barn.

"They want our land so people floatin' down the creek won't see any houses. What's it hurt to see a house?" one of the owners questioned at a public meeting held by the federal Bureau of Outdoor Recreation in the wake of the Tiadaghton letter.

"First they buy Tiadaghton, then Blackwell, Cedar Run, Slate Run, and right down the creek they'll go," said another. This was never the intent of the state, but since its intent had never clearly been presented, it was left to speculation.

The Preservation Association was formed. Its first major task was to determine DER's position on the buying of land. State officials said that no condemnation was contemplated at this time, an open-ended statement that heated the issue like bellows on a blacksmith's fire. The Secretary of the Department personally met with several residents, saying that no land would be condemned below the canyon. "That's fine, as far as his word goes," a resident said, then added, "I believe him, but how long's he going to be the Secretary?"

A written position was forthcoming as a Department policy statement which said, "The Department will continue to acquire land on a willing-seller, willing-buyer basis, hoping particularly to acquire those lands adjacent to the stream that are as yet undeveloped but which have high development potential."

The Preservation Association soon became more than a single-issue group. Amid the confusion of other events, a consortium of private utility companies proposed a statewide concept of energy "parks," where ten to twenty power plants would be grouped on one site. Ten preferred locations in Pennsylvania were selected, and one was at the edge of the Pine Creek watershed. Dams at Cammal, in the middle of the scenic river study reach, and at Keating, on the Susquehanna's West Branch, were listed as "most suitable" sites for water supply, raising adamant objections of the new group. Shortly thereafter, the Army Corps of Engineers identified Cammal with six other sites in the Susquehanna River Basin for hydroelectric studies.

A major and complex question now came before the group. The Scenic River Study by the federal Bureau of Outdoor Recreation recommended designation of Pine Creek in the National Wild and Scenic Rivers System, if

The village of Slate Run

the Governor requested inclusion. The Department of Environmental Resources would recommend the stream for designation in a State Scenic Rivers System. What will be the best for Pine Creek?

March 15, 1976
It was no surprise when the Pennsylvania Department of Environmental Resources released a statement in March of 1976, expressing opposition to the designation of Pine Creek in the National Wild and Scenic Rivers System. Some people were aware of Department's concerns since passage of the federal act in 1968, when state officials remained disinterested or downright unhappy with the idea of national rivers in Commonwealth territory. The Department stated:

> For several reasons, the Department does not recommend the designation of Pine Creek as a component of the National Wild and Scenic Rivers System. National designation would: 1) result in increased publicity, 2) attract more people to an area that is already on the brink of overuse, 3) would not provide federal funds for acquisition or development beyond those that are already

Local campers at Tiadaghton

available to the Commonwealth under other grant programs, 4) national designation would remove the flexibility and control from local government and
state land management agencies by adding an extra level of administrative control, and 5) would give decision-making power to a federal agency that is far
removed from the day to day contact that now exists between local residents,
local government, and state land management agencies.

Questions and counterpositions came from many quarters.

"Don't trust 'em," a resident said. "Look at Tocks Island Dam—Pennsylvania supported it even though the other three states didn't."

"Wouldn't the federal government be a 'court of last resort' if we have
problems?" another asked.

"They might think they can stop a dam," a local attorney said, "but there
are other states that can't."

County planners tried to document the issue of increased publicity,
which could lead to increased use. It was apparent that rivers belonging to
state or federal systems see an increase in use, but then so do streams that
are not so designated. The Youghiogheny soared from 5,000 floaters per
year in 1968 to 100,000 in 1977, and the reach in question is not in any
system whatsoever. The Allagash of Maine, which was the first river to be
federally designated, though administered and managed by the state, has
seen a general climb in recreation volume; however, inclusion in the national system seems to have caused little change in the rate of increase.
Most important, opponents of the publicity-overuse argument pointed out
that Pine Creek can normally be canoed in the springtime only—water level

is too low through summer months. If federal status were to attract more people, they would likely be coming from distant areas mostly during summer vacations rather than in other seasons. Since the creek can't be floated from June through September, summer canoeists are not likely to come. People who live close enough to canoe on spring weekends will know about the stream whether or not it's nationally recognized. The experience of Little Beaver Creek of Ohio supports this reasoning—no increase has been noticed by state officials. The creek is in the federal system, but water levels are generally too low for summer floating.

Other questions center around the wisdom of involving a federal bureaucracy. "It's a valid concern," a BOR official pointed out. "But we should look at the record of the Bureau—Ohio and Maine officials are administering national rivers, and they are well pleased with federal involvement. The federal government does not exercise any administrative control. All we do is approve of a state-prepared management plan certifying that the stream will be adequately protected."

"Once the stream is designated," says Dick Mosley, who directs Ohio's river program, "you don't know the federal government is there."

A local person, who was concerned about the Army Corps' dam proposal, argued in favor of national designation: "More government means more red tape and more difficulties in doing certain things—especially in building government dams!" But it seems that the state has too often been entangled in federal requirements and paperwork. Problems with other programs have led to fears that a river designation may be more trouble than it's worth.

The opinions of local residents vary. Distrust for the state is prevalent. "The day could come when the state won't have the power to stop a federal dam," as one landowner said.

Bill Painter, who directed the American Rivers Conservation Council, summarized the situation: "Federal involvement provides legal protection against a federal project; state designation gives political protection at the state level only," meaning that the governor would likely disapprove of a dam.

"The New Melones Dam on the Stanislaus River of California was an example," said Brendt Blackwelder of the Environmental Policy Center in Washington. "The state Water Resources Control Board attempted to restrict the activities of the federal Bureau of Reclamation, but the court ruled against them. Fortunately, the decision was partially overturned. North Carolina could not stop a dam on the New River—federal designation was required. The long-term prospects are that pressures for dams will be great. Since all of the good sites for Army Corps projects have been exhausted, the criteria may become less restrictive in the future, allowing dams where they are not considered economically or politically feasible today."

With its national river recommendation, the Bureau of Outdoor Recreation also encouraged inclusion of the creek in the state scenic rivers system, but Pennsylvania, as we shall see, has problems of its own.

August 23, 1978
Early in 1978, the Department of Environmental Resources held hearings on the
subject of state scenic river designation. Officials met a hostile audience in Tioga
County, and a few weeks later the local senator blasted the program. DER Secretary
Goddard had his fill of the controversy and called a halt to the study.

It was another public meeting, with Peter Fletcher calling people together at the Whitneyville Fairgrounds, east of Wellsboro. The intent was
to determine local sentiment about the state scenic-river study, and special
guests included the two state assemblymen, Warren Spencer of Tioga
County and Joe Grieco of Lycoming County.

Spencer denounced the scenic-river program. "The sewage treatment
that DER wants us to do in Wellsboro would make our waste purer than
rainwater," he said. His statement, besides being exaggerated, had no bearing on the river designation.

"I'm against it because of the tax base we'll lose in Tioga County,"
Spencer continued. But examination shows only 190 acres of private land
in the Tiadaghton area, the only place where substantial acquisition may
occur in Tioga County. Total tax income from these parcels would be
under $200, with less than $30 going to the township. Road maintenance
to serve the Tiadaghton owners costs the township $500 to $1,000 per
year.

Joe Grieco described how he grew up near Pine Creek, saying that these
were his people, and they were not going to be ignored or abused by DER
again. He didn't elaborate on the scenic-river program; it paled into unap-
proachable irrelevancy beside the question of liking or disliking government.

The Lycoming County Planning Commission was called upon to explain
its position: "We favor federal and state designation for two reasons: it's
the most certain way to prevent a dam from being built, and the valley
needs priority attention from the state to manage the recreation problems
that we have. DER should cope with solid waste, access area maintenance,
and other issues, and scenic-river status is the only way it'll get done."

Most of the evening was spent in a collective grumble about the tax base
and the problems of trash and township road maintenance.

The Preservation Association president spoke with uncommon clarity and
reason. "We want a better management plan—one that tells us what's going
to happen and how the problems will be solved. We want to know that
DER will have the money they need to do the job. Then we'll decide if we
want the program or not."

One township supervisor drew applause with a proposal to liquidate the
state land. Two other municipal representatives stated their disapproval of
the scenic-river program, since their townships are located above the section of creek to be designated. This added to the confusion: those who
were in the proposal wanted out, and those who were out wanted in.

Agreement was almost unanimous—"people problems" were affecting the
creek and the lands along it. Recreation creates problems that indeed need

solving, but this was seen as a reason *not* to designate Pine Creek. It was a stunning victory for ambiguity and irrelevancy. The president of the Pennsylvania Federation of Sportsmen's Clubs reported on his group's position: no more land should be bought in Pennsylvania by the federal government. However, this subject had never been proposed or considered for the Pine Creek area.

After such enlightenment, a vote was taken in democratic fashion. Results were conclusive. People at the meeting did not want Pine Creek in the state scenic-rivers system.

It may be an endless controversy, Pennsylvania's Pine Creek. If a stream as fine as this cannot be effectively dealt with and protected, can any? Can we learn from these mistakes, can we satisfy the conflicting demands? This is a simple case. Consider a complex one, where the dam-building forces are organized, where the state doesn't own half the riverfront, where urbanization is rampant, where coal reserves are ready for stripping, where the water is already polluted.

In some ways Pine Creek offers little reason to hope that we can look at the long-term future and make decisions to preserve a river. Yet the hope remains that we will do it. Many conservation efforts have struggled along without support until a major threat is upon the scene. Unfortunately, support is often too late. In the process of aimless waiting for things to get so bad that everyone recognizes a need to act, will the desirable qualities of the place be whittled away to a skeleton?

There is no such thing as no plan. When knowledge of alternatives exists, inaction is as deliberate as action, leading effectively to unwanted ends. Will elected officials be interested in the facts of the case and in everybody's future? The state is more than a device for serving immediate desires; it exists to serve the needs of all, including future generations. That's why the state has responsibilities that we as individuals, or politicians as individuals, aren't accustomed to. Many people hold the state accountable for the immediate future. Who holds it accountable for the distant future?

Maybe a new management plan will gain the support of local people and then local representatives. Maybe statewide support for protection of Pine Creek will override local opposition. Or maybe things will slide toward tomorrow, where we'll find Cammal Dam awaiting, a power plant at Cherry Flats, or a bustling Pocono resort at Cedar Run.

Troutwater, Canoewater: The Loyalsock

Loyalsock enthusiasts may well be the most avid of all river supporters in northern Pennsylvania. Few problems diminish the creek's appeal, and the smallness of the stream seems to elicit strong feelings. Many people feel that a big river can take care of itself, so to speak, and that a little more pollution won't hurt, but a narrower and cleaner stream like the "Sock" leads to more responsible conclusions. Residents, fishermen, canoeists, hikers, and campers are all interested. The Loyalsock has many excellent features:

Trout fishing is outstanding, especially in the lower creek below Forksville.

Whitewater canoeing in the springtime is hard to equal anywhere. The upper reaches are for experts only, and national slalom races have been held at Worlds End State Park.

The Loyalsock Trail is one of the finest and most popular hiking trails in Pennsylvania.

Worlds End State Park includes camping and picnicking areas with wild creek frontage and scenic views.

It all begins in a swamp above the little town of Lopez, where some waters drain to Mehoopany Creek and others fall to the west. The watery volume gradually increases, and with the addition of Lopez Creek, a larger Loyalsock is formed. At very high levels, a kayak journey can begin here and run to the West Branch of the Susquehanna River. The canoeable gradient is greater than any other waterway in Pennsylvania. After Lopez, the stream plunges and winds in Class II rapids for seven miles, over half of which has wild shorelines with no roads or buildings. Natural acidity from upland bogs is greatly augmented by drainage from coal mines, depressing the biology but not the scenery of the upper creek. Pollution eventually becomes diluted in the downstream descent.

At Route 220 the truly spectacular Loyalsock begins, with wildwater plunging over ledges again and again. Gravel and glacial boulders are brilliantly white, unlike the grey and brown riverstones found on other creeks. The Loyalsock Trail begins here, following a course through hemlocks and hardwoods to Dutchman's Falls on a tributary stream. A highlight of the Loyalsock is reached two miles east from the trailhead, where waters thunder over the Haystacks—a collection of large rounded rock outcrops that are scattered from one side of the creek to the other, creating an impassable barrier to all but the most expert paddler in any but the highest of water. The Haystacks are a popular camping area, and deep green pools above and below the rapids attract summertime swimmers. This four-mile stretch of the creek has no roads or railroads, and for a full eleven miles

Loyalsock Creek above Worlds End Park

between Route 220 and Route 87, the rapids are consistently rated a difficult Class III, for accomplished, experienced paddlers only. The gorge is wild and scenic, with foaming whitewater, glistening rock gardens of riverstone, high cliffs at water's edge, and the blackened shade of matured forests. This section and lower reaches have been recommended as high-priority candidates for the Pennsylvania Scenic Rivers System.

Worlds End Park includes campgrounds, picnic areas, a creek to explore, and views from high rocks above the Loyalsock. Whitewater races annually draw large crowds and competitors from all over the East. The "old-time" park appearance has survived at Worlds End, with log cabins, log headquarters, log guardrails, and logs everywhere.

Three more miles of heavy whitewater leads to the village of Forksville, most noted for its 126-year-old covered bridge. Below the old logging town, the mountains rise higher, but rapids are subdued to Class I and II—excellent for the experienced paddler in an open canoe. Scenery is still superb, though the valley is wider and more open, with a flood plain that is often farmed. Riverbank cabins and trailers gradually increase along the way.

Fishing on the lower Loyalsock is excellent, with a native population of brown trout, brook trout, and other species. Shaded banks, cold tributaries, and deep holes keep the water temperatures low. While most large streams warm to eighty degrees and more in the heat of August, this one usually doesn't, and its trout prosper. Along with other popular fisheries of Kettle

Creek and the Sinnemahoning's First Fork in the north central highlands, the "Sock" is big enough for excitement and variety, yet it is small enough to wade across in the summertime.

Conflicts arise between trout fishermen and canoers. Problems between the two groups have become serious on some rivers. The most notable of these is the Au Sable in Michigan, where thousands of anglers come to the cool, spring-fed waters, meeting thousands of canoeists who are attracted by the beauty and ease with which the small river can be traveled. The two factions should be compatible, one would think, since both have an appreciation for the same resource. Usually this is the case, except that boaters splash and make noise, scaring away fish. There lies the problem. In Pennsylvania the situation is seldom serious, since trout streams are usually too low to float in summertime, and since there aren't a lot of canoes in most places. Unfortunately, there is friction at times.

We were paddling through midmorning sunshine below Forksville, where a long pool stretched ahead of us and ended in a ragged-edged turbulence of Loyalsock rapids. A brown trout, motionless against the gentle current, sensed our coming and darted for cover.

"Here comes another lousy canoe." An irritable voice carried across the quiet waters from the head of the riffle. Muffled and garbled in the current below, another man said something I couldn't hear. "I said, here comes another blasted canoe!" he repeated, a little louder this time, taking his cigar out of his mouth and holding it in his left hand with his line. The trout fisherman didn't intend me to hear his remark, as evidenced by his big grin and "Fine morning, isn't it?" as we passed quickly by. We, of course, agreed, maintaining whatever social lubricant we could in a curiously strained relationship between freshwater enthusiasts.

His grievance irritated me at first. "He must think he owns the stream," Cindy said. We saw no other craft all morning, and there had been few canoes on the creek since May, when water drops to rocky levels. Knowing that neither he nor I was the worse for either of us being there, I shrugged it off. We wouldn't disturb his water—he wasn't even fishing but walking up the riffle, though that isn't always the case.

Fishermen have been knocked down by rafters who are unable to control their craft, and floaters have been stoned by shoreside anglers who aren't able to control their tempers. Ignorance is often the reason for lost trout and high blood pressure. Floaters call out, "How's the fishing?" as they paddle past, and the man in hip boots answers, "Fine, until *you* came along." I was once the guilty leader of a group who swarmed down on a peaceful angler—in front of him, behind him, and still coming from above. Having been too far ahead of the group to avoid the confrontation, I then gathered the small fleet of rafts and canoes together at the first gravel bar and gave them a few easy rules to follow:

Canoeing the Loyalsock above Worlds End Park

Never run into a fisherman.

Always pass a fisherman in single file, taking the same route as the boat ahead of you.

When the fisherman is wading deep enough, go behind him, where he's not casting.

If you can't go behind him, stay as far away as you can get.

Move as quietly as you can and quit paddling if the current will carry you.

Be friendly but don't overdo it—a lot of fishermen really don't like your being there, and there's no sense chatting when they only want you to leave.

Timing of stream-oriented recreation is critical to avoid confrontations. If floaters begin traveling no earlier than 9:00 A.M. and get off the water by 5:00 P.M., a lot of problems will be solved. The angler who is serious about his fun will be hunting trout while paddlers are breaking camp or making camp. Generally speaking, midday hours are preferable to boaters anyway, though there are exceptions. In early evening stillness and then in long shadows and the golden light of sunset, I've enjoyed paddling and fishing a six-mile reach of stream below our house. Rarely would I see another fisherman on those trips, as it was usually a weeknight instead of a weekend.

Special regulations may be necessary where boater-angler disputes are severe, or where recreational use damages the riverine environment, the life-style of local residents, or the scenic river experience itself. On some waterways, permits are now required for visitors to float the stream, with various restrictions on party size, camping sites, and use of motors. In most cases these streams are in the national or a state scenic-rivers system, and much of the shoreline is publicly owned. In order to enforce permit or river-use requirements, it is necessary that boating access points be limited in number, thus enabling a public agency to economically administer regulations from a few selected locations. Neither scenic designation, public ownership, nor limited access is the case on the Loyalsock, and so conflicts between boaters, fishermen, and other people have to be resolved voluntarily and through an understanding of one another. A little courtesy on the part of all groups can avoid confrontations and hard feelings—differences that are minor when compared to concerns for clean water, wildness, and free-flowing streams.

Water quality is clearly an issue to the fishermen and canoeists, and both groups have worked together to protect the Loyalsock. A strip mine was proposed that would discharge water into Scar and possibly Ketchum runs, both flowing into the "Sock" between the villages of Forksville and Hillsgrove. Stripping, the mining advocates say, will "clean up" a problem that was left from abandoned coal-mining operations. Many people disagree. "There's no problem that needs cleaning," says Ron Thompson, biologist and president of the Loyalsock Watershed Association. "We've tested the water to prove it, but you don't need a sampling bottle and white laboratory coat to see trout in those streams."

After a mining permit was requested of the Department of Environmental Resources in 1975, conservation groups barraged them with protests, and the Department agreed to make no decisions until a public hearing was held. This case could be significant as a guide for future actions elsewhere, for two primary arguments against the mine have great relevance to other Pennsylvania streams:

Opponents argue that surface rights to the land are of significant public value and should take precedence over mineral rights. While the land belongs to the Commonwealth as state forest, the minerals are controlled by a mining company.

The streams emanating from the mining area are of high quality, supporting native brook trout and feeding a clean Loyalsock. "Water quality of Scar and Ketchum runs is excellent but fragile," Thompson says. "Sandstone and natural acidity allow little buffering capacity, so any acid dis-

Ketchum Run, a wild tributary to the Loyalsock

charge is likely to have a devastating effect." Since these streams are clean, mine opponents say we should take special care to *keep* them clean, restricting coal extraction to watersheds that are already acid-polluted, of which there are an ample number in Pennsylvania.

Loyalsock below the village of Barbours

Below Scar and Ketchum runs, the Loyalsock passes the villages of Hills-grove, Barbours, Loyalsockville, and Farragut. A potential dam site has been identified by the Army Corps of Engineers near Barbours, though it is not being studied or recommended. Scenery, exciting rapids, and clear water continue to the Susquehanna. While 34 percent of the watershed is in public ownership, much of the lower valley is not. Access is possible at Moore's Country Store in Barbours, the mouth of Wallis Run, the Game Commission Farm at Loyalsockville, and at the Susquehanna's West Branch, where the borough of Montoursville has built a park.

Here the Loyalsock has a unique distinction, for it is the last large and unpolluted tributary to the Susquehanna. All of those below this point are muddied and clouded in comparison. Across Pennsylvania, this stream is one of the cleanest, but also one of the most fragile. Thus the effect of even minor degradation becomes important. The question is not how much pollution is added but how much quality is lost. With several groups working to protect the Loyalsock, maybe it will remain undamaged and keep its special appeal.

Moshannon and the Canyon:
A Dam Could Change It All

High in coal country near Philipsburg, Moshannon Creek curves through peaceful forests of low wetlands, then drops and rolls into whitewater before meeting the West Branch of the Susquehanna. It is sometimes said that this mountain stream has a split personality—much of the watershed is ravaged by mining, but the corridor and gorge of the winding creek remain a splendid wild path. While upper portions of the 274-square-mile drainage area offer little in scenic or recreational assets, the lower twelve miles are of rare value, as rapids push through a narrow valley that has only one bridge crossing and no paralleling roads or railroad.

We were lucky. The day we cruised, it was ninety degrees, and water roared after three inches of rain had soaked the northern highlands. More often, the necessary high water comes when snow still clings to northern slopes and ice persists in glazing rocky bluffs above the stream's edge. From the village of Winburne, we enjoyed peaceful paddling through slow water. Vegetation crowded the shorelines, like the sand rivers of northern Wisconsin or Minnesota. Hemlocks, rhododendrons, birches, and other plants hung over the banks, enclosing the traveler in a capsule of green. Now and then the water's edge was punctuated by a hugh white pine, its two-foot-diameter trunk grossly out of scale in a region where forests have been repeatedly cut. Passing through flats that looked like wetlands of the north, we could understand the Moshannon's name, which is translated as "Moose Stream" from an Indian dialect. This was probably one of the few Pennsylvania ranges that moose inhabited prior to the arrival of white people in America.

Near the towering twin bridges of Interstate 80, whitewater began. It grew and multiplied from there on, each rapids seeming to breed two more. When we reached the Route 53 crossing at the mouth of torrential Black Moshannon, we had dumped water from our canoe twice, and then the fun really began. Half a mile below the bridge, we stopped on a gravel bar to scout for an ominous-sounding rapids ahead, then ran the channel to a cautious right, staying paddle-length distance from a massive boulder that capsized a small rubber raft in front of us. When the wider Susquehanna was almost in sight, the last descending pitch of the "Mo" swept over rocks buried deep in rough current, creating a roller-coaster of buoyant highs, then thunderous falls. Half a dozen children were there with inner tubes, so we beached at the end of the rough water, where Cindy swapped a few cookies for a rubber tube and went splashing off into the rapids, this journey being a much wetter one than her first.

Even though the water level is often too low for traveling, the Moshannon has become a popular whitewater stream and a favorite for enthusiasts

Moshannon Creek near the West Branch Susquehanna

Moshannon below Interstate 80

from nearby Pennsylvania State University. There is, however, one major problem—acid mine drainage. Since low water levels show a brightly stained streambed, many people refer to the Moshannon as the "Red Mo." The orange precipitate is usually called "yellow-boy." It results from iron content in the overburden of shale that is removed when stripping bituminous coal. As long as shale stays buried, its acid, iron, zinc, and other vile components remain inert, but when it is hauled to the surface by dragline, bulldozer, or dynamite, air and water mix to form a toxic head of poison. The Moshannon is one of the most polluted streams in coal country, though it is far from unique—there are 1,350 miles of acid-bearing water in the Susquehanna basin alone. Fish cannot tolerate the acid waters, and this ironically is one reason that the wild Moshannon shorelines have survived. Without fishermen and pressure for seasonal homes, the inaccessible reaches of the waterway have remained without roads or cabins.

There is a unique advantage to designating these streams as recreational rivers: canoeing and camping can be enjoyed without the fisherman-versus-boater conflicts that are becoming more common elsewhere. By encouraging canoeing on the Moshannon, the upper West Branch, Sinnemahoning's Bennett Branch, and the Clarion, boating pressure on prime fisheries can be reduced. This presents one of the few opportunities to segregate stream uses without the necessity of regulations.

After the excitement of Moshannon whitewater, the Susquehanna's West Branch seemed slow and easy, though we enjoyed the more relaxed pace to the village of Karthaus. There the twenty-four-mile canyon began, with its steep-sloped, forested mountains rising high to the plateau above. This section of the Susquehanna is always the most enjoyable, as the road is left behind at Karthaus. Except for the railroad and a few coal tipples that are used to load trains, the traveler has the river to himself. After camping along a tributary stream that was pure and unaffected by mine drainage, we spent an easy day paddling and drifting toward the village of Keating.

In 1977 the Scenic Rivers Task Force for Pennsylvania identified the upper West Branch as the number one priority for State Scenic River Study. Moshannon, Black Moshannon, and nearby Mosquito Creek were also highly ranked. Keating Dam would flood large portions of them all. With a proposed location near the mouth of Sinnemahoning Creek above the village of Keating, the dam would be about 400 feet high and its reservoir nearly 50 miles in length. The 1976 cost estimate was $700 million—one of the costliest water projects in the country's history.

Starting in 1934, the Army Corps of Engineers identified several possible West Branch impoundment sites. Through four different studies, the dam-building agency has reviewed the idea, and in 1972 they reported a lowly 0.5 benefit-cost ratio, meaning the dam's cost equals twice its value. The Corps indicated that there was no likelihood of the project proceeding. In

June of that year, the worst flood on record blanketed the lowlands of the Susquehanna basin, and damage was widespread—$1.5 billion in federal and $290 million in state money were spent in relief. With renewed interest in a federal project, yet another analysis of Keating was begun. Strong support was voiced by the West Branch Valley Flood Control Association, a group that opposed construction of a dike around the disaster-prone city of Lock Haven. On June 28, 1976, at Lock Haven, the Army announced a new benefit-cost ratio for the dam of 0.8, additional benefits largely being an increased value of hydroelectric power.

Reaction to the new figures was rapid and madly divergent. Flood-control interests resented the attitude of Army personnel, who implied that the project would not reach the one-to-one benefit-cost ratio that is required for consideration by Congress. River protectionists raised many concerns:

Mine drainage will form an acid lake, requiring specialized hydroelectric equipment, mine reclamation, or water treatment, the costs of which were not considered.

Recreational benefits for the reservoir were being calculated, but no accounting was made of the significant natural-river recreation activity that would be lost when the rivers are dammed.

In 1972, 260,000 kilowatts of power were projected. In 1976, with a *smaller* dam proposed, 500,000 kilowatts were projected.

The value of electric power has increased, but so have costs of heavy construction. Has this adequately been evaluated?

A local official did some estimating and reported that the annual interest on $700 million would pay for the combined budgets of eleven central Pennsylvania counties, and a fee of much less than $700 million would buy flood insurance for all flood-prone property in the same region for 100 years—the estimated life of the dam. Advocates of nonstructural solutions asked, "Why not buy downstream riverfront lands that occasionally flood instead of permanently flooding upstream lands that *never* flood?" The dam's cost would be enough to acquire much of the flood plain area. Some downstream communities were in favor of the project for reasons of flood control, with upstream areas opposing the dam because it was their land that was to be flooded. Another concern related to an energy "park" proposal, advanced in 1975 by a group of Pennsylvania utility companies. Clusters of ten to twenty power plants would be located together. Pine Glen, almost adjacent to the potential reservoir, was one of ten candidate sites in the state, and Keating Dam was referenced as a "most suitable" location for water supply. "You don't ever have to worry about an impoundment *that* expensive being built," a federal official stated. Yet the Pennsylvania Department of Environmental Resources requested that the Army continue to study and evaluate possible additional benefits of water supply through low-flow augmentation to the Susquehanna River.

The West Branch Susquehanna Canyon, below Moshannon Creek

Other programs of the state run counter to the impoundment: with DER's recommendation, the Environmental Quality Board designated a wild area on state forest land at Burns Run, just above the dam site. The Fish Commission was intending to acquire boating access areas along the threatened section of the river. Pennsylvania's recreation plan identifies this reach of the West Branch and Moshannon as part of the "North Central High Mountain Area," where natural aspects of the land would be conserved for all time. The document recommends "the perpetual protection of these areas from further invasion by highways, private leases, utility rights-of-way and other forms of commercial development which remove inherent public benefits in the name of progress."

In the midst of the controversy, the House Appropriations Committee held hearings on a proposal to dike the city of Lock Haven. Dam proponents testified that a "greater" solution was needed. The Northcentral Highlands Association and the Canoe Division of Penn State Outing Club advocated nonstructural protection, recognizing the false sense of security that dams and dikes create, as illustrated by Rapid City, South Dakota, and Wilkes-Barre, Pennsylvania, in 1972. With the illusion of protection, more development occurs on the flood plain, adding to the damage potential from an exceptional storm. For Lock Haven, environmental groups supported the dike as offering faster, more complete protection with manifestly less environmental impact than the dam, at $1/23$ the cost. About half of the flood-control benefits of Keating would be due to flood reduction in Lock Haven—figures that were developed assuming there would be no dike.

The issue drags on, an indication of questions to come on other Pennsylvania rivers. The St. Petersburg Dam proposal on the Clarion was also revived after the Hurricane Agnes flood in 1972. Cammal, in the heart of the recommended National Scenic River reach of Pine Creek, was chosen by the Army Corps as one of six sites in the Susquehanna Basin for hydroelectric analysis. Sinnemahoning was another. Possible dam sites are scattered like buckshot. The upper Delaware alone has six "potential" locations as well as familiar Tocks Island. Importantly, motives for dams are likely to change. Flood-control objectives that were popular in the past have been under consistent and effective criticism, and a national consensus toward flood-plain management has developed—a "Unified National Program for Flood Plain Management," as the United States Water Resources Council calls it, stressing nonstructural alternatives toward reduction of flood losses. Section 17 of the Water Resources Development Act of 1968 authorizes funding of nonstructural alternatives such as relocation of development from the flood plain, but the Office of Management and Budget has refused to approve the programs.

Recreation benefits have likewise been under fire. With more and more impoundments for motorboating and fewer rivers to run, the evidence is clear that we need both, and wild rivers are now a scarce item. New attention is being given to hydroelectric power in a national effort to decrease dependence on foreign fuel, but the most suitable sites have long ago been developed. Furthermore, problems of coal-generated electricity have theoretical and often feasible solutions; hydroelectric dams eliminate the river permanently, for all practical purposes, and there is no theoretical or feasible way to replace the natural river.

Water supply may become critical in the future, and this may become the most important reason to build dams. With growing populations in regions where water supplies are inadequate and where nuclear power plants consume vast amounts of cooling water, something will have to be done in order to meet or to change projected future needs. The traditional water-resource and engineering approach is to build more dams in order to make more water available. Conservation of water is scarcely discussed, just as conservation of fuel was only lately given even token attention. Questions of equity will be debated as never before: should the qualities of headwater regions be sacrificed for distant urban centers? Who will make the choices, and who will gain the profit, and will those who pay the costs—financially and otherwise—be the ones who also receive the benefits? How will our social consciousness cope with trade-offs between short-term needs for electricity and the permanent loss of irreplaceable resources?

To the natural river advocates, the issues of economics or population displacement may be important, but the main issue remains the natural qualities of the stream itself—the value and the need for wild places, the beauty and the meaning that can come from a part of the earth where rivers flow free. This is an interest not quantified in the system that calculates benefits and costs. Such numbers fail to represent many real values. And for those benefits and costs that *are* calculated, the numbers can be arbitrary, easily manipulated to suit the biases of the manipulator.

It may become axiomatic that to maintain a free-flowing natural river, it must be designated as such in a national or state scenic-rivers system. If not, the waterway is "available" for other use. How do we decide which rivers should run free? Obviously, if we are to meet society's needs as now

The West Branch Susquehanna Canyon near Moshannon Creek

perceived, all streams cannot be preserved. Which have the "outstanding" qualities referred to in river protection legislation? Some questions will be answered by professionals in water-resource, scenic-river, and other fields, as evidenced by the growing effectiveness of guidelines such as the Principles and Standards of the United States Water Resources Council. But many of the answers will only come through people and the political process—all of us.

We camped for a night near the dam site at Yost Run, a churning brook trout tributary to the West Branch. This was the deepest and most exciting part of the canyon, where wooded mountainsides climbed 1,000 feet above. The river rolled on and on in moonlight, shimmering with a dark reflection of silver as I looked up toward the distant Moshannon. I thought of the Susquehanna's near-miss: this section of river was in the original National Wild and Scenic Rivers Act of 1968, but because of the local representative's opposition, the West Branch was deleted before the bill passed. Maybe there will be another chance.

Opposite: Juniata River below Huntingdon

Juniata and the Life in a River

The Juniata is a slow-moving river of central and southern Pennsylvania that is praised by people who fish for smallmouth bass, muskellunge, suckers, carp, and sunfish. It is a large watershed, 3,404 square miles, ranking in size only behind the big six of Pennsylvania: the Ohio, Allegheny, Monongahela, West Branch of the Susquehanna, Susquehanna, and Delaware. Waters parallel and then slice through the high, sandstone-covered mountains of the Ridge and Valley Province.

The landscape along parts of the Juniata and its tributaries reflects what many people feel to be a classic Pennsylvania image—a well-blended scene of farms and forests, mountains and streams, all together in a way that makes you feel good again, like you've seen a part of the older Penn's Woods and not a land that gets remodeled every twenty years. Spruce Creek is that way where farms roll across a limestone valley. Steep-sided Tussey Mountain forms the background, and fertile trout waters wind southeastward. It's a peaceful scene for folks who live at Pennsylvania Furnace, Graysville, or Seven Stars, for springtime fishermen, for children who like to swim in summer and cross-country ski in winter.

Three main branches form the Juniata: Raystown, Frankstown, and the Little Juniata. Raystown begins in the mountains near Bedford. A recently completed Army Corps of Engineers' dam floods the lower valley, an area that now attracts motorboaters as well as fishermen. Frankstown starts above Hollidaysburg, and the Little Juniata begins near Altoona, flowing northeast to Tyrone. It cuts through a scenic gorge below Spruce Creek village and then meets the Frankstown above Huntingdon. This is where the Juniata River begins, and where I began a slow-moving, six-day canoe trip to the Susquehanna.

Nearly every community has its back to the river, and Huntingdon is no exception. A vacant lot along the waterfront showed some promise of an urban park, bearing a sign that gave credit to a redevelopment authority and the United States Department of Housing and Urban Development for clearing away an area damaged by recent floods. Clearance wasn't quite complete, so amid bricks and broken glass, we set the canoe into a foam-filled eddy and loaded our gear. Eli, our black labrador retriever, looked at the water but passed on his normal pretrip ritual of swimming and jumped straight into the boat. Away we went.

While the scenic Juniata offers many interesting features, one needs to be either fishing or lazy for full appreciation. You can focus your eyes out there on nothing and let your mind recuperate. I spent a good while reading from a comfortable propped seat in the bottom of the boat, disturbed more often by Eli's sighting of a turtle than by dangerous rapids.

Clear waters now come from Raystown Branch, as most of the silt from farmland and streambank erosion has been deposited in the reservoir. While the lower reach of Raystown is almost sterile and seems to be less productive from a fisheries standpoint, the clean water helped to dilute the cloudiness and gray-colored riverbed that we saw in Huntingdon.

A pole is an excellent piece of equipment for the Juniata: often the river is shallow with a sandy or stony bottom, allowing the boater to stand in the stern and push his craft toward the Chesapeake. It's easier than paddling or rowing. Just above the Route 829 bridge, I poled through a luxuriant bloom of algae and aquatic plants; watery green leaves and yellow flowers covered the river in thick masses full of insects and riverine creatures.

Fishing access areas are plentifully provided by the Pennsylvania Fish Commission, and camp sites are easy to find. Usually an island or vacant shoreline is available where you won't bother anybody and nobody will bother you, which is a high-ranking objective of an easygoing canoe trip. One night we camped on rocks below the town of Newton-Hamilton, where waters boil over ledges and through chutes. It's the only major rapids of the river and a scenic highlight, with the houses and church of the village reflected in a long upstream pool, and a fury of whitewater and high ridges enclosing the downstream view. Killdeer, great blue herons, green herons, kingfishers, and sandpipers feed everywhere on the gluttonous supply of food that the Juniata provides.

At small towns like Mt. Union you can stop for groceries or ice cream on a hot day. We climbed craggy sandstone ridges above Route 22 for a view of the river and the community of Mapleton. Lewistown is the only urban center, followed by a long reach of flatwater where it's safest to paddle the shoreline, away from powerboats and waterskiers. While the river from Huntingdon to Lewistown is winding and often remote from the highway, the lower reach becomes wider, straighter, and in some sections crowded by four lanes of Route 322.

The real highlight of the Juniata is not the life *of* the river so much as the life *in* it. Many Pennsylvania streams are wilder, cleaner, faster, and more scenic, but no others of this size have the incredible array and amounts of waterborne creatures. A wealth of mussels, crustaceans, and fish are obvious to the traveler or angler. Smaller animals and aquatic plants are less noticeable but more essential to the Juniata ecosystem. Life changes with varying conditions: riffles, pools, sunshine, shade, shallow water, deep water, winter, summer—all lead to distinctive communities.

The food chain, as ecologists call it, begins with very simple organisms. Algae are vital ingredients, forming a slippery slime on rocks, a green carpet at the riverbed, or a swaying wave of filaments in the current. With leaves and other drifting plant debris, the basic building blocks of river life are formed. Bacteria and fungi break plant matter down, while insects and mussels are filter feeders, sifting particles and nutrients. These are primary

Juniata rapids, town of Newton-Hamilton in background

consumers, feeding on detritus or food matter of the current. The mayfly and caddisfly are two important insects that convert plant material to animal tissue.

Pale yellow wings of the mayfly are often imitated by the trout fisherman's artificial lures such as the Quill Gordon, American March Brown, Hendrickson, and Green Drake. These represent the adult phase, when thousands of the mothlike insects will rise from a watery surface. Fishermen say that a "hatch is on." Caddisfly larvae are well adapted to riffles of the Juniata and other streams, as they glue sand particles together in a protective home that may be tubular, conical, or rectangular-shaped. Pebbles will even be added to weight the larvae and assume a stable and stationary home in fast water.

Juniata below Mapleton

Secondary consumers are middlemen that eat small creatures and in turn are eaten by larger ones. On the Juniata, these include the dragonfly, damselfly, hellgramites, and some minnows. The dragonfly can be seen darting over the river on a hot summer day, though this represents only a short-lived adult stage of its life. As a nymph, the dragonfly lives in mud, on wet stems of plants, or even under rocks. Its lower lip, or labium, injects prey that includes insects, crayfish, tadpoles, small fish, and fellow nymphs. Through the year, a skin might be shed a dozen times until finally an adult emerges. Soon its long double wings stiffen for a new life of wildly acrobatic flying. No other insect has the excellent vision afforded by the dragonfly's protruding, compound eyes, used to hunt mosquitoes, the mainstay of its diet, and leading to the nickname "mosquito hawk." These and the closely related damselflies mate while airborne, and afterward they often fly in tandem. The male, now expendable as far as the species is concerned, flies above, protecting the egg-bearing female from attacks of birds. Females can sometimes be seen with only a portion of a male abdomen attached, the remainder having served as a meal to a fast-diving swallow.

Crayfish in large numbers crawl along the Juniata shore. At some places they can be found under almost every rock. These are also middlemen, scavenging leaves, dead insects, and sometimes live insects, then being eaten by fish, mink, raccoons, and birds. Favorite Juniata dinner sites of the raccoon are littered with hundreds of crayfish remains. Rocks become covered with dismembered claws.

Trout are plentiful in many tributaries and headwater reaches, but the river itself far exceeds their maximum tolerable temperature of seventy-seven to eighty degrees. Bass, on the other hand, do their best in temperatures of seventy-nine to eighty-three degrees, and they find ideal conditions here. Muskellunge are also popular game fish due to stocking programs, and some catches reach over forty inches in length. Many Juniata fish are bottom dwellers, characterized by flat bellies, underslung mouths, strong pectoral fins for propping, eyes near the top of their heads, and small swim bladders since they don't have to float to the surface. Suckers and catfish, for example, are adapted to scavenging and cleaning the riverbed. Many fish have a progressive diet as they grow larger, first feeding on algae and detritus, then insects, invertebrates, small fish, and larger fish. One challenge for the fisherman is to match bait or lures to this widely variable diet—to offer fish what, in fact, they want to eat.

Reptiles and amphibians can also be seen on the Juniata. Salamanders live in dark, damp places under stones, laying eggs in the water. Turtles often crawl onto logs that overhang the river, spending much of their time in the water but laying eggs on land.

With the abundance of aquatic life, many water-loving birds make their homes along the brushy, forested, or eroded shorelines. Sandpipers pick small insects and crustaceans from gravel or sandy edges. Kingfishers rattle their call, diving for minnows, frogs, and crayfish and living in a hole near

A young fisherman's catch, Juniata below Lewistown

swallow nests along a steep bank. Green herons and the less common yellow-crowned night herons fish the shallow waters, but showiest of all the Juniata birds are the great blue heron and the egret. An adult great blue is four feet high with a wingspan of six feet, eating small fish, frogs, salamanders, crayfish, and snakes. On land, they'll catch mice, often dunking them in the river for a Juniata dip before swallowing. Mergansers are diving ducks with sleek bodies, strong wings, and webbed feet for chasing small fish. I once removed a fishhook from a tangled merganser, and even though his wing feathers were broken from thrashing, he disappeared in an instant, swimming so far under water that I never saw him come up. To most people, mergansers are foul-tasting and inedible, and that is likely the reason so many can be seen on Pennsylvania rivers.

Along with larger fish and birds, the muskrat, mink, and raccoon are at the top of the Juniata's food chain. Plants and mussels are food for the muskrat. It, in turn, is favorite prey of the mink, a small, shy, beautiful fur bearer. Raccoons are true omnivores, eating almost anything: frogs, salamanders, crayfish, mussels, fish, nuts, leaves, turtles' eggs, birds' eggs, nestlings, corn, picnics, fishermen's fish, and garbage. Their hand-shaped tracks can be seen on sandy beaches everywhere along this and other Pennsylvania rivers.

We, of course, are also at the top of the Juniata food chain, feeding on smallmouth, musky, sunfish, and suckers, rather than algae, mayflies, and crayfish. While higher members of the chain benefit from the food processing of primary and secondary consumers, they also stand to suffer most from imbalances and toxic chemicals. Concentrations of many pollutants tend to accumulate as they rise through the food chain. While a mayfly may absorb small amounts of a hazardous substance, the minnow that eats 100 mayflies may consume 100 times that amount, the bass that eats 100 minnows receives 10,000 times that amount, and the fisherman who eats 100 bass may be dining on 1,000,000 times the pollution dosage. Since we know that toxic wastes like mercury, lead, and Kepone have been dumped into fresh water, it leads one to wonder just how safe Juniata fish are. Many people remember when you couldn't travel through the town of Tyrone without choking on the sulfur-filled air. What about the water? What is it doing to all these fish we're eating?

Bill Parsons, an engineer, and Jerry Miller, a biologist for the Pennsylvania Department of Environmental Resources, had some of the answers. "Pollution used to be severe at Tyrone, but it's greatly reduced now," Parsons said, "and the paper mill at Williamsburg closed, so we've seen pretty substantial improvement in water quality. Old paper mills used toxics like mercury, but we don't have trouble with it now. The big problem is at Roaring Spring, on a tributary to Frankstown Branch. Appleton Papers, a division of National Cash Register, is dumping copper, phenol, aluminum, color, odor, heat, and other pollutants." He paused. "Ever drink a dark brew with a nice thick head on it? Well, that's what the creek looks like. It's similar to the problem that we used to have at Tyrone, only worse. It's the worst pollution in central Pennsylvania, but Appleton is paying fines and trying to clean it up. Platinum-cobalt units of color went from 2,500 to 750 in four years, but the water standards limit is fifty, and it's supposed to be met by 1983. It's hard to see how the problem can ever be eliminated, with such a big operation on such a small stream." In 1979 agreements were reached whereby Appleton will more effectively treat their waste and will move their discharge to a larger stream.

"Sewage has been a problem in the past, but a lot of that's improving," Parsons went on. "Bedford just started their advanced treatment plant, which should do a real good job on the upper reaches of Raystown. Frankstown Branch has a tough start in Hollidaysburg and Altoona, but advanced treatment is only awaiting federal funds. Then there are local problems at Huntingdon and Lewistown, but no great impact. Near Lewistown, Honey Creek was *named* for its sewage problem, but half of that is being treated now, and the other half should be in a few years. Mining up Raystown Branch has just about sterilized Six Mile Run."

"It's hard to tell what paper mills or other industry did to fish in the past," Miller explained, "except that we know the river is extremely productive in spite of it. The Juniata's chemistry is excellent for growing things—the limestone origin of many tributaries helps, with high quantities of dissolved calcium and magnesium. There must be a new hatch of mayflies every two weeks during summer months. Crayfish are everywhere, and we found at least fifty rock bass under one boulder when we were electro-shocking during a biological survey."

While smallmouth draw fishermen and a muskellunge population is building, the Juniata could also become a key in the reintroduction of shad—a prized but nearly forgotten game fish. Susquehanna shad runs are legendary. A few old-timers recall thousands of them migrating from the Chesapeake Bay to spawn throughout the river basin. High dams blocked the shad's only route to survival. Conowingo in Maryland, and York Haven, Safe Harbor, and Holtwood Dams in Pennsylvania didn't include fish ladders, which in other rivers allow anadromous, or seagoing, species to complete their spawning run. Efforts have been made to capture and truck the fish around high Conowingo Dam, but without much success. The Pennsylvania Fish Commission is now rearing shad on the Juniata, hoping that the

Poling a canoe on the Juniata above Lewistown

problem of migration will be solved and that a new shad run will again
come to Susquehanna and Juniata waters.

Since life in the Juniata is so abundant and easily seen, this river tells us
something about all Pennsylvania waters. Ecological cycles, the food chain,
and all the life of the waterway are bound up together in a complex and
delicate system. The heron or muskellunge depend on minnows and crayfish, which depend on mayflies and caddisflies, which depend on algae that
we think of as weeds. Metals or chemicals ingested by a caddisfly are ingested by us when we have fish for dinner. While many streams are damaged and unable to support a healthy community of plants and animals, all
of them once did, and life could return to many waters as it has in the
Juniata.

The Upper Susquehanna:
A River with History

Because of its massive size, the Susquehanna is generally thought of in three parts: the wild West Branch, draining central and north central Pennsylvania, the upper river, or "North Branch," and the main stem, from the two branches' confluence at Sunbury to the Chesapeake Bay. Among other rivers of the nation, the Susquehanna ranks twelfth in average flow. The upper river is wide and winding—big, open waters with gentle riffles, pleasant scenery of farms and mountains, riverfront towns, and excellent warm-water fishing. Smallmouth bass, walleye, and muskellunge are plentiful. Several tributaries offer exciting and difficult whitewater paddling in the high flows of springtime: Sugar Creek, Towanda Creek, Schrader Branch of Towanda Creek, Wyalusing Creek, Tunkhannock Creek and its South Branch, Mehoopany Creek, and Bowman Creek.

A popular reach for lazy Susquehanna river traveling lies between Athens, near the New York border, and Tunkhannock, a small town thirty miles north of Scranton. "Tioga Point" was the earlier name for the narrow peninsula at Athens, the confluence of the Chemung and the Susquehanna. Here the rivers are dark brown, vile-looking but productive for fish. The Chemung, coming from the northwest, shows turbid evidence of Elmira and many farms. The Susquehanna originates in New York at Lake Otsega, "Glimmerglass" in the early American novels of James Fenimore

Cooper, then winds through scenic and pastoral hills, dips for thirty miles into Pennsylvania, bisects the Binghamton urban area, and then decidedly bends to the south. From Tioga Point down, water quality seems to gradually improve until the Lackawanna is reached.

Like the lower Juniata and upper Allegheny, Susquehanna shorelines are low and thickly tangled with vegetation. They are a prime wildlife habitat for often-seen herons, ducks, and shore birds. Unknowingly, we once camped beneath a great horned owl's nest, spotting the young predators late in the evening. To avoid disturbing the family more than we already had, we quickly got in our tents, while the mother sat on a distant limb, silhouetted in owlish seriousness, hooting as darkness grew.

High cliffs and rock outcrops add interest to the rolling landscape and offer good views. Best known of these are Wyalusing Rocks, just above Wyalusing and easily accessible from scenic Route 6. The wildest section of river lies below Mehoopany, as the Susquehanna drops over a sharp riffle, then wraps around a large and roadless bend, while even the railroad temporarily disappears into a tunnel. Lower sections from Wilkes-Barre to the West Branch confluence at Sunbury are more polluted, straighter, and less mountainous than the 100-mile reach in the northern counties of Bradford and Wyoming.

Etienne Brulé is largely unknown in American history, yet he was one of the great North American explorers and the first European to see much of the Susquehanna and Pennsylvania. The young Frenchman left no record of his travels and life among Indians, though a thread of his existence appears haphazardly in the writings of Champlain, Sagard, and Brébeuf. It was in 1610 that Brulé, working in Quebec under Samuel de Champlain, asked if he might winter with the Huron Indians to learn their language. Champlain agreed, and Brulé, probably eighteen years old, became the first European to travel the Ottawa and Mattawa rivers, to see Lake Nipissing and Georgian Bay, and to speak Huron. Eventually he would be the first white man to discover four of the five Great Lakes.

After aiding the Hurons against the Iroquois in 1609, the French initiated a long-lasting conflict. The significance of Brulé's involvement began in 1615, when Champlain and the Hurons were on their way southward to fight the Iroquois. Huron braves were selected to circle the southern territory and enlist aid from the Susquehannocks, allies of the Hurons from southern New York and northern Pennsylvania. Brulé sought permission to follow them, "to which I readily agreed," wrote Champlain, "since he was drawn thereto of his own inclination, and by this means would see their country and could observe the tribes that inhabit it." The mission proved unsuccessful, as the Susquehannock aid arrived at Champlain's prearranged meeting place only to discover that the Onondaga Nation of Iroquois had already defeated the combined French and Huron forces. In a

Opposite: Susquehanna below Sayre

pattern that he later adopted for life, Brulé chose not to return to Champlain's party and traveled southward with the Indians, beginning his two-year Susquehanna voyage.

Champlain later wrote of Brulé's journey:

> He employed himself in exploring the country visiting neighboring nations and lands and in passing the length of a river which discharges on the coast of Florida. The climate is very temperate and there are a great number of animals and game to be hunted. But to travel this country one must have great patience, for difficulties are to be met in its wilderness. And he continued as far as the sea along this river, past islands in it and lands that border it, which are inhabited by several nations and many savage peoples. And after he had traversed the country and discovered what was noticeable he returned to Carantouan.

In a feat of early exploration, Brulé followed the river from New York to the Chesapeake Bay (mistaken for the coast of Florida) and back again. Some historians have speculated that he may also have poled up the West Branch to the present site of Muncy. Throughout 1615 and 1616, Brulé

Foam in the Susquehanna below Towanda

passed Tioga Point, Standing Stone, Wyalusing Rocks, a crystal-clear Lackawanna, an expansive West Branch confluence, rapids full of migrating
shad at York Haven, and the great falls where Conowingo Dam now sits. A
lone white man, aided only by primitive equipment, he cruised the length
of a great river and back again. John Smith received credit for discovering
the Susquehanna in 1608, though he sailed only to the mouth of the river
and took one look at the rapids below Conowingo Falls, declaring them
unnavigable. After Brulé's voyage, over 100 years elapsed before the first
settlers arrived.

The upper river is best known in history for revolutionary war battles in
the Wyoming Valley of Luzerne County and for the Yankee-Pennamite
Wars, resulting from dual land claims by the colonies of Pennsylvania and
Connecticut.

Before the borders of the colonies were definitely established and agreed
upon, Pennsylvanians thought the upper Susquehanna and Lackawanna
valleys belonged to them, dating from a 1736 sale by the Indians to Thomas
and Richard Penn, and later by a 1768 deed that was drafted at Fort Stanwix,
New York. Meanwhile the Connecticut Susquehanna Company was formed as
the first great real-estate brokerage for the region. In 1754 it executed a
treaty with the Iroquois nations, gaining yet another title to land known as the
Wyoming Valley. It is likely that the Indians never intended the land to be
deeded, in the English sense of the word, but rather conceived of a proposi-
tion by which land would be shared. Ambiguous royal grants also complicated
the situation. New Englanders poured into the area in 1763, and with firm

Homemade raft, the Susquehanna above Towanda

occupancy, questions of colonial ownership had to wait until after the Revolutionary War. The heritage of Yankee settlers can be seen today in the distinct New England architectural styles that are common across the northern tier of Pennsylvania, extending south to the village of Picture Rocks on Muncy Creek and to the town of Muncy.

During this era the upper Susquehanna and its West Branch valley were frontier regions and as such became the target of Indian attacks, which were supplied and incited by the British. In 1778, while Washington's revolutionary army was occupied elsewhere, 400 British and 700 Iroquois embarked from Tioga Point, landed at Bowman Creek below Tunkhannock, and crossed the mountains to Wyoming Valley. The New England colonists were led by Zebulon Butler and the fanatical Lazarus Stewart, who had instigated the Paxtang Boys' killing of peaceful Indian families near Lancaster in the "Conestoga Massacre." Leaving their fort, the Yankees attacked the stronger force and lost half their men. This became known as the second Wyoming Massacre (the first having taken place in 1763) and signaled the "Big Runaway"—a movement of nearly all frontier settlers down the rivers to safety. As word of the fighting spread southward and up to the West Branch, frontier farmers packed what they could onto rowboats, rafts, and tied-together logs and drifted with the current to white settlements below.

Counterattacks came, as colonial armies followed river routes into Iroquois and British-occupied country. Thomas Hartley led 200 men from

Photo by John Lazenby

Susquehanna at Towanda

Muncy, up Lycoming Creek, down Towanda and Sugar creeks to Tioga. Then a major expedition to recapture lands and to break Indian resistance was directed by General John Sullivan. With 3,500 men and 2,000 pack horses the army walked north, sometimes wading deep into the Susquehanna. They camped at the Lackawanna River, Wyalusing, Sheshequin, and Tioga Point. James Clinton built 200 bateaux at Otsega Lake, dammed the outlet to collect a head of water, then destroyed the dam and rode the flood crest toward Tioga Point, where he combined forces with Sullivan. Without contest, the army marched north and west, destroying Iroquois villages and crops through the upper Susquehanna and Genessee basins. General William T. Sherman is generally credited with developing burned-landscape warfare as he crossed Georgia in 1864, but Sullivan perfected the style nearly 100 years earlier. After the Revolution, Pennsylvanians and Connecticuters turned to fighting one another until land claims were finally settled.

Much history has touched the upper Susquehanna. French Azilum was a colony begun in 1793 along the western shore, south of Towanda near Standing Stone. Two hundred fugitives from the French Revolution lived here, intending to bring Marie Antoinette. They traveled up the river in Durham boats and built fifty log cabins, including a sixty-by-eighty-foot, 2½-story log mansion for the Queen and Dauphin, who were unable to escape from France. An Azilum corporation is now attempting to reconstruct parts of the settlement.

Several songs of Stephen Foster deal with the upper Susquehanna, the "Tioga Waltz" and "Camptown Races," which were annually run at the small village of Camptown northeast of Wyalusing. The Susquehanna Canal was constructed along these reaches, and remains can be found in many areas.

History along the river has recorded the boom and bust of anthracite coal in the Scranton, Wilkes-Barre, and Hazelton regions. In the late 1960s, conflict raged over the planned construction of an experimental fast-breeder nuclear reactor near Tunkhannock. Though they faced a long and seemingly hopeless struggle, local residents who opposed the development succeeded in stopping the nuclear project. Downriver, at Berwick, a different nuclear reactor is now being built, but still contested.

The greatest of all American storms, Hurricane Agnes, caused flooding over much of the northeast in June 1972. Nowhere was the damage greater than in Wilkes-Barre, where the Susquehanna overtopped the city dikes. Damages to the Wyoming Valley area were estimated at over $2 billion; 80,000 people were temporarily displaced and 20,000 lost their homes. Flooding of the city began when water breached sections of the dike that had subsided over coal mines. Along with Johnstown, Wilkes-Barre illustrates the false sense of security created by flood-control structures.

Penetrating the Scranton urban area and meeting the Susquehanna between this city and Wilkes-Barre, the Lackawanna River is slowly recovering from the frenzied abuse of consecutive timber, iron, and coal eras. Mine drainage, sewage, and industrial wastes remain a problem, but the stream has improved, with new waterfront parks at Scranton and Mayfield. A springtime canoe regatta, sponsored annually by the Chamber of Commerce and the Luzerne-Lackawanna Environmental Council, draws support for the river and for preserving it. Except for the Pocono headwaters, the river does not meet water-quality standards for swimming. Someday, though, the Lackawanna could shine as a success in river reclamation.

Because of the natural, historical, and recreational values of the upper Susquehanna, designation of the river in the state scenic-river system is being sought by the Save the Endless Mountains Association, a citizens' organization that is active in a five-county region.

Susquehanna Basin River Sketches

Sinnemahoning Creek

Sinnemahoning is a major stream system of north central Pennsylvania. Its three main branches—Driftwood, Bennett, and First Fork—form the largest West Branch Susquehanna tributary. Thousands of acres are wild and unpopulated, though many southern and western regions have been strip mined.

Bennett is the largest branch and also the most affected by mine acid. Beginning near DuBois, the stream flows north and east, joined by polluted tributaries but also by clean trout waters like Medix Run. Fish are

The old Commercial Hotel along the Sinnemahoning, village of Driftwood

Trout fisherman, Driftwood Branch, Sinnemahoning Creek below Emporium

nearly nonexistent in Bennett Branch, and though orange precipitate or "yellow boy" stains the bed, views of the creek from Route 555 are very scenic, and canoe travel is excellent through early and mid springtime. There is little development along the stream, as the acid waters have never attracted fishermen. Riffles are Class I, with several fast rocky sections.

Driftwood Branch begins northeast of Saint Marys, flows through Emporium, and parallels Route 120 to the village of Driftwood, where it meets Bennett Branch. Driftwood is cleaner and still improving, with good fishing along much of its length. From Emporium or Cameron down, this makes an excellent but easy canoe voyage in high and medium-high waters of March, April, and sometimes May. The finest section is a series of wide bends below the village of Sterling Run.

First Fork is the smallest of three Sinnemahoning branches, but includes the best fishing waters. Thousands of anglers converge on the First Fork and its East Fork at the beginning of trout season. Clear waters drift through wide meadows and willow thickets with steep-sloped mountains of the north central highlands as a continual backdrop. Trailers and low-cost hunting and fishing cabins are scattered across many of the abandoned valley farms and crowd the banks of the stream, especially below Stevenson Dam.

The main stem of the Sinnemahoning is a wide, gentle stream that would be called a river in any other part of the country but Pennsylvania. Route 120 and a railroad parallel its shores, but much of the waterfront is still undisturbed. It is especially scenic below the mouth of the First Fork. This is an excellent beginner's canoe trip, with an easy take-out at Keating bridge, just before the West Branch of the Susquehanna.

Pennsylvania's only elk herd lives in the Sinnemahoning basin. This region also has an interesting history, which includes the notorious logging era of the late 1800s and tales about a legendary boatload of gold bullion that disappeared while being shipped downriver during the Civil War. It won't hurt to scratch around your camp site if you canoe the Sinnemahoning!

Little Pine Creek

Little Pine is the largest tributary to Pine Creek, entering at Waterville, which is near the lower end of the National Scenic River Study. North central forests and farmland feed water to Little Pine through a valley of unusual charm and scenic appeal. Origins of the stream lie near the town of Liberty. Pollution from a milk processing plant has been a problem here, and small amounts of acid mine drainage enter below the village of English Center, but overall water quality is excellent.

Unlike the steep and narrow gorge of Pine Creek, this valley stretches as a flat expanse, a half mile in width. Mountains border its edges, and clear water angles back and forth through rapids and pools. Little Pine is an almost unknown canoeing waterway. Its sharp bends, narrow chutes, and sudden drops make English Center to Little Pine Dam an excellent and exciting run when the flow is at high level. Thousands of fishermen come here in April. The stream and reservoir are heavily stocked, but high water temperatures will not support a year-round population of trout. A state park is maintained at the impoundment, eight miles north of Waterville, though the dam may become best known for its inordinate load of silt. The project is less than thirty years old, and mud has nearly filled the lake area to its summer pool elevation. The cost of removing the silt is prohibitive. Ironically, the flood-control dam was filled to capacity eight hours before the crest of the Hurricane Agnes flood of 1972; at the highest point of discharge, water simply entered one end of the impoundment and flowed out of the other, providing little or no flood mitigation to downstream communities.

Little Pine Creek Reservoir, with accumulation of silt

Sunrise, Little Pine Creek below English Center

Lycoming Creek

Flowing due south to the Susquehanna's West Branch, Lycoming Creek shows many contrasts of Pennsylvania. Headwaters begin on rolling dairy farms. The creek passes Roaring Branch and Ralston, small villages with wooden frame buildings typical of old-time mining and lumber towns. High slopes with rocky outcrops confine a scenic valley. Below Trout Run village, the creek passes a final gap in the Allegheny Front, leaving the northern plateau and gorge country for a gentler West Branch Valley. Here, with closely paralleling highways, development crowds the creek. Seasonal homes and cabins have been converted to year-round residences, trailer parks have multiplied, and commercial development of Route 15 spreads erratically. In spite of this, many scenic reaches of lower Lycoming

First day of trout season, Lycoming Creek at Fields Station

still remain. At Heshbon Cliffs, rocky faces and old hemlocks rise from the western bank. A relocation of Route 15 is likely to cross this area.

Lycoming Creek offers very good fishing, though excavation of flood-deposited gravel has affected lower reaches. Whitewater canoeing is excellent, with exciting Class II rapids in upper sections that can be run only during high water. Tight bends and fallen timber demand fast maneuvering.

Highlighting the basin is the scenic tributary, Rock Run. Flowing fifteen miles from Ellenton to Ralston, this crystalline stream reveals pools swirled in deep green, with rapids and small falls. Miners Run is another, smaller tributary to Rock Run, dropping from the northern mountainside in many waterfalls. Nearly all of Rock Run is on state forest land; however, mineral rights in upper reaches remain in private ownership. "Natural" and "wild" area status under state forest management has been considered to gain protection for the stream banks, but neither designation has been enacted.

Tioga River

Flowing north from Pennsylvania to New York are the Tioga, Genesee, and Allegheny rivers. While the Genesee becomes a major tributary to Lake Ontario and then the St. Lawrence, the Allegheny returns to Pennsylvania in Kinzua Dam. The Tioga joins a broad, muddy Chemung, again flowing south to the Susquehanna at Tioga Point or Athens, Pennsylvania. Though the Tioga is a large stream draining 461 square miles, it is not well-known outside the local area. Mine acid infects the river from its headwaters near Arnot and Morris Run. Deep mining was extensive; tunnels were dug into the mountains, which now discharge thousands of gallons of acid water. Modern strip-mining techniques may be reclaiming some of these areas by reexcavating the mines, then backfilling to minimize the amount of water that flows into acid-bearing shales.

During high springtime runoff, exciting whitewater flows above Blossburg and downstream toward Covington. After that, the river is slower and closely paralleled by Route 15. Efforts to remove flood-deposited gravel and to dike sections of riverbank have resulted in extensive bulldozing. A dam is under construction near the town of Tioga by the Army Corps of Engineers. Waters will be impounded for ten miles, while an adjacent dam will flood a portion of Crooked Creek, a Tioga tributary. Landslides have plagued construction efforts, though the completed reservoirs should provide flood protection to the downstream communities of Corning and Elmira. As a separate effort, the Soil Conservation Service has prepared a nonstructural flood control plan—the first of its kind to be proposed by that agency.

Towanda Creek

Most tributaries to the upper Susquehanna, or the portion above the mouth of the West Branch, are fairly short. Exceptions to this are the Chemung, which is primarily a New York river, the highly polluted Lackawanna, which flows through Carbondale and Scranton, Tunkhannock Creek, Fishing Creek, and Towanda Creek.

Towanda's watershed rises near Canton and enters the Susquehanna through broad, swampy wetlands below Towanda. Route 414 is a scenic drive through this agricultural valley, with rolling dairy farms, highland ridges to the south, and frequent evidence of glacial activity which scoured northern Pennsylvania years ago. Fishing is good, and canoeing includes a mixture of fast and gentle current, but only during high water.

The Schrader Branch of Towanda Creek is a highlight. Covering over one-third of the basin, most of this stream is within state game lands. An abandoned railroad right-of-way follows a wooded Schrader Valley as the stream twists and plunges. This is one of the few wild reaches of stream in Pennsylvania that has no road or railroad for ten miles or longer. Water quality and trout fishing are outstanding.

Penns Creek

In the central Pennsylvania country of high northeastward-pointing ridges and spacious agricultural valleys, the basin of Penns Creek includes 554 square miles. Rising in Penns Cave near Potters Mills and State College, it flows eastward past Coburn, Weikert, Laurelton, and the hamlet of Penns Creek, where Walnut Acres—a well-known organic farm and natural foods store—is located. The stream forms a western boundary of the Isle of Que, which is a long peninsula in the mile-wide Susquehanna near Selinsgrove.

Waters of lower Penns Creek often run muddy; however, the quality of its upper reaches is excellent. Vast deposits of limestone and cool spring waters make this a productive and popular trout fishery. Public acquisition of a railroad right-of-way between Coburn and Weikert has complemented state forest holdings along the stream, offering a scenic hiking trail with fishing access. Rock climbers from Penn State University also use this area, visiting a rugged set of cliffs near Coburn. Canoeing on Penns Creek is possible in early spring, but since this is a favorite stream of many fishermen, it's best to float other waters after the opening of trout season in mid April.

Penns Creek below Poe Paddy State Park

Stony Creek

Stony Creek has become known as the closest wild valley to Harrisburg and southeast population centers of the Commonwealth. Waters flow for thirty miles between Second Mountain and Stony Mountain, meeting the Susquehanna at Dauphin, only twelve miles north of the state capital. Though the basin area is only thirty-six square miles, the upper two-thirds has no public roads or vehicular access. Clean waters cross small riffles, then deep pools that offer excellent trout fishing. Heavy cobbles nearly always cover the bottom—water-worn sandstone from paralleling mountain ridges. The area has been popular with thousands of fishermen and hunters. Backpackers now hike in Stony Creek Valley, and hundreds of bicyclists use an old road that is closed to motor vehicles.

Stony Creek near the site of a proposed pump-storage reservoir project

The upper basin was protected as state game lands in the 1960s; however, 1,700 acres of Stony Creek Valley were traded to the Pennsylvania Power and Light and Metropolitan Edison companies for 5,400 road-accessible acres in neighboring Clark Creek Valley. PP&L plans to construct a reservoir for electric power generation through pump storage—a process whereby water would be pumped from a Stony Creek impoundment to a secondary reservoir on top of the mountain, then dropped from the higher storage area to generate power at peak periods, or times when demand for electricity is greatest.

Opponents to the project have been vocal, numerous, and effective. Led by the Stony Creek Valley Coalition, they include many major conservation and environmental groups. They charge that Stony is the last remaining wild valley of southeastern Pennsylvania, that its values are irreplaceable, that the pump storage project is inefficient, and that the game lands should not have been traded in the first place. Nevertheless, PP&L plans to proceed, though it has delayed development activities. Many questions remain to be resolved before construction will begin, if ever. In 1978 study was initiated for the state scenic-river designation, which would probably stop the dam.

Conestoga Creek

Much of southeastern Pennsylvania drains toward the Susquehanna through Swatara, Conewago, Conestoga, Pequea, and Octoraro creeks. This rich agricultural belt has been one of the most productive farming regions in the world.

Conestoga is the best-known stream, drifting past the historic city of Lancaster. A canal operated along Conestoga, and the remains of locks can be seen. More than anything else, the Conestoga wagon has made this a familiar name. The large, canvas-covered "prairie schooners" were invented and originally built in the area, then sold to settlers during the early westward movement.

Yellow and muddy with Lancaster County runoff, Conestoga exemplifies many of the farmland creeks. A Pennsylvania State University report estimates that twelve tons of soil are lost each year from an average agricultural acre.

Warm-water fish such as bass, suckers, carp, and catfish can be caught in the Conestoga. Canoeists can make a pleasant trip on medium or high waters from Lancaster to a park near Safe Harbor Power Plant on the Susquehanna. Several short portages are necessary.

The Ohio Basin

The Allegheny:
River of Northwestern Pennsylvania

Rainfall from northwestern Pennsylvania flows to New Orleans, and the entire path could have been called Allegheny. This river is larger than the Monongahela where they join to form the Ohio. The Ohio, in turn, carries twice the volume of the Mississippi at Cairo, where the two megarivers meet. Thus if one were to begin in the Gulf of Mexico and journey northward by always following the larger fork of the stream, one would eventually reach Coudersport in Potter County. As it happened, different names were selected for this single massive waterway. The French labeled the Mississippi, Ohio, and Allegheny from Indian dialects, which are translated as "Great River," "Beautiful River," and "Fair Waters."

The Allegheny flows gently for 314 miles to Pittsburgh. Walleye, muskellunge, northern pike, and smallmouth bass make it a popular warm-water fishery. It is a large river, attractive to canoeists, campers, and just about everybody. Brady's Bend is one of its landmarks, complete with historical marker and twenty-five-cent telescopes. Art festival visitors go swimming at Kennerdale, Boy Scouts flock to camp near Tionesta, a national forest welcomes campers at Buckaloons, motorboaters launch into Kinzua Reservoir, and deer hunters migrate to the McKean and Potter county headwaters.

Like the Delaware, its upstream reaches bear no resemblance to the lower urban ones. Industry and highways monopolize water frontage near Pittsburgh in a blanketed way that compares only to the Monongahela, Ohio, Schuylkill, and tidal Delaware. A series of nine dams and locks step upward to New Kensington and Kittanning, drawing barges of the Mississippi and Ohio to the north and the rural core of Pennsylvania. Parts of the lower river are being restored to an undevastated condition. The Western Pennsylvania Conservancy is acquiring wooded islands, and opportunities for public access to the water are improving.

If one were to segregate the Allegheny of northern Pennsylvania from the rest of the river, East Brady could be the boundary. Here, seventy-two miles above the Ohio River, the backwater of dam number nine stops, and one can see a smooth, winding current. Without a navigation channel, the industrial conglomeration of the waterfront terminates and only reappears

Opposite: Potter County Courthouse and the Allegheny flood channel, Coudersport

Sunrise and Labrador Retriever, Allegheny River
near Franklin

at sporadic intervals. Emlenton lies twenty-one miles upstream, and thousands of canoeists and fishermen use a thirty-five-mile section that reaches
farther northward to Franklin. Cottages and cabins are scattered here and
elsewhere on the middle and upper Allegheny, as the current weaves in
distended coiling bends. Green herons nest by the dozens in a riverine
cover of willows and birch. Yellow sneezeweed colors the shorelines in August, and wet-rooted, white-flowered "lizards tail" blurs the boundary of
water and land, blooming in a profligacy that rivals the dandelions of my
backyard. Kennerdale is a village and cabin complex where an art and music festival is held each August. Here 3,140 acres of the west shore have
been acquired by the Commonwealth for Allegheny State Park, but no facilities have been developed.

In the 1830s a canal was constructed up French Creek, a tributary that
meets the Allegheny at Franklin, the site of historic Fort Venango. French
Creek Canal was the ultimate in poor planning, as there wasn't enough
water to float a boat. The dry canal, however, represented the beginnings
of a more ambitious idea—an inland commercial waterway from Lake Erie
to Pittsburgh, with "an escalation of poor planning," as one local critic said.
In 1919 the Allegheny River Improvement Association was formed to promote advancement of locks and dams upstream from Pittsburgh and to
support a route of commerce to the Great Lakes.

A similar proposal was advanced for canal construction from the port city of Ashtabula on Lake Erie to the industrialized Ohio River via Youngstown, New Castle, and the Beaver River. The project has been criticized for its projected cost, farmland consumption, resident displacement, and ecological impact on streams and Lake Erie. The benefactors would be industries along the way, primarily in Youngstown. It was known as "Mike's Ditch" after Michael Kirwan of Ohio, senior member of the U.S. House Appropriations Committee. Kirwan supported it, while freshman Representative Joseph Vigorito of Pennsylvania objected, saying the project included "cynically juggled figures to justify an indefensible boondoggle," yet in 1968 it gained the credibility of $2 million in planning funds.

The more eastern Allegheny Canal route attracted renewed attention after Kirwan ended his last term in office. Through the project, industrial traffic would be extended above dam number nine at Brady's Bend, through Emlenton to Franklin, and then up French Creek to Erie. The canal was long regarded as the primary reason for opposition to National Scenic River designation of the Allegheny, protection that would prohibit canal construction within the designated reach.

While the canal has been a threat so unlikely and long-debated that few people get excited any more, dredging of sand and gravel from the middle and upper Allegheny was an issue that exploded statewide in 1974.

For years commercial operators had been dredging sections of the river above Oil City. When temporary permit extensions were granted in 1972, the Pennsylvania Department of Environmental Resources included three stipulations under the Dams and Encroachments Act and Clean Streams Act: dredging was prohibited within fifty feet of shorelines, during weekends or holidays, and in natural or undisturbed areas. Operators appealed the restrictions, raising questions that were not resolved until 1976. Opponents of dredging sought to eliminate all mining from the river, stating that land-based sand and gravel should be extracted. A United States Fish and Wildlife Service report recommended a phase-out of dredging, identifying what many people recognized as obvious: game-fish populations in natural reaches of the river were far superior to those in disturbed areas. The study also counted sixty-nine species of fish, three of which are endangered in the state. Regional benefits of a $113 million recreational economy were regarded by fishing and recreation interests to be far more significant than those of river excavation. Pennsylvania's Federation of Sportsman's Clubs supported the dredgers' fight, saying that no permanent harm to the river would result from continuing to dredge. The Department of Transportation, largest purchaser of gravel, testified in support of the sand and gravel companies.

A newly formed Allegheny River Protective Association worked to restrict the dredging, but statewide attention was not apparent until introduction of House Bill 685, proposed legislation that would have eliminated the Department of Environmental Resources' authority to deny or adequately regulate river-based mining operations. Reaction was incensed from all corners of the Commonwealth, as this bill was not limited to the Allegheny but included waters throughout the state. Environmentalists became active in fighting the "Allegheny River dredging bill," a measure that ultimately passed the House, where Representative John Ladaddio had sponsored it, but not the Senate.

In 1976, when the heat of controversy subsided, the Department published a new policy and new regulations. A five-year phase-out of all dredging above East Brady was announced and praised by river enthusiasts. The waterway was clearly recognized as a significant natural resource: "No other stream in northwestern Pennsylvania has the recreational and fishery value of the Upper Allegheny." The Department's position was greatly enhanced by national and state scenic-river systems. DER stated: "The Upper Allegheny River . . . has been named as a potential addition to the National Wild and Scenic Rivers System, under proposed Federal legislation, and has been designated for in-depth study as a highest priority river under the Pennsylvania Wild and Scenic Rivers program."

Both the canal and dredging issues have stimulated support for the scenic-river programs. Federal designation would prohibit the use of federal funds for the canal, and the mere potential for designation helped the state adopt a policy against dredging. In 1968 the entire river from Kinzua Dam (built before the Wild and Scenic Rivers Act was considered) to Pittsburgh was recommended for federal study by Congressman John Saylor, but upper Allegheny Representative Albert Johnson deleted his section, leaving only the industrial flatwater below East Brady. The lower Allegheny study attained notoriety as the easiest one that the Bureau of Outdoor Recreation ever did. One glance told them that the river was ineligible because of pollution, dams, and development. The federal agency went through the motions, however, and in 1973 produced a thirty-two-page report, which significantly recommended another study, the same one originally intended by Saylor. "As a result of the feasibility investigation, it is recommended that the Upper Allegheny, between East Brady and Kinzua Dam, be considered for future in-depth study to determine whether it qualifies for inclusion in the National Wild and Scenic Rivers System."

Armed with an official report, Paul Bohlander, Lud Haller, and other members of the Protective Association gained support from Senators Hugh Scott and Richard Schweiker. George Reese of Greenville testified before a Senate committee in 1975, pointing out the recreational values of the river and the pressures that threatened them.

The state Department of Environmental Resources also supported a bill that would authorize federal study of the Allegheny. A 1974 comment of the governor was repeated: "I would like to recommend that the upper section of the river, from Kinzua Dam to East Brady, be included for future study for possible designation in the National Wild and Scenic Rivers System."

Deputy Secretary Clifford McConnell of the Department also referred to the state planning report, "Outdoor Recreation Horizons": "Those guidelines are explicit in support of the National Wild and Scenic Rivers Act and identify this particular river segment as a potential candidate for detailed study."

Resistance came from Representative Johnson and from local economic interests, such as the Warren County Chamber of Commerce. "This three-year study is a narrow, one-shot deal and would practically paralyze all activities on and along the river for the duration of the study," the congressman said.

"In fact," Protective Association spokesman Reese replied, "the study would only place a moratorium on federal funds for water resource projects, such as the canal." The next election saw the congressman soundly defeated. In 1978 the National Parks and Recreation Act authorized a study of the upper Allegheny for the national rivers system.

Allegheny River below West Hickory

Below Kinzua the Allegheny has two exceptionally scenic areas: the thirty-five-mile reach between Franklin and Emlenton, and fifty miles of river from Buckaloons to Oil City. While great falcated bends characterize the lower and shorter reach, the more northern passage is uncommonly rich in islands. This is a favorite section of the Allegheny, for here are many rivers in a maze of miniature, convoluted channels. Travelers are drawn into

Allegheny River near Oil City

wooded backwaters and a mystery of twisting riffles that flatten into maple-crowded pools. Turtles as big as serving platters lie on sun-warmed rocks, great blue herons wade into the shallows, and kingfishers rattle their call from one bank to the next. The islands offer a liberty of separation from other lands and people. They are a world apart, and you can relax in confidence that no trucks or locomotives will run you down. Euell Gibbons called an island "a small body of land surrounded by the need for a boat."

As in the Susquehanna below Sunbury, islands are everywhere, a result of the river's tireless energy in clutching soil fragments from above, carrying them downward in a brown current, then dropping the oozing earth in quiet eddies. Like drifting snow, watery lands continually change; more soil settles on leeward sides, while floods rip at the upper extremities. Long and slender forms have outgrown themselves when high water rattles the brush and breaks into the land, digging one spot, then consuming another, eventually bursting forth on the opposite side. The land is split, and afterward the incision may grow deeper. As a constricted passage, the new channel may trap unearthed trees and the infinite assortment of debris that floats in a flood. Keelboat and steamboat pilots had names for all the islands: Brokenstraw, Clark's, Thompson's, Steward, Charley Smith's Bars, Mill Stone, Goose Flat, McGee's Bar, Courson, Maguyer's Bar, Tidioute, White Oak, Hemlock, Hickory Town, and many more.

"Islands are a highlight of the Allegheny," said John Oliver, president of the Western Pennsylvania Conservancy, a private, nonprofit conservation organization that has done remarkable work to protect sections of the Youghiogheny, Slippery Rock Creek, and this river. Recognizing the waterway's vast importance, the Conservancy has undertaken a task that only it could effectively accomplish. David Fahringer, a noted landscape architect, was hired to prepare a comprehensive study of the riverine corridor, identifying scenic, wild, or recreationally valuable areas. Then, with a technique that had matured over many years, the Pittsburgh-based organization launched an effort to buy selected lands of the Allegheny.

Crulls Island was acquired and later resold to the federal government as an addition to Allegheny National Forest. "We're also acquiring vacant shorelines, adjacent hillsides, and access areas for boaters and fishermen," said Oliver. "The Allegheny represents one of the most significant features in the natural heritage of western Pennsylvania, and our goal is to save what we can of the remaining undeveloped lands." Usually the Conservancy resells its newly acquired property to a state or federal agency, which agrees to protect the land. So far 6,500 acres have been secured as open space.

In 1977, 1,355 Allegheny acres were protected in a way that exemplifies the Conservancy's importance and unique role. The Forest Service owned seven acres of commercial real estate in Radnor, near Philadelphia. Originally the site was intended to become a new Forest Service headquarters, plans which the government later dropped. By law the Forest Service cannot sell land, but exchanges of property are allowed. After two years of negotiating, the Conservancy acquired five parcels of Allegheny River frontage, traded them for the seven commercial acres that were appraised at a similar value, then sold the commercial land to a tennis-court developer. This recovered the original Allegheny investment, which again jingled in the Conservancy's pocket, burning a hole for another sandy bank with silver maples.

The Western Pennsylvania Conservancy's acquisition program may be an important indicator of changing trends and strategies in open-land preservation and recreational development. The river has been recognized as a focus, and efforts are made to preserve pieces of shoreline, scattered as they might be. Clearly this differs from the "buy-and-build-a-park" technique that was more common for many years. The new approach incorporates several important features:

It is based on the riverine environment rather than on establishing a consolidated management unit where access and activity can be tightly controlled. By securing key sections of riverway, environmental protection and water-oriented recreational objectives may be best accomplished, since these lands are the most fragile and also the most desirable for leisure-time activities. A project is likely to be regional in scope, crossing many counties and involving different kinds of landscapes and communities.

The final result will be a patchwork of publicly and privately owned lands, not a solid "block of green" on the map. Public ownership will be important for access, recreational sites, natural areas, and wild lands. Otherwise, private use will prevail, probably with local zoning and flood-plain regulations. Efforts are long-term, reflecting the complexity, the lack of condemnation powers, and the broad goals of the programs.

Legal action such as scenic-river designation may be sought to protect the river—a much larger resource than a park. Many difficult questions are involved: Is a dam needed for flood control, water supply, or hydroelectric generation? Is a canal feasible and in the best interest? The river, in essence, *is* the park, and there are frequent conflicts regarding its most appropriate use.

Recreation is not regarded as an independent activity but as a total experience. It incorporates a variety of skills and interests, such as camping, canoeing, fishing, outdoor cooking, hiking, nature study, and photography. It is not dependent on one particular site but upon a high-quality natural environment. It can involve many degrees of social togetherness from solitary wilderness to a group outing.

Cost alone has become a major deterrent to many conventional programs of park acquisition and recreation facility development. Construction and maintenance are very expensive. To buy large blocks of land is difficult, not to speak of the hostility and objections that accompany the threat of condemnation. "One favorable aspect of an inflationary economy is that it benefits the natural environment, and all government agencies must now recognize this," Oliver said. "To establish a river protection and recreation program, only inexpensive facilities need to be developed, and a relatively small percentage of shoreline may be essential for public acquisition." With the Western Pennsylvania Conservancy and with the access and open-space

Industrial discharge, Allegheny River at Emlenton

programs of the Pennsylvania Department of Environmental Resources, the United States Forest Service, and the Pennsylvania Game and Fish Commissions, many of our streams may remain available for public use.

Closer to the headwaters, Kinzua Dam formed northern Pennsylvania's longest impoundment in 1967 when it was hailed as an economic boon to northwestern counties and as a salvation to Pittsburgh through flood control. Recreation and flood reduction were the main purposes of the 180-foot dam, and it effectively provided both. The Flood Control Acts of 1936, 1938, and 1941 authorized the project, which had a 1.3 to 1.0 benefit-cost ratio: for every dollar spent, $1.30 would be returned. This was a close ratio, where at least a one-to-one comparison was needed for Congressional action. If the dam were being considered today, its construction would be questioned more seriously because of economics and escalated costs, environmental impact analysis, and perhaps most important, new social views.

The reservoir flooded a Seneca Indian Reservation given to Chief Cornplanter through the oldest treaty in the Congressional archives—an agreement that George Washington signed. The Seneca Nation would hold the lands "so long as the Allegheny flows and the sun and moon shine," the 1794 agreement read. Indians and their consultant, Arthur E. Morgan, argued that a better alternative to provide Pittsburgh's flood control was available. A legal battle ensued between the 482 Indians and the federal government, and while the court did not determine that the sun and moon would no longer shine, it was decided that the Allegheny would indeed cease to flow. Now the village sites of Jennesadaga and Kinzua are deep under watery brown silt.

After a long upstream journey from Pittsburgh, we finally enter the headwaters of the river that early French explorers called "La Belle Riviere." Steamboats once went as far as Salamanca and Olean, New York, where the river shrinks and shallow sand bars grow. In geologic history, the river once went north from Olean to Lake Erie, a route that became blocked by continental ice masses that forced the current into new paths southward. Similar reversals of flow happened at Warren and French Creek.

Rolling uplands of the basin are vastly different from the mountainous shorelines below, for this is hill-farming country, much of it now abandoned but showing many signs of past activity. Above Eldred the river penetrates deep woodlands of the "Allegheny Flats." Currents weave through a low, boglike forest that seems primeval in its wetness. With yearly floods, the flats have been unaffected by cabins and roads. This is the wildest part of the entire Allegheny, twisting in a serene monotony of miles. I've floated on the high waves of March when braids of river escape the muddy streambed and filter through the woods. Ponds lie everywhere, as lands behind the riverbank slope downward to the remains of ancient

Unloading at a campsite, upper Allegheny River

High water in the Allegheny flats below Port Allegany

channels. The phenomenon is unique to flatlands: when the stream is running bank-full, the canoeist can look *down* into the woods that lie at each side.

Like diagrams in geography books, meanders loop erratically, recurved upon themselves so that the traveler loses all accurate sense of direction. The river borders Port Allegany, called "Canoe Place" in earlier days. Here the long portage began—an Indian trail that connected waters of midland America to an eastern flow of the Sinnemahoning and Susquehanna. The river is drawn smaller, attenuated between sharp-cornered bends, and then Coudersport is bisected by a concrete channel that was created for flood protection. From there, an ascent begins toward the high divide of forest and farms where rainwater flows north to Lake Ontario, east toward the Chesapeake Bay, and southeast on a long voyage to the Gulf of Mexico.

Opposite: Clarion River below Ridgway

The Clarion: Clear Water Again?

It was one of those first springtime evenings. Warming us from a cold winter detachment, a breeze along the river carried the scent of soil, pine, and life. We sat on a flat rock that had been covered by high currents of early March and felt a new freshness as the last light of day glowed from ridges above. The Clarion churned mildly, just enough that the surface danced in watery agitation and most other sounds could be forgotten.

Behind us, on the road to Piney Dam, a sports car shifted down, coming to a stop. "It was a little too peaceful to last," Cindy said, as she turned to see what kind of company we had. Where a clearing had been cut along the banks of Deer Creek, just before it dumped a load of acid water into the river, the car was carefully parked. To our surprise, the hulking frame of Ken Linton, a limnologist from Clarion State College, emerged. He waved, smiled a little, and ambled toward us, stopping deliberately to peer into the stream in the manner of his trade. We had been friends for a while, and as the three of us talked, he turned stones, hunting a stonefly or a caddisfly nymph.

"There isn't a crawlin' thing in there," he concluded. "If you're looking for a sunset, you've found one, but I'm looking for life in that water, and there isn't any."

Linton agreed, however, that if you wanted to sit by a river, this was the only one. "This place is what keeps me going," he said a little later, as he

crawled back into the vehicle that seemed half his size, like the parson whose boots scuffled on the trail because his mule was too short. "It's got to be better. It can't go on like this. Right *there* is something that's got to be changed." He pointed to the orange-stained rocks, squinting seriously. Five years later, on the same beach where Cindy and I had enjoyed a spring evening, we loaded the canoe one morning for a twenty-mile cruise to the end of the river. At ten o'clock the water rose like a flash flood on the South Platte. Knowing that the release gates had been opened at Piney Hydroelectric Dam just upstream, we embarked from a glistening sand bar. As Ken Linton says, this reach of the Clarion is an ecological disaster with a pH of 4.0. Within this measure of acid or alkalinity, a rating of 6 or 7 would be normal. Lower scores mean more acid: a pH of 5 is the limit for keeping any fish alive. Piney Creek, Deer Creek, and Licking Creek pour their lifeless runoff from both sides; however, in all other respects, the lower river is a prize to the canoeist. Riffles are fast, and scenery is almost unmarred. For fifteen miles there are no roads or railroads.

We passed the proposed dam site near St. Petersburg. A 1969 Army Corps of Engineers' report calls for a structure nearly 300 feet high, which would impound waters for thirty miles to Cook Forest. Optimistically, the purposes are listed as "flood control, quality control, water supply, hydro-electric power, recreation, conservation, fish and wildlife enhancement, other environmental quality improvements, and economic development." Downstream groups such as the Three Rivers Improvement and Development Corporation in Pittsburgh have supported the dam, stating that it would have reduced flooding in June 1972 by three feet. Public benefits are claimed for industrial development of open space that lies downstream—lowlands of the Allegheny that now flood too frequently for private business to risk its investment. The Project Analysis report states, "In view of land now idle and potentially available for industrial develop-ment, flood plain regulation would not be an acceptable solution to the flood control problem." Fiscal conservatives and flood-plain management advocates objected, saying that it's one thing to claim benefits for protec-tion of *existing* development but quite another matter to list benefits for development of currently *vacant* land.

"The main problem is one of flood plain *development* control," says John Sweet of the American Canoe Association. "I don't agree that the public is to benefit from industrialization of flood plains and that tax dollars should be used to make these 'benefits' possible. Floods are a natural part of the life cycle along a river; if we don't want wet buildings, then we shouldn't build them there. Flood plains are less than five percent of the land—there are plenty of other places to go."

Economic development, however, has been a selling point, endorsed by the Appalachian Regional Commission and local individuals. Supporters of the reservoir recognized that cleaner water is a prerequisite for dam con-struction, and they began backing efforts to reduce mine drainage pollution. The Federal Water Resources Development Act of 1976 authorized a more detailed study of acid abatement for Clarion tributaries.

The lower eight miles of the river were especially enjoyable as it twisted in horseshoe bends with wild shorelines. Occasionally we could see evidence of coal stripping, but from the water one would never imagine the feverish activity that was taking place above. The return trip from Parker to Deer Creek by way of country roads seemed like a macabre tour of earthen surgery where the patient died. It occurred to me that the effect of coal mining on rivers is the inverse of urbanization. In mining country, uplands are ravaged, but the stream corridor is often untouched; with cities, the waterfront is the first land to be paved or industrialized, while highlands remain vacant. To pollute, both ways have been effective.

The troubles and values that I saw on the lower Clarion are reflected elsewhere along this 150-mile stream, but judging the rest of the watershed from these twenty miles would be like the blind man describing an elephant after feeling one leg. In Pennsylvania this is one of the major rivers and one of the most interesting.

The East Branch begins near Clermont and the West Branch near Mt. Jewett, high headwaters, as both names suggest. Similar streams run north to the Allegheny, west to Tionesta, or east to the many-branched forks of Sinnemahoning Creek, but these Clarion waters flow southward toward a confluence at Johnsonburg. The West Branch is the cleaner of the two, though chloride content, possibly from oil drilling, has been high in the past. Mine drainage runs into the East Branch, loading a small Army Corps dam with acid. Water quality has been improved through treatment at Bogardy Run and the covering of acid-bearing shales with soil. Sandstone that caps the upper Clarion basin is very high in acid content; thus a pH of 5 is possible on an undisturbed stream.

As if these problems weren't enough, evidence points to yet another: acid rainfall. "Northcentral Pennsylvania is in the rain shadow of Pittsburgh and midwestern industrial centers," says Ken Schoener of the Department of Environmental Resources, "and we know that acid content of the rain is increasing." Hydrochloric, nitric, and sulfuric acids are thought to stem primarily from gaseous, man-made pollutants such as sulfur dioxide and nitrogen oxides produced when burning fossil fuels. Prevailing winds sweep up these wastes of industry, power plants, and automobiles, while precipitation brings the odious elements earthward again. Maps have been drawn showing the acid content of rain; highest incidence in the nation is near Ithaca, New York, in a zone that includes much of northcentral Pennsylvania.

East and West branches meet at Johnsonburg, a small town with an old papermill. Downstream people used to ask, "Who can enjoy reading the *Saturday Evening Post* when we have to drink it too?" They were referring to the New York and Pennsylvania company's mill where the paper for the

Rapids of the Clarion near Hallton

Post was made. Effluent is pumped to the largest waste lagoon in the state, a lake of 400 acres or more. Different degrees of discharge have occurred in past years, prompting a series of state orders to clean up. Most recently, the Sierra Club filed legal action with effective results. "The mill seems generally to be in compliance with state regulations," a Department of Environmental Resources official from the Meadville office said. But there are days when the pulp mill smell still lingers with the river for twenty miles or more below Johnsonburg. Sewage wastes have been a major problem here and at Ridgway, six miles below, though secondary treatment is now effective in both towns.

Toby Creek is the largest tributary on the upper Clarion, churning through a wild gorge from Brockway but carrying a deadly load of acid, iron, and other residue from the mines. The Toby Creek Watershed Association has been active in reclamation efforts, and with continued involvement, theirs may be one of the better stories in stream improvement. Much of the lower creek is protected as State Game Lands.

Toby reaches the Clarion at Portland Mills, where a finer section of river begins. For eight miles the waterway is uninterrupted by roads or railroads, except for an old iron truss bridge at Arroyo. This area offers ideal camping for canoeists who run a three-day trip from Ridgway to Cook Forest on the high waters of springtime. Ledges rise from the shorelines with

Canoeing the Clarion below Cook Forest

clusters of aged pines. Rhododendron spreads everywhere, impenetrably tangled, leaves glistening in the rain or curling tightly in the frigid cold of winter.

Generally speaking, the Clarion has good riffles but few rapids, except for a drop five miles downstream of Hallton. The river transcends its peaceful character and plunges madly over deep, hidden boulders. On a cold, rainy morning in April, we beached above the whitewater for a good view, then ran the rapids through the center, our canoe pointing sharply up toward the sky and then down into the next trough.

Much of the western bank from Ridgway to Cooksburg is within Allegheny National Forest; with state parks, forests, and game lands, public open space comprises one-fourth of the stream's shoreline. Cook Forest is unquestionably the highlight. Many people are familiar with the Clarion from hiking cool, shaded trails of the state park. Aged pine and hemlock stand as one of the finest remnants of primeval woodland in Pennsylvania. Anthony Wayne Cook and A. Cook Sons Company had delayed the logging of over 6,000 acres until 1927, when a bill was signed by Governor John S. Fisher for $450,000 to acquire the virgin timber. Another $200,000 was needed and finally raised through public subscription and contributions. Boxes were placed in local schools, and in this way the pennies of children helped to preserve a magnificent eastern forest.

Strip mine

After investigating ninety miles of the Clarion, the federal Bureau of Outdoor Recreation reported in 1971 that the river did not meet National Wild and Scenic River standards. Water pollution from the paper mill, municipal sewage, and coal mines were listed as major problems, but the federal study added, "At such time as the water quality is improved to permit suitable outdoor recreation activities which are now precluded, the Clarion should be reconsidered for possible addition to the National System."

Spoil piles and erosion from strip mining, lower Clarion River

In reviewing the federal report, the governor of Pennsylvania expressed agreement: "I want to emphasize my interest in reconsidering the Clarion River in the future." Governor Milton Shapp also cited recent improvements to water quality, particularly on the East Branch.

Five years later, further advances were evident. "We've seen four-foot-long muskie," said Bob Cortez, a tough, likable, pollution-fighting patrolman for Pennsylvania's Fish Commission. "Rainbow trout and a twenty-two-inch wall-eye were caught at the Route 322 bridge," he added. "Cooksburg to Mill Creek is now a good fishery. A Commission survey found twenty-seven different types of minnows." Cortez feels that improvements at the paper mill have made a difference. "It's like the Juniata River—someday the Clarion will be just as well known for its recovery."

While there is less acid on the East Branch and upper Toby, pressure for mining has grown incredibly. "During 1970 I reviewed twelve or fifteen strip-mine applications," said Cortez. "In 1975 there were a hundred, and nearly all of them were approved." Out of 126 tributaries in Clarion County, only eight are suitable for fish stocking. "We fought to keep mining away from Beaver Creek and Turkey and Leatherwood, but Beaver's the only one we saved," he said. Ken Young of the Department of Environmental Resources' Meadville office reported receiving nearly 450 mine applications for the Clarion and Allegheny basins in one year.

A 1976 study showed 474 sources of acid in the Clarion watershed.

While much of the problem is from old abandoned mines, new ones also contribute. Strict enforcement of Pennsylvania regulations would minimize but not eliminate the problem. "But good enforcement's what we don't have," Cortez added. "I found weeds eighteen inches high where a siltation pond was required to be, and the inspector had been there only one week before."

Cortez stopped the car at Gravel Lick bridge, just below Cook Forest, and we walked down to look at the river. He pointed back over the ridge where lands above Maxwell Run were being stripped. "The best we can do is to try and save the clean streams we have left. That leaves plenty of choices for mining—118 out of 126 watersheds in the county!" Maxwell had been wild and unpolluted, an exception that may not last much longer. It was depressing, and there wasn't much else to say.

Cortez changed the subject. "You should see the canoes now—it's a beautiful river, and I just lean back on this bridge and laugh, the people who come down love it so much. I'd like to see national river designation; the scenery and fishing to Mill Creek are too good to change—let it be." But pressures for the St. Petersburg Dam could also arise again. "If there's money being spent to clean the Clarion, my guess is that a dam will go in," Cortez said. "It could provide for a lot of flatwater recreation." In addition to fifteen miles of wild river on the lower Clarion, the dam would flood ten miles between Cook Forest and Mill Creek, a section that is interrupted only by Gravel Lick bridge.

It was on this reach that the annual Clarion River Float began in 1970. Sponsored through an environmental education and action program at Clarion State College, the event was a river promotional effort in which 200 people cruised together. It would make the seeker of solitude shudder, but the event served effectively to bring attention to the waterway as a valuable resource. Prefloat publicity was intense, drawing canoeists from the local area and more distant places like Pittsburgh, Erie, Sharon, and State College. Free shuttle service was provided with pickup trucks, and information was distributed concerning the river and its problems. Two high school students won the trash collection contest; grating to a stop on the sandy Mill Creek beach, their canoe was top-heavy with an oil drum, three old tires, and miscellaneous cans rolling from bow to stern. Congressman John Saylor was there to express his regret that the Clarion was not yet in the National Rivers System.

It was like a celebration in many ways, with lots of happy people. There were original designs in water craft: five kids had three different sizes of inner tubes linked together, an American flag flew from the stern of one canoe, and a huge rubber duck was towed behind another. A golden retriever seemed to swim most of the way. While in a limited sense the float trip achieved little more than fun, it also represented a very significant turning point. For once the river was regarded as more than a route for floating logs to market, more than a wasteline for sewage, pulp debris, and acid, and more than a cause of flooding. The Clarion was recognized as a living river that can provide recreation and a special, essential kind of satisfaction. Use of the waterway will increase sharply over the coming years as trout return to many places above Mill Creek. Support for designation in the Pennsylvania Scenic Rivers System and in the National System will grow, but the Clarion's future is uncertain. These waters can show success, proving our ability to reclaim losses and preserve the best of Pennsylvania rivers. Or a history of abuse could repeat itself again.

The Clarion River below Cook Forest

Congestion of rafts, Swimmer's Rapid, Youghiogheny River

The Youghiogheny:
Pennsylvania's Whitewater

Along with seventy-eight other folks, we took seats on the side of a black rubber raft. "Welcome to Whitewater Adventurers," the guide announced. "Today we're going to have a lot of fun on an eleven-mile float. There are lots of exciting rapids. First of all, we'll talk about your equipment. The most important thing is the life jacket. Put your arms through the holes and tie the straps in a knot—don't tie them in a bow." He spotted a misfit without seeming to hunt and pointed to a young girl. Embarrassed but determined, she was struggling with a tangle of straps, arm holes, and metal clips, trying to put the vest on upside down. "Better turn that jacket over; it'll float you feet-up that way." A friend offered some help.

"Okay, each raft should have four people, with the strongest two in back. Your paddles are the most dangerous thing, more dangerous than rocks or the water. Some people wave their paddles in the air to calm the rapids, but instead they calm other people by knocking them out. Keep the paddles down—they belong in the river. We use two kinds of strokes: forward and backward. Paddle on the right side to turn left and on the left side to turn right. You'll have to paddle to get through the rapids—hoping and wishing isn't good enough.

"Today you'll have a chance to get your raft stuck on a rock. You'll know when that happens because your friends will wave as they go floating past. Don't worry—they'll be hung up in five minutes too. Push on the rock with your paddles, and if you still don't move, you've done a splendid job. Don't sit there admiring your work, push harder, and if the raft *isn't* tilted up against a rock, move your body to the end of the raft that's *not* stuck, then try pushing again.

"If you fall out, and some of you will, tell the other people. Otherwise the splashing around that you'll do will sound just like all the rest of the river splashing around, and they might not miss you 'til later in the day. People in the raft should grab the person and pull him in. There's no graceful way—grab arms, legs, and (ahem) pants. Ladies, don't be offended—they'll be saving your life. While you're in the water, stay away from the front of the raft, and keep your feet high and pointed downstream, otherwise you might get a foot stuck in the river, which can be very dangerous.

"If your raft starts making funny 'hissing' noises, tell one of the guides. Okay, grab your raft and follow me, and don't let a car hit you when you cross the road."

With this ten-minute introduction, 60,000 people each year begin their trip down the Youghiogheny. Counting the legions of independent paddlers who don't go with an outfitter, there are over 100,000 rafters, kay-

Canoeing the Youghiogheny below Confluence
(paddling without life jacket is not recommended)

akers, and canoeists. This is the most floated whitewater in the United
States. Exciting rapids, spectacular scenery, clean water, adequate flow
throughout summer, and closeness to Pittsburgh are all conditions that
make the Yough popular.

Delaware or Lenni-Lenape Indians called the river "Yohoghany," meaning "stream flowing in a roundabout course." And it does. Beginning in
Maryland, the river is wild rapids until it's impounded by Youghiogheny
Dam, an Army Corps of Engineers' structure at the southern Pennsylvania
town of Confluence. Here the clean waters of Laurel Hill Creek and the
siltier, mine-acid drainage of the Casselman join the Yough. From Confluence to Ohiopyle, twelve miles of river are scenic and undeveloped, with
several Class II rapids that challenge beginning canoeists.

Swimming at Ohiopyle

Ohiopyle is the small remnant of a mountain town, the site of the river's best scenery and fullest recreational use. The Youghiogheny drops ninety feet in a boiling mile that includes hazardous rapids and the cataract of Ohiopyle Falls. Far more water flows over this falls than any other in Pennsylvania.

In 1754 George Washington's Indian guide wisely refused to lead a small army of colonists down the river, even though a loaded gun was said to be pointed at his head for encouragement. The French and Indian War skirmishes of Jumonville and Fort Necessity both took place nearby. Settlers arrived at Ohiopyle in the early 1800s, and from time to time they operated a saltworks, saw and pulp mill, spoke factory, shook (barrel parts) factory, and grist mill. The lumber and coal eras supported the most people, with the town's population peaking at about 700.

Old-time Ohiopyle was different from the place we see today. To hear what the river was like then, I looked up Shelby Mitchell, a "native" who grew up at the edge of the Yough fifty years ago.

"I've seen plenty of change since then. We swam in the river most every day, I guess, but that's about all it was used for. There weren't no fish, what with the tannery and acid from the mines, including our own Potter mine." He paused and reflected. "What we did up there ruined Cucumber Run. Then there was the industries that dumped their stuff in, and the sewage from Confluence. We used to cut ice and store it, y'know, and then people'd get diphtheria or typhoid when they drank the ice water. Nobody gave the river much thought; this rafting didn't start 'til about ten years ago.

"Oh, I s'pose the falls did make things a bit different around here. Us kids swam into it all the time, from the Ferncliff side, understand. God, you wouldn't want to go in from the side the mill was on. It was the strangers who'd come in and drown themselves, and then all the town'd go down there and watch for 'em to bring the body up."

I questioned why the town would be so entertained. "There just wasn't much else happenin', understand?"

"Who would look for the bodies?"

"Well, we all did, that is, me and my brother Udie, and old man Tharpe, and other guys in town. We pulled a lot of folks out, dead ones, that is. At night we'd drag hooks at the falls after someone drowned, and whenever the hook'd get stuck, one of us kids'd jump in and follow the hook down and pull it loose. If we couldn't find the body, we'd drop a charge into the water, and the blast'd sometimes bring 'em up. One fella didn't show up until he floated to Connellsville the next spring, but nine days seemed to be a normal time. That is, if we couldn't find 'em, they'd generally come up in nine days anyhow.

"That's all changed now. The park ranger won't let anybody swim at the falls. There's a hellish lot of people around, more, of course, than we'd ever seen. And there's more trouble, too, places broken into and such. Back then we'd have four or five drunks who'd fight with each other, but you knew who they were, and they didn't give anybody else trouble. I think the Kennedys got this raftin' stuff started, goin' down the Colorado and what not."

I asked about the state park and land that the Western Pennsylvania Conservancy bought in order to preserve the natural features of the area.

"The Conservancy I think has done a good thing in protectin' this land. Some folks get pretty upset about it all, but the way I see it is that Ohiopyle did its job—lumber, coal and the like, and now we've got recreation. But things go to extremes. Just how much land's the government need, anyway? Don't let anybody kid you, this social government's no good. Now there's even talk of buyin' land from Ohiopyle Park to Fort Necessity, about six miles on out the road, and that'd go right through this area."

The Ohiopyle Falls

"You don't really believe that, do you?" I knew this was not in the state's plans.

"Well, who knows? Guys'a been walkin' around here with maps and stuff, and nobody knows what'll happen. If they want to do something for the environment, why don't they stop this strip minin'?"

Bill and Adalene Holt also have spent their entire lives in Ohiopyle. Their families have lived in the area since the early 1800s. They ran the local store for forty years, and now they rent rooms in their antique-furnished guest house that sits with an older-era charm on a high bank overlooking the new park.

"We've had two waves of tourism in Ohiopyle," Bill began. "From 1900 to the thirties, and what you see here today. Things were pretty quiet in between times." That was how I remembered the town from visits I had made ten and twenty years ago. "At about 1900, excursion trains began bringing passengers, two trains from Pittsburgh and one from Cumberland. People'd come up and back the same day, or they'd sell their return trip ticket for fifty cents and then stay overnight."

"The ladies wore long ruffled dresses, and they carried parasols," Adalene added. "Local folks would board visitors, meeting them with fringe-covered surreys at the train station. The three hotels would be filled, and at the Ferncliff they'd have outdoor dining and dancing with good orchestras. Bill's uncle ran the Ferncliff."

"What happened to the hotels and the people?" There are no hotels today.

"You're looking at it right there," Bill answered before I finished asking. He waved a hand toward the cars along Main Street. "The automobile put an end to the railroad's profits, and they quit running excursion trains."

"It's different now, isn't it?"

Adalene and a few visiting neighbor ladies agreed. The way they shook their heads, it was clear they liked it a lot more the way it used to be. "How did all this get started?" I asked, as we looked down at the park, at four boys carrying a rubber raft, a mother with her children coming out of the store, and a young girl wearing a T-shirt lettered "JanSport"—one of the backpacking equipment manufacturers.

"Lance Martin was the first outfitter," Bill began. "For his first year, he took fifty people all summer, using one raft that he blew up with my Electrolux sweeper. He'd sleep overnight in the garage, back over at the old house. That was about 1965."

"As the town changed and the park was developed, what affected local people the most?"

"Well, the *land*," Adalene said, wondering why I didn't have a better grasp of the obvious. "Twenty-nine houses on Main Street were taken."

"Most of the people didn't want to sell," Bill added. "Many were old, with nothing much to live for after their places were gone." I wanted to talk to some of these people. "They're mostly all dead now," Bill explained, "and a lot of the younger people weren't here to really know what it was like. Some people got $3,000, which might have been the value of their building, but how could those folks ever buy a new house for that price?"

"Why did they have to do it *that* way?" Adalene asked, as if I would know. "The town could have been fixed up nice, with shops and places for people to go."

"And if they'd left the picnic area at Ferncliff Park, across the river, they wouldn't have needed all that land in Ohiopyle," one of the neighbor ladies added. "Oh, the picnics and ball games we used to have over there!"

I tried to answer. "I think that a lot of government agencies are taking a softer approach now, without buying up so many homes, and relocation assistance is now better, but none of that helps you people."

I changed the subject. "What do folks think of the park now—does all the activity bother you?" I was thinking of the 800,000 visitors, the parking lots, and the vast cultural gulf between the people of Ohiopyle and the melange of whitewater enthusiasts, urbanites, and other people who storm through town.

"Not so much anymore," one of the neighbor women said, "but there used to be all kinds of riff-raff down there." She pointed at the park again. "People would even swim—well, nude."

"There's really not much of any problem now," Bill said. "Of course, some people'd complain if you mowed their grass for them, but by and large, visitors stay down there and we stay up here."

Cucumber Rapid of the Youghiogheny, below Ohiopyle

Cucumber Falls, a tributary to the Youghiogheny

Rafters in Cucumber Rapid below Ohiopyle

I wanted to hear more about the Youghiogheny and the state park, so I drove out the old Dinner-Bell Road to Meadow Run bridge where the state park headquarters is now located. The receptionist was friendly and asked me to be seated. A few minutes later, Larry Adams, the superintendent, said I could step in his office.

"What can I do for you?" he asked.

I was a little surprised at how young he looked, with a cool but helpful, honest air about him. We began talking about the river, the park, and whitewater rafting.

"Actually, rafting and kayaking amount to only 10 percent of our use," Larry said. "About 800,000 people come here during the year, and most of them just look around, maybe have a picnic."

"Do you have problems with overuse?"

"Crowds are heavy only on major holidays. Overuse or crowding is not a limiting factor, generally."

I could see that I was going to get answers, but the superintendent wasn't the rambling type and I'd have to ask a lot of questions. "Permits and quotas are now established and enforced for commercial outfitters. Do you see a permit requirement coming for private individual boaters as well?"

"No, but it's hard to tell for sure."

"Do you find many people disappointed when they meet crowds of other floaters on the river?"

"Sometimes the kayakers and canoeists find that a problem. It doesn't seem to bother the rafters. Most rafters, of course, are less experienced. Most people who come seem to be really pleased. They like the park."

"What special kinds of problems do you face here that you didn't have in the other parks where you've worked?"

Pause. "This is a unique park. Safety is the biggest thing, the biggest issue. We've cut down on the number of drownings—no swimming is allowed at the falls, no inner tubes in the rapids. Life jackets are required, and rafting is closed when water level is over three feet at the launch site."

The outfitters on the Yough were up for relicensing in 1977, and it looked as if it could become a hot subject. Under past "temporary" agreements, only four companies were allowed on the river, taking a maximum of eighty people per trip and two trips per day. The Commonwealth assumed authority to regulate the operations, since the access area is within park boundaries. The rafting companies limited their numbers, with the state providing assurance that no new competition would be allowed in. "It's difficult to regulate commercial operators," was about all the superintendent would say.

"How do you identify outfitters who bring their people and equipment in for one day? They could look like a church group or the YMCA."

"They do, and sometimes we don't."

"What's the state's position on the proposed national scenic-river designation?" I asked.

"The state's not for it," he answered. "We'd rather administer our own program. All the federal government would do is add an extra level of administration."

"What complaint do you hear most often, and what do you think could be the biggest problem in the park?"

He thought for a few seconds and fidgeted with his cigarette. "Ferncliff Park. The old picnic area and ballfield was closed after the area was designated a National Natural Landmark. It's a unique area, biologically speaking, and the park was not consistent with landmark status. Some people were used to going there for picnics and other activity, and now they can't do that. Things are going pretty well now, but new coal mining that could pollute the river is always a threat."

Cindy and I left our camp site early for a sunrise photo of the Youghiogheny, then we went to the store for a cup of coffee. While substantial block letters at the top of the building still say "Holt's Department Store," it's obvious that a switch has been made over the last five or ten years. The snack bar is now located where a good selection of clothing and hardware had been. Bill Holt even carried appliances for the townspeople and mountaineers, but now there were pinball machines: "Wildlife, A Game of Skill," with a picture of an apeman and a full-bosomed female wearing a small fraction of a leopard's skin. An older fellow who worked in a nearby strip mine sat across from us, and we talked a little, mainly about fishing in the Yough, which has improved incredibly over the past few years. The waitress came out. Without speaking, she poured a cup of coffee for the man and didn't quite seem to notice us.

"Ja hear about the drownin'?" she asked but didn't wait for an answer. "I just knew it'd happen; there hasn't been one *all* year." Details of the report had stuck in her mind. "They say her life jacket was ripped right off, and it took a half-hour to pull her out. There's *no way* I'm goin' down that river!"

Cass Chestnut is a river guide. Running whitewater is his livelihood. It's hard to be a good guide—an expert's skills in paddling are needed, along with a thorough knowledge of safety, equipment, and the river. A flair for entertaining is essential. In spite of cold weather, soaking clothes, and a few folks who are scared out of their shivering skins, the guide has to keep the clients happy, or at least try. Cass's head is full of river experience that comes out unwinnowed, unstrained.

"It was a real bummer. I had three months to go before the Peace Corps, and so I figured, 'Cass, you really enjoyed that trip down the Yough—why not get a job for a few months?' So I wrote to this outfitter, and he said, 'Sure, come on down.' You guessed it, I've been here ever since. Back in

Rowing a raft on the Youghiogheny below Ohiopyle

those days, if you wanted to be a river guide, you lived a river guide's life—what I mean is, you got $300 a year, and you hoped it came by December. Nowadays, if you want to be a river guide, you have to live a river guide's life, if you know what I mean." He motioned to his old silver trailer, provided free to the guide staff. "The place is—well, I spend most of my time outside anyway. Say, can I get you a cup of tea?"

Cass came out of the trailer armed with a hot cup of red zinger and a bag of oatmeal cookies, flipping a thumb toward a rusty metal bed that sat under a maple tree. "Lately I've even been sleeping out here. I quit drinking altogether. I feel great. I quit smoking except for special occasions, and this is a special occasion. Want a buzz?"

I didn't want to smoke. "No, thanks."

"Where was I? Oh yeah, I could write a book about the river—'The Death of the Yough,' how's that sound? You get tired of some of these guys, the macho types, know what I mean? A few years ago it was different, for sure. People came 'cause they wanted to see the river and have fun. They looked at the trees. Now it's the thing to do; they heard about it at a party. 'Well, *I* rafted the Yough.' You know, some of the girls around are really good in their kayaks, and these goons'd meet 'em in town and brag about how they were going down the river, trying to make an impression or something. The 'quasi wilderness experience' gets a little more 'quasi' all the time. Some days I'd just rather patch rafts. But people make it interesting, too. Once in a while I leave the kayak in the garage and go in a raft to be with some other folks."

"Isn't that slow and not much fun?" I asked, but there's more to running a river than whitewater.

"You should have seen the young lady in that raft! Really, the people are okay so long as they're not bummin' off the rest of the trip. They gotta keep their water splashing battles to themselves, in other words.

"People come from all over—Cleveland, Baltimore, especially Pittsburgh, and some even from Chicago. Once we had this double group—a gang of gay weightlifters along with a bunch of deaf-mutes. The weightlifters would do their gestures, you know? and the deaf-mutes rattled off their sign language. Then there's our guides standing on the rocks waving which way to go—" and he did a quick imitation of half a dozen arm motions that were commonly seen on that day. "Then once in a while something really neat happens, like this picture. Hold on." Cass disappeared again into the trailer and emerged holding a snapshot. "I met this dude on the Slippery Rock—now there's a good stream. You seen it?"

"Yeah."

"Anyway, this guy took my picture doing an ender. A few weeks ago he showed up with it as a gift. I don't know how he even found out I was here. The only neater thing was the lady who claimed to be my wife in a former lifetime."

We talked for a while about the outfitters' operations and the way guides handle safety. "At first when they started talking about sixty or eighty people per trip, the guides said, 'My God, no, what will we do with them?' But it worked out okay, I guess, with more guides on the river, Each outfitter is allowed to take eighty people per trip, see, in order to not overrun the river. You know how they came up with that number? That's what two shuttle busses hold. The outfitters' contracts are up this year. I mean, a new contract has to be made. Everybody's kind of anxious and waitin' to see what'll happen."

He went on. "You know none of the outfitters has ever had a drowning on the Yough?"

"That's kind of amazing, isn't it?" I said.

"Don't get me wrong; we have had some people die on us. Two heart

Double Hydraulic Rapid, Youghiogheny River

Kayakers in Cucumber Rapid

attacks, both at the bottom of Swimmer's Rapids. You know Swimmer's don't you?"

"Sure."

"The first was on the day the Goodyear blimp was over the river. Yeah, we came around a bend, and there it was. We got to Swimmer's, and the guy just kind of slumped over in his rubber kayak. We pulled him in and gave him mouth-to-mouth resuscitation. His lunch kept comin' up, and I think it was a month, no, probably two, before I had any peanut butter sandwiches again. A doctor was on the trip and pronounced him dead after forty minutes or so.

"The guides've saved a lot of other people too—independent, private boaters, I mean. Like the duffers who rent a raft from this guy in town. It's gotten so we just can't babysit everybody. We've quit throwing his people ropes. . . . That's his job.

"We keep backboards hid at six places along the route, in case we ever get a broken back or something like that. We now use type five jackets— the safest kind—it's the law for inflatable boats." At last Cass stopped talking for a second.

"When we went down with you," I said, "there were people who really didn't belong out there. They weren't in very good shape, and some of the older women looked terrified. What do you do when someone just doesn't want to go any farther?"

"They mostly just last it out. Once a girl fell out at Cucumber and didn't want back in, so I got in her raft and kind of calmed her down for a while." Cass winked at me but really at the memory. "That was an exciting day; half the rafts were flipping at Dimple Rock.

"That's where the California girl drowned yesterday. They had a big rowing rig, seventeen feet or so. Great on western rivers, but here it's a little too tight." I had just rowed my twelve-foot Avon raft down the river, and Cass was right—there are a lot of rocks to maneuver around, and oars require a little more width of river than paddles. Worse problems, however, came from other rafts that would get too close, immobilizing the oars.

"Is the number of boaters increasing?"

"Oh, sure. Commercial use, I think, will level off, but independent boaters just keep coming and coming. There'll probably be a permit requirement for them in a few years. Some days the river's too crowded— seventeen or eighteen hundred people might go down on a weekend. People ought to come during the week. You know, those folks are different, too—the ones on Monday through Friday seem to see more, to enjoy it more. They're more interested."

He paused for a second, but it was never much more than that. "One of the neatest things is just being here. You know, it's a good place to *be*. I've thought of building a cabin. The people are great; we really get along well. They accept the guides, like the lady who runs the post office. No problems like you might run into other places. Some of the local young people are now paddling too. There are some really good local paddlers, for sure."

I always figured a river runner would take to running rivers everywhere. "Have you thought of guiding in the West, on wild rivers out there?"

Cass thought a little longer than his usual split second. "No, it pays pretty good here, $45 or $50 a day for a good experienced guide. But I'm thinking of moving on. I've got an application for Hershey Medical Center for medical assistant training, you know, do a lot of doctor-type jobs in rural areas. Being a guide all your life would be a little tough, for sure. Jumpin' into a wet suit to paddle a freezin' river when you're forty or fifty years old? I figure we each ought to be the best person we can, and so some day I'll be movin' on, to do something better. For people, I mean. That's what I like about guiding. Wilderness belongs to everybody, and this is a way to get them there. If you enjoy it, it can do something *to* you—it's expansive. People who enjoy it might even want to save it. They'll know it better. They'll know it's worth something."

The Youghiogheny below Railroad Rapid

Tionesta Creek below Sheffield

Ohio Basin River Sketches

Tionesta Creek

Tionesta Creek is probably best known for its scout camp where many thousands of western Pennsylvania boys have gone for weekends and week-long summer camping sessions. Most of the watershed is in Allegheny National Forest, including an outstanding tract of virgin timber at Hearts Content, a smaller stand at Tionesta Scenic Area, and a recreational site and wilderness valley at Minister Creek.

Below the small town of Sheffield, Tionesta and its South Branch join and follow a south and westerly course to the backwaters of Tionesta Dam, where the Boy Scout camp is located. The creek meets the Allegheny only a few miles below the impoundment. Fishing is good, attracting many anglers from western Pennsylvania and eastern Ohio. There are no major rapids, and the stream makes an excellent canoe trip in early spring. The confluence of Tionesta and the South Branch is an interesting and scenic lowland area, and massive hemlocks can be seen above the eastern bank, a half mile downstream.

Oil Creek

The oil industry began along this stream of northwestern Pennsylvania. Drake's Well, the first to be drilled, is located on the creek's east bank near Titusville. Evidence of old drilling is seen everywhere—well casing, rusting pipes, and abandoned machinery. Active wells continue, and refineries are crowded in the highly industrialized lower creek, which meets the Allegheny at Oil City. In this part of the state chloride pollution is extensive, resulting from oil and gas recovery operations and from natural upwelling of deep brines.

A state park has been established along the stream from Titusville to Petroleum Center, a distance of about eighteen miles. Both sides of Oil Creek are included, and a bicycle trail is being built through the park's entire length. While the area has been repeatedly logged, drilled, and farmed in past years, development has not occurred in this reach. Canoeing can be done in springtime, and fishing is possible above the industrialized areas.

French Creek below Utica

French Creek

Flowing southward through farmlands that are only twenty miles from
Lake Erie beaches, French Creek is one of the largest Allegheny tributaries.
The stream's origins are in New York; then its waters drift in a great arc to
Meadville and southeastward to the town of Franklin. During the geologic
past, prior to the Wisconsin Ice Age, the Allegheny River flowed north
toward Lake Erie through the approximate channel of today's French
Creek. The direction of flow was reversed when continental ice masses
blocked the water's northern escape.

Uplands and headwaters of French Creek are sometimes swampy or
marshy, serving as an excellent waterfowl habitat. Most of the stream is
slow, winding through pastoral farmlands, but the lower reaches are more
confined and enclosed by wooded hillsides. A pleasant and easy canoe trip
can be run in the springtime from Meadville, and the creek is popular for
warm-water fishing. Another French Creek, near Philadelphia, is a small
stream being considered for the state scenic rivers system.

The Conemaugh and Flood City

The Conemaugh is a major stream of western Pennsylvania, where its waters form the Kiskiminetas, then join the Allegheny. Mine acid, Bethlehem Steel, and raw sewage devastated the Conemaugh and Kiski years ago, in a pattern that continues. The river causes fish kills in the Allegheny.

High water was inevitable at Johnstown, on the low terrace between Stony Creek and the Little Conemaugh. Mountainsides flushed their rains to this urban meeting place; flooding occurred fifteen times between 1808 and 1888. May of 1889, however, was a different case. Heavy rains filled South Fork Lake. At the time it was the world's largest earthen dam, seventy feet high, originally built for the state canal system. Pittsburgh industrialists bought the lake and settled at their comfortable summer retreats, but only after repairing a breach. They filled it with dirt, rubble, and cow manure, leaving a low spot in the center and partially filling the spillway to block in the fish. On May 31 waters flowed over the repaired dam. The rubble loosened, then burst. A forty-foot wave reached town without warning one hour later. Twenty-two hundred people drowned or burned in a fiery mass that congealed above the great stone railroad bridge. It's the same bridge you see today, just below the point where the two rivers meet.

People rebuilt, of course, to be flooded again in 1936, when water levels surpassed all records. After this the Army Corps of Engineers played an important role, channeling the rivers in concrete walls, and concluding, "We believe the flood troubles of the city are at an end."

Boosterism caught hold for "flood-free Johnstown," and this was largely true until July 19, 1977. Nearly twelve inches of rain fell in seven hours. It was a freak storm, like others that occur once or twice every year, somewhere in the country. The 1936 record was surpassed, and five small earthen dams failed. Laurel Run sent fifteen feet of water through the flood-plain neighborhoods. Eighty-seven people were killed. Incredibly, communities had decided that flood insurance and zoning were not necessary.

So much for a false sense of security.

What's happening now? A ride up the Johnstown incline can show you the birds-eye view. There's rebuilding, but there are plenty of vacant lots, too. A developer proposes an elevated shopping mall near the confluence. Bethlehem Steel, its tracks and buildings and furnaces winding beyond the horizon along the Little Conemaugh, threatened a shutdown after the flood, but is hanging on with an Environmental Protection Agency extension for pollution abatement. Faced with unnecessary hardship and cost, people's willingness to stay and rebuild is being shaken.

Of 2,800 communities in Pennsylvania, 2,468 are partially in the flood plain. Statewide, $7 billion worth of property has been lost to floods through the years. In spite of $3 billion which has been spent on flood-control works, damages continue to grow. Local government fails to prevent new building on lowlands, while logging, urbanization, and some modern farming techniques vastly increase the magnitude of storm-water problems.

Along with the Hurricane Agnes flood of 1972, the submerged dikes of Wilkes-Barre and the inadequacies of the flood-insurance program, Johnstown points to the need for an effective, obligatory flood-plain management program. Senator Franklin Kury has championed the issue since Agnes waters subsided, but local government and developers staunchly kept the legislature from action. In 1978 a Pennsylvania flood-plain management law passed, but in a weakened form.

Little Conemaugh at Johnstown

The Conemaugh also includes a gorge 1,350 feet deep. Above Johnstown is Stony Creek (not to be confused with Stony Creek north of Harrisburg). Though pollution is severe in this stream, whose waters range from coal black to bright orange, the valley is undeveloped and scenic in some places. A formidable gorge forms north of U.S. Route 30.

Loyalhanna Creek joins the Kiskiminetas near Saltsburg. Beginning on Laurel Hill near Linn Run and Laurel Mountain state parks, water of Loyalhanna is better than that of other tributaries, since coal mining has been less extensive and many acres are publicly owned.

Slippery Rock Creek

Like the Youghiogheny of southwestern Pennsylvania or Pine Creek in the north central highlands, Slippery Rock Creek is an outstanding stream of its region. In the northwestern portion of the state, no other waterway has the scenic appeal of moss-covered boulders, churning whitewater, and deep green pools that are found in the gorge below Route 422. At the end of the Wisconsin Ice Age, the gorge was formed when a terminal moraine holding a massive meltwater lake eroded, releasing waters in a torrent and carving the rocky passage that the creek now follows. Recognizing the need to preserve the scenic, geological, and historic landmark, the Western Pennsylvania Conservancy acquired 2,000 acres along the Slippery Rock, including an abandoned grist mill. Later the Conservancy resold the land to the Commonwealth, and McConnell's Mill State Park was established. The restored mill is now open for public touring, and scenic trails can be hiked upstream and down. A maze of boulders and rocky cliffs are found on the western side of the creek, where crevasses and tunnels can be explored and climbed, with adequate safety precautions.

The Slippery Rock's plunge through the gorge involves highly "technical" rapids. The stream is not large, and expert maneuvering around many rocks and obstacles is essential if the kayaker or canoeist is to stay afloat. Good trout fishing is also returning to the Slippery Rock after years of acid pollution.

Headwaters include Muddy Creek, where 3,200-acre Lake Arthur was built in the late 1960s near the site of the ancient meltwater lake. Moraine State Park, another Conservancy project, surrounds the new impoundment and draws large crowds of Pittsburghers and other western Pennsylvanians on summer weekends. National Boy Scout jamborees have been held here several times. To improve water quality, the state engaged in costly mine reclamation programs. Additional stripping remains a threat. After heated debates, a new mine was opened along the boundary of McConnell's Mill Park.

Slippery Rock Creek below McConnell's Mill

Above the Beaver River, the Slippery Rock meets Connoquenessing Creek. This stream is a popular warm-water fishery where bluegills, bass, and sunfish thrive. While most of the Connoquenessing meanders through farmland, the creek forms a formidable set of Class III rapids in its lower reaches.

Beaver River

Much of the land in northwestern Pennsylvania drains toward the Beaver River, which begins at New Castle with the confluence of the Mahoning and Shenango. Over 3,000 square miles are in this system, the Mahoning and Shenango River basins draining about 1,000 square miles each. Characteristically, rivers of industrialized western Pennsylvania are sluggish and foul, with a few exceptions. The Shenango begins in Pymatuning Lake and marsh areas of the north, incomparable for their populations of migrating water birds. Coming from Ohio, the Mahoning is exceptional too in another way—noted as one of the dirtiest, most fetid of American waterways, regarded as a sewer more than a river. In 1977, the state of Pennsylvania and the Sierra Club won a lawsuit against the federal Environmental Protection Agency. The U.S. Court of Appeals' decision disallowed EPA's unprecedented water quality control exemptions to eight Mahoning steel mills.

The Beaver River is slow moving, impounded, and highly developed. Though the water can be unhealthy to swimmers, the lower river provides recreation; boating activity has exploded over the past fifteen years. Motorboats were uncommon when I grew up along the Beaver and Ohio rivers in the fifties and early sixties. A high school friend had a boat that we cruised in, daring each other to jump in the foul broth. Now the water is a little better and packed with expensive fleets. An annual regatta near the mouth of the Beaver draws thousands of people each summer.

Casselman River

The Casselman rises near Grantsville, in the state of Maryland, and flows counterclockwise in a large arc around Mt. Davis to Confluence, Pennsylvania, where it meets the great Youghiogheny. Through much of its course the Casselman is a rugged and wild river, but acid mine drainage has nearly decimated aquatic life and has stained an orange riverbed.

Mine drainage does not eliminate the thrills and challenge of a whitewater canoeing experience, and several reaches from Garrett to Confluence are favorites of canoe and kayak travelers when water is at medium and high levels. Boulders are plentiful, forming powerful chutes of water and pockets of bubbling eddies where boaters can stop to rest and plan their next moves through the current. Visitors should not park vehicles or use private land for access without asking permission from landowners, as problems regarding trespassing have occurred. Rapids are rated Class II and III, a good choice for experienced paddlers who might travel to Ohiopyle and find the Youghiogheny too high to comfortably run.

Much has been done to reclaim areas of strip mining and to improve water quality. Better fishing on the Youghiogheny is evidence of this, but the Casselman still has a long way to go.

Wills Creek

The Potomac tends to be a forgotten river system in Pennsylvania, though its tributaries include a total of 1,582 square miles in the south central mountains. Waters of the Allegheny ridges flow southward to feed the "National River," as it was called by President Lyndon Johnson. At one point, the Potomac's north shore is only a few miles from the Pennsylvania state border.

Major tributaries include Conococheague Creek, largest in length and in letters, Monocacy Creek, which runs through Gettysburg, Tonoloway Creek, Evitts Creek, and Wills Creek.

Wills is the wildest and most rugged of the group. It cuts a stony gorge eastward through the mountains before joining broader and southward-tending valleys that are typical of the region. The basin begins east of Myersdale, where two remote forks switch back through an erratic topography, then plunge together from Fairhope to Hyndman, where the stream bends southward to the city of Cumberland. Dark and rounded boulders characterize much of the upper stream bed. Trout fishing is generally good. Kayaking and whitewater canoeing in covered or decked boats is possible during very high runoff, but the creek is extremely difficult and only for experts.

Laurel Hill Creek

While many of the waterways of western Pennsylvania have been developed, mined, and polluted, Laurel Hill Creek has retained many qualities of the natural river. The stream has been "saved," in effect, by Laurel Mountain, a long backbone of the Appalachians that angles northeastward from the Ohiopyle area to Johnstown. This is the second in a rugged set of paralleling ridges, and as such, headlong development of the greater Pittsburgh area comes to an abrupt stop on mountain flanks to the west.

Recognizing the beauty of the land and its recreational value to the metropolitan area, the Commonwealth has acquired many acres on the mountain. Kooser and Laurel Hill state parks form the headwaters of Laurel Hill Creek, while state forest and game lands cover western portions of the basin. Dairy farms blend with forested passages of the stream, and trout fishing is excellent. Just below Route 653, west of New Lexington, is a Burr Truss-type covered bridge, built in the 1800s. With high water, canoe runs on Laurel Hill Creek are a challenging Class III.

In 1975 the "Laurel Hill Study" was prepared by University of Pennsylvania graduate students, under the sponsorship of the Western Pennsylvania Conservancy. Important environmental features of the region were identified and evaluated, leading to recommendations for overall protection and use. To implement the study, the Laurel Highlands Conservation and Development Project was formed with William Curry as its director. It is hoped that this type of long-range view, with combined action of private and public interests, will be successful in preserving Laurel Hill and its creek.

The Monongahela River

The Monongahela is one of the six largest waterways in Pennsylvania. Most people know the river as a flatwater industrial pool at Homestead, McKeesport, and Pittsburgh, where riverboat cruises can be taken through the Three Rivers urban area. The basin encompasses over 7,000 square miles, though much of this is in West Virginia, where the Cheat River, a tributary, incorporates a wild-water canyon and outstanding streams for the paddler and naturalist. Some of these are the forks named Shavers, Glady, Laurel, and Dry. Red Creek drains the Dolly Sods wild area. Otter Creek is another wilderness area, and the Blackwater is famous for its falls.

The "Mon" forms at the West Fork and Tygart rivers near Fairmont, West Virginia, and runs 128 miles to the Allegheny at Pittsburgh. All of this is navigable to motorized, commercial craft.

Like other big rivers, the "Mon" has a share of the nation's history. George Washington explored its upper reaches, looking for a colonial northwest passage—a waterway from the Potomac to the Ohio. Local folks advised the Virginian that the Cheat was navigable. Luckily for the nation, George didn't try it. That style of river running has been better left to Kennedy on the Colorado and Carter on the Middle Fork of the Salmon.

One of the first flatboats was built and launched from Brownsville in 1782. Jacob Yoder spent two months drifting 2,000 miles to the lower Mississippi. Commercial shipping came early: the Monongahela Navigation Company was formed in 1808 to build dams but the company failed before its impoundments were constructed. A second company formed in 1836 and had six locks and dams in place by 1844. Similar developments on the lower Youghiogheny, a major tributary, washed out in 1854 and were not rebuilt.

The Navigation Company did well until the government interfered in 1886, when Congress stipulated that no tolls could be charged for shipping that originated above government dams in West Virginia. So began the pork-barrel/special interest lobby of river navigation, whereby shippers run for free with the government doing the work. The political and economic forces generated in this way have drag-lined themselves up many a stream, dredging, channeling, and damming the big arteries of riverine America. Ongoing controversy about the Tennessee-Tombigbee waterway of Alabama and Lock and Dam 26 on the Mississippi are one of the results. The government bought the Monongahela Navigation Company in 1897 after a year of condemnation proceedings.

As a centerpiece of intensive use and abuse, the Monongahela may be unsurpassed. One hundred sixty miles of tributary streams are acidic with coal-mine waste. Sewage and industrial pollution are rampant, and thermal discharges overheat the water at power plant and industrial sites. Burrell and Davidson's guidebook to West Virginia rivers calls the "Mon" the sewer of northern West Virginia. Yet it has improved. Powerboating is popular through the length of the river, with access and marinas at Millsboro, Rice's

Monongahela at Pittsburgh

Landing, Point Marion, and other sites. Some communities show a renewed interest in their riverfront, with open space and park developments.

Appropriation of water is burgeoning as a major issue on this southwestern river. Steel mills, seventeen public water suppliers, and three power plants have a deep and lasting thirst. Much of the flow in drought periods comes from Tygart Reservoir in West Virginia, which was built to augment navigation flow. The federal government has control of these waters and may prohibit any diversion that would interfere with the quantity needed for commercial barge traffic. The state of Pennsylvania recommends another reservoir in West Virginia—Rowlesburg Dam on the Cheat. The target reach, from Rowlesburg to Parsons, is an easy rolling river, scenic

Monongahela at Pittsburgh

with farmland, bluffs, and a healthy family of bass. West Virginia opposes the dam, arguing successfully to the Ohio River Basin Commission, which dropped the site from its Level B study. Pennsylvania holds fast, as with the Tocks Island Dam proposal on the Delaware, identifying some extreme options for times of drought: a moratorium on growth, relocation of major water users, importation of water, and temporary abandonment of commercial navigation. Consumptive use of water—using it and not returning it to the stream—is on a sharp increase through much of Pennsylvania, due largely to electric power-plant cooling, especially nuclear plants. The question looms greater and greater, here and on other Pennsylvania rivers: who will get the water when it starts to run short?

Ohio River, with Pittsburgh and the confluence of the Allegheny (left)
and Monogahela (right) in background

The Ohio River

The Ohio's volume of water is second only to the Susquehanna's among Pennsylvania streams. This becomes one of the largest American rivers; it carries twice the volume of the Mississippi where they join in Cairo, Illinois. It is a historical river—Fort Duquesne, a French frontier outpost, was strategically located at the Ohio's origin, where the Allegheny and Monongahela join. The site was one of highest importance, marking the gateway to interior American travel as well as routes north and southeast. The French and English fought repeatedly over this location during the French and Indian War. Upon English capture, Duquesne was renamed Fort Pitt; hence the frontier town was called "Pittsburgh." With nearby coalfields, rail lines, and commercial navigation throughout the Ohio's length, the city eventually became the industrial giant of the nation.

Flatboats carried many western settlers from busy Pittsburgh wharves to the Mississippi, where they boarded steamboats for St. Louis and routes west. Luxurious stern-wheeler riverboats churned up and down the Ohio through the nineteenth century. To facilitate river commerce, a continuous series of nineteen locks and dams was completed in 1929. The 981-mile river carries more cargo than the Panama Canal, and 29 million people now live in the fourteen-state basin. The Port of Pittsburgh is the largest inland waterway port of the United States.

Today the "Golden Triangle" marks the Ohio's source, where tall buildings show Pittsburgh's successful efforts to reclaim and reuse an area of abandoned structures and warehouses. Point State Park includes an interesting reconstruction of Fort Duquesne, though it is surrounded by freeways that may pose hazards greater than French guards. Downriver, development of heavy industry is nearly continuous—Jones and Laughlin steel mills at Aliquippa envelop miles of water frontage, and the Conway railroad yards, once the largest in the world, are still heavily used.

Most natural values of the river have been utterly destroyed. Industry, railroads, and highways allow only a weedy growth of vegetation to meet the water's edge, and pollution is severe. Manufacturing wastes include toxic materials: cyanide, phenolics, PCB's, and other effluent; however, water quality has improved over the past era, which was marked by total indifference to the environment.

Allegheny County has 20,023 registered motorboats, more than the next three Pennsylvania counties combined. The Three Rivers Regatta attracts several hundred thousand people. Downriver, motorboating and water skiing are also popular in places like the big southward bend where the towns of Beaver, Rochester, and Monaca border the river.

From a distance the Ohio remains an impressive sight. The three rivers—Allegheny, Monongahela, and Ohio—can be seen from overlooks on Mt. Washington, south of downtown Pittsburgh. In the town of Beaver, River Road follows the rim of a high terrace, with attractive houses on one side

Ohio River at Beaver

and scenic river views on the other. Sandstone cliffs rise from the southern shore, and riverboats push their barges of freight. At Georgetown, a small settlement near the state border, one can see an old river village and an uncommonly natural view of the wide Ohio waters.

The Delaware Basin

High on the Lehigh

In northeastern Pennsylvania, the Pocono Mountains have been a popular recreation area for nearly 100 years. Brown boggy waters signify land that used to be a maze of glacial lakes, now bordered by Scranton and Wilkes-Barre's urban fringe. New York City and Philadelphia are not far away, and so the trade in lodges, golf courses, car racing, skiing, motorboating, and honeymooning has been a vigorous one, overshadowing but certainly not eliminating the more traditional fishing and hunting. The lakes of Tobyhanna, Bear, Bradys, Arrowhead, and Pocono lie at high headwaters; together with hundreds of swamps and wetlands, they join to form the Lehigh River.

One can accurately picture the Lehigh in three distinct sections, the first being headwaters and a small but turbulent river, growing with amber swampwater and cutting an ever deeper valley into the glaciated plateau. Notable tributaries are the rapid Bear Creek and the famous trout stream, Tobyhanna.

At Francis E. Walters Dam, the continuum of river is broken with a mile-long pool that extends far upstream when flood gates are shut. Below the reservoir begins the wild course of the Lehigh River Gorge, where the stream drops 735 feet in thirty-three miles. The first seven miles offer excellent Class II and III whitewater, though the topography of the gorge has not yet fully evolved and shorelines are sometimes developed with roads, railroads, and homes. Below Lehigh Tannery, the gorge begins in earnest, and whitewater continues to mount in a crescendo, reaching its exciting peak at Mile-Long Rapids above the town of Jim Thorpe. Scenery becomes spectacular, with jagged outcrops on ridge-lines that rise 1,000 feet. In Pennsylvania only the canyons of Pine Creek and the upper West Branch of the Susquehanna compare, although the Lehigh is many times more turbulent than either.

Much of this ends at Jim Thorpe, where the Lehigh becomes a river of man, with highways, railroads, switchyards, industry, and commerce crowding its banks. The lower river penetrates the industrial metropolis of Allentown-Bethlehem.

Of the three sections, the gorge is clearly the highlight. If you are look-

Opposite: Rock climbing above the Lehigh, lower gorge

ing for wild whitewater, here is the place to go. Next to the Youghiogheny of southwestern Pennsylvania, this Pocono river is the roughest big stream in the state. For years it has been a mecca to whitewater enthusiasts.

Protection efforts in the Lehigh Gorge began with the Game Commission's acquisition of much acreage on the east shore. The Penn Haven Rod and Gun Club retains control of twelve miles on the west side, an area members zealously guard with firearms, preventing boaters and other strangers from setting foot on it.

In 1970 the statewide planning report titled "Outdoor Recreation Horizons" recommended that the Department of Forests and Waters (now the Department of Environmental Resources) acquire most lands in the gorge for a state park. "This area should be preserved in its present condition," the report added, "with development primarily limited to construction of scenic hiking trails and primitive camping areas." The Horizons report recognized the Pocono region of the Commonwealth as one of the major recreation areas of northeastern United States, but identified the gorge as a place that "should be left relatively undeveloped." Plans proceeded for establishment of a Lehigh Gorge State Park, but acquisition of property became entangled, and interminable delays set in. Instead of the Department of Environmental Resources, where Secretary Goddard would have acted with dispatch, the Department of General Services was given money to buy lands, assuring a snail's pace to protection while property values soar. Some owners will reap windfalls at public expense. It was not the park but another state program that was to bring renewed and concentrated attention to the middle Lehigh.

In December of 1972 Governor Shapp signed into law a Pennsylvania Scenic Rivers Act, which established a framework to designate streams for special protection and management. Efforts had begun several years earlier when, in the wake of the National Wild and Scenic Rivers Act, a number of states began to enact their own programs. Conservationists from State College and Williamsport collected samples of bills and forwarded them to Representative (now Senator) Franklin Kury, who began the long and tedious process of lawmaking.

The bill was supported by environmentalists, though some were skeptical. "The Pennsylvania law will allow for appeasement of conservation interests while providing a means of river protection that is less secure than national designation," some people said. "It will be used as a reason to oppose the federal program." In support of the bill they added, "Nationally significant streams can be included in the national system, but we have scores of rivers that deserve protection, though they are only of statewide significance. They are the ones that should be in the state system."

Legislators carefully avoided questions of which river in which system. The act simply stated that "the Department of Environmental Resources shall study, conduct public hearings . . . and from time to time submit to the Governor and to the General Assembly proposals for the designation of rivers or sections of rivers as components of the Pennsylvania Scenic River System." In a very important but often overlooked paragraph, the law refers to the national system: "The Secretary of Environmental Resources is directed to encourage and assist any federal studies for inclusion of Pennsylvania rivers in a national scenic rivers system."

A task force was formed to assist the Department in completing recommendations for waterways that should be studied under the new law. Two hundred forty-five streams were identified, and sixty-one were recommended as highest priority. The Secretary of the Department chose three of these for study in 1976—Pine Creek, the Schuylkill River, and the Lehigh Gorge.

Kayakers, Lehigh at Mile-Long Rapids

The intent of the Scenic Rivers Act is clear: "to protect these values and to practice sound conservation policies and practices within this Scenic Rivers System." Details, however, are largely absent from the law. While a stream must be free of dams to be classified as "wild" or "scenic," the act does not specifically prohibit consideration or construction of new impoundments. Assumptions are that state designation will guarantee state opposition to dams and that state agencies will become better funded and more capable in solving recreation and resource management problems. State zoning of private lands is not permitted under the law, nor is condemnation of land, though the Commonwealth can use the right of eminent domain to acquire right-of-way easements to the water.

Crossing the pipeline, lower Lehigh Gorge

Year-long studies are being undertaken to determine if the streams should be designated and to draft guidelines for managing the rivers and their adjacent landscapes. A number of issues were to become apparent on the Lehigh Advisory Committee's float trip—a field investigation by people involved in preparation of the Scenic River Study.

In two vans driven by local outfitters, we rumbled down the stony road to Rockport. While this area is acceptable for the commercial operator, it is not recommended for private or individual access—your car will likely be sacked by local residents who have had their fill of floaters. At the bottom of the hill, doors burst open, and a parade of government people and Lehigh enthusiasts poured forth. I was especially anxious to see the river. This was my first visit to the gorge, and I had heard lots of tantalizing stories. Four rafts carried Department of Environmental Resources officials, Fish Commission personnel, county planners, and citizen members of the study committee. Charlie Walbridge, representing the American Canoe Association, and Roger McCay of the Forest Service took a C-1 (decked canoe) and a kayak, dancing circles around our lumbering "rubber ducks." I had very nearly brought my sixteen-and-half-foot open canoe but cautiously followed the advice of some Lehigh experts and left the boat atop my car at the campground. While a lot of people use conventional open canoes in the gorge, many of them foolishly risk losing their boat and maybe more.

After two minutes of cruising, we made the first stop for reasons I could not imagine and then did not believe. "Someone had an idea for a parking lot over here," Katie Gavan said. She worked for DER on the Lehigh study. It didn't take long to conclude that no road went to the potential parking area. "There would have to be a bridge across the river, but don't worry about it," Katie added. "There'll never be enough money to do it, even if it had been possible. Though the Lehigh qualifies for 'scenic' designation, the intent is to manage it as a 'wild' river, which would likely mean opposition to any new crossings."

Access and parking are important problems that the Scenic River Study is addressing. Currently the only major points for putting in or taking out of boats are at White Haven, Lehigh Tannery, and Jim Thorpe, for a minimum trip of about twenty-five difficult miles. Minor points of access are at Rockport, where cars frequently are vandalized, and Drakes Creek, where an obscure dirt road turns into a jeep trail, then stops 200 feet short of the river. Portage under a railroad bridge is required, and that often means wading in the creek. The solutions will be difficult ones; however, with limited access come opportunities for management of recreational use and related problems. Outfitters on the intensively floated Youghiogheny are controlled by the state, but only because embarkation points are on state-owned land. To regulate use of the river, public control of major access points is imperative.

Local outfitters feel that Rockport should be reserved for commercial float trips, since the guides don't have to leave cars and since they can police the area to minimize litter and other problems that make local residents unhappy. Spokesman Ken Powley added, "We recommend the development of the unpopulated Drake's Creek access area for use by private boaters only, where they wouldn't be interfering with the daily lives of local residents." An additional advantage of this plan is that commercial and independent boating traffic would largely be segregated, since White Haven to Rockport would be an easy shuttle for the outfitters, and Drake's Creek to Jim Thorpe would be good for independents. "We have over thirty miles of excellent whitewater rapids," Powley said. "There's no need for everyone to be paddling up each other's backs." Drake's Creek is far from a simple solution, as a four-wheel-drive vehicle is now needed, and to significantly improve the road would be very difficult.

After looking at the "parking" area and the Drake's Creek access, we entered some wilder rapids, and I got to thinking that I did the right thing in leaving my canoe at the campground. I'd be plenty wet by now. Half a dozen times we passed corpses of canoes which had been, no doubt, the pride and joy of enthusiastic owners. It makes a miserable day when you

Overturned kayaker, Lehigh River

wrap a $400 boat around a rock and leave it there to become shredded in the coming floods. It's also a long walk out of Lehigh Gorge, providing you're able. Three weeks before, a man had drowned in these rapids. After swamping his open canoe, the thirty-four-year-old paddler apparently wedged his foot under a rock while trying to free the pinned boat. After falling into the water, he was held under by the force of the current. Wise advice is to stay clear of the Lehigh in your open canoe unless you're an expert. Better to go by raft, or if you're experienced, by whitewater (decked) canoe or kayak.

When we stopped for lunch, Bob Steiner of the Fish Commission mentioned that an estimated 1,200 people floated the gorge on the busiest day of the year. That's an incredibly high figure, but it's easy to see why the river is popular. For the kayaking enthusiast, the Lehigh is ideal. Like the Delaware, it's within easy traveling distance of one-fourth of the nation's people. For the expert canoeist, the Lehigh still presents challenges, and for the novice in a raft, it's perfect. The big waters of the Cheat River in West Virginia and the Youghiogheny in Pennsylvania are *too* wild for many beginners, often leaving them in fright and outright peril. People who have never cruised whitewater should not begin on the biggest and wildest rivers, any more than a casual jogger should enter the Boston Marathon. The Lehigh offers thrills, wildness, and scenery and can be safely run by any healthy person in a big rubber raft.

It was October, and we didn't see a single fisherman, but as elsewhere on scenic rivers, there are conflicts between floaters and anglers. Unique to the Lehigh, the main concern is the release of water from Walters Dam. For a number of years, the Army Corps of Engineers has been releasing extra water on the third weekend of July, August, September, and October, creating a high flow that boaters can rely upon and allowing them to schedule trips accordingly. Fishermen maintain that extra water destroys invertebrate bottom life that is critical to the food chain. Invertebrates have been sampled twice after releases, one survey showing a reduction in bottom life; however, recovery was rapid. With inconclusive results, the Corps continues to release under an agreement with the Fish Commission and the Department of Environmental Resources. Boaters argue that natural floods of far greater magnitude don't significantly harm the fishery, and fishermen say the river is being destroyed. The Fish Commission and the Scenic River Study team are trying to get all the facts that they need to make their management decisions.

As we floated further down the gorge, the scenery became more and more spectacular. Remains of the Lehigh Canal could be seen, and then mountains rose high at Oxbow Bend; rocky outcrops hung all around in a grandeur unlike any Pennsylvania stream. At Mile-Long Rapids, the river rolled and roared, pitching us over boulders and haystacks and rinsing gallons of water into the raft. One cannot remain unenthusiastic about the Lehigh.

Delaware Basin River Sketches

Lackawaxen River

A large Delaware tributary in the northeastern part of Pennsylvania, the Lackawaxen is formed by its West Branch and Van Auken Creek at Prompton village. The upper river is fast and includes two impoundments. Just below Seelysville Dam, a 250-yard rapids drops twenty feet. Honesdale is an old northern industrial village.

Early spring sunshine, Lackawaxen River near Kimbles

Wallenpaupack Creek enters at Hawley, draining Lake Wallenpaupack. With 5,760 acres of water, it's the largest Pocono lake and attracts a heavy tourist trade. Water is clear, and fifty-one miles of shoreline are forested, with cabins and four public camp sites operated by Pennsylvania Power and Light Company, the owners. Though this is a reservoir, it has the attractive appearance of a natural lake and is one of the finest large flat-water canoeing sites in the state. Wallenpaupack's East Branch is a rushing woodland stream that carves through small gorges and drops over an unboatable falls, one mile above the lake.

Below Hawley, the Lackawaxen is at its best and attracts many fishermen. Outstanding scenic areas are near the Kimble Road Bridge and through the rapids that run for five miles above the Delaware confluence. Pennsylvania Power and Light Company's powerhouse for the lake is located above

Lackawaxen River below Kimbles

the Kimble Bridge, causing flows to fluctuate greatly. Releases are not scheduled, making it impossible to predict water levels. The river drops eighteen feet per mile through this reach, becoming even steeper as the Delaware is approached. At medium and high levels, paddlers can run from Hawley, but rapids are a challenging Class II and III.

State Route 590 and smaller roads follow the river but detract little from a rocky beauty of the shoreline. Zane Grey did much writing in the historic hotel at the village of Lackawaxen, where an archaic suspension bridge spans the Delaware.

Shohola Creek and Upper Delaware Tributaries

Though Shohola is only a small stream draining eighty-six square miles, it deserves special attention because of its extraordinary ruggedness and beauty. The creek rises on the high and boggy plateau of the Poconos near

Shohola Falls

Resica Falls, Bushkill Creek

Lords Valley and Greeley, then flows northeast to the Delaware, which it joins at the village of Shohola. Route 6, which many people consider Pennsylvania's most scenic highway, crosses just below Shohola Falls, one of the state's most picturesque cascades. Three hundred yards above the falls, an ancient glacial lake has been reimpounded on state game lands, but at the falls, waters plunge madly over broad sandstone ledges, darkened tannin color contrasting sharply with white aerated foam. Massive, glistening rock outcrops and deep shade of hemlocks all add to the scene. Below the falls, Shohola churns downhill through a gorge that is almost impassable on foot and totally impassable on water except for the most expert kayakers who float during high runoff. Fishing is good, with many anglers at the lake, a few who cast into the deep black pool at the foot of the falls, and rarely anyone in the rugged gorge where pools are much smaller.

Like Shohola, other tributaries to the northern Delaware are small streams, with the exception of the beautiful Lackawaxen. Big and Little Bush Kill are special attractions. On the larger stream, Resica Falls is a highlight that can be seen at the Boy Scout camp along Route 402. Bushkill Falls is a very long drop, located on a private, commercially operated site north of Bushkill village.

Brodhead Creek is also an upper Delaware tributary, well known as an excellent trout stream. Proposals to construct small dams have threatened the Broadhead in recent years, though they have thus far been successfully fought by environmental groups such as Trout Unlimited.

The Schuylkill River

The Schuylkill is best known for its broad reach of flatwater behind Fairmount Dam in Philadelphia. This is a rowing center of the world, and racing shells can almost always be seen with their crews of one, two, four, or eight men or women. In 1876, 800 acres were taken from industrial, residential, and vacant space along the Schuylkill and used for the nation's Centennial celebration. Two hundred buildings were constructed and later removed to create Fairmont Park, the largest urban park in the United States. It includes both sides of the river and lower Wissahickon Creek, a small tributary with a history of protection activities that has involved many generations.

Schuylkill water quality has a reputation of being poor. It was long a

Eight-man crew, Schuylkill River and Fairmont Park

joke, and perhaps a fact, that an overturned oarsman should get typhoid shots immediately. The last twenty years have brought improvements. The riverbed and shores were black with coal sludge until much of it was removed in the 1940s. Fish passages are now being built for the ocean-migrating shad at Fairmont Dam and Flat Rock. Wastes from mining have largely been curtailed, but many industrial and municipal problems remain. Swimming is limited indefinitely due to high fecal coliform. Philadelphia draws 180 million gallons of Schuylkill water per day for municipal use. Four other communities tap the lower river for consumption. Increases in power plant cooling and irrigation are projected, with conflicts over appropriation. Water is now utilized six different times before it reaches Fairmont Dam, and by the year 2020, water will be used a minimum of eight or a maximum of sixteen times.

Floating debris, Schuylkill River in Philadelphia

Yet the river is in a strategic place for recreation. It flows through the nation's fourth most populous city, and 28 percent of Pennsylvania's residents live in the five counties that face the waterfront. Some of the river is noxious and carries the noise and cemented banks of industry, like the reach below Norristown Dam. Other areas are fine assets: the scenic Blue Mountain Gap below Port Clinton, the recreational pool above Felix Dam, and the edge of Reading's riverfront park. Philadelphia plans to restore a section of the Schuylkill Canal in the Manayunk section of the city.

Under contract from the state Department of Environmental Resources, the Pennsylvania Environmental Council prepared a recreational river study and a greenway proposal for ninety miles of the river. PEC found that one-third of the riverfront is public or recreational land. The proposal emphasizes establishment of access areas, natural area protection, and the use of special-interest sites, such as the old canal. A Schuylkill River Greenway Association was formed to foster open space and recreational improvement. Importantly, the effort had local political support. Though Pennsylvania has dozens of wilder, more scenic, more open, and cleaner streams than this, the Schuylkill was designated a "recreational" and "modified recreational" river—the first member of the state scenic rivers system. You can't get much closer to the people than this.

The Brandywine and Its Landscape

Brandywine Creek and its resident conservationists have gained special status. Here, in 1945, a group of thirty-five people formed the nation's first major watershed association. Led by Clayton Hoff, the organization sought to eliminate problems of erosion, industrial and municipal water pollution, and flood damage. Their efforts led to substantial success, as 96 percent of industrial waste and 94 percent of sewage wastes are now treated, and soil losses by erosion are reduced by 60 percent. In 1958 the first flood-plain zoning in Pennsylvania was enacted here. The organization supported small dams for recreation, flood control, and low-flow augmentation, maintaining enough water in dry periods so that pollution is diluted and less noticeable. Bob Struble, who headed the association for years, says that their key was to "get people together and work in a quiet, constructive way. Water quality is better now than it's been in one hundred years. Though the process of improvement is slow, we've come a long way."

One effort that didn't go very far was an ambitious proposal for easement acquisition, whereby the Chester County Water Resources Authority would buy certain development rights from landowners of flood plain and steep-sloped areas. The program was developed by the University of Penn-

Brandywine Creek above Lenape

sylvania, the Regional Science Research Institute, the United States Geological Survey, and the Academy of Natural Sciences. Its intention was to prevent environmental damage and to maintain the existing rural character of the upper East Branch. Specialists prepared background materials, information brochures, and, in 1968, "The Brandywine Plan." An introduction stated:

> Urban development is coming to the Brandywine Valley just as it has to neighboring valleys. If this development takes place in flood plains, near streams and on steep slopes, if erosion occurs during construction and sewage pollutes the water, the stream and the general environment of the valley will deteriorate. The purpose of the work currently being undertaken by the Water Resources Authority is to prevent this from happening in the basin of the Upper East Branch by restricting development to areas where it will do the least damage.

For a variety of reasons, the proposals were rejected by most of the local governing bodies. Few residents had any apparent and serious concern that the future would bring problems demanding new approaches to land management. Local organizations were not highly active or supportive, leaving a vacuum to be filled by the Chester County Freeholder's Association, a new group whose goal was to defeat the program. The conflict was similar to many that involve new attitudes about land. As John C. Keene and Ann Louise Strong described it, "Followers of an old way of life . . . confronted proposals that promised change and called for cooperation, a sense of community, and use of governmental power." Condemnation authority was an unfortunate recommendation, serving to fuel fears, arguments, and persuasiveness of opponents. While eminent domain provisions were later dropped, damage had already been done, and many people's minds were not to be changed.

"Too much, too fast, is how I sum it up," explained Struble, who at the time was executive director of the Water Resources Authority and who later ran successfully for county commissioner. "Though the program failed, some of its goals are being achieved by using good conservation practices, local zoning, and easements which are donated to the Brandywine Conservancy for protection as open space."

While efforts at conservation and planning have given notoriety to the Brandywine, the valley is also well known for its history and for artists who have lived there. The sixty-mile-long stream was ideally suited for mill sites, with steep falls and rapids just above Delaware Bay at Wilmington. One hundred thirty-three water-powered industries were in the watershed during the early 1800s. At Chadds Ford the Battle of the Brandywine was fought, British General Howe defeating Washington during the Revolutionary War. The battlefield is now a state park. Many artists have worked and lived along the Brandywine, including the well-known Wyeths. Historic sites can be visited through use of a taped driving tour, produced by the Brandywine Valley Association, the Chester County Library, and the Chester County Tourist Bureau, available at the County Library, 235 West Market Street in West Chester.

For a better view of the stream itself, canoe the Brandywine from Northbrook on the West Branch or from Lenape, below the confluence of the East and West branches, to Chadds Ford. Flow is usually high enough throughout the summer. Waters are quiet with small riffles, but stone rubble from old mill dams sometimes creates short, exciting rapids. Above Wilmington, waters become too rough for boating, with waterfalls, dams, and a 120-foot drop in four miles.

Opposite: Skinner's Falls

Travels on the Delaware:
Whitewater, Herons, and Kids from the Bronx

It was like a festival, and everybody was excited. "There's only *one* of these places," I said to myself as I pulled the Delaware River backward with my paddle, then drifted toward the gravel beach near Skinner's Falls. The kids! There must have been a hundred altogether, and thirty of them hopped around on the shore as impatiently as my labrador retriever when there's something to fetch.

"What's his name?" one of the boys asked.

"Eli," was my answer, and then the dog's torment began.

"Eli! Here, Eli," a twelve-year-old girl squealed, but the black lab stayed put in the bow of my canoe.

That Tuesday afternoon was the highlight of a 130-mile canoe journey. Water roared through the rapids for 100 yards, churning up foam and pulling down canoes of the inexperienced and careless, which seemed like most of them. Wherever water falls, an alluring magic fills the air and electrifies those nearby. I thought of the million-dollar fountain-building industry that strives to create and transport a tiny piece of Skinner's Falls to the center of a shopping mall someplace.

It wasn't just children at the falls; the blend of visitors could have competed with Mardi Gras. Everybody seemed to be represented. The lead

show was a stream of young adventurers who tried their best to float through the whitewater, but some sun-loving local girls also attracted attention. I got out my camera and took pictures of both as Eli and I walked downriver to scout the rapids. Rocks that reached into the water were an anthill of activity—kids on inner tubes would spin with the current, then swim into an eddy and hustle back to do it all over again. Three or four canoes were always being carried upriver so that the Delaware roller-coaster could be run again. Young faces peered out from beneath aluminum boats turned upside down over their heads. Mom and the children had found some shallows in which to swim, and a gang of guys with a radio and a case of beer moved stealthily one rock closer to the girls, who used sunshine to the limits of accepted dress codes. A tourist in a red shirt and blue socks was rolling movies from an outer vantage point. Suddenly he turned to shoot Eli and me as we zigzagged in his direction, up one rock, down another.

Just in time, he took a new bead on the river, aiming his camera for a comic sequence of four guys in an overloaded boat that was headed toward the center of troublesome water. The first big wave splashed over their bow. The second added two more gallons of the Catskills and Poconos, and then the woeful canoe entered a series of four or five haystacks—large standing waves about three feet high. With each roller the boat sank lower into the river until the gunwales could barely be seen. The next wave showed only four men from the chest up. Their craft was sinking irrevocably toward the bottom, but with futility they continued to paddle in unison.

Sunbathing, Skinner's Falls

Below Skinner's Falls

After I had advanced my film for another frame, the paddlers and their possessions were scattered from Pennsylvania to New York on either side of the borderline river. Reassembly looked like a hopeless task.

Actually, the fun should be regarded with deathly seriousness. It's no wonder that two, three, or four people may drown at Skinner's Falls in a year. The next boat through the rapids scared me. Two boys who might have been fourteen years old overturned to the *downstream* side. They splashed through the rapids and were pursued by their own canoe; that is, their canoe was drifting through the rapids *behind* them. It looks as harmless as when the sunken boat is in front of its dislocated operator, but a boat to the rear is infinitely more dangerous. If the waterborne paddler hits a rock, the canoe may in turn hit him, pinning him tightly and possibly with his head underwater. As I watched those children flailing at the river and yelling in frenzy, their 2,000-pound, water-laden Grumman rolled and tumbled, side over side, just behind them. It was a silent, unseen death trap. Like bad etiquette, the problem is recognized only by those who understand it. The boat rumbled as it scraped rocks, moving inevitably and powerfully like the impersonal giants in fairy tales. Before I tell a beginning canoeist which end of the paddle to put in the water, I tell him to fall out on the upstream side if the boat goes under. Somebody should have said that to everyone who went down the Delaware.

After the children drifted into stillwater, I spotted my route through the rapids. With camping gear, $800 worth of camera equipment, and my only canoe for the trip, I wasn't anxious to overdo it. A thrilling descent would be enough, without big chances on swamping or cracking into the hard earth that separated the Delaware's flow. Before we run Skinner's Falls, maybe we should go back to the beginning.

The Delaware always appealed to me, maybe because it's the name given to the eastern Pennsylvania Indians or maybe because I didn't grow up with the river's tidal stench at Philadelphia. I decided to start as far up as the water level would permit. My route would include the section of river being considered for National Scenic River status and the reach that would be flooded by Tocks Island Dam.

On Catskill waters of the East Branch I embarked with Eli. Scenery was magnificent, the water fast and clear. I had never seen so many great blue herons. They would wade in backwater shallows or go soaring off downstream. After beaching on a small island, I took some photographs, Eli fetched sticks out of the river, and I had my first meeting with other canoeists. Scraping and grating they came. Along with the Wisconsin Glacier, their rearranging of the river-bottom landscape must be one of the more profound changes in geologic history.

"How far to Hancock?" one asked in a weary tone of voice, each word a little lower than the one before it. I said I didn't know. "Well, *about* how far?"

"Maybe five miles." He gave me the blankest stare I've seen, the same stare I used to give Mr. Moore in high-school algebra class. I must have demoralized them. I hoped that they didn't get out to hitchhike, since it turned out to be only a mile and a half to town.

We met the West Branch late in the day. In a golden sundown I looked back up at Point Mountain and the confluence of two branches—the beginning of the whole Delaware. A current whipped around the downstream end of an island, and I followed it into a sharp eddy turn. There lay an idyllic site—a high sandy bank with aged pines clustered all around. It was the most beautiful grove I'd see on the entire trip and also the best camp, except for the last night, when we settled upon a wooded bank and looked out at the Delaware through old-time sugar maples above Tocks Island.

Monday morning was misty—a sunny day coming for sure. I like to travel silently in the fog, and so I drifted without effort toward Equinunk, Long Eddy, and Callicoon. The upper reach of the Delaware is one of the most scenic sections. Even though a road sometimes follows the valley, it's rarely seen, nor is its traffic heard. McCoy's Knob and Jensen Hill are high, splendid backdrops to a moving current. Except for smaller trees today, much of the river must look as it did when Indians called it Poutaxat, Makiriskitton, Makarish-Kisten, or Whitiuck.

It is easy to see why the upper Delaware was included in the National Wild and Scenic Rivers System. With designation has come a prohibition against dams, a restriction that could be important someday. Potential res-

Historic Lackawaxen Bridge, Delaware River

ervoir sites are listed at Hankins, Callicoon, Tusten, Hawks Nest, and Skinner's Falls. Federal status is also to result in maintenance of recreation areas and more attention to trash and litter disposal, sewage waste, and other recreation-related problems. In 1977 Representative Peter Kostmayer of Pennsylvania and Senator Clifford Case of New Jersey introduced bills to designate this and middle reaches of the river—action to prevent construction of Tocks Island Dam. The 1978 Parks and Recreation Act finally designated the upper and middle Delaware.

Long Eddy was the first town after lunch. From a picnicking family I sought directions to the village store and permission to use the access area. After buying a pint of ice cream, I returned to the beach and watched the arrival of two vans and canoe trailers. I'd heard there were some big liveries on the river, one with 600 boats and a few others that rent over 200. Pandemonium broke loose, and the picnicking family was inundated with canoes, kayaks, life vests, happy people eager to get on the river, canoe trailers turning around—you name it. I took off downriver and ended up spending much of the afternoon floating along with the fun-loving group that included the lifeguard, canoe rental girl, and stable boy from the Upper Delaware Campground at Callicoon. I asked about people's feelings on National Scenic River designation, which was pending at that time. "Some want it, but they don't want more people coming here. They don't want a dam, either."

One would think that people who take the time, trouble, and expense to canoe our rivers would do so without leaving trash behind, but that isn't always so, as I found out Monday night. The eastern shore looked like a perfect camp site—a sloping beach, a higher wooded bank with sugar maples, and just for extra measure, an evening view of Callicoon and the old seminary that stands high above the town. I was tired and ready to camp, but as I beached I caught a strange odor, the kind that revolts me but excites my labrador retriever. With differing anticipation, we both climbed the bank to see what it was.

I never really figured it out, and neither did the dog, though leaving that place was my choice and a hard thing for him to do. A fire still smouldered, and at least part of the bad odor came from it. The amazing thing was that behind the fire sat half a dozen garbage bags bulging fuller than a stuffed turkey at Thanksgiving. People must have been proud of the care they had taken to put all that trash together and package it so nicely that it would be no problem for the pickup man in the morning.

Awakening on Tuesday morning, I knew it was early, because when I raised my head, Eli didn't raise his. Later a cool gust of heavy mist blew through the mosquito net of the tent door. It's like having your face washed by the morning itself. I didn't know what time it was but didn't care either. Canoe trips allow you to depart from the normal procedure of checking the morning clock. A watch is something I never take; that way I do what I want instead of what I'm supposed to do.

In a leisurely way I prepared breakfast, then we started our journey as sunshine began to penetrate the fog. After paddling half a mile, I turned to inspect the upstream view. It looked like the Spanish Armada coming behind me, in the distance, at the beginning of a long flatwater reach that I was now leaving. I couldn't see them or their boats, only wet blades of paddles flashing silver as the sun struck them. First one boat, then three, and when I turned the next time to look, there must have been twenty. Forty paddles were blinking on and off through the last remnant of mist that clung to the river. It didn't take long for the group to pass us.

At Cochecton, a public access area of the New York Department of Natural Resources attracted me to the shore. This welcome was appreciated after passing so many "no trespassing" signs. With the camera gear over my shoulder and the dog held tightly on a nylon rope, we started off to town for supplies. I tied Eli to a post at the store front, though he was never happy that way—especially here, as a half-pint dog kept yapping at him from the second-story window. I thought I heard Eli say, "You come within three feet of this post and I'll swallow you whole." I went inside.

While the owner was ringing up my three-dollar order, Eli let out a bark that just about shook the jelly jars off the shelf. "There's so many damn dogs in this town I can't keep track of 'em," the man said. I just sort of agreed and got out of there as fast as I could.

When we reached the canoe, I opened my new sandwich. A little kid on

Trash left by campers, Delaware River near Callicoon

a minibike whipped down the bank and onto the gravel bar. "You goin' to Skinner's?" he asked.

"I've already been there." This really set him back. "I'm going *up* the river."

"Without a motor?"

"The dog pulls—see this harness?" I held up my usual tangled mess of rope. He blinked, looked at the dog, and then a big toothy grin spread from one ear to the other. He knew I was joking.

"There's really big waves. You better watch out!" I thanked him as we drifted away, under the bridge. "You better watch out," he repeated. His voice was faint now from the space between us.

Skinner's easier side is on the right, so that is where I ran. I went cautiously, not wanting to ship water or hit any rocks. After standing for a good view, I picked my way around two outcrops of sandstone. The big waves were coming, so I backpaddled to slow the boat, floating up on the first wave, bracing heavily with the paddle so the boat wouldn't sink into the next haystack. The second and third rollers came closely together. To avoid burying the bow in the lower wave, I canted the canoe a little sideways, and we dipped and rolled parallel to the waves, with only a pint of water slurping over the gunwale and onto Eli. I told him it wasn't much, all considered, but he still didn't like it and gave me an indignant look, as if I'd accused him of not being a pure-bred lab. I couldn't tell for sure what was ahead until I stood up again. Hardly any whitewater remained, so just for fun I reached to the left and drew hard, pulling the boat into heavier rapids.

It was then that we hit a flat rock, the kind that lurks a few inches under so that water slicks over them without much evidence. The real danger is beyond, since a minor collision on a flat rock can throw the canoe off course or destroy a sequence of moves intended to guide you past the next obstacle, and the next one and the next one. That's what happened, so I scrambled to go right where I had intended to go left, while I yelled at Eli to sit instead of trying to turn around each time a wave approached from the opposite side. I smiled as we passed the last rock and swung the canoe into an eddy so we could beach. Hearing a yell, I turned to look and saw a dismembered Grumman and crew headed toward me. I picked up a drifting paddle for them while staying clear of the boat, and then we went for a long, cool swim.

We had come only three days down this great eastern river, but already I had seen so much and done so much. The Delaware drifted and plunged and in many ways created or designed all that was around it. Ahead lay Narrowsburg, Shohola and Mongap rapids, the cliffs at Eddy Farm Hotel, a long winding course past Milford to the Tocks Island Dam site, and then the Delaware Water Gap where we would have to stop. Like life, the river changed every minute; each day would bring a new world, and I would leave an old one behind. It's a fascination that seizes me on all trips, especially after the second or third day out—the movement and life that travel *as* a river, and the places and lives *along* the river.

A whole new riverine perspective appears at Narrowsburg. In a strange pattern, the shorelines bulge to a wide, circular basin that is constricted at its lower end in a narrows for which the town was named. Rocks protrude on either bank, supporting a high arched bridge that connects Pennsylvania to New York. After passing under the bridge, waters of the Delaware are again freed of shoreline encumbrances, forming a lakelike basin beneath clustered homes and shops of the small New York town. Rising from the cliffs and partially encompassed by the river, Narrowsburg looks like a medieval fortress, and sure enough, it was a challenge for me to dock my boat and enter the town without wading, sliding, and falling back into the water.

The effort was worthwhile, for Main Street had an unusual small-town charm. While there were excellent river views, the "downtown" area was well above flood levels. Recognizing a happy group of city kids who had passed me a few miles upriver, I got one of them to hold Eli while I ordered a sandwich. The children were staying in town for a movie that night. Their counselor told them the name of the show, and one asked, "You mean there's only *one* theater in town?"

Into the evening I paddled, passing other groups of young people who were having the time of their lives canoeing, camping, swimming, and cooking supper.

One of the finest sections of the Delaware lies below Narrowsburg, though I was able to enjoy it the least since it rained for a half day. Shohola Rapids were my favorite of all. Less celebrated and without the high excitement of Skinner's Falls, they still offer challenging whitewater, particularly to the novice paddler. Boulders are strewn like buckshot, more like the glacial streams of New York and the north than the smoother-bedded rivers of Pennsylvania.

Seldom would I overtake another party, as I enjoy the slower pace of the river and give priority to bird watching, listening to kingfishers and hawks, and just looking around. So it surprised me that I was gaining on a group of eight aluminum canoes that were spread thin from the east shore to the west. Nearing one of the boats, I noticed its unusual crew. In front were two little girls whom I guessed to be in second or third grade. Never before had I seen two people sitting on one canoe seat. Neatly packed gear was piled amidships, and in the stern was a girl who couldn't have been older than fourteen. We began talking, and I learned that Virginia was a camp counselor—in all likelihood the youngest one on the Delaware. Fred, who runs the summer program for the Putnam School of Greenwich, Connecticut, paddled over to get acquainted and then drifted off to check on another one of his boats. With two college students, Fred and Virginia guide six trips each summer for students of all ages.

"My dad taught me how to canoe," Virginia explained, "but not in rapids. I learned that pretty much by myself." We talked about Skinner's Falls, and I explained the dangers of swimming through the rapids with a swamped canoe behind you. "Hey!" she said, getting the attention of the two second-graders. "Did you hear that?" She explained the danger to her crew exactly as I had done, concluding that they should bail out on the upstream side if the boat goes under.

After a while Fred yelled over, "Virginia, get your friend to have lunch with us—I want to talk to him about Pennsylvania rivers," and so we beached at the mouth of a trout stream.

The children fussed over Eli and were impressed with his swimming demonstration. I said that he had webbed feet to help him, which of course they didn't believe. While I held a paw and pointed to the layer of skin that connects a lab's toes, Fred asked about other rivers that he and his students could run. "The Delaware's great, but this is our fifteenth cruise!" I was amazed that he had no rivers to run in New England. "Except for northern Maine, we don't have a single free-flowing stream for a long trip," he explained. "The Delaware is the closest."

I mentioned the Susquehanna above Wilkes-Barre, and the West Branch. "But you won't find the Delaware's rapids," I warned, "and while the upper West Branch is wild and scenic, it's another three hours from Connecticut."

Everyone depended upon Virginia for lunch; while others casually talked and ate, she spread jelly on top of peanut butter over and over again and at the same time passed out fruit and equitably rationed a pile of candy bars. I didn't want to leave, but as the rain started, I did, draping an extra jacket over Eli's back so that he looked like a racehorse who had just won the Kentucky Derby. We joined the current again, and I waved goodby to new friends.

After a few hours of flatwater paddling, we came to rapids where the Mongap River has built a delta and pushed the Delaware against a cement wall of the railroad on the opposite side. Currents are deep and fast, creating haystacks, any two of which could swamp an open canoe. I eased off to the left and then splashed through the lower rapids that lie half a mile below. It was twilight when we approached Cherry Island. Looking into the river, I saw a half-dozen enormous trout and countless fish of other species. It was like an aquarium.

At Cherry Island we floated through more riffles; then as nighttime neared, we entered the long set of rapids below Millrift. This whitewater came unexpectedly. In growing darkness, the force of an unknown river shook me in a way that recurs often enough that I maintain a healthy fear of water. I intended to make camp half an hour before, but all semblance of a reasonable schedule faded as we came upon Eddy Farm Hotel.

One should understand that my reaction at seeing the hotel was influenced by the circumstances: this was the fourth day of a journey through sparsely developed country, and it was the end of a day that seemed to

The Putnam School canoe trip, Delaware River above Mongap

Virginia, paddling the Delaware below Shohola

have begun forty-eight hours earlier. Only twilight remained as I dropped from rapids into a deep green pool with fern-covered cliffs on the western shore. First I noticed a boat dock and manicured beach. Sun umbrellas called to mind scenes of leisure that are atypical of any Pennsylvania river. Lights shone through dense foliage, and there stood the hotel. The towering wooden frame building seemed to ramble on forever with wings and dormers and porches. I think that the sounds were the most alluring aspect of all, for across the quiet waters came laughter and delight, the crisp noise from glasses and dishes, and occasionally a voice that stood apart from the rest. Then I saw the style of luxuriant recreation that had been so popular fifty and eighty years ago in the Catskills, Adirondacks, and at Eagles Mere above Muncy Creek. A camp site could wait—any poison ivy field would do. "Let's go take a look," I said to Eli, and so we walked up from the beach, water seeping from my ragged sneakers.

Delaware fisherman near Port Jervis

First we met an elderly woman with a twinkle in her eye. She fussed over the dog and graciously told me the name of the place. Our inspection of the grounds was uneventful until we reached the shuffleboard courts. A big man with a shiny bald head looked up from a row of chairs he was straightening and said flatly, "Who are *you*?" I told him. "Do you know that this is private property?" I explained that I was canoeing and photographing the Delaware River, and the trip wouldn't be complete if I passed this place by. He liked that.

"We have nothing against *you*, understand; it's just that we have thousands of canoeists passing by, and we have to say 'no' sometime." He ended up saying it was all right for me to return in the morning to take some pictures.

Early on Thursday morning, we reached Matamoras on the Pennsylvania side and Port Jervis in New York. A foul smell rose from the water, and I was happy to keep passing through. Fishermen were all around on the shore and in rowboats. As we cruised under the Interstate 84 bridge, New York ended and New Jersey began.

The Delaware became a lazier river, and the sun appeared in full force, so that I became a lazier paddler, content to lean back in the canoe and close my eyes as we drifted, occasionally splashing cold water or going for a swim to cool off. The slow river was elegant if not exciting, a friendly sea to turn to, a ribbon of life through the palisaded valley that divides New Jersey mountains from the Pocono Plateau. As we floated to the end of Namanock Island, voices broke through the trees. Reaching the downstream point of the island, I saw a dozen canoes and a lot of young girls. Looking closer for a leader, I could find none. The oldest one was about Virginia's age. They had come four days from Lackawaxen and would finish at Dingman's Ferry—a trip of over forty miles. I paddled away, wondering why there weren't more older people traveling and vacationing by canoe; the pleasures of river voyages shouldn't be reserved for the young. In winding corridors everywhere, waterways show open land, public property, and fine scenery. The experience is almost painless, unlike the rigors of backpacking. Floating a river is the only way to really see it and experience its life. Cars are of limited value, since the most beautiful streams are where roads are not, and usually when rivers can be seen from the highway, the view is marred by the road itself. The canoeist almost always has a choice of excellent camp sites and good opportunities to see wildlife. One can view the rivers as a vast public transportation network that penetrates the most beautiful Pennsylvania countrysides, while augmenting instead of detracting from the scenery. Roadside clutter, exhaust fumes, and noise that are created and tolerated in "pleasure driving" are nonexistent. Rivers are the focus and the highlights of our lands, lacing them together in a web of life and serving as an unmatched recreation system.

For some time we had been floating through the thirty-seven-mile section of river that would be flooded by Tocks Island Dam. Authorized by the Flood Control Act of 1962, the project was designed for flood control, water supply, power generation, and recreation. A lack of funds delayed it for ten years, at the end of which the forces of environmentalists and river protectors were gathered. An initial eight-page environmental statement by the Army Corps of Engineers was rejected, and in the course of intensive study that followed, a proposal to use the National Recreational Area without the dam gained favor. By 1975 all the involved states but Pennsylvania opposed the dam and in 1978, National River designation set a congressional barrier. Efforts are now being made to deauthorize the reservoir—an action that would formally reverse Congress's 1962 commitment. Only two projects in the nation have been deauthorized.

The Pennsylvania Department of Environmental Resources maintains that storage is needed for assurance against Delaware Bay salt intrusion, though the state's criteria are far more stringent than federal standards. The middle Delaware's future has been contested for sixteen years, and while the advocates of free flow have won some important rounds, a counterforce may continue for a long time.

After camping on a shaded sugar-maple bank at Wallpack Bend, we drifted in a light drizzle during the last day of our trip. The base of Kittatinny Mountain rose from the east shore, and 1,000 feet above stood the summit, Sunfish Pond, and the Appalachian Trail. While a party of fifteen canoes went past, I beached on Tocks Island and photographed the immense maples and hardwoods crowning fertile lowlands that were built by centuries of silt and sand deposits.

Six miles ahead lay the Water Gap and the towering cliffs that would mark the end of our 130-mile voyage. With changing waters, the traveler himself changes, and I recalled the perceptions and moods that I had met. First was an excitement of traveling and of moving through the current. Then a smooth contentment came again and again with misty mornings, the plunging dive of a kingfisher, afternoon sun, and the shimmering of water late in the day. To this, people were added in a kinship as citizens of the river—a companionship unlike that of neighbors or old acquaintances. All of the travelers seemed to be one collective friend, and the relationship built with each new face. The Delaware's rhythm replaced the routine of my other lives.

Beneath us the current surged up again, casting us further to the south. River traveling had become more than a canoe trip, more than recreation or seeing new lands. The experience suddenly expands beyond its appearance. Drifting in the widening rapids and eddies becomes a way of life as one leaves the common molds and joins the pace of the waterway. For a while I was lost from the other world, insulated by shorelines and mountainsides. We were exploring a continent, and each mile showed us land that we had never seen before. One can do far worse than to spend a lifetime traveling rivers.

Swimming from the canoe, Delaware River above Tocks Island

Above: An urban river — the Susquehanna at Harrisburg

Photo by John Lazenby

Below: Pine Creek below Blackwell

The Future
of Pennsylvania Rivers

Pennsylvania's rivers are a valuable resource, with qualities difficult to find elsewhere. For residents of the valleys and for visitors who canoe, fish, hike, and camp, many of the streams offer wildness, clean water, and outstanding scenery. A person can experience peace in solitude or share with others the companionship of the river.

Streams have also been ravaged, polluted, and dammed. We have progressed in some respects, achieving better sewage treatment, less industrial waste, recovery from mine drainage, enaction of flood-plain regulations, and a program to designate scenic rivers; but most of the problems from the past remain. The early 1970s have shown a net improvement in 670 miles of major streams, but thousands of waterway miles still do not meet established standards. Future changes are likely to place even more stress on certain aspects of the riverine environment. With more people there is more waste.

Leetonia, on Pine Creek's Cedar Run, used to have fifteen hundred people; now it has half a dozen. Without the sawmills and tanneries and boom towns of the nineteenth century, some waters of the north central highlands are cleaner. But the backwoods and rural reaches of Pennsylvania are entering a new era today, growing with urban emigrants. Escapees from cities and suburbs are reversing seventy years of exodus from the countryside, small towns, and quiet villages. People clamor for land. In many mountainous counties they find 95 percent of the soils poorly suited for on-site sewage disposal. The state Department of Environmental Resources had barely finished tightening enforcement to prevent pollution from poorly sited septic tanks when pressure from bankers, developers, and local governments forced a liberalization. "Alternate" disposal techniques, such as sand mounds, now account for half of the new systems in some areas, but over 40 percent of these malfunction and overflow.

Rural Pennsylvania is ill-equipped to cope with the coming tide of popularity. No sewage permit is required by the state if the new owner has ten acres of land. The township can require a permit, but few do. These new settlers can dump wastewater as they please, affecting the environment as much as the owner of half an acre. It makes the difference between drinking and not drinking from many mountain streams.

More graphic is the problem of municipal and industrial disposal, though improvements have been made. The Ohio River, where I grew up, was a sordid conduit of waste that no one thought could be clean. You were considered nostalgic to think about a clear forest-shored Ohio; the river was obviously meant to transport sewage and steaming overflow from the steel mills. It's said to be better now, but far from good. The first time I canoed the Susquehanna's West Branch, sewer gas at Williamsport smelled like a trapless bathroom drain. Today the river is usually green and odorless, with bass and walleye, though some sewage overloads persist. Throughout the state, the job of municipal clean-up is still onerous, and without subsidies from the federal government little will be accomplished. Galeton, in Potter County, can't afford to install adequate sewage treatment, even with 80 percent funding assistance from state and federal agencies. It's a low-income community, bustling only with the invasion of deer hunters and trout fishermen.

Galeton is a small problem; consider the enormity of waste on the lower Delaware, the Schuylkill, the lower Allegheny, the Monongahela, and worst of all, the Mahoning River as it flows down from Youngstown. To reclaim these waters would require fortunes of investment. With scarce financial resources and enforcement personnel, the best approach may be to first eliminate the toxic waste and serious health hazards wherever they occur, then try to keep the clean waters clean. It's a difficult question of priorities. We could reclaim the Schuylkill and gain 100 miles of less polluted water, or we could prevent pollution and correct more minor problems on perhaps 1,000 miles of nonurbanized river.

Some progress has been made with industrial wastes. Eighty percent of industry's treatment plants are reported to be in compliance or satisfactorily working toward requirements, but with 2,200 treatment works and another 2,900 sewage plants in the state, who knows for sure? Corning Glass was credited with a 650 parts per million discharge of fluoride—highly poisonous to life—but the factory is now meeting Department of Environmental Resources regulations. Environmental Hearing Board action was scheduled with Hammermill Paper Company, but improvements are now being instituted at their Lock Haven mill. United States Steel spent $30 million to treat a water discharge near Pittsburgh, but when the question involved air emissions, they responded with attorneys and a long siege of resistance. Bethlehem Steel begged clean-up extensions from the federal Environmental Protection Agency, finally receiving an exemption after the 1977 Johnstown flood, as the company threatened to lay off 7,000 flood-stricken employees. Legislators introduced a bill to fire DER's Deputy Secretary for Enforcement William Eichbaum, who forced reform on many of the state's worst polluters. Big industry is tough, and while the Commonwealth dealt seriously with environmental protection under DER Secretary Goddard and Deputy Eichbaum, there is no guarantee that commitment to clean up the big, well-financed problems will continue.

Nonpoint sources of pollution are some of the most troublesome. These are wastes from large land areas and not from a single discharge. Silt from farmland is the greatest source, such as the suspended soil that makes the Conestoga and other agricultural rivers opaque brown or yellow with mud. Farmers are worried that there will be new, costly controls for things like manure-spreading. "Conservation plans," prepared by the Soil Conservation Service, are now required for erosion control.

Pesticide and herbicide wastes have effects that we aren't even aware of. Most applications of DDT have stopped, and already the osprey and eagle populations in some parts of the nation are increasing. More of these raptors are appearing along Pennsylvania waters. The safety of herbicide 2,4,5-T has been seriously questioned, though it was widely used by the state Department of Transportation in border spraying and by utilities to kill plants along power lines. In 1979, most uses of this poison were banned.

Storm water and runoff from urban areas contributes in ways that individually are imperceptible. Oceanographers estimate there is more oil in the sea from drained crankcases than from wrecked tankers. After high school, when I worked at the wire mill along the Ohio River in Monaca, I'd collect the milky-gray metallic sludge from wire-grinding machines and dump it out the back window of the plant.

Acid mine drainage degrades over 2,000 miles of major streams in Pennsylvania. Old abandoned mines are responsible for much of the problem, a

Industrialized river: the Ohio and J&L Steel at Aliquippa

West Branch Susquehanna above Williamsport

point much touted by today's mining interests, but far from the full truth. In the last sixteen years, ten clean streams between Karthaus and Renovo became polluted, and it was no horse-and-buggy deep mine from 1890 that did it. "Operation Scarlift" has spent $193 million to abate acid and restore land, but the job seems endless. Pennsylvania was long recognized as having the best strip-mine regulations in the nation, but the streams didn't get the message: they're still turning orange and acidic. Enforcement is the problem, as many sites are rarely inspected, and some inspectors have done their job on an "appointment" basis. In recent years stripping activity has increased dramatically. "New mining doesn't mean pollution," it's often said. Believers are plentiful, but evidence is scarce. Cooks Run is a good case: after conservationists protested, a mining permit was issued on the West Branch Susquehanna stream above Renovo. A year later, with two-foot-high grass, the reclamation was said to be exemplary. Then aluminum-polluted groundwater burst out through a spring, decimating life in eight miles of excellent trout water. In another case, the Jersey Shore community water supply is threatened by aluminum from a mine that's been scratched and blasted at the municipal watershed's border.

Clean streams in coal country are scarce and of great value to many people. With demands to get the coal out, the most important approach may be saving the undisturbed watersheds while mining the ones that are already polluted. Wilderness trout streams designated by the Fish Commission and the basins of clean streams where DER has tried to discourage mining include less than 5 percent of Pennsylvania's coal. At current mining rates, there are about 600 years of known coal reserves in Pennsylvania; the clean-stream coal could be saved until the year 2450. Society doesn't need it, but only the owner of the minerals and the miner, who want the money now. Their reasoning sounds identical to that of the rural developer who argues for the right to do whatever he pleases with his land. No matter that the miner doesn't own the land or the trees, the soil and the water. If he owns only the minerals, courts support his right to turn the surface upside down so he can haul his glittering black cargo off to the coal tipple.

Regulations to reserve undisturbed streams are now incorporated in the "conservation stream" classification of the Environmental Quality Board, but custody is very weak. New federal strip-mine regulations call for the protection of clean-stream areas. We need to do the job now.

Power generation bridges the issues of water quality and supply. Thermal pollution has been a problem at electric plants, where the river is heated far beyond natural levels, killing native fishes. To avoid some of this, cooling towers are designed so waste heat goes into the air instead, generating steam and often consuming a significant share of the river. At the extreme are nuclear plants, where excessive heat demands vast amounts of water.

Where does it come from? The natural volume of our streams is limited. To maintain adequate in-stream flow for other users and for wildlife, regulations have been effected that require the river level to drop no further than the lowest average consecutive seven-day flow that's likely to occur once every ten years (Q-7-10). Major consumers, like power plants, will have to provide "make-up" water—stored water that can replace their cooling water. That will likely mean dams, either private ones or public ones where the consumers "buy into" the project.

Water supply is becoming more critical than ever before. Per capita consumption is sixty-five gallons per day. Major urban centers face potential shortages, highlighted in the Monongahela basin. Today New York City gets water from the neighboring Delaware basin, and the lower Delaware gets water from the Susquehanna. These "interbasin transfers" may become a major controversy in the future. Will Keating Dam on the wild canyon of the Susquehanna's West Branch be justified by supplying water to Philadelphia, 200 miles away? Will Tocks Island Dam on the Delaware be constructed someday? And what end is there? Pennsylvania proposed Rowlesburg Dam on the Cheat River in West Virginia. In 1966 the Army Corps of Engineers identified Barbours, on Loyalsock Creek, as one of the ten best sites in the state. River protection depends on energy and water conservation, which can greatly extend our ability to get along without sacrificing additional natural streams.

Besides water supply, common objectives of the dam builder are flood control, hydroelectric production, recreation, wildlife enhancement, and economic development. These issues have been discussed in the Moshannon and Clarion chapters and others. Without adequate flood-plain management, high-water hazards will only become worse, leading to yet more river destruction and more flood-plain development in a cycle of ever-fewer flowing rivers and ever-greater flood disaster potential. Benefit-cost ratios are used to justify public water-resource projects, but there is a need to recognize the less tangible costs of forsaking the natural river, and the broader economic costs of building dams: timber and agricultural yields that are lost, recreation loss, maintenance through dredging, repair of the dams, and disposition only one hundred years from now when they become public hazards and monumental white elephants.

Human needs and wants inevitably affect rivers. This book does not argue for restoration of nature as though people don't exist. Nor does it argue that our desire for recreational or metaphysical experience should override demands for food, shelter, and other important goods and services. My plea is for a balance among competing pressures—for responsible stewardship. Although these chapters criticize special interest groups, I recognize that progress toward environmental quality has been made, and that there are environmentalists everywhere, including concerned persons within the industries and agencies that I have criticized.

While pressures mount for the use of rivers, an evolution of attitudes is

Mobile homes on the flood plain, West Branch Susquehanna below Jersey Shore

Flood damage to mobile homes located on the flood plain

another phenomenon we are facing. The commitment of people to maintain the quality of natural rivers continues to grow. In future years many decisions will be made about the waters that have been described in this book. The National Wild and Scenic Rivers System and the Pennsylvania State Scenic Rivers System will likely include some of these streams—Pine Creek, the Lehigh Gorge, and others. Additional rivers such as the Clarion, Upper Allegheny, and West Branch Canyon of the Susquehanna should be studied and designated. National river status provides the most certain protection for free-flowing qualities—to see that dams aren't built. Pennsylvania already has over 600 impoundments of twenty acres or more. State scenic-river status may be the only way to assure a Commonwealth policy of protection for our best remaining streams, and for adequate attention to management of public recreation and the problems that it brings.

A state water plan is being prepared by the Department of Environmental Resources, which could form the basis of many decisions regarding protection and exploitation. The Commonwealth also plans for statewide recreation programs, and the Army Corps of Engineers plans for dams and water-resource developments. Counties and local governments plan for land use, flood plains, and related concerns. All of these programs will have an effect on the future of waters, and nearly all effects will be a result of compromise, determined through some degree of public debate. You can and should be a part of it. Responsible compromise recognizes the needs and desires of the whole citizenry, present and future, and of the limits beyond which important values have been lost. To have all rivers half-polluted or half-dammed would be a loss. Comsumptive needs are not so vast, nor is our thirst so great that we cannot save the best of our free-flowing streams. But even if that were the case, could one find better proof that our society asks for too much?

Knowledge of our rivers and our needs is essential if we are to make the right decisions. Equally important is a consciousness of values to be protected, so that the next generation and all people in the future will enjoy and prosper through an environment that meets our spiritual as well as material needs. Unless people are willing to learn and perceive and protect, the rivers will never again be as wild and scenic, as enjoyable and impressive as they are today.

For months and years I've explored the rivers of Pennsylvania. They've led me to rainy nights, snow-covered mornings, high and muddy waters of a half dozen floods, and a wild exuberance with sunshine and rapids on a hundred afternoons. The rivers run on and on, over and over again in a pattern that has molded a continent. In learning to live with their seasons, to respect their nature, we can guarantee their qualities and their use in the future. The rivers are here for themselves and for us to travel and admire; they are the shining life of our land.

West Branch Susquehanna below Williamsport

Information for River People

Recreation along Pennsylvania Rivers

Fishing, canoeing, rafting, camping, hiking, picnicking, swimming—all
these kinds of recreation can be enjoyed along the rivers of Pennsylvania.
People are attracted to the freedom of open spaces and the scenery of
these flowing streams. As with other liberties, recognition of responsibility
is important—to ourselves, to other people, and to the environment.

Safety
We owe ourselves reasonable precautions for safety. Common sense is the
most important ingredient. Canoe, kayak, raft, or inner-tube travelers
should know how to swim. Meet a person who knows lifesaving techniques
for water rescue; they make good paddling partners! Better yet, learn the
rescue skills yourself. Techniques in mouth-to-mouth respiration and car-
diopulmonary resuscitation may save your best friend's life. An American
Red Cross first aid course is a good way to learn these and other lessons.
The Red Cross handbook, *First Aid and Emergency Care,* is a reference for
most problems.

When you're on the water, wear a life jacket (technically termed a "personal floatation device" or PFD), especially if the water is deep, fast, or
cold. The law requires one vest per person in each craft, a rule that should
be taken seriously. Fish Commission deputies have inspected my canoe
twice. High waters and floods magnify hazards. Quiet riffles become a
course of haystack waves and whirlpools. Logs, stumps, and springtime ice
can complicate an already vexing current. If there's a chance of extremely
high water, investigate conditions before beginning your trip. Never wear
hip boots or fisherman's waders in a boat. If the craft capsizes, they fill
with water and pull the wearer straight to the bottom. Powerful currents
handicap any fast-change artist who tries to escape from his footgear. Don't
overextend yourself. Know the difficulty of your water and the level of
your personal skill. Ten miles per day is enough for many paddlers,
though some may want to go twenty or more.

If your boat has overturned in the current, stay on the *upstream* side of it.
The importance of this cannot be overstressed. If you're not upstream,
then swim *away* from the boat. Contrary to this warning, many paddlers
have been told to stay with the canoe if it capsizes, since it will float. This is

Opposite: Fisherman on Penns Creek below Poe Paddy

flatwater advice; it could cost you your life in the current of a river. Many whitewater fatalities are due to entrapment: the capsized swimmer hits a rock or tree, then his boat hits *him,* pinning him tightly and possibly with his head under water. To fall out on the upstream side should become second nature, like falling backwards when skiing. Don't walk in fast water that is more than knee-deep; a foot can become stuck between two rocks. If the current pushes you over, a broken foot may be the less serious consequence, and your chances of drowning are good. Immediate aid to victims of entrapment is essential but often impossible. Whitewater boaters should see the article titled "Avoiding Entrapment," by Charles Walbridge, in *Canoe* magazine, June 1976.

Hypothermia, when the body loses more heat than it generates, is perhaps the most common and greatest danger of all. Uncontrollable shivering is a sign of danger. Keep dry or get dry; warm up fast. Much is written about hypothermia. For important details, see the editorial in the January 1977 issue of *Wilderness Camping* magazine, or almost any book on canoeing. Springtime is especially dangerous; a person who falls into forty-degree water will be unconscious in fifteen to thirty minutes. Be cautious, and consider wearing a wetsuit when waters are cold.

Except for people with special allergies, biting insects are more of a nuisance than a safety problem. Nonetheless, one should be prepared. In Pennsylvania we're fortunate, being north of most ticks and chiggers and south of the black flies. At certain times we have mosquitoes, no-see-ums,

Youghiogheny, Entrance Rapid

Owassee Rapid, Pine Creek

deer flies, and biting "house" flies, though these are just a mild sampling from boggy bug country in the Adirondacks, Maine, Minnesota, Canada, Alaska, and other lands of the river lover. A good repellent will keep mosquitoes from penetrating. It's best to ignore their nerve-wracking, high-pitched song. No-see-ums have waked me many a night, chomping into the epidermis after climbing through the tent's mosquito net. Until I got a tent with a fine mesh screen, I sweated through summer nights with the nylon door zipped shut to keep the tiny pests out. Deer flies bite like an alligator, only more so. My biggest problems are with the dog. The flies burrow into his fur and send him howling. Aboard ship, a furious eighty-pound labrador retriever is a tough force to reckon with. He becomes determined to catch that fly.

Most concerns about wild animals are remnants of the medieval understanding of the wilderness as a place of mystery and werewolves. Snakebite is about the only valid concern in Pennsylvania. The bite of a rattler or copperhead can cause critical illness, especially in a child. Watch out, particularly when rock climbing, berry picking, or engaging in other activities with your hands or head near the ground. Look where you step. The worst places are where it's rocky, sunny, or near still water in the dry season. Everyone should read first aid instructions regarding snakebite; see the Red Cross manual.

Water pollution, unfortunately, is a safety hazard that cannot be ignored. All but the small, undeveloped, and unmarred tributary streams are too polluted to drink. Coliform bacteria from sewage waste often exceed state standards for swimming, though I've survived many a substandard plunge. Except where toxic wastes may be a problem, most people do well when relying on their senses to determine adequate quality for a summertime dip.

Safety is the individual's responsibility, but other people assume a share. Paddlers have risked their lives in saving their wet companions or strangers. Government agencies have been held accountable for accidents and thus have assumed a paternalistic view on some issues of safety. Requirements regarding equipment, the timing of float trips (such as no cruising in high water or cold weather) swimming, and other facets of the river experience could be expanded to stifling levels. Nobody wants more regulations, but unless the users themselves show the caution necessary for their own safety, the government will be abrogating more and more of the individual's right to travel and play as he pleases.

Recreation Problems

It is ironic that the great movement to enjoy our rivers is creating its own problems. On some streams, the very values that attract people are jeopardized by popularity. With small amounts of recreation, the riverine environment can withstand abuse without showing much strain, but with more activity, high standards of responsible behavior are critical.

Many visitors come to the public lands and mountain rivers of rural Pennsylvania to get away from people, to be alone, or to do things they aren't allowed to do in their crowded home town. The fact is, there *are* people here, and their rights to privacy deserve respect. Before using populated lands for access to a stream, stop and ask permission. There's no sense in creating a bad image or getting shot at. Most owners will say okay if the visitor has the courtesy to inquire.

In heavily used areas, local residents accumulate a common list of complaints: fishermen park in front of driveways, and trespassers roam about or camp without permission. On the Delaware, canoeists stop to ride a farmer's horses! The less inhibited visitors will change clothes in front of homes, and there is always the sewage problem. Worst and most prevalent is trash and litter. Visitors should take their trash home. Never bury it at camp sites; frost or raccoons will bring it to the surface. Many people have the idea that garbage collection at any access area is someone's responsibility. Usually that isn't the case. Some outfitters and landowners haul trash from publicly used sites, which is most generous of them. Some public sites are maintained, such as Fish Commission access areas, but these are rare or nonexistent on smaller streams. As for the person who throws his soda bottle, beer can, or plastic tackle wrappings along the stream, to break a Norse paddle or an Orvis fly rod on his head would be worth the cost and the risk of aggravated assault charges.

As much as we seek solitude, experiences on rivers in Pennsylvania are usually social to some degree. To be alone, I run rivers on weekdays, especially in the spring. Most often we're sharing the stream with people, and a respect for their wishes is important. Boaters should try to avoid fishermen and to pass them quietly. Motorized recreational vehicles are usually offensive to everyone but the user of them. People who are seeking to escape urban problems and a pervasive gasoline-powered technology take no pleasure in more exhaust fumes, noise, and abuse of trails or fragile landscapes. All wild-country visitors should be as inconspicuous as they possibly can.

Our touch on the land need not be a heavy one, weighted with change and the increasing spread of trash and noise. Concern for safety, environmental quality, and the rights of other people can lead to recreational activity that serves important needs without degrading the resource or other people's experience.

There are many places to go. Most streams are specialists offering particular values, and recreational visits should be planned accordingly. Consideration of travel time, safety, visitor facilities, and degree of remoteness may be important to any outing. All recreational opportunities cannot be listed here. The intent is to present selected highlights that are only an introduction to thousands of waterway miles.

Canoe camping, upper Susquehanna

Camping and General Recreation

Pennsylvania state parks provide many opportunities for picnicking, camping, swimming, fishing, and stream access. Rustic riverfront cabins are available for rent at several state parks, including Clear Creek on the Clarion and Worlds End on the Loyalsock. Reservations must be made in advance with the Department of Environmental Resources, Bureau of State Parks. For more information, write to the Department of Environmental Resources, Bureau of Parks, P.O. Box 1467, Harrisburg, PA 17120.

Other riverine recreation facilities are located in Allegheny National Forest and the Delaware Water Gap National Recreation Area. Many state forests offer public land for hiking, stream-side camping, and fishing. Public access areas are provided along some rivers by the Pennsylvania Fish Commission. The maps in this book show the location of public lands, parks, and access areas.

Many private campgrounds can be found along the rivers, such as several large sites along the upper Delaware and Allegheny. For information on private recreation establishments, write to the Pennsylvania Bureau of Travel Development, Box X, South Office Building, Harrisburg, PA 17120, or the chamber of commerce of any county or large town.

Hiking

While there are hundreds of trails on public lands in Pennsylvania, they generally do not follow a major waterway for any great distance. Several trails parallel rivers for short distances, offering outstanding hiking experiences and excellent scenery. A few favorites include:

Slippery Rock Creek at McConnell's Mill State Park.

Clarion River at Cook Forest State Park.

Spring Creek, a tributary to the Clarion in Allegheny National Forest. Old railroad grades are rough but can be hiked, and trout fishing is good.

Youghiogheny River at Ohiopyle State Park. Short but unusually scenic trails lead to the river from Cucumber Falls and Ferncliff Park.

Grove Run, a small stream in Linn Run State Park.

Hammersley Fork of Kettle Creek, a small but wild stream in Susquehannock State Forest. The Susquehannock Trail is eighty-five miles long and includes the Hammersley. Hiking is best done as an overnight backpack trip. For trail maps, write to the Susquehannock Trail Club, Susquehannock Lodge, Ulysses, PA 16948.

Pine Creek at Colton and Harrison Point State Parks. The Turkey Path and Four Mile Run Trail wind precipitously from canyon rims to the valley floor. These trails are especially hazardous in early spring and should be avoided until the ice melts.

Loyalsock Creek, accessible from the Loyalsock Trail, which runs southwest from Route 220 near Laporte. The northernmost two miles parallel the creek, leading to the rugged Haystack Rapids.

Penns Creek, where an old railroad grade can be hiked for eight miles, accessible at Weikert or one-half mile south of Coburn.

Schrader Branch of Towanda Creek, a small stream that can be followed along an abandoned railroad grade on state game lands, beginning near Wheelerville. Fishing is excellent.

Kitchen Creek in Ricketts Glen State Park, west of Wilkes-Barre. Thirty-three waterfalls range from 6 to 100 feet in height. Many people feel this is the most scenic hike in Pennsylvania.

Schuylkill River and Wissahickon Creek in Fairmount Park, Philadelphia. Paths and bike trails are plentiful and uncommonly pleasant for a major urban area.

Hiking across the Hammersley Fork of Kettle Creek

Many other short hiking trails can be discovered along hundreds of streams. Detailed information regarding trails is available from the Pennsylvania Bureau of Forestry, P.O. Box 1467, Harrisburg, PA 17120, or the Pennsylvania Bureau of Travel Development, South Office Building, Box X, Harrisburg, PA 17120. United States Geological Survey maps also show hundreds of trails. Many require bushwhacking but lead to excellent river views, camp sites, and fishing streams. A useful guide to trails in the central part of the state is Tom Thwaites, *Fifty Hikes in Central Pennsylvania*.

Fishing

Fish can be caught in nearly all Pennsylvania waterways, except those with mine acid* and the most polluted streams near major urban areas. Many of the accessible streams are stocked by the Pennsylvania Fish Commission, which has also developed access areas. Fishermen are notably reticent about their favorite streams, so if you want to know about the really good places, better ask a friend who's willing to share, or just start casting. While cold-water or trout fishing is often more popular than warm-water, Pennsylvania has six times as many acres of warm-water fishery as cold (including lakes). A few of the best and most-used waterways are the following:

Allegheny River from Kinzua Dam to East Brady for bass and walleye.

Clarion River above the town of Clarion. This stream is now improving after years of unrestrained pollution. The West Branch of the Clarion, above Johnsonburg, has always been good trout water.

Youghiogheny from Confluence to Connellsville, another river that has improved greatly in recent years.

First Fork Sinnemahoning Creek, a favorite trout stream that is crowded with anglers early in the season. Driftwood Branch is also becoming a good fishery.

West Branch Susquehanna River from Williamsport to Sunbury. This waterway was affected by mine drainage as recently as 1970, but now offers good walleye and bass fishing.

Susquehanna River from New York state to Scranton. This is a large river with excellent warm-water fishing.

Upper Kettle Creek, Penns Creek, and the lower Loyalsock—all good trout fisheries in the northern and central areas.

Juniata River. Warm-water fishing is good almost anywhere, but especially in the lower reaches.

---

*Coal mining has resulted in the pollution of over 3,000 miles of waterways in Pennsylvania.

Yellow Breeches Creek, an excellent limestone stream popular among trout fishermen.

Delaware River from Hancock to Easton. Don't look for solitude on weekends—there are many, many canoes.

Lackawaxen River, a large tributary to the Delaware.

Other streams are also heavily used. Hundreds of cold, wooded waterways are a prime habitat of the small native brook trout. For the angler who wants to get away from the crowds, these are the places to go.

A fishing license is required for anyone over twelve years of age. Creel limits, seasons, and other regulations must be strictly followed. In "Fish-for-Fun" areas, trout fishing is allowed year round, under special regulations that vary from stream to stream. For more information, write to the Pennsylvania Fish Commission, P.O. Box 1673, Harrisburg, PA 17120. Pamphlets on fishing locations are available, with county maps that show stocked streams. See the map inside the back cover for further information.

River Traveling

People enjoy canoeing, kayaking, and rafting on many Pennsylvania streams. The popularity of river traveling and whitewater cruising has increased greatly in recent years and is likely to continue. The map inside the front cover identifies selected streams and indicates their degree of difficulty. Canoeing guidebooks offer detail on access sites, whitewater difficulty ratings, lengths of various reaches, and other information. Guides can be very helpful, but all river travelers should beware of hazards that may not be discussed in the books or indicated on our map. Owassee Rapids in the Pine Creek Canyon is not mentioned in Burmeister's guide, yet it is significant, dangerous, and unexpected, lying two miles south of Ansonia. Paddlers should consult the following:

Canoeing Guide to Western Pennsylvania and Northern West Virginia
Pittsburgh Council of American Youth Hostels, Inc.
6300 Fifth Ave.
Pittsburgh, PA 15232

Appalachian Waters 1: The Delaware and Its Tributaries
Walter F. Burmeister
Appalachian Books
Oakton, VA 22124

Appalachian Waters 3: The Susquehanna River and Its Tributaries
Walter F. Burmeister
Appalachian Books
Oakton, VA 22124

Select Rivers of Central Pennsylvania
Penn State Outing Club
4 Intramural Building
University Park, PA 16802

A short brochure, which includes major canoeing streams of Pennsylvania, is "Canoe Country Pennsylvania Style," available from the Pennsylvania Bureau of Travel Development, Box X, South Office Building, Harrisburg, PA 17120. Due to low water levels, only a limited number of rivers can normally be floated in the summertime:

Allegheny River, which always has sufficient flow from Warren down.

Youghiogheny River from Confluence down, including many Class IV rapids below the Ohiopyle Falls, which can't be run. Only experts should attempt to canoe or kayak below the falls. Inexperienced paddlers should travel in a raft with a guided party.

The Monongahela and Ohio rivers, though they are dammed, polluted, and developed, more suited for motorboats than canoes.

The West Branch Susquehanna, from Lock Haven to Sunbury. Water volume is usually adequate from Karthaus (between Renovo and Clearfield), though in dry periods the river will require some wading.

Susquehanna River from the New York border down.

Juniata River from Huntingdon down. One difficult rapids is below Newton-Hamilton.

Lehigh River, a whitewater stream where releases from Walters Dam are sometimes planned for the third weekend of each summer month. At other times during the summer, flow is usually not sufficient for floating. For water level information, call the Army Corps of Engineers, (717) 443-9493. The Lehigh is a difficult and dangerous river. Inexperienced paddlers should cruise by raft, preferably with a guide.

Brandywine Creek, from Lenape to Chadds Ford. Old mill dams create short and sudden rapids.

Delaware River, though dry periods will require wading through shallows in northern reaches. Here and on the upper West Branch of the Susquehanna, it's best to plan summer trips for the month of June. The Delaware has some difficult Class II rapids.

Scores of medium-sized streams are excellent for springtime floating or for canoeing after heavy rains. The guidebooks already mentioned list most of these. Some of the finest waters are Tionesta Creek, the Clarion River, Casselman River, Bennett and Driftwood branches of the Sinnemahoning, Moshannon Creek, the upper West Branch of the Susquehanna, Pine Creek, Loyalsock Creek, and Tunkhannock Creek. Intermediate paddling skills are needed for these.

Whitewater streams that offer excitement and challenge to the experienced boater include Slippery Rock Creek, the Youghiogheny River, the Pine Creek Canyon, Little Pine Creek, upper Loyalsock Creek, Schrader

Branch Towanda Creek, Wills Creek, Stony Creek (near Johnstown), Lehigh River Gorge, Lackawaxen River, and some sections of the Delaware. The Slippery Rock, Youghiogheny, upper Loyalsock, Lehigh Gorge, Wills Creek, and Stony Creek are the most significant and difficult of these; only true experts should attempt them in canoes. Two outstanding rafting rivers are the Youghiogheny at Ohiopyle and the Lehigh River Gorge.

Kayakers, Youghiogheny below Ohiopyle

River Rating System
For Whitewater Difficulty

Degree of rapids and whitewater difficulty is expressed in "grade" or "class" ratings of I through VI, developed in Europe and known as the International Scale. It is not a perfect system, but does much toward simplifying and standardizing a river description. Water levels often change the condition of rapids, usually making them more difficult, but not always. Flow characteristics also change from year to year: gravel bars and boulders are rearranged by high water, and trees fall into streams, creating new hazards. While the classification can help in planning a river trip, never rely totally on the books. If there are big rapids, look for yourself before paddling through. The following description is taken from the American Whitewater Affiliation's safety code:

Class I   Moving water with a few riffles and small waves. Few or no obstructions.

Class II   Easy rapids with waves up to 3 feet, and wide, clear channels that are obvious without scouting. Some maneuvering is required.

Class III Rapids with high, irregular waves often capable of swamping an open canoe. Narrow passages that often require complex maneuvering. May require scouting from shore.

Class IV   Long, difficult rapids with constricted passages that often require precise maneuvering in very turbulent waters. Scouting from shore is often necessary, and conditions make rescue difficult. Generally not possible for open canoes. Boaters in covered canoes and kayaks should be able to Eskimo roll.

Class V   Extremely difficult, long, and very violent rapids with highly congested routes which nearly always must be scouted from shore. Rescue conditions are difficult and there is significant hazard to life in event of a mishap. Ability to Eskimo roll is essential for kayaks and canoes.

Class VI   Difficulties of Class V carried to the extreme of navigability. Nearly impossible and very dangerous. For teams of experts only, after close study and with all precautions taken.

Major Stream Basins of Pennsylvania*

Stream	Square Miles in Watershed
DELAWARE RIVER BASIN	
Delaware River including Lackawaxen River	2,626
Delaware River including Brodhead Creek	4,717
Delaware River including Lehigh River	6,085
Delaware River at Pennsylvania-Delaware state boundary	10,370
Lackawaxen River	597
Wallenpaupack Creek	228
Bush Kill	158
Brodhead Creek	287
McMichaels Creek	113
Lehigh River	1,368
Tobyhanna Creek	128
Pohopoco Creek	111
Little Lehigh Creek	190
Tohickon Creek	112
Neshaminy Creek	232
Schuylkill River	1,912
Little Schuylkill River	137
Maiden Creek	216
Tulpehocken Creek	219
Perkiomen Creek	362
Brandywine Creek to Christina River in Delaware	304
West Branch Brandywine Creek	135
East Branch Brandywine Creek	124
SUSQUEHANNA RIVER BASIN	
Susquehanna River including Chemung River	7,528
Susquehanna River including Lackawanna River	9,887
Susquehanna River at West Branch (but not including West Branch)	11,302
Susquehanna River and West Branch	18,257
Susquehanna River including Juniata River	23,091
Susquehanna River at Maryland state boundary	27,132
Tioga River	461
Crooked Creek	132
Cowanesque Creek	300
Cayuta Creek	140
Chemung River	2,595
Sugar Creek	190
Towanda Creek	278

*Figures indicate watersheds 100 square miles or more, including neighboring states' areas that drain into Pennsylvania. Tributaries are indented.

Source: Pennsylvania Gazetteer of Streams

Wysox Creek	101
Wyalusing Creek	219
Meshoppen Creek	114
Mehoopany Creek	123
Tunkhannock Creek	413
Bowman Creek	120
Lackawanna River	348
Nescopeck Creek	174
Fishing Creek	385
Huntington Creek	114
Catawissa Creek	153
West Branch Susquehanna River	6,955
Chest Creek	129
Clearfield Creek	393
Moshannon Creek	274
Sinnemahoning Creek	1,035
Bennett Branch Sinnemahoning Creek	367
Driftwood Branch Sinnemahoning Creek	319
First Fork Sinnemahoning Creek	267
Kettle Creek	246
Bald Eagle Creek	770
Spring Creek	143
Beech Creek	172
Fishing Creek	181
Pine Creek	981
Babb Creek	129
Little Pine Creek	180
Lycoming Creek	272
Loyalsock Creek	494
Muncy Creek	194
Buffalo Creek	134
Shamokin Creek	118
Middle Creek	175
Penns Creek	554
Mahanoy Creek	157
Mahantango Creek	164
Wiconisco Creek	116
Juniata River	3,404
Frankstown Branch Juniata River	395
Little Juniata River	343
Spruce Creek	109
Standing Stone Creek	132
Raystown Branch Juniata River	963
Dunning Creek	197
Aughwick Creek	323
Kishacoquillas Creek	191
Tuscarora Creek	270
Sherman Creek	244
Conodoguinet Creek	506
Yellow Breeches Creek	219
Swatara Creek	571
West Conewago Creek	515
Bermudian Creek	110

Codorus Creek	278
South Branch Codorus Creek	117
Chickies Creek	126
Conestoga Creek	477
Cocalico Creek	140
Pequea Creek	154
Muddy Creek	138
Octoraro Creek	176

POTOMAC RIVER BASIN
(figures include area in Maryland)

Wills Creek	194
Tonoloway Creek	112
Licking Creek	189
Conococheague Creek	503
West Branch Conococheague Creek	199
Antietam Creek	113
Monocacy River	240

GENESEE RIVER BASIN

Genesee River at Pennsylvania-New York boundary	136

OHIO RIVER BASIN

Ohio River including Little Beaver Creek	23,487
Allegheny River including Potato Creek	603
Allegheny River including Sandy Creek	6,433
Allegheny River including Clarion River	8,937
Allegheny River at Ohio River	11,748
Potato Creek	224
Oswayo Creek	195
Tunungwant Creek	139
Kinzua Creek	182
Conewango Creek	898
Brokenstraw Creek	329
Tionesta Creek	474
Oil Creek	318
Conneaut Outlet	101
French Creek	1,232
Sugar Creek	167
East Sandy Creek	103
Sandy Creek	161
Clarion River	1,252
East Branch Clarion River	108
Little Toby Creek	126
Redbank Creek	573
Sandy Lick Creek	229
Mahoning Creek	425
Little Mahoning Creek	113

Crooked Creek	292
Kiskiminetas River	1,887
Conemaugh River	1,372
Stony Creek	467
Little Conemaugh River	190
Blacklick Creek	418
Two Lick Creek	192
Loyalhanna Creek	299
Buffalo Creek	171
Monongahela River	7,384
Cheat River	1,422
Dunkard Creek	235
Tenmile Creek	338
South Fork Tenmile Creek	199
Redstone Creek	109
Youghiogheny River	1,763
Casselman River	590
Laurel Hill Creek	125
Indian Creek	125
Sewickley Creek	168
Turtle Creek	148
Chartiers Creek	277
Beaver River	3,153
Mahoning River	1,140
Shenango River	1,062
Little Shenango River	109
Pymatuning Creek	171
Neshannock Creek	242
Connoquenessing Creek	838
Slippery Rock Creek	408
Wolf Creek	101
Raccoon Creek	184
Little Beaver Creek	503
North Fork Little Beaver Creek	193
Buffalo Creek	114
Wheeling Creek	164
LAKE ERIE BASIN	543
Conneaut Creek	152

Recommended Streams (High-Priority Candidates) for Pennsylvania Scenic River Study*

Stream Name	Location

DELAWARE BASIN

Brandywine Creek   Chester, Delaware counties
  East Branch Brandywine Creek
  West Branch Brandywine Creek
Bush Kill (Big Bushkill Creek)   Monroe, Pike counties
Delaware River   Bucks, Monroe, Northampton,
                                        Pike, Wayne counties
Lehigh River   Carbon, Luzerne counties
  Glen Onoko Falls
  Jeans Run
  Mud Run
Schuylkill River   Berks, Chester, Montgomery,
                                        Philadelphia counties
French Creek   Chester, Berks counties
  South Branch French Creek
Tohickon Creek   Bucks County
Bushkill Creek   Northampton County
Cooks Creek   Bucks County
Jordan Creek   Lehigh County
Lehigh River   Carbon, Lehigh, Northamp-
                                        ton counties
Maiden Creek   Berks County
Perkiomen Creek   Montgomery County
Wissahickon Creek   Montgomery, Philadelphia
                                        counties

SUSQUEHANNA BASIN

Beech Creek   Centre, Clinton counties
Black Moshannon Creek   Centre County
Hammersley Fork   Clinton, Potter counties
Juniata River   Huntingdon, Mifflin counties
Laurel Run   Perry County
Lick Run   Clinton County
Loyalsock Creek   Lycoming, Sullivan counties
Moshannon Creek   Centre, Clearfield counties
Mosquito Creek   Cameron, Clearfield counties
Muddy Creek   York County
Octoraro Creek   Chester, Lancaster counties
  East Branch Octoraro Creek

*Compiled by the Pennsylvania Scenic Rivers Task Force, Department of Environmental Resources

West Branch Octoraro Creek
Stewart Run
Penns Creek   Centre, Mifflin, Snyder,
                                                  Union counties

Pine Creek   Lycoming, Tioga counties
Schrader Creek   Bradford, Sullivan counties
Sinnemahoning Creek   Cameron, Clinton counties
   Driftwood Branch Sinnemahoning
   Creek
Spruce Creek   Huntingdon County
   Little Juniata River
Stony Creek   Dauphin, Lebanon counties
Susquehanna River   Bradford, Lackawanna,
                                                  Luzerne, Wyoming counties
Susquehanna River   Dauphin, Juniata, North-
                                                  umberland, Perry, Snyder
                                                  counties
Tuscarora Creek   Huntingdon, Juniata counties
West Branch Susquehanna River   Centre, Clearfield, Clinton
                                                  counties

OHIO BASIN

Allegheny River   Clarion, Forest, Venango,
                                                  Warren counties
Brokenstraw Creek   Erie, Warren counties
Casselman River   Somerset County
Clarion River   Clarion, Elk, Forest,
                                                  Jefferson counties
French Creek   Crawford, Elk, Mercer
   Cussewago Creek   counties
   Muddy Creek
   South Branch French Creek
   Sugar Creek
      Lake Creek
   West Branch French Creek
Kinzua Creek   McKean County
Laurel Hill Creek   Somerset County
North Fork Redbank Creek   Jefferson County
Slippery Rock Creek   Butler, Lawrence counties
   Connoquenessing Creek
Squaw Run   Allegheny County
Tionesta Creek   Forest, McKean, Warren
   East Branch Tionesta Creek   counties
Wolf Creek   Butler, Mercer counties
Youghiogheny River   Fayette, Somerset,
   Cucumber Run   Westmoreland counties
   Dunbar Creek
   Indian Creek
   Jonathan Run
   Meadow Run
Bear Creek   Elk County

Buffalo Creek	Armstrong, Butler counties
Buffalo Creek	Washington County
Dutch Fork	
Dunkard Fork Wheeling Creek	Greene County
Enlow Fork Wheeling Creek	Greene County
Oil Creek	Crawford, Venango counties
Youghiogheny River	Fayette, Westmoreland counties
Allegheny River	McKean County
Allegheny River	Allegheny, Armstrong,
	Clarion counties
Aunt Clara Fork Kings Creek	Washington County
Connoquenessing Creek	Beaver, Butler, Lawrence counties
North Fork Little Beaver Creek	Beaver, Lawrence counties
Youghiogheny River	Allegheny, Westmoreland counties

Selected Bibliography

Allen, Barry, and Haefele, Mina Hamilton. *In Defense of Rivers: A Citizen's Workbook.* Stillwater, N.J.: Delaware Valley Conservation Association, 1976.

American Youth Hostels, Pittsburgh Council. *Canoeing Guide to Western Pennsylvania and Northern West Virginia.* Pittsburgh: Pittsburgh Council, American Youth Hostels, 1975.

Amos, William H. *The Infinite River.* New York: Ballantine, 1970.

Banta, R.E. *The Ohio.* New York: Rinehart, 1949.

Beak Consultants. *Wild and Scenic River Survey, Physiographic Provinces 8D & 8E,* vol. 1. Atlanta, Ga.: United States Department of the Interior, Bureau of Outdoor Recreation, January 1976.

Bradford, Willard. *Pennsylvania Geology Summarized.* Pennsylvania Department of Environmental Resources, 1973.

Burmeister, Walter F. *Appalachian Waters 1: The Delaware River and Its Tributaries.* Oakton, Va.: Appalachian Books.

Burmeister, Walter F. *Appalachian Waters 3: The Susquehanna River and Its Tributaries.* Oakton, Va.: Appalachian Books, 1975.

Canby, Henry Seidel. *The Brandywine.* New York: Rinehart, 1941.

Carmer, Carl-Lamson. *The Susquehanna.* New York: Rinehart, 1955.

Chester County Water Resources Authority. *The Brandywine: A Place for Man/A Place for Nature.* West Chester, Pa.: Chester County Water Resources Authority, 1967.

Clement, Thomas M. Jr.; Lopez, Glen; and Mountain, Pamela T. *Engineering a Victory for Our Environment: A Citizen's Guide to the U.S. Army Corps of Engineers.* San Francisco: Sierra Club, 1973.

Directory of Canadian Biography, Volume 1. Toronto: University of Toronto Press, 1966.

Erdman, Kimball S., and Weigman, Paul G. *Preliminary List of Natural Areas in Pennsylvania.* Pittsburgh: Western Pennsylvania Conservancy, 1974.

Fletcher, Peter W. *Man in the Ecology of a Mountain Stream.* University Park: Pennsylvania State University, College of Agriculture, 1971.

Frank, O. Lynn. *80 Miles of Wilderness Adventure on the West Branch of the Susquehanna River.* Clearfield, Pa.: Clearfield District, Bucktail Council, Boy Scouts of America, 1970.

Hornberger, Marlin L. *A Geological, Chemical and Biological Survey of the Effects of Land Use on Little Pine Creek, Lycoming County, Pa.* University Park: A report sponsored by the National Science Foundation and The Pennsylvania State University, 1971.

Kauffman, John M. *Flow East: A Look at Our Eastern Rivers.* New York: McGraw-Hill, 1973.

Keene, John C., and Strong, Ann Louise. "The Brandywine Plan." *American Institute of Planners Journal* (January 1970), 50–58.

Likens, Gene E. "Acid Precipitation." *Chemical and Engineering News* (22 November 1976).

Myers, Barry Lee, Esquire; Bumgarner, Harry L.; and Shirey, Elizabeth G. *Legal Problems Associated with Planning Land Uses in a Riverine Area, Pine Creek, Pennsylvania.* University Park: A report of the Center for the Study of Environmental Policy, The Pennsylvania State University, March 1973.

Naturalist, volume 16, no. 3, 1965.

Northern Environmental Council. *Preservation of Wild and Scenic Rivers from Overuse and Deterioration.* Ashland, Wis.: Northern Environmental Council, 1973.

Outdoor World. *Rivers of North America.* Waukesha, Wis.: Outdoor World, 1973.

Palmer, Timothy T. *Pine Creek, A Summary of Reports.* Harrisburg: Lycoming County Planning Commission and the Pennsylvania Department of Environmental Resources, 1975.

Palmer, Timothy T. *Pine Creek Tomorrow.* Harrisburg: Lycoming County Planning Commission and the Pennsylvania Department of Environmental Resources, 1974.

Palmer, Timothy T. *Recreation on a Wild and Scenic River: Pine Creek.* Harrisburg: Lycoming County Planning Commission and the Pennsylvania Department of Environmental Resources, 1974.

Palmer, Timothy T. *Susquehanna Waterway, The West Branch in Lycoming County.* Williamsport, Pa.: Lycoming County Planning Commission, June 1975.

Pennsylvania Department of Environmental Resources. *Programs and Planning for the Management of the Water Resources of Pennsylvania.* Harrisburg: Pennsylvania Department of Environmental Resources, November 1971.

Pennsylvania Department of Environmental Resources and United States Department of the Interior, Bureau of Outdoor Recreation. *Northeast Regional States Scenic Rivers Planning Workshop: Summary of Proceedings.* Philadelphia: United States Department of the Interior, Bureau of Outdoor Recreation, 1976.

Pennsylvania Department of Forests and Waters. *Outdoor Recreation Horizons.* Harrisburg: Pennsylvania Department of Forests and Waters, 1970.

Pennsylvania Department of Forests and Waters. *Water Resources Bulletin No. 6, Pennsylvania Gazetteer of Streams, Part 1.* Harrisburg: Pennsylvania Department of Forests and Waters, December 1970.

Pennsylvania Fish Commission. *Fishing in Pennsylvania.* Harrisburg: Pennsylvania Fish Commission, n.d.

Pennsylvania Governor's Office of State Planning and Development. *Pennsylvania's Recreation Plan: Summary.* Harrisburg: Pennsylvania Governor's Office of State Planning and Development, March 1976.

Pennsylvania State Planning Board. *Pennsylvania's Regions: A Survey of the Commonwealth.* Harrisburg: Pennsylvania State Planning Board, 1967.

Pennsylvania Wild and Scenic Rivers Task Force. *Pennsylvania Scenic Rivers Inventory.* Harrisburg: Pennsylvania Department of Environmental Resources, 1975.

Power, John, and Brown, Jeremy. *The Fisherman's Handbook.* New York: Charles Scribner's Sons, 1972.

Pringle, Laurence. *Wild River.* New York: J.B. Lippincott, 1975.

Riviere, Bill. *Pole, Paddle and Portage: A Complete Guide to Canoeing.* New York: Van Nostrand Reinhold, 1969.

Schaefer, Thomas G. *Technical Report No. 5: Management Alternatives for the Importance of Canoeing Opportunities and the Resolution of Problems Relating to the Recreational Use of Rivers.* Ohio Department of Natural Resources, May 1975.

SEDA Council of Governments. *SEDA-COG Regional Flood Recovery Plan* (draft). Lewisburg, Pa.: SEDA Council of Governments, 1975.

Susquehanna River Basin Commission. *Comprehensive Plan for Management and Development of the Water Resources of the Susquehanna River Basin.* Mechanicsburg, Pa.: Susquehanna River Basin Commission, December 1973.

Susquehanna River Basin Study Coordinating Committee. *Susquehanna River Basin Study Summary.* Susquehanna River Basin Study Coordinating Committee, 1970.

U.S. Army Corps of Engineers. *Acid Mine Drainage Abatement Program for the Clarion River Basin, Pa.* July 1976.

U.S. Army Corps of Engineers. *Development of Water Resources in Appalachia.* Part III Project Analysis, volume 9, chapter 2. November 1969.

U.S. Army Corps of Engineers. *Environmental Statement: Lock Haven Flood Protection Project, West Branch Susquehanna River and Bald Eagle Creek, Pa.* October 1974.

U.S. Army Corps of Engineers. *A Vacationscape for Appalachia: A Comprehensive Out-*

door Recreation Study of North Central Pennsylvania. Washington, D.C.: U.S. Government Printing Office, 1968.

U.S. Army Corps of Engineers. *Water Resources Development in Pennsylvania.* Washington, D.C.: U.S. Government Printing Office, 1975.

U.S. Congress. *Wild and Scenic Rivers Act as Amended Through Public Law 93-621.* 3 January 1975.

U.S. Department of the Interior, Bureau of Outdoor Recreation. *Clarion River Study: The National Wild and Scenic Rivers Act.* Philadelphia: U.S. Department of the Interior, Bureau of Outdoor Recreation, May 1971.

U.S. Department of the Interior, Bureau of Outdoor Recreation. *The Lower Allegheny River Study.* Philadelphia: U.S. Department of the Interior, Bureau of Outdoor Recreation, April 1973.

U.S. Department of the Interior, Bureau of Outdoor Recreation. *Pine Creek: A Wild and Scenic River Study.* Philadelphia: U.S. Department of the Interior, Bureau of Outdoor Recreation, November 1975.

U.S. Department of the Interior, Bureau of Outdoor Recreation. *Preliminary Environmental Statement: Proposed Pine Creek National Scenic River.* Philadelphia: U.S. Department of the Interior, Bureau of Outdoor Recreation, 1975.

U.S. Department of the Interior, Bureau of Outdoor Recreation. *A Survey of Rivers in the Ridge and Valley Physiographic Province.* Philadelphia: U.S. Department of the Interior, Bureau of Outdoor Recreation, 1976.

U.S. Department of the Interior, Bureau of Outdoor Recreation. *The Upper Delaware: A Wild and Scenic River Study.* Philadelphia: U.S. Department of the Interior, Bureau of Outdoor Recreation, December 1973.

U.S. Department of the Interior, Bureau of Outdoor Recreation. *The Youghiogheny Wild and Scenic River Study.* Philadelphia: U.S. Department of the Interior, Bureau of Outdoor Recreation, 1977.

U.S. Department of the Interior, Fish and Wildlife Service. *Allegheny River Survey: Final Report, August 1, 1969 to April 30, 1975.* Washington, D.C.: U.S. Government Printing Office, 1975.

U.S. Environmental Protection Agency. *Cooperative Mine Drainage Study: Selected Areas in the Clarion River Basin.* June 1971.

U.S. Forest Service, North Central Forest Experiment Station. *Proceedings: River Recreation Management and Research Symposium.* January 24–27, 1977.

Way, Frederick. *The Allegheny.* New York: Farrar and Rinehart, 1942.

White, Gilbert. *Strategies of American Water Management.* Ann Arbor: University of Michigan Press, 1969.

Wildes, Harry Emerson. *The Delaware.* New York: Farrar and Rinehart, 1940.

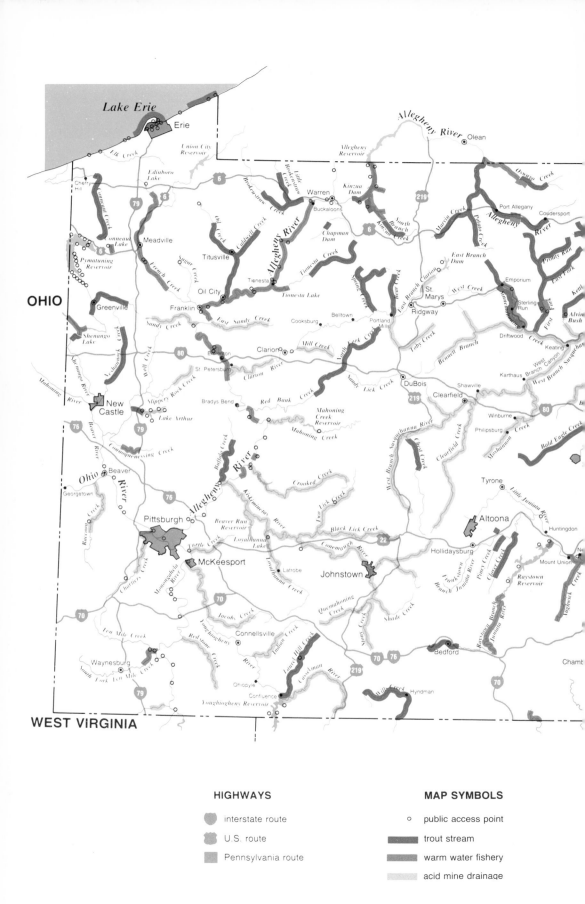

Lake Erie

Erie

OHIO

WEST VIRGINIA

HIGHWAYS

- interstate route
- U.S. route
- Pennsylvania route

MAP SYMBOLS

- ○ public access point
- trout stream
- warm water fishery
- acid mine drainage